MW01633591

HISTORY

OF

DURHAM,

CONNECTICUT,

FROM THE FIRST GRANT OF LAND IN 1662 TO 1866.

By WILLIAM CHAUNCEY FOWLER, LL. D.

"I have considered the days of old, the years of ancient times."—Psalm lxxvii 5.

"Fair scenes for childhood's opening bloom,
For sportive youth to stray in;
For manhood to enjoy his strength;
And age to wear away in!"

Wordsworth.

PUBLISHED BY THE TOWN.

HARTFORD:
PRESS OF WILEY, WATERMAN & EATON.
MDCCCLXVI.

Ke

PREFACE.

The four primitive Towns on Connecticut River, namely, Wethersfield, Hartford, Windsor, and Saybrook, the four primitive Towns on Long Island Sound, namely, Stratford, Milford, New Haven, and Guilford, were all settled by Companies of Englishmen, thrown out and off from the mother country by its internal convulsions. They resembled the great primary formations of Geology, thrown up by powerful convulsions of the earth, retaining, for a long time, the heat derived from their igneous origin, and showing, in their structure, the marks of the violent forces to which they had been subject.

On the other hand, Durham, a derivative town, settled more than sixty years, or more than two generations later, in more quiet and less heated times, resembled the secondary formations of Geology, which are composed of the fragmentary contributions from the primary, under the working of gentle forces.

In the primary formations of Geology, there is more that is grand, striking, and peculiar, in the scenery. In the secondary formations, there are more of the elements of fertility, and a richer outgrowth of vegetation

In the primitive Towns mentioned, the spirit of dissent was rife, nearly as much so, in some cases, as when the settlers left England. Parties arose, measuring themselves by themselves, and comparing themselves among themselves, requiring legislative interference in order to settle their religious differences. Secessions took place from the Churches and from the Towns, for the purpose of forming other Churches and other Towns, where the favorite opinions and measures of the seceders might prevail.

Durham, on the other hand, was settled after the spirit of dissent had, to some extent, died out; after the jealousy of Ecclesiastical encroachment on the rights of individual Churches was somewhat weakened; after the controversies about Episcopal forms had passed by, after the evils of separatism, independency, and Church isolation, and the advantages of the Consociation of Churches, recommended by the great synod in Massachusetts, in 1662, and adopted in Connecticut in 1708, were beginning to be felt. It is not known that a single emigrant to Durham came from out of a heated controversy, or was detached from his former residence, in a primitive town, by the repellency of dissent. A considerable number were attracted to one another by personal friendship and the ties of blood.

Guilford and New Haven, and Milford, and Stratford, and Hartford, and Windsor, and Farmington, and Northampton, furnished settlers to Durham, so that it showed the average character of those several Towns and Churches, and not the marked peculiarities of any one of them. Several of those Towns sent some of their best inhabitants to Durham.

Thus it appears that Durham had the advantage of the collected wisdom of these several Towns, wisdom derived from the experience of two generations in this country. It was settled chiefly by the grand-children of the Pilgrim Fathers of Connecticut. It was settled by Americans, by those who had grown up under Colonial institutions, civil, social, and religious, such as Connecticut had adopted; and was not as were the primitive Towns, settled by Englishmen, who had every-thing to learn in a new country. The history of Durham shows the progress that had been made in the third generation from the settlement of the two Colonies in Connecticut; what had been lost that was English, and what had been gained that was American. In this respect, if not as interesting, it is more instructive, than that of a primitive Town.

In the primitive Towns, at their first settlement, there were those who looked back, with yearning hearts, across the waters to their first home. Some actually returned thither. Others wished to do so. And numbers who left England under the monitions of conscience, in the spirit of adventure, in the hot blood of controversy, or in the bad blood of resentment for injuries, real or threatened, would, in the sun-set and twilight of age, look back with softened hearts and tearful eyes to the home of their childhood; to the Church-yard, where their parents were sleeping, to the Churches and Cathedrals in which they had offered their youthful devotion. Methinks some of those aged pilgrims, in moments of fond recollection, exclaim,

"Oh thou queen,
Thou delegated Deity of earth,
Oh dear, dear England!"

But their grand-children, such as settled in Durham, knew but one country, that of their birth and of their residence. Theirs was no divided love. Under these western skies, on colonial soil, amid institutions formed here, they had their birth and breeding. They knew nothing better. They breathed no sigh for the past and the distant. They did not, from their grand-sires, inherit the incompatible ideas, the incompatible feelings generated in the religious and political ferments of England. They did not inherit all the diversity of sentiment in the minds of the leaders in the two Colonies in Connecticut. Their ideas were practical, their feelings were chastened in the school of daily labor, under the teachings of the stern monitress, necessity. They had become largely assimilated to one another in their opinions and feelings, by their common experience and by their common destinies. Marriages had extensively united families together. The people were bound together by something more than a common love of religious liberty, and a common hatred of prelacy.

By these remarks, I do not mean to detract one particle from the preeminence of a single primitive Town, but only to show what is the true position of Durham. I would not, willingly, fall into the mistake of the simple shepherd, Tityrus, in Virgil, who fondly imagined that Mantua was equal to or like great Rome. Still, Mantua has its place in Roman history, though not as large a one as Rome.

In the course of events, it so happened, a few years since, that a large number of documents, connected with the early history of Durham, fell into my hands. Ever since I first examined these documents, many years ago, there has been a growing conviction in my mind that they ought to be put into some permanent form for preservation, before "decay's effacing fingers" shall have done their work upon them, or the accident of fire shall have reduced them to ashes.

Was I not bound to do something for their preservation? My ancestors, on both sides of the house, were proprietors of the Town. My ancestor, Deacon John Fowler, of Guilford, for public services, received the grant of a farm in Durham, from the Colonial Legislature. I spent the years of my boyhood, and am now spending the years of old age, here. Here I am expecting to sleep the long sleep, on a sunny slope in "God's acre."

Accordingly, I digested these documents, and other materials collected elsewhere, into a shape for publication, and offered them to the Town in Town Meeting assembled. *The Town readily accepted of the offering, and promptly provided the means for the publication.* This action of the Town deserves especial notice and commendation, inasmuch, as it is believed to be the first instance in the State, and in the United States, of a Town's publishing, at its own expense, its own History The Town having acted thus, measures were taken to canvass all of the School Districts for subscribers for the book, which they were to receive at cost, or not above cost. In this way, so many subscribers were obtained that the Town Treasury is relieved from what might be deemed a burden In this movement, Durham is a *model Town.* Let other Towns go and do likewise. If all the Towns in the State should do thus, the History of the State would be written.

It should be stated that the whole subject of publishing was placed under the direction of the following Committee —William C. Fowler, William Wadsworth, Joseph Chedsey, and Simeon S Scranton. The following is their Report:—

"TO THE CITIZENS OF DURHAM.

The Committee appointed in accordance with the Resolution adopted by the Town, have had the subject of publication under consideration, and, as the result of their examination, they herewith present you with the HISTORY OF DURHAM, written and compiled by Professor William C. Fowler.

WILLIAM WADSWORTH,
JOSEPH CHEDSEY,
S. S. SCRANTON."

In acknowledging my obligations to the other Members of the Committee, for their attention and assistance, I would beg leave to say, that I have endeavored to write a history composed of facts and not of fancies. Had I introduced fewer prosaic facts, and more poetic fancies, it might be more read, and yet be less valuable, because less reliable. President Timothy Dwight used to repeat a story of Voltaire, who in his histories sometimes sacrificed truth in order to be readable. When an Abbé, in gentle terms, charged him with this literary sin, he replied,— "Monsieur L'Abbé, I must be read." There are editors of newspapers, and letter writers, and reviewers, and even historians, now-a-days, who seem to have adopted the rule of Voltaire, in their compositions, whether they ever heard of it or not. It should be kept in mind, that a principal object of the Town, in publishing this book, was to *preserve the Records, and place them in the hands of the inhabitants in a form convenient for reference.*

The spelling, I have adopted as I found it. In acknowledging my obligations to many for aid, I ought especially to mention Ralph D. Smith, Esq., of Guilford, Rufus W. Matthewson, M. D., of Durham, and Leveret Norton, Esq., of Suffield.

W C. F.

CONTENTS.

HISTORY OF DURHAM.

CHAPTER I.

TERRITORY

GEOGRAPHICAL POSITION.

THE TERRITORY between Middletown on the North, Haddam on the East, Killingworth and Guilford on the South, and Wallingford on the West, was, for a long time, supposed to belong to these Towns. It was a *terra incognita*, an unknown region. But when these Towns were surveyed, it was found to belong to none of them. Even after this discovery, as it was considered too small for a Township, it did not attract very much attention.

COLONIAL GRANTS.

But the Colonial legislature granted in it a large number of farms to distinguished men, in different parts of the Colony, for civil, military, and ecclesiastical services. As early as 1662, the General Court made a grant of land to John Talcott and others, and in 1669 to Samuel Talcott; in 1670 to soldiers that had served in the Pequot war; in 1672 certain lands were surveyed, and assigned to Governor William Leete, Rev. Israel Chauncey, and others. For a period, if a public man merited the gratitude of the Colony by wisdom in council, bravery in battle, in the Pequot war, or by preaching a good election sermon, he was rewarded by the grant of a farm in COGINCHAUG, as the territory was called. In this way the Colony could show its gratitude to public men, without taxing the people; and those men could keep the lands, thus granted, until they should become valuable for themselves or their heirs.

2

The Colonial Assembly, styled the "General Court," granted th south eastern part of the territory to Killingworth. In the *Col onial Record*, 1686, is the following entry: "The Court grant to the Towne of Kenilworth, all the lands north of their bound and Guilford, and west of Haddam bounds up to Coginchau swamp, which are not formerly granted to any Township or per ticular person." This tract was, after considerable negotiation restored to Durham by Killingworth, that is the jurisdictio of it, in 1708, for the consideration of sixty acres, in fee simple paid by Durham. Henry Crane lived in Killingworth which had been taken off from Coginchaug, where Henry E Nettleton now lives. In 1773 a tract from Haddam was added to the northeast part of Durham, which is still called "Haddam Quar ter." The inhabitants there, for a long time, perhaps from the first, attended meeting in Durham. Thus in 1734, Thomas Fair child, Stephen Smith, Abner Newton, Nathaniel Sutliff, John Smith, John Coe, Simeon Parsons paid their ministerial tax in Durham.

Thus it appears that Durham is made up of territory belonging to Coginchaug or Durham propriety, Killingworth propriety, and Haddam propriety. Moreover portions of it belonged to three Counties, namely, the Coginchaug portion to New Haven County, the Killingworth portion to New London County, and the Haddam portion to Hartford County. Afterwards for a long time, by the request of the inhabitants, the whole town belonged to New Haven County. It was, at the request of the inhabitants, annexed to Middlesex County in May, 1799.

This territory was, by the Indians, called *Coginchaug*, a name in their language descriptive of the *long swamp*, or the *thick swamp*, in its central portion extending from south to north. In 1704 it was, by the act of the General Assembly, called DURHAM, from a city and county seat in the north of England, according to some tradition the residence of the Wadsworth family.

OWNERSHIP.

The Indians were the original owners of the soil, namely, the Mettabesset Indians, who resided in and about Middletown, and who frequented Coginchaug as a hunting ground. Of these Indians the grantees of land in Coginchaug purchased the territory. In 1672, January 24th, in the *Colonial Record of Lands*," Vol I, p. 411 is the following: "Mr. Samuel Wyllis, Capt. John Talcott who, besides his own grant, had purchased the right of a soldier by the name of Bunce, Mr. James Richard, Mr. John Allyn, all of whom held lands in Coginchaug under grants from the General Court, purchased the native right of the whole tract from the Sachem *Tarramuggus* and others. They valued these signatures of the natives, notwithstanding Governor Andros had said that the "signature of an Indian was no better than the scratch of a bear's paw."

The General Court also granted farms, in addition to those already mentioned, to Rev. Samuel Russell, James Steele, Esq., Commissary of the Connecticut forces, in Phillip's war, Rev. John Whiting, Governor Gurdon Saltonstall, Gov. William Leete, Deacon John Fowler, Deacon William Johnson, ancestor of the celebrated William Samuel Johnson, Lieut. Joseph Seward, Deacon John Graves. The farms of the last four were called the *Guilford Farms*, and lay in one piece in the southwest part of the town. Two hundred acres also were granted to Rev. Joseph Elliott of Guilford, son of the apostle John Elliott, and one hundred acres to Abraham Pierson, the first president of Yale College. John Stone, Esq., Rev. Timothy Woodbridge, and others, received similar grants. Besides these, there was the ungranted land in possession of the General Court. The high character of these owners of lands inspired confidence and attracted respectable men to settle in Durham. Such owners, too, could hardly fail of being successful, in their application to the General Assembly, especially when one of their number was Governor of the Colony.

PRESENT OWNERSHIP.

The present ownership, or title to the lands in Durham is derived 1. From purchase of the Indians. 2. From the patent of Connecticut under the great seal of England. 3. From the grants made by the Colonial Legislature to individuals, which those individuals had power to convey by deed. 4. From the patent of Durham under the seal of the Colony, which gave power to the proprietors of Durham to make allotments of land to individuals, who had power to convey these lands thus allotted, by deed.

PETITION FOR A TOWN PLAT.

A petition dated April 29, 1699, was addressed to the General Court, by a number of inhabitants of Guilford, some of whom were owners in the above named grants, as follows:

"To the General Court sitting in Hartford, May 1699:

We whose names are underwritten, do humbly request of this Honorable Court, that you would grant that the tract of land commonly called Coginchaug, bounded northwardly by Middletown, easterly by Haddam, westerly by Wallingford, and southerly by Guilford, and Kenelworth, may be by this Honorable Court granted, and settled for a Township; and to that end, and for the encouragement of your humble petitioners, and such others as shall be thought meet to join with them, that you would grant that all the common lands unlaid out, be granted to this Township. The Grounds and Reasons of your humble petitioners moving thus to petition are as follows:

1st. It having pleased this Honorable Court formerly to grant sundry farms which have been laid out in the forementioned Tract of Land, the Country filling up with People, one family having already gone from Guilford to that place, and sundry more having strong inclination moving that way, Provided this Honorable Court would so far favor it, that it may be probable with all convenient speed, the ordinances of God might be settled there, it being considerably remote from any other town, and looks to be very difficult if not almost impossible for any comfortable attainment of them, which should be the greatest thing that we should have regard to in our settling here in this Wilderness.

2d. If people should settle out on the great farms already laid out, it must always be very scattered and distant from each other, and very probably be long before they can imbody themselves either for the enjoyment of ordinances, or for defending themseles if any trouble should arise in the country, which this Honorable Court has seen the sorrowful experience of formerly; now if this Honorable Court should in your wisdom think meet to grant our petitions, we desire there may be a Committee by this Court appointed and empowered to make search for, and lay out a Town plat where it may be judged most advantageous to accommodate those farms already layed out. And your petitioners will ever pray.

Caleb Seaward, William Stone, John Collins, Jr., Joseph Grave, William Jones, Abraham Bradley, Thomas Maycock, Nathaniel Stone, John Collins, Sr., John Parmele, Thomas Cook, John Hall, Sr., Nathaniel Grave, James Benton, Abraham Fowler, John Seaward, Josiah Rossiter, William Johnson, Comfort Starr, Peter Tallman, Joel Parmele, Jacob Doude, Ezekiel Bull, Joseph Seaward, Stephen Bradley, Sr, John Grover, Thomas Wallstone, James Hooker, Samuel Johnson, Obadiah Wilcoxen, John Hall, Jr.

THE PETITION GRANTED.

This petition was granted. A committee appointed by the General Court made their report, November, 1699, "that they had laid out a Town plat in the south part of Coginchaug, bounded north by Caleb Seaward's land, east by John Stone's land, south by Abraham Pierson's land, and west by the Guilford Farms." The Committee that laid out the first Town plat, Nov. 1699, were Nathaniel White, Thomas Yale, John Griswold, and Daniel Brainard. This Town plat was evidently laid out under the Guilford influence. Another committee was appointed by the General Court, May 13th, 1703, namely Mr. John Griswold, Mr. Caleb Stanley and Mr. John Hooker, to act with the inhabitants of Coginchaug. These laid out a new Town plat, evidently under the Hartford influence, where the town was afterwards built. As a motive to induce settlers to come in, it was, at the advice of this General Court, agreed by the owners of the farms already granted, that they would surrender a "fourth part of their lands," so that such persons as should come in to settle as inhabitants, should have a common right to all the undivided and ungranted land and to the fourth part thus surrendered. This arrangement was a wise one, and proved to be satisfactory to immigrants, as it was likewise to the owners of the farms.

CHANGE OF TOWN PLAT.

The Committee who laid out the second Town plat, performed their duties judiciously. The old plat was given up by Legislative enactment for the new one. The ground on which the new Town plat was laid, was admirably adapted to the purpose. It was a ridge of land running North and South, a mile and a half in length, sloping off towards the East and the West. On the summit of this ridge running North and South, a street was laid out by the Committee, eight rods wide, as stated in the Town Records, reaching from the Wadsworth place on the South, to the Swathel place on the North, called the "Broad street" and the "Great street." Parallel to this, at a suitable distance, was laid out another street of the same length, as it appears, six rods or more wide, which has been called the "Back lane." East of the Broad street, and parallel with it, at a suitable distance, a third street was laid out, now known as "Brick lane," or "Cherry lane;" it was of the same length as the Broad street, but what was the original width of it, does not appear. Other streets were also laid out; near the Wadsworth place, opposite the Green, at the Quarry, at Simeon S. Scranton's, and at the site of the North School House. The street past the house now known as having belonged to Dennis Camp, was substituted for the street laid out by the Committee past Francis Hubbard's house. Many years subsequently to the laying out of the Town plat, a narrow street was laid out by the town from the Broad Street to Crooked lane, so called, after much delay and opposition. The breadth of these cross streets appears to have been something like five rods. I have not been able to find the exact width put down in the record. The proprietors or the Town seem in some cases to have used their discretionary power as to adhering to the action of the Legislative committee. Individuals have also encroached on these streets, thus sacrificing the rights of the town to their own interests.

DOINGS OF THE GENERAL COURT RESPECTING THE TOWN PLAT.

"It is agreed by the proprietors and owners of ye farms, granted by the General Assembly at Coginchaug, that each proprietor or owner, shall lay out of the two ranges of Farms, such a part of their respective proprieties on that side of their respective farms which adjoined Mr. Talcott's land, as shall be judged sufficient for a good Town plat, and that house lots shall be laid out in the said Town plat for a convenient number of inhabitants, and a reasonable value to recompense for the first cost of the said land and laying the same out, shall be set upon each of said lots, which each inhabitant that takes up a lot there, shall pay to the proprietors, and the money, so received be divided among the respective proprietors, according to the number of lots which each of them shall so throw up to make the Town plat; wherefore the proprietors or owners of the said ranges of farms, who, for the settlement of a plantation at the said Coginchaug, have relinquished and thrown up a proportion of their lands, in the only convenient place there for a settlement of inhabitants, do pray this Honorable Court that whereas in March, 1700, the Assembly did grant that a township should be laid out at Coginchaug, whereupon a Town plat hath been laid out in such a place, of the said Township, as cannot receive many, or encourage any inhabitants who are to settle there; so that the land thereabouts is like to lay waste and unimproved; this Assembly would now grant that the Town plat should be removed from ye sd place, where it hath been and is laid out and carried to ye place so set apart by the proprietors for the sd use; which all persons that have viewed the sd lands consider as the only convenient place for erecting houses and settling inhabitants, and may be the means of procuring a flourishing plantation there in a short time."

Passed in the upper House.

E. KIMBERLEY, *Secretary.*

Passed in the lower House, May 22d, 1703, provided the land be sold at a reasonable price."

ELEAZAR STENT, *Secretary.*

THE NAME CHANGED.

"At a Court of Election holden at Hartford, May 11th, 1704. This Court grants the petition of Mr. Samuel Russell, Mr. Gurdon Saltonstall, Mr. James Steel, Mr. Benjamin Talcott, Mr. Nathaniel Talcott, and the rest of the proprietors of the farms of Cocinchauge, concerning the settlements of the said Cocinchauge, they laying down the one fourth part of their several farms for the better accommodation of inhabitants to be received there, which quarter part, together with such common land there that hath not already been granted away by the General Court, shall be laid out by the said farmers as a committee in house lots, and other allotments to such persons as shall offer themselves for inhabitants there, and are qualified for inhabitants according to law, which plantation shall be called by the name of Durham, and have this figure for a brand for their horse kind, viz: D———. And whereas, the town of Killingworth have formerly had a grant of land within the bounds of Cockinchauge, it is ordered that if they will lay down a quarter part thereof for the accommodation of the plantation as the above farmers do, then they shall have liberty to appoint a proportionable number of themselves to be joined with the Committee of Farmers for the laying out and disposing of the land to inhabitants as is before expressed."

The town of Killingworth preferred another arrangement to the one here offered by the General Court.

"A court of election held at Hartford, May 11th, 1704. Ordered and enacted by this Court that the Farmers or proprietors at Caukinchauge, viz: those proprietors on the east side do run their lines and mark their bounds within one year, and give notice to their adjoining Neighbors, but that if they do not so bound their farms, that then the surveyor of the County of Hartford shall measure and bound said farms upon the charge of the proprietors"

"At a General Court held at Hartford, May ye 13th, 1708. This Assembly doth grant unto Mr. Hezekiah Talcott, Joseph Seaward, Caleb Seaward, David Robinson, John Sutliff, Samuel Fairchilde, and James Wadsworth together with ye rest of ye inhabitantes and Proprietors in the Township of Durham, excepting the town of Killingworth, or any Proprietors of Land in Durham, yt are Inhabetantes of Killingworth, and concerned in ye Agreement heareafter mentioned, their Heircs, suckcessors and Assignees, that Tract of land lying and being between ye township of Middletown and ye townshipes of Guilford and Killingworth, and ye Township of Haddam and ye Township of Wallingford ye said Tract of Land being bounded as followeth: to ye east or eastwardly by ye Township of Haddam aforesd; to ye west or westwardly by ye township of Wallingford aforesd; to ye north or northwardly by ye Township of Middletown aforesd; to ye South or southwardly by ye Townshipes of Guilford and Killingworth together with all and singular Rights, Preveledges, Profites, Members and Timber, Timber Trees, Wood, underwood, Mines, Mineralls (reserving only ye fifth Part of ye Silver and Gold Oare to her Majestye) Stones, Quarries, Water, Water Courses, and all other Apurtenances thereon or thereunto belonging, or in any wise thereunto apurtaining, be by ye major Part of ye sd inhabitantes and proprietors, (excepting as above excepted) granted and disposed of, not prejudising former Grantes of Farmes unto pertecular Persons (particularly not to prejudis ye farmes formerly layde out unto Mr. Samuel Willyes, Esqr., Mr Samuel Talcott and Mr. John Whiting, as they were lately survayed anew by Willyam Tomson, surveyer of ye County of New Haven, Octobr ye 17th, 1704 which sd Farmes are heareby saved to ye sd oregenall Grantees or thos yt now clayme under them) all ye Owners of ye aforementioned Farmes within ye Township to allow necessary Highways through sd Farmes, also not prejudising Artecles of an agreement made and concluded Janewary ye 29th, 1707–8 by Cometes impowered by sd Townes of Killingworth and Durham. And also this Assembly doth grant unto ye sd inhabitantes, viz: unto thos of them which are or hereafter shall be quallefied ackording to law annually, (being regularly called together) ye liberty of chuseing their own ordenary offesers as fully and amplely as any Town in this Collony of Conecticut and ye sd Offesers being so chosen and quallefyed acording to Law, shall have power to act (within their own precencts,) as fully and amplely as Offesers in any Town in this Colony And this Assembly doth also order yt ye above sd Persones shall for themselves and ye rest of ye Inhabitantes in ye sd Township of Durham their heirs, sucksessors and Assignes as above sd, shall have a Pattent for ye more full and ample Confermation of ye sd Tract of Land, together with all and singular ye Rightes and Preveledges thereon, or thereunto belonging as above is mentioned, the sd Pattent to be signed by ye Honerable ye Governer and Secretary in ye name and Behalf of ye Governer and Company.

A Trew copie of ye Act of ye Generll Assembly of May ye 13th, 1708, conserning ye Town of Durham acording to ye import thereof.

TST. ELEAZAR KIMBERLY, *Secretary.*

DURHAM PATENT.

"To All People unto whom this present Act and Deed shall come, Greeting: Whereas, by letters patents from his late Majesty King Charles the second, under the Great Seal of England, bearing date at Westminster, in the fourteenth year of his Reign, his said Majesty was pleased upon diverse good considirations therein mentioned to give and grant for himself, his Heirs and Successors to John Winthrop, Esq., and several others his loving Subjects in the said Letters patent named and and incorporated by the Name of Governor and Company of the English Colony of Connecticut in America their Successors, and assigns forever all that part of his Dominion, contained, comprehended, and being within certain limitts sett and fixed for the Bounds and Extent of the said Colony of Connecticut, with all firm Lands, Soyles, Havens, Ports, Rivers, Waters, Mines, Minerals, fishings, precious Stones, Quarries, and all singular other Commodities, Jurisdictions, Royalties, Priviledges and preliminaries, Franchises and Hereditaments whatsoever within the Tract of Land, Islands and Bounds of the said Colony.

To Have and to Hold unto the said Governor and Company their Heirs and Successors, and assigns forever in Trust and for the use of themselves and their associates the freemen of the said Colony their Heirs and Assigns forever to be holden of his said Majesty, his Heirs and Successors in free and Common Soccage, &c, reserving only the payment of One fifth part of all the Gold and Silver Oar, &c, which shall happen to be found-had, gotten &c, unto his said Majesty his Heirs and Successors; as in and by the said Letters Patent, Relation being thereto had, doth and will more fully appear. And Whereas, the proprietors, Inhabitants of the Town of Durham within the said Colony, Have granted unto them by the Governor and Company in General Court assembled, May 13th, 1708, all that tract of Land, both upland and meadow Grounds and Soiles, with the members and Appurtenances thereof called and known by the Name of Durham, which said Tract of Land is butted and bounded as followeth, viz: East or Eastwardly by the Township of Haddam; West or Westwardly by the Township of Wallingford; North or Northwardly by the Township of Middletown;

South or Southwardly by the Townships of Guilford and Killingworth. AND WHEREAS they having for some years past stood quietly and peaceably possessed thereof, and the same now being in their lawfull peaceable and Quiet, Seizen and Possession, and now applying themselves to the Governor and Company aforesaid in General Court assembled for a more full Confirmation by Patent Deed or Conveyance according to Law KNOW, THEREFORE, All Men that for further and full Confirmation and sure making of all the aforesd Tract of Land, granted at aforesaid, with all the Rights, Members and Appurtenances thereof and the improvements made thereupon, and that the same be held by the Grantees hereafter mentioned, according to the true Import and intent of the aforesaid Letters Patent from his Majesty King Charles the second. We the said Governor and Company of the aforesaid English Colony of Connecticut, in New England in America, being now assembled in General Court, in discharge of our Trust and by Vertue of the Power derived to us in and by the said Letters Patent, have Given, Granted, Conveyed, Confirmed, Enfeofed and firmly made over, and do by these Presents for Ourselves our Heirs and Successors fully and absolutely give, Grant and Convey, Enfeof, Rattifie, Confirm and make over unto Mr. Hezekiah Talcot, Joseph Seward, Caleb Seward, Mr. David Robinson, John Sutliff, Samuel Fairchild and James Wadsworth and all others the present proprietors and inhabetants of Durham aforesaid, (excepting the town of Killingworth or any Proprietor of Land, in Durham that are Inhabitants of Killingworth, and are concerned in the agreements made Janry the 29th, 1707–8, between the Towns of Killingworth and Durham) their Heirs and Assigns forever.

All the afore mentioned Tracts of Land, both Upland and Meadow Grounds and Soiles whatsoever contained within the Limitts and Boundaries above expressed to be by a major Part of of the Proprietors and Inhabitants disposed off, not prejudceing former Grants of Farms nor Articles of Agreements as aforementioned, made January 29th, 1707–8, (being fully Expressed and Limitted unto the said Proprietors and Inhabitants by the aforementioned General Court,) and now in their Actual and peaceable possession called and known by the Name of Durham with all the Wood and underwoods, Commons, Pastures, Herbage

Feeding, Stones, Rivers, Rivuletts, Ponds, Waters, precious Stones, Quarries, Emoluments, Commodities, Heredetaments, Priviledges and appurtenances thereto belonging or any wise appertaining and therewith Used, Occupied and enjoyed also all the Estate, Right, Title, Interests, Claim or Demand which We the said Governor and Company by Vertue of the aforesd Letters Patent ever have have had, or which we our Heirs and Successors can or might Have or Challenge in time to Come of in or to the said Land and premises or to any part or parcell thereof, or the Housing, Buildings and Appurtenances thereof.

To HAVE AND TO HOLD all the above granted Premeses to the said Hezekiah Talcott, Joseph Seward, Caleb Seward, David Robinson, John Sutliff, Samuel Fairchild and James Wadsworth and to the rest of the Proprietors and Inhabitants of Durham aforesaid, (except what is above Excepted) their Heirs and Assigns, or others lawfully Deriving from them, forever to be holden in free and Common Soccage, and not in Capita nor by Knight Service, rendering and paying unto our Sovereign Lady the Qeen, her Heirs and Successors, one fifth part of all Gold and Silver Oar, which shall be there had or gotten in any part thereof, in Lieu of all Rents, Services and Demands whatsoever.

IN WITNESS whereof, We, the said Governor and Company, have caused the Seal of the Colony to be hereunto affixed the Twenty and first Day of May in the seventh Year of the Reign of Our Sovereign Lady ANN of Great Britain and Ireland's Queen, Anno Dom. 1708.

G. SALTONSTALL, *Governor*

By order of the Honble the Governor and General Assembly.

ELEAZAR KIMBERLY, *Secretary.*

We can easily understand with what exultation the inhabitants of Durham received this patent from the Governor. They were now a TOWN in the full sense of the word They now had the right to discuss in Town meetings all matters of public interest, to enroll all the able bodied men in the militia, to raise money to support the ministry, and schools and highways and the poor; to elect and instruct their representatives. They had now all the rights of the other Towns of the State, greater rights than the Towns of England. The township was a territorial parish; the town was the religious congregation; the independent church was established by law, the minister was elected by the people, who annually made grants for his support. See Bancroft's History, Vol. IV., p. 149.

THE PATENTEES OR PROPRIETORS.

At the time the patent was issued, the number of adults males, was thirty-four, most of them heads of families Their names were Caleb Seaward, John Seaward, Joseph Seaward, David Robinson, and Joel Parmelee, from Guilford; the Rev. Nathaniel Chauncey, Isaac Chauncey, Robert Coe, Joseph Coe, Samuel Fairchild, James Curtis, Ezekiel Hawley and Benjamin Baldwin, from Stratford; Richard Beach and Benjamin Beach, supposed to have been from the same place; James Baldwin, Samuel Camp, William Roberts, Samuel Sanford and Thomas Wheeler, from Milford; Joseph Gaylord, Joseph Gaylord, Jr., John Gaylord, Joseph Hickox and Stephen Hickox, from Waterbury; Joseph Norton and Samuel Norton, from Saybrook; John Sutliff and Nathaniel Sutliff, from Deerfield, James Wadsworth from Farmington: Jonathan Wells, from Hatfield, Henry Crane, from Killingworth; Hezekiah Talcott, from Hartford, and Ezekiel Buck, from Weathersfield. These were regarded as *original* proprietors.

They were joined by John Norton, from Saybrook; by the Ancestors of the Lymans, Parsons, and Strongs, from Northampton, of the Newtons, Guernseys, Tibbalses, Merwins and Canfields from Milford; of the Pickets, from Stratford; of the Bateses, from Haddam; and of the Hulls from Killingworth, and of the Fowlers from Guilford. In later periods, families have settled in the Town by the name of Hall, Hart, Bishop, Scranton, Chedsey, from Guilford; of Smith and Johnson from Middletown, of Chalker and Loveland from Saybrook, and of Butler from Branford. The first white child born in the Town was Ephraim Seaward, son of Caleb Seaward, the first settler, who lived just north of where George Atwell now lives. He was born Aug. 6, 1700; and died in 1780. In 1756 there were 799 inhabitants, exclusive of Haddam quarter, in which there may have been 100 or 150 more. In 1776 there was 1076. In 1840 —1095. In 1860—1131.

THE FIRST TOWN MEETING HELD AT DURHAM.

"Dec. 24th, 1706 Mr Nathaniel Sutliff was chosen Constable for the Town of Durham for ye year ensuing. Caleb Seaward was chosen Towne Clerke for ye Town of Durham.

At ye same meeting Joseph Seward, Joseph Gailord, and Samuel Fairchild were chosen Selectmen for ye year ensuing.

Thomas Wheeler and Joseph Hickox were at ye same meeting chosen Surveyors of Highways for ye year ensuing, also Samuel Sanford and Joel Parmalee were chosen Fence Viewers for ye year ensuing.

At ye same meeting Joseph Seward and Robert Coe were chosen listers for ye year ensuing.

At ye same meeting Caleb Seward was chosen Collector for ye year ensuing. Also John Sutlief was at ye same meeting chosen Culler for ye year ensuing for the town of Durham

At the same meeting it was voted, that the place for ye Town Pound shall be for ye time being between Nathaniel Sutliff and John Sutliff on ye east side of the street.

At ye same meeting ye desire of the town was voted for the town of Durham to be annexed to ye County of New Haven."

This first town meeting was held before the patent was issued or any act of incorporation was passed by the General Assembly, but not before that Assembly had acted so far as to afford evidence that a patent would be granted. The settlers were in haste to become a town, but they acted with due submission to the Assembly.

"At a Town meeting April 7, 1707. The town by voate declare their minds that they would have, and by this vote empower ye Selectmen, by themselves, or by an atturney empowered by them, to make application to the General Assembly in May next, that the sd General Assembly would decide to settle ye bounds between ye Town of Kenelworth, and the Town of Durham, and explain the meaning of the clause, [up to Coginchaug swamp] which clause is in a former and additional grant to Kenelworth aforesaid, and under color of which grant they do pretend to the land within the Township of Durham."

"At the same meeting James Wadsworth was appointed to prefer this application on behalf of the Town of Durham to the General Assembly in their session in Hartford in May next."

Thus Durham at the very first and before being incorporated found itself involved in a dispute with Kennelworth as to territorial boundary The above vote was a very judicious one; Kennelworth acted liberally, and the Assembly very properly returned to Durham what had been taken from Coginchaug When the annexation of Haddam Quarter was pending, Durham, by a vote in Town meeting, refused to make application to the Assembly that the transfer from Haddam should be made. In the first case Durham stood upon its rights; in the other it respected the rights of Haddam.

LANDS GRANTED FOR PUBLIC USES.

"At a town meeting, Feb. 16, 1707. The Town by vote doth grant two allotments, in every division of land herein granted, for the encouragement of the ministry; and one of said allotments the town by vote doth grant unto the minister and his heirs forever who shall here be settled in the gospel ministry; and the other allotment to be and *remain for the support of the ministry* in the Town of Durham forever, but only with that proviso, *that if there should be not, or so often as there should be no orthodox dispenser of the word resident here*, that doth publicly dispense the same here in this Town, that then the *whole profit* of said allotment shall be unto the town, and is hereby reserved for the Town." The condition of grant was that the land should "remain," and that the "profit" only should be unto the Town, if there should be and so often as there should be no "orthodox dispenser of the word *resident* here." Under this vote, and as a gift from the proprietors, to the Town, as many as five pieces of land were allotted to the support of the ministry forever.

As many as five pieces of land were allotted by the proprietors to the Town, and by the Town given to Mr. Chauncey, the first minister, and his heirs forever

Lands were granted by the proprietors for a burying ground between the Broad street and the Back lane, reaching from a certain point on the north to Allyn's brook on the south. South of this end of Allyn's brook, and of the same width between the two streets, land was granted to the first minister to belong to him and his heirs. Four other pieces of land were allotted to him. Land was also granted south of the ministers' lot, and of the same width between the same streets, reaching to Samuel Camp's land, now Mr. Canfield's land, for a public green, described in the language of the proprietors' clerk as the "Meeting house place."

The gift of five pieces of land to Mr. Chauncey, the first Minister, on condition that he should *continue* as their minister, was in accordance with the primitive practice of the congregation of Connecticut to give land or money, or other property, to a minister as his "settlement." This "settlement" is based on the idea that the minister should *stay* where he is ordained, not that he *alights* there for a temporary resting place A "settlement" thus served to bind the contract, as earnest money does other contracts.

When my minister in my youth, the Rev. John Elliott of Madison, sitting with the Committee of the parish at a table in negotiating terms of his settlement, accepted of the terms they offered—"It is done," said he bringing his hand down on the table, "I will live with you and die with you, and lay my bones with you." His bones lie in the grave yard there with the bones of his people. A "settlement" indicated a union for life between a minister and his people, almost as sacred as the marriage union.

Before dismissing this general topic, I would state, that the parsonage land north of the burying ground, the burying ground itself, the ministers' lot south of it, and the public green, were taken from the land which was owned by John Talcott, the whole tract thus lying in one body, being a portion of that fourth part of the several farms, granted by the legislature, which was surrendered to the proprietors of Durham by the owners of the farms, when the General Assembly established the Town plat.

HIGHWAYS AND ROADS.

The roads connected with the Town plat have already been mentioned. At a Town meeting September 2, 1707, the town ordered three public highways to be laid out across Coginchaug swamp four rods wide. These three roads were one from the

Broad street to the north "west side," one to the middle "west side," one to the south "west side" The term "west side" means the west side of Coginchaug river, and not the west side of the Town, though it is in the west side of the town. At a Town meeting, August 23, 1709, a committee was appointed by the Town to lay out a highway, four rods wide, across the swamp, westward of Joseph Hickox. His house stood near where Bela Davis's house now stands. The committee in their report, March 28, 1710, say that they "had laid out the road across the swamp four rods wide, and one mile in length" This is the road south of the place ownedby Col Samuel Camp, now owned by Phinehas Meiggs

"At a Town meeting, Sept. 24, 1712 The Town by voate made choyse of the selectmen for the time annually, to take effectual care that the several highways throughout the Town bounds be not encroached upon by any person, and that the said ways are to be kept free their full width." Other acts of a similar kind were afterwards passed.

BOUNDARY LINES.

In 1701 the boundary line was run between the Town of Wallingford, and the Town of Durham or Coginchaug. The Guilford committee were Josiah Rossiter, Abraham Fowler and John Collins. The Wallingford committee were Thomas Holt and John Merriman

In September, 1705, Caleb Stanley, surveyor of lands, by the desires of the committees appointed by the Towns of Haddam and Killingworth ran the line between Haddam and Killingworth and between Haddam and Durham.

In 1707 the boundary line was run between the town of Guilford and the town of Durham. The Guilford committee were John Fowler, brother of Abraham, and Daniel Evarts, and Andrew Ward. The Durham committee were Caleb Seward and James Wright.

In June, 1708, the agreement was made between Killingworth and Durham in regard to the restoration of the land to Durham which had been granted by the General Court, 1686, to Killingworth. The Killingworth committee were Henry Crane, Samuel

Buel, John Buel, Robert Lane and John Crane. The Durham committee were Joseph Seward, John Sutliff, James Wadsworth.

In March, 1708, the line was run between Killingworth and Durham The Killingworth committee were William Wellman, John Lane, Henry Crane. The Durham committee were Joseph Seaward, John Sutliff, James Wadsworth.

In April, 1711, the boundary line was run between Middletown and Durham The Middletown committee were Hezekiah Wetmore, William Harris, Thomas Miller. The Durham committee were James Wadsworth, John Sutliff.

It should be added that it was the practice, for many years, for suitable men appointed by the selectmen, to "perambulate" the borders or bounds of the Town, and renew the boundary where necessary.

PROPRIETORS.

Before the patent was issued the owners of the farms granted by the Legislature, were called proprietors, that is of the *land granted.* They were absentee owners or non-residents.

After the patent was issued, only those were henceforth considered as original proprietors of Durham, who were *inhabitants of Durham at the time the patent was issued.* They became owners of all the land in Durham which had not been granted to the above named grantees, and also of one-fourth part of what had been granted, which was surrendered by the owners of the farms for the benefit of the first inhabitants. A list of the original proprietors has already been given.

OTHER PROPRIETORS VOTED IN.

Others were afterwards, by vote, admitted as proprietors, some to a full and some to a half share The following is a list of the proprietors in 1724: Nathaniel Sutliff, Ministry, David Robinson, Sen., Josiah Fowler, Joseph Seward, Sen , Jonathan Wells, Samuel Fairchild, James Baldwin, V. Clement's heirs, Thomas Wheeler, John Camp, 1st, Noadiah Graves, Joseph Tibbals, David Robinson, Jun., Hezekiah Talcott, John Gaylord Caleb Seward, Samuel Camp, Joseph Coe, Daniel Merwin, Samuel Parsons, John Seward, Nathaniel Chauncey, Joseph Norton, Henry Crane, John Norton, James Wadsworth, William Seward, Stephen Hickox's heirs, Joel Parmelee, Samuel Norton. The following were half share proprietors: Richard Beach, Noah Lyman's heirs, Moses Parsons, Benjamin Beach's heirs, Nathan Camp, Thomas Lyman, Timothy Parsons, James Curtis, Isaac Chauncey, Ebenezer Lyman, David Fowler. Some of the rights were afterwards transferred, so that in 1742 the list differs considerably from the list above.

The reason why the original proprietors consented to admit others to a full or a half share with themselves was, that they wished to induce them to become inhabitants of the Town Some of those thus admitted, owned farms under the original grants from the Assembly.

PROPRIETORS' MEETINGS.

Even before the above named agreement was made, and before the patent was issued, the owners of land in Durham had meetings in Guilford. Dec 28, 1700, they had a meeting at which Abraham Fowler was appointed a committee on the lands, and was appointed a grand juror, and Hon. JOSIAH ROSSITER, of Guilford was appointed Recorder or Clerk Besides being an owner, he had been appointed by the General Court to lay out some of the farms, granted to individuals He acted as clerk until Feb. 10, 1707–8, when Hon. JAMES WADSWORTH'S name first appears as clerk. He in turn, appears to have acted until his death in 1756, when his grandson, Gen. James Wadsworth, was appointed clerk. He acted as clerk until January 6, 1819, when Worthington G Chauncey was appointed clerk. He performed the duties of the office until 1824, since which time there have been no meetings.

PROPRIETORS' MEETINGS DISTINCT FROM TOWN MEETINGS

After the grant of Town privileges in 1708, the proprietors held their meetings in Durham, and occasionally admitted new members by name, some whole share, and some half share members. They generally held their meetings at the same time that the Town held their meetings, but these meetings were kept distinct, and committees were generally appointed by one body to confer with committees appointed by the other body. When a grant of a certain number of acres was made to each proprietor, a committee was chosen to make Surveys, or rather give them. The committee was clothed with power to keep off encroachments, commence suits, exchange and lay out highways, and occasionally to lease certain tracts of common land or a useless highway.

For instance, in 1762, the selectmen, under instructions from the Town, made application to the proprietors for the Green and the Burying Ground. Their language is, "The favor requested is of a public nature and is not greater than is necessary and convenient to answer the purpose asked for." The Green is asked for "the purposes of a parade to perform military exercises, musters, &c. upon, and also for building public houses as Meeting houses, Court houses, Town and School houses, or the like, as the inhabitants of said town may have occasion. The Burying hill asked for is not larger than is necessary for the purpose of a burying ground." In this, as in other cases, the Town understood what were the rights of the proprietors and what were the rights of the Town, and that these rights were not in all respects the same.

Besides the Durham proprietors, there were also the Killingworth proprietors, and the Haddam proprietors, that originally owned land in what is now called Durham

ENCROACHMENTS UPON PUBLIC LANDS.

We have seen that the Town was laid out and settled by men of enlarged views and generous purposes Liberal donations of land were made by the proprietors for highways, for a Burial Ground, for a Public Green, for the support of the ministry. The first generation of settlers were generally animated by the enlightened views which they endeavored to carry out, under the influence of an enlarged public spirit. Committees were from an early period appointed to watch over the lands thus given, and prevent all encroachments by individuals. The public weal was cared for. But it has to be confessed that some who came after the generous fathers of the Town, endeavored to obtain for themselves what had been given to the public. Encroachments were made, some of them more than a century ago and some later, upon the streets in closing them and removing them; upon the Green by enclosing half of it or more than half and placing private houses upon it, upon the old Burying Ground by enclosing and cultivating a portion of it, and by cutting a road through it without the shadow of a right.

Encroachments, if such they may be called, have been made by virtually selling, under the name of a lease for 999 years, the land which was granted for the support of the ministry. That there was no authority to sell is evident from the wording of the grant by the proprietors' clerk, Col. James Wadsworth. See p. 31. He was their clerk and Town clerk for nearly fifty years. Gen. James Wadsworth was after him proprietors' clerk until his death, and Town clerk for thirty years. Worthington G. Chauncey was proprietors' clerk after him and Town clerk twenty years. These men all agreed in the declaration that neither the Town nor the Ecclesiastical Society had any right to sell the parsonage lands.

THE EVIL OF THESE ENCROACHMENTS.

Had these Parsonage lands been retained, they would, at the present time, have been much more valuable than any money obtained for them, and would have been a bond of union. By selling these lands in violation of the trust, the Ecclesiastical Society must have weakened confidence in the public mind, so that cautious men would hardly dare to convey property to such societies in trust, lest the trust should be violated, when they are sleeping in their graves.

Several of the first proprietors of Durham were the sons or grandsons of emigrants from England, where trusts of this kind were held sacred.

Had no encroachments been made on the Burying Ground hill, there would have been ample room for the burial of the dead of the present generation, and for a long time to come.

Had no encroachments been made upon the Green, as laid out originally, what a convenience, what an ornament it would have been, adorned with rows and groups of trees! Beautiful, for situation, is the Town plat of Durham, skirted by a prairie on one side, and by a cultivated valley on the other, and girded about by mountains, neither too near nor too remote! Beautiful is the village of Durham with its long, broad, street, studded with neat habitations, the abodes of peace and virtue, and contentment and religion. But how much more beautiful would it have been, if the ideas of the first fathers of the Town had been carried out without any encroachments!

MODE OF DISTRIBUTION.

I would add that the lands in Durham were distributed according to the mode adopted in Guilford. A settler had a home lot of six or eight acres upon which he lived, while the principal part of his land was elsewhere in the township, sometimes at a distance. This mode of distribution in Guilford and in some of the other older towns, perhaps grew out of the exposed condition of the first settlers, which rendered it necessary that they should reside in close proximity for mutual defense. Whether this is a more convenient mode than what is common in England and Virginia, may be doubted. It is remarkable that most of the settlers from Guilford lived on their farms and not on the Town plat.

THE PICTURESQUE APPEARANCE OF DURHAM.

The Territory of Durham, as already remarked, has a good deal in it to gratify the taste, and it may be the pride of the inhabitants. Just north of the Swathel House, on Bare Rock, on Pisgah, or at Frederic Parmelee's house, you can see the whole or nearly the whole of Durham, as you do a picture. When the Town was on the great mail route between Boston and New York and six stages daily passed through it, passengers, as they stopped for breakfast, or dinner, at the Swathel House, would often declare they had seen nothing on their way which for beauty of landscape surpassed it. Here General Washington and other distinguished men stopped for rest and refreshment. When Silas Deane, the minister to France, passed though, in a private carriage and four, which was a new thing in this country, he was met by a troop of boys, a mile beyond the limits of the territory of the Town on the north, and after dinner a troop of boys trotted before and after his carriage, as far as the causeway below the Wadsworth place.

As we in this generation are surrounded by our comforts and conveniences, our County lines, our Town lines, our titles to our lands recorded, our farms separated from others by fences, our religious, our literary, our civil institutions all established,—we can hardly appreciate the amount of our obligations to our fathers, who obtained and transmitted these advantages to us. They labored, and we have entered into their labors. They sowed the seed, and we are now reaping the abundant harvest, abundant beyond their brightest visions. They looked forward to us with hope, let us look back upon them with gratitude.

CHAPTER II.

MINISTRY OF REV. NATHANIEL CHAUNCEY.

TOWN ACTION.

"AT a Town Meeting, June, 1708, the Town by vote agree and grant to pay unto the much esteemed Mr. Nathaniel Chauncey for the present year's labor in the work of the ministry, provided he continueth with us in said labor, the sum of fifty-five pounds in grain, at country price, also the sum of sixty pounds in grain, at country price, yearly, so long as said Mr. Chauncey shall continue in the work of the Gospel ministry as above."

"Also at the same Meeting, the Town, by vote, did enact, agree, and grant, unto Mr. Nathaniel Chauncey, his fire wood, that is, so much fire wood as shall be needful for the said Mr. Chauncey and a family, if he should see cause to have one; the said fire wood to be brought unto Mr. Chauncey upon a day appointed yearly by the Select-men."

"At a Town Meeting, October the 4th, 1708, the Town, by a full vote, did agree and desire the much esteemed Mr. Nathaniel Chauncey to settle with us in the office of Pastor."

"At the same Meeting, the Town, by vote, did agree and grant that the much esteemed Mr Nathaniel Chauncey should have, and do by these presents grant unto the said Mr. Chauncey, the house and all the appurtenances thereunto belonging, that was built for the first Minister, and the lot upon which said house standeth, with all the several tracts and parcels of land formerly set apart for the first Minister, to be and remain to be, unto Mr. Chauncey, and his heirs, forever, on the condition following, viz. :—That the said Mr. Chauncey shall and doth continue with us to be our Minister, during the term of his natural life, provided, nevertheless, that if the said Mr. Chauncey shall at any time expire his natural life, he being from us upon his occasions, and intending to continue in said work, or that the said Mr. Chauncey shall continue with us in the work of the Ministry until he be disenabled, by age or weakness, from being any farther serviceable in said work, that then no advantage shall be taken of said Mr. Chauncey, or his heirs, in their holding said house and lands. But if said Mr. Chauncey shall fail in his performing said condition, in his removing or otherwise, then the said land with all and every part thereof, together with said house, shall return unto the Town, to be disposed of as they think meet."

Mr. Chauncey declined this call, but continued to preach in the Town. The reasons for his declining the call may be understood from his statement, of the "relations between him and his people," given in the following pages.

LIBERTY TO FORM A CHURCH.

"At a Town Meeting, October 4, 1708, ye Town by voate did order and empower ye present Select Men to petition ye Honorable General Court, at their next sitting, to grant liberty yt a Church may be heare embodied acording unto ye rules of God's holy Word."

"At a General Assembly holden in New Haven, October 14, 1708, This Assembly grant their consent and full liberty to the Town of Durham, to embody themselves into church estate with the approbation of the neighboring churches."

No Church was formed for more than two years after this permission was granted. It is to be noted that the Town, that is, the inhabitants of the Town, have liberty to form themselves into church estate. This was done at the ordination of Mr. Chauncey, when pastors of neighboring churches ordained him. "The approbation of the neighboring churches" was expressed by the pastors of the churches.

RENEWED CALL OF REV. NATHANIEL CHAUNCEY.

"Dec. 10, 1710. Wee, the inhabitants of Durham, having desired the much esteemed Mr. Chauncey to settle with us, in the office of pastor, and also several persons have showed their willingness both to embody into church estate and also to desire Mr. Chauncey to take upon him the office of a pastor, and we are now informed that Mr. Chauncey doth at present decline settling with us by reason that there are several of our people against his settlement; unless he be advised thereto by a council called heare for that end, and accordingly Mr Chauncey doth advise ye Town to joyne with him in calling a council both to advise him what may be his duties in the matter, and also to direct the town in what may be necessary respecting his settlement, the Town having seriously considered Mr. Chauncey's advice, do thankfully accept the same, and do earnestly, by voate, desire the Rever'd Mr. JAMES PIERPONT, the Rever'd Mr. TIMOTHY WOODBRIDGE, the Rever'd Mr. NOADIAH RUSSELL, in conjunction, to give us advice in relation to the above settlement. We hope we shall always show a hearty Readiness and willingness to comply with what advice shall be given to us; and also we desire Mr. Chauncey to write to the said Reverend Elders to pray their help and advise, and also we desire James Wadsworth and Caleb Seaward to write in ye behalf of the Town earnestly to beg the help and advise of the ye said Rever'd Elders in our difficult circumstances."

"Also the Town, by voate, did appoynt James Wadsworth and Caleb Seaward to take care about calling said counsell and take care of their entertainment, and what may be necessary respecting the premissees."

"At a Meeting of the Inhabitants of the Town of Durham, December 22, 1710, Mr. Pierpont's letter being read, wherein he expresseth his unwillingness to serve us in a counsell, as he was desired by a voate at a Town Meeting on the 12th of this instant

5

December, the said inhabitants, by vote, did earnestly pray the Rever'd Mr. SAMUEL RUSSELL for to joyne with the Rever'd Mr. TIMOTHY WOODBRIDGE, the Rever'd Mr. Noadiah Russell, in a counsell to be heare attended on ye first Tuesday in January in giving us direction and advise according to the Town voate which is above mentioned: Also it was voated yt ye Rever'd Mr. Thomas Ruggles should be addressed to be heare and joyne in ye above sd counsell if Mr Russell should fayle in coming."

ORDINATION OF MR. CHAUNCEY.

"At a Meeting of the inhabitants of Durham, Dec. 26, 1710, ye sd Inhabitants by voate did agree yt ye much esteemed Mr Chauncey should be advised in all convenient speed, provided he consent thereto, while they earnestly desire him to comply with all, the ministers to advise Mr. Chauncey he hath already propounded, viz.: ye Rever'd Mr. TIMOTHY WOODBRIDGE, Mr. NOADIAH RUSSELL, Mr. SAMUEL RUSSELL, and ye Rever'd THOMAS RUGGLES, which ministers the Town do pray to ordaine Mr. Chauncey and also to be helpful to us in ye affair, by advising us, or in gathering a church and what may be necessary. Also the Town by voate do make choyce of DAVID ROBINSON, CALEB SEAWARD and JAMES WADSWORTH as a comittee to take care yt ye sd ordination be attended as above sd, and also to make what provition may be necessary for sd ordination and to take such methods relating to said ordination as they shall think best."

It should be noticed that the Council who ordained Mr. Chauncey, *were invited by the Town*, or the inhabitants, and not by the church. There was no church, at that time, in Durham. It was an act of the *Congregation*, and was thus *Congregational*. A church was formed the same day on which Mr. Chauncey was ordained. It should also be noticed that in the permission granted by the General Assembly to the "Town of Durham to embody themselves into a church estate," a condition is inserted, namely, "with the approbation of the neighboring Churches." The Town performed the condition by acting under the authority of Ministers, who, as pastors, represented the neighboring churches of Middletown, Guilford, Branford and Hartford.

OF LAYING OUT FOR YE ORDINATION OF REV. NATHANIEL CHAUNCEY.

	s	d.
From Joel Parmerly 15 lb Pork and ½ Bushel Mault,	4	4
By Beef from Mr. Wadsworth, - - - - -	16	0
By 20 lb Butter, 10, - - - - - -	10	0
By 20 lb Sugar, 10, - - - - - - - -	10	0
By 4 Bushl Wheat, - - - - - -	17	0
By Cheese, 4 2, - - - . - - - -	4	2
By Hens, Goose, Turkie, - - - - - -	16	6
By a Sheep and fetching from Town, - - -	9	0
By 3 Bushel Apples, - - - - - -	3	6
By 2 Quarters of Mutton, - - - - - -	3	0
Mault for Beer, - - - - - - -	4	0
Barrel of Cyder, - - - - - - - - -	8	0
Chocolate, Pepper, Spice, Currant, Nutmeg, -	6	0
Metheglin and Rum, - - - - - - -	12	6
Two Piggs, fresh Pork, Salt Pork and Beef, -	6	6
Hiring 5 Horses, - - - - - - - - -	2	0
Labor and trouble of my Family, - - - -	10	0
Four Neats' Tongues, - - - - - - -	2	8
To ye Camp's girl, 5 6, - - - - - -	5	6
Good wife Taylor, - - - - - - - -	′6	0
Good wife Seward, - - - - - - -	3	0
Good wife Hecox, - - - - - - - -	3	0
Good wife Squire, - - - - - - -	3	0
£8	5	8

An ordination was, in those days, a great event in the history of a Town. The generous provision here made shows that they expected friends from other Towns to rejoice with them.

THE WOOD FURNISHED.

"At a Town Meeting, Dec. 9, 1740, voted that one hundred loads of wood is the number of loads which the Town thinks sufficient for Mr. Chauncey, and that all the loads be viewed and approved by some one of the Committee hereinafter to be named."

The persons chosen by a Major vote to view the wood to be furnished by the Town to Mr. Chauncey, namely, Sergt. Ebenezer Guernsey, Serj. Daniel Merwin, Sergt. John Camp, the Second, Deacon Israel Burritt, Jonathan Wells, Ebenezer Robinson, James Wadsworth, Jun., and Samuel Fowler.

Those that undertake to get and carry the wood to Mr. Chauncey, are Henry Crane, Jun., who undertakes to carry 10 loads, and Isaac Norton, 10 loads, John Norton the first, 6 loads, Noadiah Graves, 4 loads, Sergt. Joel Parmeley, 8 loads, Thos. Seymour, 3 loads, Sergt. Joseph Seward and Ensign Nathaniel Seward, 20 loads, Deacon Israel Burritt, 6 loads, Jonathan Wells, 4 loads, Samuel Norton, 4 loads, John Norton, 2d, 5 loads, Samuel Picket, 10 loads, Josiah Fowler, 4 loads, John Parmely, 8 loads, Caleb Seward, 3 loads, Silas Crane, 2 loads; in all 100 loads, which are to be carried to Mr. Chauncey's house."

The Town, by the terms of settlement, were to furnish Mr. Chauncey with fire wood, besides the annual salary of sixty pounds. The above vote shows their liberality in carrying out the agreement.

HOW THE SALARY WAS PAID.

His Salary of £60 was, to a large extent, paid in the products of agriculture, which was the chief business of his people, at "Country price." "Country," in those days, meant the Colony of Connecticut. Sometimes in the annual vote of the salary, the prices of articles are given, as Wheat, five shillings a bushel; Indian Corn, two shillings and sixpence. The wheat which he received, he sent to merchants in Boston, by vessels from Middletown, to be disposed of at Boston prices. With his own wheat, and other articles, he sometimes sent his parishioners' for their accommodation. The following is a letter to a merchant in Boston, showing his lively gratitude for the favors thus received —

To Mr. Jonathan Belcher,
Merchant in Boston.

Sir,—I have sent you by Mr. James Lewis, as the enclosed will show sixteen bushels of wheat, hoping it may, if the Market has not fallen, answer the four pounds I am in your debt; and herewith the most thankful acknowledgement of your kindness therein, and of your other free and unmerited regards and favors; since there could be no previous obligation, or indeed worth, it bespeaks your manifest goodness and my deeper engagements. It is said there are three degrees of gratitude, to requite, to deserve, and to confess a benefit received; surely your bounty aimed at no requital, in that it chose an object of so little worth, and so little ability, the utmost reach of whose gratitude can but acknowledge such bounty, and beg the blessing of heaven on his benefactor. And may this truly rest on your person, your family, your wider affairs. May you increase by scattering. May he that hath given you both a large estate and a large heart, continue long in peace and honor to enjoy and wisely improve it, and then remove you to a more full, satisfying inheritance above, is the hearty prayer of him who should account it a happiness to do you the least service.

From your most obliged humble Servant,

Durham, July 25, 1717. NATHANIEL CHAUNCEY.

From the time that Mr. Chauncey came the second time to Durham, namely, May 23, 1706, to the time of his marriage, he boarded with his parishioners, first with Mr. David Robinson, and after the 24th of October, of the same year, with Mr. Joseph Norton, for a period. Mr. Chauncey was to receive from the Town, 1, a salary of £60; 2, his fire wood, 3, five pieces of land, or one allotment of land in the several divisions, to be his in fee simple. Four acres of this land the Town cleared, and cultivated, free of expense to him, giving him the produce. 4, the use of the allotment, or five pieces of land set apart for the Ministry, as parsonage lots.

HIS MINISTERIAL AUTHORITY.

In the Town of Durham, in the State of Connecticut, about a hundred years ago, the following usage prevailed:—Whenever a child, or youth, was discovered playing, or in any way disturbing the order of public worship, the Minister would pause, and calling him by name, would publicly direct him to repair to his house Monday morning, to give an account of his conduct. In the study of the Minister, the offense, with its aggravating or mitigating circumstances, was canvassed, and such admonition and discipline imparted to the offender, as the overseer of the flock deemed wise.

So well established was this order of things, that few if any parents demurred sending their children. Nor would a child have presumed to decline obeying the summons of the sacred functionary.

It happened one Sabbath, that a certain boy, named Charles ———, then about twelve years of age, played during Divine service The eye of the Minister caught the action He paused, and audibly pronouncing his name, directed him to come to his house on Monday morning at nine o'clock. His parents were present, and witnesses, if not of the offense, of the solemn summons.

What was said by them to their son, after service, is not stated; but it was at once admitted that the call must be obeyed. Accordingly, the following day, his mother directed him to put on his Sunday suit, and prepare to go to Mr. Chauncey's. When ready, and about to go, she thus addressed him:—

"Charles, you now see what you suffer for being a naughty boy, and playing at meeting You have grieved your father and mother, and greatly displeased Mr. Chauncey. Go to him, my son, and confess your fault, and, more than all, ask forgiveness of God, whose command you have broken. I know you feel bad, but you deserve to suffer. Your conduct no one can justify, and you yourself would condemn in another what you have done."

"Mother," said Charles, "will you not go with me?"

"No, my child," she replied. "You must go alone, and tell Mr Chauncey that neither your father nor mother wish to screen you, and do you submit to whatever punishment he may inflict upon you."

With a heavy heart, Charles proceeded to Mr. Chauncey's. Having reached the house, he went round to the back door, and gave one or two gentle taps. This he did, as he afterwards said, in the hope that no one would hear him, and that he might be able to say, that he knocked, and found no one to admit him. Thus he was tempted to screen himself; but the rap, gentle as it was, was heard by Mrs. Chauncey, who happened to be near by, and who opened the door. Before her stood Charles. She knew him well, and immediately inquired,

"Charles, is it you? and what do you want?"

"Mr. Chauncey told me," said the guilty boy, "to come and see him this morning."

"Oh! you are the boy that played at meeting, yesterday, are you? Mr. Chauncey is in his study. I will speak to him."

Accordingly, advancing to the chamber stairs, she called to her husband.

"Mr. Chauncey, here is Charles ———, who played at meeting yesterday, come to see you."

"Tell him to come up to my study."

Charles soon stood in the presence of the kind-hearted, but now, somewhat stern Mr. Chauncey. Laying aside his pen, he cast a severe look upon the offender, but noticing his meek and humble mien, he immediately relaxed all appearance of the judge, and gently drawing Charles toward him, mildly inquired:

"Charles, can you repeat the fourth commandment?"

"Yes, Sir. Remember the Sabbath day," &c.

"And did you not break this commandment yesterday, when you played at meeting?"

"Yes, Sir."

"Well, and are you sorry that you broke one of God's commandments?"

"Yes, Sir."

"Do you feel willing to ask God to forgive you?"

"Yes, Sir."

Other questions followed, and were answered by Charles to the acceptance of Mr Chauncey, who was satisfied, as well he might be, of the sincere repentance and good resolutions of the offender. At length Mr. Chauncey inquired:

"Charles, who sent you here?"

"My mother."

"And was she not sorry that her son should play on God's holy day, and that in the house of God?"

"She was; and she told me to tell you, that neither she nor father wished to screen me."

"Charles," said the worthy divine. "Charles, you should be thankful for such a mother. Can you repeat the fifth commandment?"

"Honor thy father and thy mother," &c.

"Well, now look to it, Charles, when you play on the Sabbath-day, you offend God, who says, 'Remember the Sabbath-day to keep it holy;' and you offend your parents, and then you break the fifth commandment, which says, 'Honor thy father and thy mother.' Are you willing to promise that you will never play at meeting again?"

"Yes, Sir; I never will."

"Now, my son, you may go, and remember your promise."

Upon this, Mr. Chauncey arose, and opening the study door, called with quite a strong voice—

"Mrs. Chauncey! here is Charles coming down; give him a piece of cake. He says he is sorry for playing yesterday at meeting, and has promised that he will never do so again."

Charles took the cake and retired. In after years he often related the above incident, and always added that his interview with Mr. Chauncey, was blessed to his good, through the grace of God. At first, his distress, which was great, arose from the fear of the man; but the kind and affectionate manner of Mr. Chauncey's address, added to the serious questions which he asked, at length convinced him of the dishonor which he had done to God.

Never, afterwards, did he exhibit a light or irreverent manner in the sanctuary.

And in maturer years, and upon other occasions, the faithful dealings of Mr Chauncey had its influence upon his conduct.

Such was the custom, a hundred years ago, in the Town of Durham. Who admits not, that it was a salutary custom? What friend to the order of divine worship, and the proper observance of the Sabbath would not wish it had descended to the present time?

A SPECIMEN LETTER OF DISMISSION.

NORTHAMPTON, June 8th, 1710.

To THE REV. MR. NATHANIEL CHAUNCEY and the rest of the brethren in Durham, Reverend and beloved about to gather into a church there,

The church of Christ in Northampton sendeth greeting:

God having fixed the habitation of Capt. Samuel Parsons among you, he hath desired letters of dismission for himselfe and his wife unto yourselves, and accordingly we commend them both unto you as persons qualified for your holy communion. They have been in fellowship with us for many years, and are without offence. We heartily desire that God would smile upon your beginnings and make his ordinances mighty for saving good to many souls. Thus begging an interest in your prayers, we remain your brethren in the fellowship of the gospel.

SOLOMON STODDARD,

In the name and with the consent of the Church.

HIS RELATIONS TO HIS PEOPLE.

In the year 1706, on the 23d of May, I came to preach to the people of Durham. After a considerable time of trial as to my public doings, I remember not much dissatisfaction. Yet some were minded to know my judgment as to matters of discipline and came to discourse with me about that point. Whatever has been the practice of others, or whatever is most prudent in itself, I determine not. I think I dealt plainly from the very first, in showing my own judgment, and my purpose to act according to it, and a resolution not to be imposed upon. When the practice of some worthy ministers and churches has been cryed up to me, I have been free to say that my Master's copy is to be minded, and not the copy of my mates. Such a spirit was to be seen in sundry upon this account, and such a division appeared that I had thought of removing, having at that very time invitations to several places.

But, before I had actually concluded to leave this people, I desired the town should come together, that I might have some discourse with them. I told them plainly upon what terms I would serve them, and if could not be received and accepted upon those terms I would not abide with. It was then voted to accept of me as enjoying my own judgment, which was then expressed. I think there were six persons who did not vote, one of which was Mr Robinson. Upon these terms and no other I concluded to abide. And the people concluded then to make over to me what they had designed to give to the first minister, in order to settlement. It being thus concluded, I let those opportunities go of settling elsewhere. I thought there was enough done to make way for peace.

But before many months were passed there came a man to me, and told me some were uneasy about that matter, and desired to have an opportunity to have discourse with me, which I yielded to, and the time was appointed, but it proved foul weather; none came then.

The difference and dissatisfaction continuing, if not growing (I believe growing, for the devil's bellows did not fail,) when I heard of the general meeting of the Elders to be held at Saybrook, I told some of them I thought it was wisdom to tarry until that was over. It may be, somewhat would be done there, in which there might be union. As soon as I could get a copy and let them have it, which they took a time to read among themselves. And having read and considered it, all those that were members in full communion came to me, and told me that their business was to tell me that they were all suited, and desired to know of me whether I could be suited, to which I manifested my assent, saying they had little reason to think I should stand out from the whole country. There being now such a friendly agreement they invited me to take the pastoral charge.

At this meeting something was said about the understanding of the articles, to which I replied, If difficulty should be there, we must refer ourselves to the same power which drew them up, which was not objected against, but backed by one of them as a way proper. I reckoned here was a full agreement.

The next news I had was of their drawing many articles which they were resolved to stand for, and getting hands thereto; so that when the town began to move for my ordination, a considerable number held back. After a while I proposed the issuing of difficulty by a council, and proposed that the town should choose one, the dissatisfied persons one, and I should choose one. This was agreed upon; the ministers were chosen, and sent to the time appointed, &c. But before that time came, sundry persons fell in and desired there might be no council; so that there remained but four or five unquiet, so few that it was a small matter for a council to meet about. Therefore it was concluded to put by the council, and it was proposed that the same ministers should be impowered about the ordination, adding Mr. Ruggles of Guilford, and that the difficulty respecting those four or five men should be issued by them I took it that this was agreed to, and after they and others who had pretended to be dissatisfied had taken time at the council, the result was this: I was called for and asked whether in difficult and weighty cases I was willing the mind of the church should be known by some sign. I replied I never designed any other but to be tender in such cases, and should like to have the concurrence of the church. But it may be, that might be insisted on by some in trivial matters, whereto reply was made. "To things that I might judge or account best." This I duly assented to.

This is the whole of what I was obligated to at that time, namely, that the mind of the church be known by some sign in things that I, myself, should judge to be weighty and difficult.

Now if there is any one instance that can be given, wherein I have swerved, either from the articles at Saybrook, or from the settlement at my ordination, or from my own judgment, or from the word of God, I am ready to answer it.

N. Chauncey.

A PRIMITIVE PLEDGE.

Whereas, the great and glorious God hath by many awful rebukes of his holy Providence, testified his just displeasure, agst his People in this Land, as particularly by unexpected frustrations of our Military undertakings, with ye sad disasters yt have attended or followed the same; as also by the Malignant distemper wch hath proved so Mortal in sevl of our towns, whereby many Pious and useful Persons have been taken from us.

And, Whereas, all the frequent and solemn Addresses to Heaven for ye Averting his judgment and obtaining his favr, and Blessing, against wch God has manifested much anger, answering us by terrible things in Righteousness. All which tremendous dispensations as they speak us an Apostatizing and sinful people, do seem to call for some more than Ordinary endeavours after ye Reformation of those God-provoking evils, wch are so gen'l and prevailing among us.

And, WHEREAS, there are, even with us, many of those sins agst the Lord God of Israel, wch we have reason to Reckon among the procuring causes, of those Judgments, and Consequently yt we orselves are under special Engagements to use all proper means to that end. Accordingly in Order hereunto we do all before the Lord this Day declare upon the Cov. obligations that we are under that we will watch unto the Dutys and Carefully avoid ye Evils now to be mentioned.

1st. We will constantly attend the dutys of God's worship in Publick, Private, and secret, not allowing ourselves in ye neglect of any of his Holy Ordinances, through Carelessness, Contempt or any sinful excuse.

2d. We will carefully watch against all Irreverence in ye worship of God, and all profanations of his glorious and fearful name by Causeless Imprecations, Rash swearing, or any other way in wch it is, or may be taken in vain.

3rd. We will strictly observe the Christian Sabbath, viz: One whole Day in seven seasonably beginning and duly continuing ye same and Carefully watching against worldly thoughts, words and work on that day.

4th. We will carefully endeavor to discharge the several Dutys of our several Places, and Relations, as our Superiours, Inferiors, and Equals. Particularly we will Honour, Submit to, and obey those whom God hath set over us; whether in family, Church or Common-wealth. We will look well to our Household, and keep our Children and servants in subjection, Instruct them in the principles of our Holy Religion, and Endeavr to Restrain them from all Profaneness and Immorality.

5th. Wee will as much as in us lye, live peaceably with all men.

6th. Wee will be careful to maintain a Chaste Conversation watching agst all ye Occasions and preventives to uncleaness, especially.

7th. Wee will mind or own Business, and strictly observe ye Rule of Righteousness, in our Commerce, and dealing one wth another, watching agst all violations of it by Deceit, Oppression, and all unjust and dishonest dealing wsoever.

8th. Wee will Carefully take heed to speak ye truth in our Converse one wth Another, Carefully avoiding all Lying, Slandering, backbiting, Reviling and Promise breaking.

9th. Wee will mutually watch over one another, giving and receiving Reproof as becomes Christians.

10th. Wee will in our sevl Capacity bare due testimony or witness agst all Profaneness and Immorality, and not wthhold our Testimony when it shall be necessary for ye Convicting and Punishing Offender unless some Religions Tye of Conscience founded on ye word of God do require Secrecy.

11th. Wee will watch agst the prevailing of a worldly Covetous Spirit.

12th. Wee will watch agst all Intemperance in ye use of Lawful things, and in particular agst excessive drinking.

13th. Wee will not allow ourselves in unnecessary frequenting Public or Private drinking houses; and,

In order to our faithful and more acceptable performance of ye above expressed, we will set ourselves seriously and Diligently to seek all needful Grace and help from God.

NATHANIEL AND SARAH CHAUNCEY,
SAMUEL AND RHODA PARSONS,
THOMAS AND RUTH LYMAN,
HENRY CRANE,
RICHARD BEECH,
TIMOTHY WALTON,
JOSEPH NORTON.

THE LIFE AND DEATH OF NATH'L CHAUNCEY.

Rev. Nathaniel Chauncey of Durham, Connecticut, the son of Rev. Nathaniel Chauncey of Hatfield, who was the son of President Chauncey, was born in Hatfield, Sept. 21, 1681 Having lost his father when he was between four and five years of age, he was taken to Stratford, Conn., with his father's library, for the use of which his uncle, Israel Chauncey, agreed to educate him. Being thus placed under the best influences, his ancestral love of learning led him to prepare himself for college, under the training of his uncle.

Yale College, had just been founded. His uncle, who was one of the founders, placed him in that institution His name stands on the Triennial Catalogue as the *first who received a degree from that College.* As the first born of Yale, he reflected no dishonor upon his Alma Mater. He was admitted to the church in Stratford, January 16, 1698

After his graduation he taught school for a period, in Springfield, Mass , and in the Hopkins Grammar School, Hadley He pursued his theological studies, probably, partly with his uncle, and partly with Rev Mr. Brewer of Springfield, who married his sister. In May 23d, 1706, he commenced preaching in Durham, "the second time," when there were but fourteen families. To these were added ten or twelve from Stratford, where Mr. Chauncey was bred, and several from Northampton and Hatfield, where he was known. The Strongs and Parsons, and Lymans, were relatives, inasmuch as they were related to Elder Strong, his grandfather, by blood or marriage

Mr Chauncey entered with great earnestness on the prosecution of his professional duties. His sermons, the result of severe study and well digested thought, were carefully written out in a neat, legible hand , and so distinctly impressed were they upon his memory, that he never carried his notes into the pulpit, until quite the latter part of his life, when he used, in his preaching, an abstract of his sermons, containing little besides the heads and the subordinate divisions of the written discourse. These abstracts were carefully placed for preservation in the written sermons, with which the present writer has compared a number of them. His elocution was distinct, his tones earnest, his addresses solemn and pungent, and his whole bearing grave and dignified. Said one of his intelligent and admiring hearers to the writer, many years ago, "He was not a large man, but he was a man of great presence. He looked like a man. When he was approaching the meeting-house on the Sabbath, we were all careful to be in our seats; and when he entered the house we all rose to receive him, and continued standing until he took his seat in the pulpit."

When Colonel Elihu Chauncey, in his youth, was in New

Haven, he attended Church one Sabbath morning with his friend Chauncey Whittlesy, Jun. "How did you like the preaching?" said the latter, when they were returning from Church "Preaching!" said Col. Chauncey, "I don't call this preaching!"

At noon, when this was reported to the father of Mr Whittlesy, who was the preacher, he said to Mr. Chauncey, "Your father preaches without notes."

"Yes, Sir, one reading in the morning will give him one sermon, and one reading at noon will give him the other."

He deeply interested his audience. On one occasion, in his preaching, he had not cleared up some points to the entire satisfaction of Deacon Henry Crane, who rose after the service and said, "Reverend Sir, will you please to explain further on that point of doctrine in your sermon?" "Deacon Crane, if you will walk to my study, I will explain it to you," was the reply.

Accordingly Mr. Chauncey went immediately to his study, when lo! the whole congregation followed to hear the explanation, which he gave.

Personal religion, family religion, the duties of parents and children, of husband and wife, of brothers and sisters, of neighbors, the great doctrines of the cross, the broad distinction between sin and holiness, the necessity of regeneration, and the terrible condition of the wicked in this and the life to come; these were the topics on which he dwelt. So successful was he in promoting family religion that many in his congregation who were not members of the church maintained family worship.

He was entirely devoted to his profession. His brother Isaac, who was bachelor, took care of his farm, and his wife, a notable housekeeper, relieved him of all trouble about temporalities. To show his love of knowledge, it is related of him, that on the occasion of his son, Col. Chauncey, receiving from Dr Chauncey, of Boston, Wollaston's Religion of Nature, in virtue of his paternal relation, he took the book without ceremony to his study and kept it a fortnight, and then brought it down, and gave it to his son, who had not yet read it Upon his son's asking him what he thought of the work, he replied, "Think, sir? I think I don't know anything Forty years I have been studying, and this book has told me more than I ever knew"

In the early part of his ministry, he was inclining to high Calvinism, but afterwards his views became somewhat modified, though Calvanistic still, in consequence of reading various learned authors. Through his friends abroad he obtained the library of a deceased clergyman abroad. When landed at Middletown it was so large that it amounted to two cart loads drawn by a strong team. These books, with those which he received by inheritance, constituted one of the largest private libraries in the State of Connecticut, if not the largest.

He interested himself in promoting the welfare of his people generally. The trade of Connecticut River was connected chiefly with Boston. By means of his friends and correspondents there, especially of his relatives, Mr. Charles Chauncey, and his son, Dr Charles Chauncey, and Mr. Frank Willoughby, he assisted his people to dispose of their wheat and butter, with the wheat he received for his salary, in Boston, and to receive, from thence, necessary dry goods and groceries. I have in my possession a number of these mercantile letters, addressed to him from Boston, in which there are bills of Canary wine, and Psalm books, and pepper and ginger, and pewter ware and silk, and other goods which were in common use.

At every annual Thanksgiving, he regularly came down from his study, and carefully inquired whether portions had been sent to the poor, naming certain individuals.

In building the second meeting-house, besides, other contributions, he was at the expense of building the pulpit of the richest and widest cherry boards. He also boarded a joiner a year, gratuitously. In gratitude, the Society voted, that he and Col. Wadsworth, who had also contributed largely to the erection of the church, should be entitled to a pew, each of them, for themselves and their heirs, to be selected by themselves.

When an elderly man, Deacon Burritt, of his church, made application to him for permission to marry his daughter, who was much younger; he gave his permission, but remarked to his daughter, "I give my consent to Deacon Burritt to marry you. You will have a pleasant forenoon, but your afternoon will be rather dark and gloomy."

Such was the estimation in which he was held by the public generally, that he had great influence in the neighboring churches; was a Fellow of Yale College, was in correspondence with distinguished clergymen of his times; by appointment preached *two* election sermons, the first in 1719, the second in 1734; is mentioned by President Edwards as a successful minister, in the great revival in New England.

With some of the ablest and best men of New England, he was, in the time of Whitfield and Davenport, in sympathy with the Old Lights rather than the New Lights, especially in the latter years of his life, when he had become acquainted with the disastrous tendency of the new measures, adopted by some of the New Light preachers As moderator of the Consociation of New Haven County, he took a decided stand with his brethren in respect to the matter at issue in the Branford Controversy, with respect to Mr. Robbins, of which Dr. Trumbull has given an account in his History of Connecticut, not entirely candid, being himself a partisan.

His immediate, as well as his permanent influence, was powerfully exerted in favor of learning as well as religion. As a fruit of his efforts education was prized, sought for, and promoted among his people, whether in primary schools or in Yale College. The celebrated missionary, David Brainard, dates his "frequent longing" after a liberal education from his year's residence in Durham, and he commenced his classical studies while under the preaching of Mr. Chauncey, or immediately after returning home. The Town of Durham, in the great number of educated men which it sent forth, and in the high character of these men, bears testimony to the value of his influence.

The Rev. Timothy Mather Cooley, D. D., in his life of Haynes, alludes to the happy influence of Mr Chauncey upon the emigrants from Durham, who settled the town of Granville, Mass., and in an interesting letter to the present writer, more fully proves that that influence has been transmitted in successive generations in that town, in the intelligence of the people, and in their love of learning and religion.

The influence of Mr. Chauncey's preaching and counsels can be traced distinctly in Hartland, Connecticut, Greenfield, Sandisfield and Granville, Massachusetts; Durham, New York, towns which received some of their early inhabitants from Durham, and from under the pastoral care of Mr Chauncey.

From many circumstances it is evident that he was greatly respected throughout the State I have in my possession a letter from the Governor of Connecticut, in the year 1734, in which he is requested to preach a *Second Election Sermon.* This request is couched in very respectful and flattering terms.

On the occasion of his death two sermons were preached by Rev. JONATHAN TODD, of East Guilford, of which the following is on the title page: "Public Mourning at the Death of Godly and Useful Men, and solicitous enquiry after their God. Two sermons preached at Durham, Feb. 8, 1756, occasioned by the much lamented death of the venerable Mr. Nathaniel Chauncey, pastor of the Church there, who departed this life on the first instant, in the 75th year of his life, and the fifty first of his ministry; by Jonathan Todd, A. M, pastor of the church at East Guilford."

Besides two "Election Sermons," Mr. Chauncey published a sermon on "Regular Singing;" and also a sermon on the death of the Rev. John Hart, of East Guilford.

Mr Chauncey married Sarah Judson, daughter of Capt. James Judson of Stratford, Oct. 12, 1708. Their children were I, Elihu; II, Sarah, who married Israel Burritt; III, Catherine was married to Benjamin Stillman, of Wethersfield; IV, Abigail, who married Jabez Hamlin, V, Nathaniel; VI, Elnathan.

The first settlers of Durham came, some of them from Guilford where Thomas Ruggles was pastor, some of them from Stratford where Israel Chauncey was pastor, some of them from Milford where Samuel Andrew was pastor, some of them from Northampton where Solomon Stoddard was pastor, some of them from Saybrook where Thomas Buckingham was pastor, some of them from Killingworth where Abraham Pierson was pastor. These clergymen were above the common level of ministers. Three of them were appointed President of Yale College, and one of them accepted of the appointment. Coming together from under the ministrations of such men, they were not willing to leave their religion behind them Deeply imbued with the Spirit of the Bible they wished to have their own Pisgah, their own sacred tabernacle in the wilderness, their own ark of the Covenant, their own Shekinah, their own priest to minister at the altar.

They were strongly attached to Mr. Chauncey, as he was to them. But difficulties arose which delayed his settlement.

These difficulties grew out of the old question among Congregationalists, namely: What is the power of the pastor in his relations to his people? Mr. Chauncey in his remarks heretofore quoted, shows what were his opinions on the subject. His grandfather, President Chauncey, came to this country to escape the domination of the "Lords Bishops," and he was not willing to place himself under the domination of the "Lords Brethren." He insisted upon retaining some substantive power as a pastor. He refused to surrender everything to the church as some few of the people wished him to do. He was willing to come into the wilderness to preach the gospel, but not into the "wilderness of Congregational principles."

This difficulty was settled by the "*Saybrook Platform*" which had been recently adopted by the Synod of Connecticut. His people were willing to take that as a religious constitution, to be interpreted if need be by the "Consociation," a permanent body. He too, was willing to do the same. In giving his assent to this constitution he says, "they had little reason to think that he should stand out against the whole country." In this remarkable expression he signifies that there was a general satisfaction with the Saybrook Platform throughout the colony, which was equivalent to "the country." Difficulties generally existed before the Platform was adopted. That Platform was adopted in order to remove those difficulties. It had that effect in this case It may be added that the Congregational Church in Durham has ever since clung to that standard of faith and practice.

CHAPTER III

MINISTRY OF REV. ELIZUR GOODRICH, D. D

STATEMENT BY REV. ELIZUR GOODRICH, D.D.

"A short account of the Proceedings of the Town, and Church of Christ, in Durham, in Relation to my Settlement in the Work of the Ministry with them, taken either from the original Papers or Attested Copies.

At a Town Meeting held in Durham on the second Tuesday of June or the 8th in 1756, it was voted and resolved to apply to the *Committee* of the Reverend Association to ask their Counsel and Advice with respect to the obtaining a candidate for the Ministry to preach with them on Probation for a settlement, and for that purpose appointed Col *Elihu Chauncey*, Deacon *Joseph Tibbals*, Deacon *Ezra Baldwin*, Mr. *Nathan Camp* and Mr. *Caleb Seward*, as a committee, who, upon application, received the following advice *Verbatim*, (viz)

We the subscribers being Members of the Committee, of New Haven Association being applyed to, by two of the Committee of Durham to Advise to a suitable person to apply to, and preach among them, as a Probationer in order to settle among them in the work of the Gospel Ministry, do advise them to apply unto Mr. Elizur Goodrich for that purpose, as witness our hands.

Joseph Noyes, Jonathan Merick, Isaac Stiles, Sam'l Whittlesy.
N. H, June 9th 1756.

Upon this advise and Counsel from the Committee of the Rev. Association, the Town by a Vote resolved, on the third Tuesday the 17th of June, 1756, to choose, and did choose a Comittee, namely, Col. *Elihu Chauncey*, Dea. *Jos. Tibbals*, Dea *Ezra Baldwin*, Mr. *Nathan Camp* and Mr. *Caleb Seward* to apply to and desire me to preach with them as a Probationer for Settlement in the Ministry, until the 13th day of the September following, with which Invitation I complyed, and accordingly preached with them till that time On the second Monday or the 13th day of September, A D. 1756, the Town having met, voted and resolved to give me a Call to settle in the Ministry with them, and appointed James Wadsworth Esq, Col Elihu Chauncey, Mr. Silas Crane, Dea Joseph Tibbalds, Dea. Ezra Baldwin, Mr. Caleb Seward, and Capt. Timothy Parsons, as a Committee to inform me of their Votes, and desire my Complyance as also to consider and confer with me, about Terms of Settlement, which Committee having made such proposals* to me, which appeared reasonable, and layed them before the Town, who voted the same, I complyed with and accepted their Call, and wrote to them in the following words:

"To the Inhabitants of Durham assembled in Town Meeting held by adjournment this 8th day of October, A D 1756.

Gentlemen:

I take this opportunity to acknowledge with gratitude, your kind and generous treatment since I have preached with you as a Candidate for settling in the work of the Ministry with you, and having taken into serious consideration your Invitation to a Settlement with you in the Gospel Ministry, I do hereby signify my thankful acceptance of the encouragement proposed by your Note, and my Complyance (provided nothing discouraging should hereafter appear) to settle with you in the work of the Gospel Ministry.

That abundance of spiritual blessings in heavenly things, through Christ Jesus our Lord, may rest on you and your children, is the sincere prayer of

Gentlemen,

Your obliged Servant,

ELIZUR GOODRICH.

"Upon which the Town chose, fully empowered and authorized, Col. Chauncey, Dea. Joseph Tibbals, Dea. Ezra Baldwin,

---

*The Committee reported on the 17th of Sept., "that after having taken into our consideration the matter referred to in our appointment have thought proper to submit to the consideration of Mr Goodrich whether the sum of £70 lawful money for settlement to be paid in three years in three equal and annual payments, one third part of said sum paid each year, and the sum of £72 lawful money for his salary yearly and the use and improvements of the five lots called parsonage land in Durham Said £72 to be paid in lawful money or produce at the ready money market price, equivalent to said sum, will be sufficient encouragement to him to comply with the call of the Town to settle in the work of the Ministry here, in answer to which Mr. Goodrich has signified to us that he does not object against said proposals, all of which is submitted by your humble servants" Elihu Chauncey, Joseph Tibbalds, Caleb Seward James Wadsworth, Timothy Parsons, Silas Crane, Ezra Baldwin.

James Wadsworth Esq, Mr. Henry Crane, Capt. Abraham Bartlett, and Mr. Nathan Camp, as a Committee in behalf of the Town, to take all proper measures, and make suitable provision for the ordination.

The proceedings of the Church of Christ in Durham in relation to my settlement was as follows:

At a meeting of the Church of Christ in Durham held in Durham the 30th day of September, A. D. 1756.

Elihu Chauncey was chosen Moderator.

The Church voted (nemine Contradicente) to give Mr. Elizur Goodrich a call, to settle in the work of the Gospel Ministry in this Church, and take the charge and oversight thereof as their Pastor, and Messrs. Elihu Chauncey, Dea. Joseph Tibbals, Dea. Ezra Baldwin were by a major vote chosen a Committee to wait on Mr. Goodrich, with this vote of the Church, and request his acceptance and compliance therewith, and lay his answer thereto before the Church at their next meeting, then by a Major vote this meeting was adjourned to Friday, the eighth day of October next at 3 o'clock P. M.

Test, ELIHU CHAUNCEY, *Moderator.*

A true Record. Test, E. GOODRICH.

DURHAM, Friday, 8th of Oct., A. D. 1756.

"The Church met according to adjournment. The Committee laid before this meeting Mr. Elizur Goodrich's answer to the call of the Church, contained in a letter from him (viz):

"To the Church of Christ in Durham, assembled this eighth day of October, A. D. 1756," which was read as follows:

"Beloved:

"Having seriously considered your invitation and call to settle in the work of the ministry in, and take the pastoral charge of this Church, I do hereby thankfully acknowledge your unanimity of choice, and, provided nothing hereafter discouraging should arise, am willing to devote myself to your service in the Gospel, and comply with and accept of your call and invitation.

That grace, mercy and peace may be multiplied unto you from our Lord, Jesus Christ, the great King, Head, and Redeemer of his Church is the sincere desire and prayer of, brethren, your devoted servant,

ELIZUR GOODRICH."

"Then the Church by their major vote made choice of Messrs. Elihu Chauncey, Dea. Joseph Tibbalds, Dea Ezra Baldwin, Mr. Nathaniel Seward, Mr. Silas Crane, Captain Timothy Parsons, and Mr. Caleb Seward, to be a Committee with full power in behalf of the Church to proceed to take all proper and necessary measures, in order to have Mr. Elizur Goodrich ordained Pastor in and over this Church, and the meeting was dismissed

Test, ELIHU CHAUNCEY, *Moderator*.

"At a meeting of the Church of Christ, in Durham, held in Durham, the 19th day of November, 1756.

The Committee of the Church laid before this meeting a letter from Mr. Elizur Goodrich as follows; (viz):

To the Church of Christ in Durham, assembled this 19th day of Nov., A. D. 1756.

Beloved:

According to the Motion and Desire of the Committees of both *Church* and *Town*, I do hereby signify my approbation and willingness to be settled upon the *Ecclesiastical Constitution* of the Churches of this COLONY which I look upon to be consistent with and agreeable to the Gospel of our Lord, and therefore, according to said *Constitution* that in all Church Acts, there shall be the joint act and consent of the Pastor and Church, and that all *Differences*, *Difficulties*, or Grievances, shall be finally issued and Determined according to the Rules prescribed in said Constitution, and desire the Church to signify their minds hereupon. I desire and pray that every one may study the Things which make for Peace, and the Edification of the Body of Christ in love, and am Beloved, your souls' well wisher. ELIZUR GOODRICH."

"The Church, after taking the Subject Matter of the above Letter into their serious Consideration, unanimously voted their approbation of and Willingness that Mr Goodrich should be settled in the work of the Gospel Ministry to which he is called in this place upon the Ecclesiastical Constitution of the Churches of this Colony, and consent that Mr. Elizur Goodrich, be settled in the work of the Ministry in this Church according to sd Constitution as expressed in his letter.

Test, ELIHU CHAUNCEY, *Moderator*.

ORDINATION OF REV. ELIZUR GOODRICH.

"In consequence of the foregoing Votes and Resolutions of this Church and Town, and my Complyance therewith, the Committees of the Town and Church often met to consider proper Measures, in order to finish the matter by Ordination, and appointed Wednesday the of November to be observed as a day of Fasting, by the Church and People preparatory thereto, which was accordingly observed. The Rev. Mr. Jonathan Merick of North Branford preached.

Matters being thus far concluded, the Committees of both Town and Church joined in writing Letters to the Rev. Elders and Churches, near, desiring their assistance in the solemn transaction of Ordination, which they appointed to be on Wednesday, the 24th day of Nov., A. D 1756, desiring the Council to meet the day before.

The Council accordingly met at Durham, Nov. 23rd, 1756, at the House of Col. Elihu Chauncey, before whom the Committees of the Church and Town laid their Proceedings, and desiring me to appear before them, they required a Certificate of my License to Preach, which I gave them as follows:

These may certify that the associated Ministers of the southern part of the County of Hampshire having examined Mr. Elizur Goodrich, as to his Qualifications to preach the Gospel, do approve of him, on that Regard, and accordingly recommend him to that work, wherever divine Providence shall open a door for his Improvement.

Springfield, Jan. 9th, 1755.

STEPHEN WILLIAMS, *Moderator.*

A true copy of the original.

NOAH MERICK, *Scribe.*

"The Rev. Council also requiring a Certificate of my Church Membership, I presented one as follows:

To the Church of Christ in Durham.

Hon'd and Beloved:

This may certify you, that Mr. Elizur Goodrich was admitted to full Communion with us. His conversation with us, was as becomes a Christian: upon his Desire is dismist from us, and recommended as meet for your Holy Fellowship. We hope that in him, you will have a rich gift of our Ascended Lord.

Yours in the Faith and Fellowship of the gospel,

JOHN BALLANTINE, *Pastor*.

In the name of the Church of Christ in Westfield.

A true copy of the original.

Westfield, Oct. 19, A. D. 1756.

"Then the Council, having examined me, I retired and the Council drew up, and executed the following Result the next Day being Nov. 24th, 1756."

"At an Ecclesiastical Council convened at Durham by the Call of the Church and Town of Durham, Nov. 23rd, 1756, in order to ordain Mr. Elizur Goodrich to the pastoral office and work of the Ministry in said Church and Town.

"ELDERS PRESENT.

New Cheshire, Rev. Mr. SAMUEL HALL
North Haven, " " ISAAC STILES.
Guilford, " " THOMAS RUGGLES.
North Branford, " " JOHNATHAN MERICK.
East Guilford, " " JONATHAN TODD
North Guilford, " " JOHN RICHARDS.

MESSENGERS OF CHURCHES

New Cheshire, Dea. STEPHEN HOTCHKISS.
North Haven, Capt. SAMUEL BARNES.
Guilford, Col. TIMOTHY STONE
North Branford, Dea. ITHIEL RUSSEL.
East Guilford, Dea. JOSIAH MEIGGS.
North Guilford, Dea. THOMAS ROSSITER.
Meriden, Capt. AARON LYMAN.

The Rev. Mr. Hall was chosen Moderator.

Thomas Ruggles chosen Scribe.

The Council was opened with Prayer.

"The Committee of the Town and Church appeared before this Council, and layed before the Council, Records of their Proceedings in inviting, and calling Mr. Goodrich, to the Pastoral Office and Work of the Ministry, which appearing to the Council, to be regular and unanimous, was accepted. Mr. Elizur Goodrich appeared before this Council, and was examined and approved, and professed his assent to the Religious Constitution of this Government in Doctrine and Discipline to the acceptance of this Council."

"*Voted* that Mr. Elizur Goodrich be set apart to the work of the Ministry, and be ordained to the pastoral office over the Church in this Place to-morrow, Nov. 24th, at half an hour past Ten O'clock, before Noon.

"*Voted* that the ordination be carried on in the following order: (viz.): The Rev. Mr. Merick to make the Prayer before sermon. Thomas Ruggles to lead in the affairs preparatory to the ordination. The Rev. Mr. Hall to make the prayer before and give the Charge The Rev. Mr. Stiles to make the concluding Prayer, and the Rev. Mr. Todd to give the Right Hand of Fellowship, and the Ordination was attended and performed according to the above order of Council.

Test, THOMAS RUGGLES, *Scribe*, faithfully transcribed from a true Copy of the order of Council, by ELIZUR GOODRICH.

N. B.—The Rev. Mr. Edward Eells, of Middletown preached the Sermon."

The Town took the lead in the call given to Mr. Goodrich, and the Church followed the lead of the Town in its action.

Mr. Goodrich was in religious opinions much the same as his predecessor, a moderate Calvinist; using the same confession of faith, baptising the children of those who themselves had been baptised, and who owned the covenant into which their parents had entered for them. In his preaching his topics were justification by faith, the evidences of Christianity, and the duties of the first and second table of the law. He was discriminating in his statments and clear in argumentation, and impressive in his appeals.

LIFE AND DEATH OF REV. ELIZUR GOODRICH, D. D.

Rev. Elizur Goodrich, D. D., was born the 26th of October, O. S. 1734, in Rocky Hill, the south part of Wethersfield, Conn. He was placed at an early age with the Rev. James Lockwood of Wethersfield, one of the best scholars in the colony. Here he was taught the languages with that peculiar thoroughness which came down from the first ministry of New England, from men who had been trained in the school of Erasmus. He was made to speak Latin from childhood much like a mother tongue. Having entered College at the age of fourteen, he took his degree of Bachelor of Arts at the age of eighteen, 1752.

He now studied Theology and began to preach, but was called back to the tutorship, 1755. This office he held only a year, being invited to the pastoral charge of the church in Durham.

Being amply provided with books which came from the library of his predecessor, on his settlement, he devoted himself with great diligence to study, that he might qualify himself to meet the large congregation that every Sabbath assembled in the house of God. He had become familiar with the Hebrew while in college; and was accustomed during most of his life to read directly from the original of the Old or New Testament, giving a translation in his own language, with such comments as the case required. Most of his labor was spent for the first ten years of his ministry, upon difficult passages of the Scriptures There were two physicians in adjoining towns, of a skeptical turn of mind. Both of them had an extensive practice through the country, and wherever they went, they were throwing out insinuations against religion, on the ground of alleged difficulties and contradictions in the Bible. This led him to study the passages referred to with the closest attention. This he was enabled to do on a broad scale by means of his ample library. The conclusions he reached were drawn out in extended disputations, of which there were said to be more than two hundred.

After spending ten years in patient study, he found a young family growing up without adequate means for their support. He had received from his people what is called a "settlement," that is, a sufficient sum of money to procure a convenient house and homestead. But his salary was only $333 34, with the use of the parsonage lands He lived on one of the great thoroughfares of New England, at a time when clergymen always travelled at the expense of their brethren along the road, and his house was every where known for its generous hospitality. He was compelled, therefore, to seek more ample means of support, and now began to prepare students for College. His thorough scholarship made him a highly successful teacher. Among the great number of his pupils were the celebrated Eli Whitney, inventor of the cotton gin, and William Botsford, Chief Justice of New Brunswick. In this way he was enabled to educate five sons at College, and prepare them for public life; in addition to which he left an estate of six or seven thousand dollars

In the exact sciences as well as in mental and moral philosophy he was distinguished No exercise gave him more pleasure, than to sit down to the solution of some difficult problem, as he was wont to do in his hours of leisure. Having the use of the valuable library of his predecessor, many of the works in which library were written in Latin, he read extensively in that language. Divinity, however, was the great study of his Life. He took large, comprehensive views of the doctrines of Christianity. He loved the Bible, and especially those truths which go to exalt and illustrate the grace of God. Salvation by a crucified Redeemer, without merit on the part of the sinner, and the duties of the moral law were the burden of his preaching. At the same time he exerted a commanding influence in the churches of Connecticut, as a friend and a counsellor.

In 1776 he was elected into the corporation of Yale College. The next year a President was appointed. The votes were equally divided between him and Dr. Stiles. He then magnanimously used his influence in favor of Dr. Stiles, who received the appointment. Like his predecessor he exerted a powerful influence in favor of education. His five sons were all educated at Yale College. He was devoted to the interests of common schools; was for many years clerk of the Durham Book Company. There was a young farmer in Durham, who had heard so much about the study of the Hebrew that he was eager to undertake it. He asked assistance, which was freely given him for two or three winters, so that he was able to read the Old Testament in that language.

The death of Dr. Goodrich occurred in November, 1797, and was sudden and unexpected. On the 17th of that month, he left home for the purpose of examining some lands, which belonged to Yale College, in the county of Litchfield. On the Sabbath following he preached at Litchfield, and on Monday proceeded to Norfolk, where he was entertained by the hospitable family of Captain Titus Ives. At this time he was in the enjoyment of good health. The evening was spent in pleasant conversation. On the following morning he rose early, as was his custom; had dressed himself, with the exception of putting on his coat, which he was evidently in the act of doing, proceeding during the same time towards the door, when he fell in an apoplectic fit, and expired in the sixty-fourth year of his age, and the forty-second year of his ministry. His remains were carried to Durham, on the succeeding Saturday, and were followed to the grave by his family, the Church, and the congregation and a numerous concourse of strangers. President Dwight of Yale College delivered a solemn and affecting discourse from Ecclesiastes ii. 1: "The righteous and the wise and their works are in the hands of God."

In addressing the clergy present, he used the following language:

"My beloved brethren, a great man has fallen in our Israel to day; a man of distinguished learning and understanding, of unusual prudence, and of singular skill and experience in the councils of congregations, churches and ministers. Recommended by tried wisdom, he was, you well know, very extensively employed, and confided in by both ministers and people throughout the State. By both were his useful labors acknowledged in composing their differences and directing their interests. To you, to me, to all with whom he was connected, the loss was great and affecting. In the Congregations, in the Churches, and especially in the University of this State, every weighty concern will remind us of his important services and force us to feel what we have lost. His talents were not only great and distinguished, but they were also of that most useful kind which we call *practical* Such talents are eminently fitted for the service of God, and for usefulness to mankind. In whatsoever he was called to judge or act, he made it his first business thoroughly to examine, and fully to understand. This he accomplished by diligent scrutiny, close attention to both sides of disputable points, a careful investigation of principles, and a cautious consideration of consequences For this important business, his thorough knowledge of the human character qualified him in an eminent degree, as did also his strong powers of judging, and his peculiar coolness and self possession. Not less important were his attention, patience and perseverance in investigation. In these most useful things he was at once an eminent blessing to mankind, and a most profitable example to us. No man living so well understood the interests of our university, or for more than twenty years took so active and important a part in its concerns. Few so well knew the interests of our churches, or so ably and extensively served them"

To this I would add that he left on the minds of the people of Durham a deep impression of his prudence, wisdom, and sagacity. For years after his decease his remarks were treasured up and repeated as the lessons of wisdom. Some of these remarks I have often heard and admired in my boyhood

As already mentioned, Dr. Goodrich being a man of great wisdom and prudence, he was eminently successful in retaining in harmony the congregation which his predecessor, Mr. Chauncey had gathered. He adhered to the same doctrines, and the same measures which that able, eloquent and venerable man had taught, and employed during the fifty years of his ministry. If he was not as earnest and eloquent, if he was not as zealous and impressive, he equalled him in devotedness to study, and surpassed him in general scholarship. Among his people he was dignified yet affable and bland in his manners.

By his candor and impartiality, he was able to reconcile conflicting opinions, and settle dangerous disputes in his congregation. On one occasion a parishioner brought to him grievous complaints and heavy charges against a neighbor, and then asked Dr. Goodrich for his opinion in the case. In his reply, he said to him, "I have two ears. One of them I have lent to you, the other I must keep for your neighbor." The parishioner went away satisfied with the answer.

In the year 1774, there were only six "Dissenters" in the town of Durham, in a population of a thousand and thirty-one. This was about the number when he died.

The published works of Dr. Goodrich are, *A Sermon at the Ordination of Rev. Roger Newton; A Sermon at the Ordination of Rev. Benjamin Boardman; A Sermon at the Ordination of his Son, Rev. Samuel Goodrich; An Election Sermon*, at Hartford, 1787. *A Sermon at the Ordination of Rev. Mathew Noyes.*

February 1, 1759, Dr. Goodrich married Catherine Chauncey, the grand daughter of his predecessor, who was born April 11th, 1741.

Mrs. Goodrich survived her husband for many years, honored

and beloved by a large circle of friends and relations. For the church and congregation of Durham, she cherished the highest regard, and continued to receive from them the respect and affection to which by her character, her love for them and her example among them, she was eminently entitled. Her death occurred April 8th, 1830.

Their children were, I. Chauncey, II. Elizur, III. Samuel, V. Charles Augustus, VI. Catherine, who married Rev. David Smith, his successor.

CHAPTER IV.

MINISTRY OF REV. DAVID SMITH, D. D.

STATEMENT OF MR. SMITH RESPECTING HIS SETTLEMENT.

"ON ye application of ye Committee of the Town, namely, Deacon Dan Parmelee, Deacon John Johnson, General James Wadsworth, Simeon Parsons, and Elnathan Camp, I came here and began to preach as a candidate, Feb. 10th, 1799. I tarried three Sabbaths. I was then absent four Sabbaths, and returned as a Candidate for settlement.

"The following are ye proceedings of ye Town and Church, respecting my call and settlement here, copied from ye Town records and votes of ye Church:

"At a Town meeting legally warned and holden in Durham on ye 20th day of May, 1799.

"At ye same meeting, ye Town voted to give Mr. David Smith a call to settle in ye work of ye Ministry in this Town. Then voted that Gen. James Wadsworth, Simeon Parsons, Esq., Mr. Elnathan Camp, Dan. Parmelee, Esq., and Dea. John Johnson, be a Committee to inform Mr. Smith of ye preceding vote, and request his compliance with ye same, and treat with him on terms of settlement, and make report to this meeting. And also to engage him to continue preaching in ye Town for a season. Then ye Town adjourned ye meeting to ye second Monday in June next, at 3 o'clock in ye afternoon. Then ye Town met according to adjournment, and ye Committee made report in ye following words, viz.:

"To ye Inhabitants of Durham, in Town meeting assembled, the subscribers, a Committee appointed to confer with Mr. David Smith on the terms of his settlement in ye work of ye Ministry in this Town, and make report to this meeting, take leave to report, that we waited on sd Mr. Smith, made him acquainted with ye votes of ye Town, at their last meeting, respecting his settlement in ye work of the Gospel Ministry among us, and have conferred with him on ye subject matter of said votes. That Mr. Smith, on his part, manifests a willingness to comply with ye request of this Town; but conceived that there was an impropriety in his setting a price on his services previous to any offer that might be made by the Town—that he wished only a decent and comfortable support—that he had no desire for agricultural pursuits—that his wish is to be placed in such a situation as that he might devote his time and attention to the discharge of ye office and duties of a Gospel Minister.

"The Committee beg leave further to report, that they have taken into consideration ye advanced prices of provisions, and other necessary articles of subsistence, beyond what they were forty years ago; also ye great difference in ye style and manner of living in this State, and ye consequent increased expense—also ye situation of this Town, whereby a minister will unavoidably be liable to more expense to support a decent character, than in many other places; and also to accommodate Mr. Smith it will be very convenient and necessary that a greater sum should be paid him, in a short time after his settlement, than may be necessary afterward. The Committee, therefore, take liberty to recommend to ye Town that, as an encouragement to Mr. Smith to settle in ye work of ye Gospel Ministry in this Town, and for his support, they should pay him annually, the first three years of his Ministry here, 500 dollars, and after ye expiration of said three years, to pay him annually 400 dollars, so long as he should continue to be their Minister, and that he shall have ye use and improvements of ye parsonage lot, adjoining Col. Camp's home lot—also, ye parsonage lot opposite the dwelling house of Robert Smithson; and that ye Town improve ye other parsonage lands, and apply ye annual avails thereof in part payment of ye annual sums above mentioned; all of which is hereby submitted by your most obedient humble servants,

James Wadsworth, Simeon Parsons, Elnathan Camp,
Dan. Parmelee, John Johnson,
Committee.

"The Town voted to accept and approve the above report, and voted ye same.

"At ye same meeting:—Whereas, ye Town, by their vote, have requested Mr. David Smith to settle in ye work of ye Gospel Ministry in this Town, and have voted to pay to him annually, for the first three years of his Ministry, 500 dollars, and after ye expiration of three years, to pay him annually 400 dollars, so long as he shall continue to be their Minister; and that he shall have ye use and improvements of ye parsonage lot adjoining Col. Camp's home lot, and also ye parsonage lot opposite ye dwelling house of Robert Smithson, during said term, provided he shall settle in said work.

"At ye same meeting, ye Town voted that ye same Committee, that made report to this meeting, should wait on Mr. Smith and lay before him ye votes of ye Town, and request his answer to the same.

"The following are the doings of the Church At an adjourned Church meeting, holden in Durham, on the 3rd of July, 1799.

"It appearing to this Church that the Town of Durham have called and invited Mr. David Smith of New Marlborough, Commonwealth of Massachusetts, to settle with them in the Gospel Ministry, and have made provision for his settlement and subsistence during his continuance with them. This Church do now approve of said choice, and do now, by their Major vote, invite ye said Mr. David Smith to take ye pastoral care and charge of this Church, to teach, guide, and direct us according to ye rules and directions given by Jesus Christ, ye great Head of ye Church, and his Apostles, revealed to us in ye Gospel.

"Then ye Church, by a very full vote, voted ye same in ye affirmative.

"A true copy, Test, SIMEON PARSONS,
Moderator."

"At ye same meeting of the Church, I presented a confession of faith and covenant, which wholly excludes the practice of what is called the half-way covenant, for their acceptance, without which I could not answer them in ye affirmative."

"The following is my answer to ye call I received from ye Church and Town of Durham to be their Minister:

"DURHAM, July 3rd, 1799.

"Beloved brethren of the Church of Christ, and the members of ye Congregation in ye Town of Durham:—

"I have received and taken into consideration the call which you have given me, to settle with you in the important and arduous work of the Gospel Ministry. I have, also, seriously and attentively considered your situation, and the proposals you have made me, to become your Minister, and have deliberately weighed the matter, I hope, with a real and prayerful desire of complying with duty. And, after much painful anxiety and serious deliberation, I have come to the following determination, viz.: That considering the situation of the Town, and the present prospect of union and harmony, which now subsists, I think it my duty to accept your proposals and settle with you And depending on Divine Providence for assistance, direction, and support, I am willing to take upon me the sacred and solemn office of a Gospel Minister in this place.

"The connection, my friends, which is now contemplated between you and me, is solemn and interesting. It is connected with eternity, and will come up to view, should it take place, in the solemn day of retribution.

"Let us, in all these transactions, go to God and seek direction from Him. Let us seek His glory as our supreme object; trust in His providence, and rely on His promises. Earnestly beseeching the great Head of the Church to direct us all into the path of duty, and dispose us to walk therein.

"I subscribe myself your sincere friend,
and fellow-traveller to Eternity,
DAVID SMITH."

"Having received and heard ye above answer to their call, ye Church and Town, with my consent, appointed Thursday, ye

13th of August, for ye day ordination, and made arrangements accordingly.

"The following are ye doings of ye Council :—At an Ecclesiastical Council, convened by letters missive, in Durham, at ye house of Mr. Elnathan Camp, August 14, 1799. Present, Rev. Messrs. Enoch Huntington, Benjamin Trumble, D. D , Ephraim Judson, Thomas W. Bray, John Foot, David Huntington, James Noyes, Jacob Catlin, and Matthew Noyes.

"And ye following Delegates from ye respective Churches which they represent, viz.:

"Capt Seth Wetmore, from ye 1st Chh. of Cht. in Middletown. Dr. Elisha Chapman, from ye Chh. of Cht. in North Haven. Capt. Amos Porter, from ye Chh. of Cht. in Sheffield. Deacon Joel Rose, from ye 3rd Chh. of Cht. in Guilford. Dea. Israel Bunnel, from ye 1st Chh. of Cht. in Cheshire. Rev. Wait Cornwell, from ye 3rd Chh. of Cht. in Middletown. Dea. Oliver Stanley, Esq., from ye 1st Chh. of Cht. in Wallingford. Dea. Samuel Shelden, from ye 1st Chh. of Cht. in New Marlborough. Dea. Phinneas Baldwin, from ye 3rd Chh of Cht. in Branford. Rev. Enoch Huntington was chosen Moderator, and ye Rev Matthew Noyes, Scribe."

"The Council was opened with prayer, by ye Moderator; after which ye letter missive was read, specifying ye design for which this Council was called, viz.: to set apart, consecrate and ordain Mr David Smith to ye pastoral office of ye Church and Congregation in this Town.

"The Committee from ye Church and Congregation then appeared, and laid before ye Council their votes and transactions relative to their call of Mr. Smith, to settle with them, as their Gospel Minister, and his acceptance of the same.

"The Council, by vote, expressed their approbation of their proceedings. Mr. Smith then appeared, and produced a certificate of his being an approved candidate for the Gospel Ministry, and suitable testimony of his regular standing, as a Church member, in ye 1st Chh. of Cht. in New Marlborough.

"The Council then proceeded to examine him in his knowledge in divinity, soundness in ye faith, and qualifications for ye work of ye Ministry; together with his views of entering upon the same. *Voted*, that he is approved, and that ye Council proceed to ordain him, on ye morrow, at half past ten o'clock, A M.

"The Council then arranged ye several parts of his ordination in ye following order: and voted that ye Rev. Mr. Catlin make ye introductory prayer, previous to the sermon to be delivered by ye Rev. Mr. Judson; that ye Rev. Dr Trumbull make ye ordaining prayer, and that Rev. Messrs. Huntington, Judson and Bray join with him in ye imposition of hands, that ye Rev. Moderator give ye charge; that ye Rev. Mr. Foot give ye right hand of fellowship; and that Rev. Mr. Bray make the concluding prayer. In ye foregoing votes and arrangements, ye Council were unanimous.

Test, MATTHEW NOYES, Scribe.

"The Council then adjourned until to-morrow morning, then to meet again at this place at nine o'clock.

"August 15th, 1799. Met according to adjournment, and proceeded to ye house of God, where, after ye sermon delivered by Rev Mr Judson, from Jonah 3rd, 2,—'Preach unto it ye preaching that I bid thee,'—Mr. Smith was ordained according to ye foregoing arrangements.

Test, MATTHEW NOYES."

In the settlement of Mr. Smith, as in that of Dr. Goodrich, the Town or Congregation took the lead, and the Church followed that lead.

With what feelings he entered on his work, may be seen from the following record, penned by him on the day of his ordination:—

"This day I have been consecrated by the laying on of the hands of the Presbytery, and by prayer, to the solemn and important work of the Gospel Ministry. How great the work! How inadequate am I to perform it! I feel my own insufficiency, and I pray for Divine assistance. O that God would make me faithful, and use me as an instrument, though unworthy, of promoting the cause of the Gracious Redeemer, and of saving the souls of some of my fellow-men."

STATEMENT OF REV. DAVID SMITH WITH RESPECT TO HIS SALARY.

"A brief statement of facts in relation to my salary, in Durham:—

"My salary was originally, for ye first three years, $500, and after three years, to be $400, and also the use of the parsonage lots, one seven acres and ye other five acres. In 1811 I requested some addition to my salary, as ye expenses of supporting a family had much increased. A subscription of about $30 was raised, and was to be as permanent as the life, or the residence of the subscribers should be.

"In 1816, I proposed to give up the subscription, as it operated unequally, and also the five-acre lot, from which, by selling it, the society could realize $102 a year, and have my salary fixed at a definite sum. Accordingly the society voted that my salary should be in future, $550, and ye use of the seven-acre lot. But in 1824, the society requested me to relinquish $50 a year, with which I complied, to aid and encourage the society.

"In 1827, the society requested me to relinquish another $50, making my salary $450. With this request, by the advice of some of the principal members of the Church and society, I did not feel it my duty to comply.

"In 1828, the subject of salary was again brought up, and ye request that I would relinquish another $50 was repeated. With this request, I finally complied, on condition that it should be punctually paid, and the subject should be no more agitated.

"In Autumn, 1831, a few individuals, who had secretly endeavoured to create uneasiness in the society appeared more bold, and manifested a desire for a dissolution of the connection between me and my people.

"At no time could a greater number than eighteen be found to vote their consent that I should be dismissed; and most of them professed to be satisfied with my labors.

"A Committee was finally chosen to confer with me on he subject. The Committee came, and after a free conversation, I communicated the following answer:—

"To the Church and First Ecclesiastical Society in Durham.

Gentlemen :

In consequence of your vote presented to me by your Committee, bearing date Oct 7th, 1831, I feel myself under the painful necessity of addressing you on a subject deeply interesting, both to you and myself. More than thirty-two years I have labored here in the work of the Ministry, and with what fidelity and desire for the spiritual good of my people, the day of judgment will show. I know I am far from being perfect, and have to acknowledge my deficiency in many respects. But I am conscious that I have sought the best interests of the Church and society for whom I have so long labored and prayed. And I would acknowledge with gratitude, the goodness of God, in so far blessing my labors, however unworthy of such a blessing, that five special revivals of religion have been enjoyed among my people, besides some special drops of mercy experienced since the year commenced. (Thirteen were added to the Church, and several others entertained a hope that they have embraced the Saviour, this year.) And during my Ministry, two hundred and seventy-three have been added to the Church. For this object, I have labored both by night and by day; and have spent the greatest part of my life in your service.

"Though I enjoy good health, and am as well able to discharge my parochial duties as I ever was, yet at my age, it cannot be expected that I should have the charge of another people. My desire would be to remain in peace, and sleep with my people.

"When I relinquished the last $50 from my salary, I had strong assurances that all would be satisfied and I should remain in peace. Nor did I know, until recently, that any discontent existed among my people. Nor am I now able to discover the ground of discontent which has been recently manifested.

"As I have ever felt, and I think, *manifested* an anxious concern for your spiritual good, and have made many sacrifices to promote it, I still feel disposed to pursue the same course.

"For the information of the younger part of the Church and society, and in justice to myself, I will make a brief statement of a few facts.

"When I accepted the call to become your Minister, I reserved four Sabbaths in each year, to be absent on visits to my relatives and friends. But when I had labored here three years I had not left my people destitute, but one half day, giving them thirty-five and a half Sabbaths more than I was under obligation to do. Nor during the whole time since, have I left them more than one half as much as I had a right to do according to agreement. In 1811 I had an eligible offer to leave Durham, and settle in another State, which I declined from the affection I had for my people and ye obligation I felt myself under to remain with them. A few years after, I had another offer, in this State of a situation with a salary of $700, paid semi-annually from a friend. This, also, I declined; I have also for several years past, relinquished $100 a year of salary, for the sake of peace and harmony, and of remaining in quiet. This, I had a strong assurance, *should* be the case But as efforts are making by *some*, to dissolve the pastoral relation, between me and my people, or to have me give up my salary and labors, proposing to make me some remuneration, I am still disposed to do every thing which is reasonable, to gratify the feelings of the society. I will, therefore, make the following propositions, from which the Church and society may make their selection.

"If the society will secure to me $550, and let me retain the lot I occupy, the ensuing season, as the society had the avails of it the first season of my ministry, it having been previously let; and will also pay me for my labors till a dissolution shall take place, I will unite in calling a council for the purpose. Or I will leave it with the association to say what I shall receive, and abide their decision.

"Had ye proposition been made to settle a collegue with me on condition of my giving up my salary and labors, I might have proposed some different terms. The terms I have proposed, I do not consider as a compensation, which I might in justice claim, considering my situation, and what I have already sacrificed. But I do not wish to burden the society, but shall ever rejoice in their prosperity.

"That you may have wisdom from above, to direct your deliberations, and be prospered in your spiritual concerns is the desire and prayer of your afflicted pastor.

Nov. 1831. D. SMITH."

DISMISSION OF DR. SMITH.

"The society having voted to comply with my proposal, I united with them in calling a council to dissolve the connection between me and them.

The following is a true copy of the result of council.

"At an Ecclesiastical council convened at the house of the Rev. David Smith, D. D., in Durham, Jan. 11th, 1832, by letters missive, from the pastor and the committee of the Church and society in said place, for the purpose of dissolving the pastoral relation, between him and them.

"Present, the Rev. Messrs. *Matthew Noyes*, from Northford, *Aaron Dutton*, from Guilford; *Zolva Whitmore*, from North Guilford; *Charles J. Hinsdale*, from Meriden; *Samuel N. Shepherd*, from Madison; *James Noyes, Jun*, from Middlefield.

"Mr. M. Noyes was chosen Moderator, and Mr. Dutton scribe. The council was opened with prayer. The committee of the Church and society presented to the council, documents of a correspondence between the society and the pastor relative to a dissolution of the pastoral relation, by which it appears that a mutual agreement has been entered into, between the parties on this subject. Therefore, voted unanimously, that we ratify the agreement between Rev. David Smith, D D., and the Church and society of Durham, relative to his dismission; and the pastoral relation between him and them is hereby dissolved. At the same time the council would bear their united testimony, to the ministerial talents and qualifications of Dr Smith—to his fidelity in the discharge of his pastoral duties, and to his success in his labors, witnessed in the repeated revivals of religion, as the fruit of which, more than two hundred and seventy have been added to his church.

"As an *able* and *faithful* minister, we cheerfully recommend him to the Churches, and to his brethren in the ministry.

"And while we deeply regret that any thing should have occurred in the society to render the above proceedings neecssary; we feel peculiarly solicitous for the future peace and harmony of the society, and devoutly hope that all existing difficulties, may from this time be settled, that no root of bitterness may be permitted hereafter to spring up and occasion divisions; and that ere long, they may be united in resettling the gospel ministry.

Unanimously voted as the doings of this Council.

Test, MATTHEW NOYES, *Moderator.*
AARON DUTTON, *Scribe.*

Durham, Jan., 1832."

LIFE AND DEATH OF REV. DAVID SMITH, D. D.

The Rev. David Smith was born in Bozrah, Connecticut, Dec. 13, 1767. He died at Fair Haven, in the house of his daughter, Mrs. Catherine Ellsworth, March 5, 1862, aged ninety-four years, two months and twenty days He was the son of Ebenezer and Sarah Smith, who spent their last years in New Marlborough, Massachusetts. His father was a valuable officer in the Army of the Revolution, and at the close of the war, after a service of more than eight years, was the oldest captain in the Massachusetts line. Mr. Smith spent the years of his youth and early manhood in laboring on a farm. After losing his wife, Mr. Smith commenced his preparation for college While engaged in a school, he studied for a time without an instructor. In 1791 he placed himself under the care of Rev. Jacob Catlin, of New Marlborough, Mass In 1792 he entered the Sophomore class in Yale College, where he enjoyed the confidence of his instructors and fellow students. Having as an excellent scholar, taken his first degree at the college in 1795, he taught school for a time in Sheffield, Mass. In June, 1796, he commenced the study of theology with Rev. Ephraim Judson of that place. At the meeting of the Association of Berkshire County in October, he was licensed to preach the Gospel. After preaching in several places, he came to Durham and preached for the first time Feb. 10, 1799, when he soon after received a call, and was settled August 15, 1799.

Dr. Smith was the pastor of the congregation and church in Durham thirty-three years, and was distinguished for zeal and activity, and ability in the performance of his professional duties During his ministry there were six revivals of religion.

For many years, like his predecessors, he received youth into his family and fitted them for college. Among his pupils were Hon. Samuel D. Hubbard, afterwards member of Congress, and

Post Master General; Dr. James E. Dekay, a distinguished naturalist, and Commodore George Dekay. Between him and them there was always a continued friendship. Like his predecessors, he was a fellow of Yale College; and such were his habits of punctuality, that for forty years he was not absent a single time from the meetings of the Board. In 1830 he received the degree of Doctor of Divinity, from Hamilton College.

Besides his professional and scholastic employments, he cultivated a farm with good judgment and success, laboring with his own hands, rising at early dawn.

The strong features of his character he preserved to extreme old age, but mellowed and improved by time. His social feelings always fine, grew finer, more genial and attractive as he grew older, and as he became disengaged from the exciting cares and anxieties of life.

He could say, "My last days are my best days, and my last comforts my best comforts." He enjoyed eminently a green old age, and was able to preach in the Capitol at Washington with ease to himself, and with edification to his hearers, and to act as the Chaplain of the Cincinnati Society in Boston, when past ninety years of age.

His religion was of the type that became common, at the close of the last century, and the commencement of this, which was then called New Divinity. But he lived so long that what was then called New Divinity, was, when he became old, called Old Divinity. In the faith and practice of this religion he lived. In the consolations of this religion he died—to enjoy the rewards promised to the faithful.

Dr. Smith was united in a second marriage to Catherine Goodrich, daughter of his predecessor. In this way the pulpit of Durham was in the possession of one family one hundred and twenty-six years. Mrs. Smith died on the thirty-first of July, 1845, in the 70th year of her age. The following is an extract from an obituary notice published soon after her death:

"With a natural disposition of uncommon tenderness and affection, a cultivated intellect, and a heart early sanctified by divine grace, she spent a long life in continued acts of kindness to those around her, which will be remembered with gratitude not only by the circle of her immediate friends, but by hundreds who have shared, at different times, in the hospitalities of the household over which she presided. In all the relations of the family, the neighborhood, and the parish, it was her constant aim to promote peace and mutual affection, and such was the force of her self denying consecration to the good of others, that she probably never had an enemy; but enjoyed the spontaneous testimony of all, however they might differ from each other, to the purity of her motives, and the healing influence of her example. The close of such a life was, as might be expected, one of peace and spiritual consolation. During four months of suffering she enjoyed the presence of the Divine Comforter. Deeply sensible of her lost condition as a sinner, and the imperfection of her best service, she cast herself on the merits of Christ alone for pardon and acceptance. She could say with humble confidence 'I know in whom I have believed' And when the hand of death was upon her, she was enabled to whisper, as the last words she uttered, 'In my father's house are many mansions.'" To this I would only add, that as there was a life-friendship between her and my mother, and in my childhood I was taught by her to call her "Aunt Caty," I entertained for her, from my earliest years strong affection and deep respect which time only increased Her silent and unconscious influence was felt in the parish in the ties that kept it together.

Dr Smith was married to Betsey Marsh before he went to college. David Marsh, was a child of this union. The children of Rev David, and Mrs. Catherine (Goodrich) Smith were, I Catharine, she married Hon. Henry L Ellsworth, but is now a widow. II. Elizur Goodrich; III. Elizabeth Marsh; IV. Chauncey Goodrich, who was born October 17, 1807, and died September 27, 1825, an amiable and promising young man. He was in a store in Hartford preparing himself for mercantile life. V. Simeon Parsons, born July 31st, 1809, became a merchant in New York, had good business talents, and courteous manners, was a professor of religion Married Hetty Hosford Smith, daughter of Walter D. Smith, Esq, who died Jan. 23d, 1840 She left one daughter, Hetty Hosford. He married for his second wife, Eliza Van Ness Lyle, June 27, 1842. He died after a short illness, Feb. 6, 1848. Their children were, I Henry

Lyle, M. D, II. Catherine—deceased, III. Gertrude Van Ness VI. Gustavus Walter, who was born June 16, 1815, and died at Lafayette, Indiana, August 8, 1840.

Mr. Smith on his settlement in Durham, showed more than common ability, enterprise and energy. And he brought with him the evident desire to consecrate himself to the duties of his office as a minister of Christ. And yet, it is well known, in Durham, that he did not enjoy the full measure of success in his professional labors which he desired.

Many causes over which he had no control, conspired to disturb the harmony which had hitherto existed in ecclesiastical matters in the town. The times had changed. The principles of the American Revolution and of the French Revolution, circulated in books and newspapers, and in conversation, were beginning to produce their legitimate effects in the minds of men in lessening a respect for constituted authority, whether civil or ecclesiastical. The right of private judgment in matters of faith and practice, became prominent in the minds and conversation of men, as if they were disposed to do their own thinking. And in order to show that they were thus independent, some would be tempted to oppose current opinions, both in politics and religion, merely because they were current. Some of the abstract doctrines of human rights in a state of nature, were beginning to agitate society in their application to existing civil and ecclesiastical organizations.

The puritan clergy, generally, while the colonies were subject to Great Britain, secretly or openly advocated the rights of the colonies against the Government of the mother country. They were in favor of local law in opposition to imperial law. In so doing they were in harmony with the great body of the people in the several colonies. But under the State Government formed at the Revolution, and under the Federal Government formed in 1788, differences of opinion grew up among the people themselves, so that the position of the clergy became delicate in relation to different political parties in their parishes. In this difficult position, Mr. Smith found himself placed among a reading, thinking people, both political parties being equally intelligent, and sincere.

Moreover, there was in the town a suspicion that some of the young clergymen, near the close of the last century, and the beginning of this, differed from the fathers in the ministry, in their opinions on theological doctrines, and rites, and discipline, and measures. Mr. Smith was exposed to this suspicion from the circumstance that he had studied theology with the Rev. Ephraim Judson, of Sheffield, Massachusetts, who was a strong Hopkinsian. Hitherto in Durham the same confession of faith had been used from the first. Hitherto the ministers of Durham, like most of the ministers of Connecticut, had baptized the children of those who had themselves been baptized, and who "*owned the Covenant*" into which their parents had entered for them, though they did not unite with the church at the table of the Lord. Having in a public manner "owned the covenant," into which their parents had entered, they were permitted to have their children baptized. This was a privilege earnestly coveted by many who had scruples about their fitness for full communion. This was what was called baptizing under the "*half-way covenant.*" Hitherto extreme discipline in the church in Durham had been confined chiefly or entirely to those who were guilty of admitted immoralities; so that the offender and his friends, and the community would acknowledge its justice. Hitherto personal and family religion was chiefly urged upon the people, and evening meetings had not been greatly encouraged.

It was alleged against Mr. Smith that he had brought in a new confession of faith, and refused to baptize under the "half way covenant," thus debarring some of a privilege;—was in favor of discipline in cases in which there was no immorality, but only the violation of an arbitrary by-law recently enacted; and had introduced conference meetings, at which unprofitable and ill-natured discussions took place. On the other hand, it was alleged against the opposers of Mr. Smith, that they did not love experimental religion, and were inclined to infidel opinions; even though a considerable number of them were members of the church.

From these and other causes a large secession took place from the church and congregation, to other denominations, especially the Methodist and the Episcopal. Dr. Smith after going through these troubles, come out from them all, in his old age, as gold tried in the fire. Few men have lived so long as he. Few have enjoyed so much, both of temporal and of spiritual good, and very, very few have exhibited such beautiful old age, "frosty but kindly," fresh with the remembrance of the past, bright with the hopes of the future.

CHAPTER V.

ECCLESIASTICAL SOCIETIES

SEPARATION OF THE ECCLESIASTICAL SOCIETY FROM THE TOWN.

Until November, 1804, the Town of Durham was an Ecclesiastical parish. It, or to use the language of the Record, "they" had given a call to their ministers, had provided for their settlement and maintenance, had annually voted and paid them salaries, had felt competent to pass votes in order to settle Ecclesiastical difficulties, and preserve harmony. The following gives an account of the separation, between the Town and the Ecclesiastical Society.

"Whereas, the Town of Durham from its origin has been one Ecclesiastical society, and done their Ministerial business in Town meetings, till of late there has been a number of the Inhabitants of said Town certificated themselves to other Denominations, whereby it becomes inconvenient to do said business in Town meetings: And as the General Assembly in their sessions in May, 1804, gave liberty to any Ecclesiastical society, which had hitherto exercised this power in town meetings, or through the agency of select men, to meet together and organize themselves into a Society, and do any other business proper to be done: And on the request of several of the Inhabitants of said town, to warn a meeting for said purpose, a warrant was granted signed by Gen'l JAMES WADSWORTH, Esq, SIMEON PARSONS, Justice of the peace, DAN PARMELEE, Esq., and Deacon JOHN JOHNSON, to warn all the Inhabitants of said Town, legal voters excepting those that are exempted from paying Ministers taxes in said town, to meet at the school house near the Meeting-house, on the 19th day of Nov. 1804: And accordingly the Inhabitants met on said day, and the necessary officers were chosen according to Law in said Meeting for said society.

At the same meeting DAN. PARMELEE, Esq., was chosen Moderator; SIMEON PARSONS, Esq., was chosen society's clerk; GUERNSEY BATES was chosen society's Treasurer; JOSEPH TUTTLE, Jun., was chosen society's collector; General JAMES WADSWORTH, DAN. PARMALEE, Esq, and Capt. JOHN JOHNSON were chosen society's committee."

SIMEON PARSONS, *Society's Clerk.*

When Durham was first settled, as religion was acknowledged to be a public benefit for all, it seemed reasonable that all should be taxed for the support of it, just as all were taxed by the town for the support of schools, which are for the benefit of all But when after the experience of a hundred years, men came to differ as to what religion is; what are its articles of faith; to whom should baptism be administered; what are the measures for promoting religion; for what shall members of the church be disciplined—the case was changed. In March, 1800, as many as twenty men, most of them men of property, made an application to the town, to have their ministerial tax abated; which application was granted. These applications continued year after year. In the Town Record for Dec. 27, 1803, is the following entry: "Whereas sundry persons have represented to the Town that they are dissatisfied with the preaching of the Rev. Mr. Smith, and request some measures may be adopted by the town respecting the same to give satisfaction; *Voted*, that Messrs. Stephen Norton, Jun, Eliphas Parmelee and Charles Coe, be a committee to apply to Jonathan Bull, Roger Newton, and Nathaniel Rosseter, Esq. to hear all persons, who are dissatisfied and advise those persons what measures are best to be adopted, to preserve the peace and harmony of the town; and to be done as soon as may be convenient."

After the action mentioned above, the Town was relieved from those embarrassments; but the breaking up of the old systems, and the introduction of the new, was attended in Durham as elsewhere in the State, with a good deal of sadness, and discouragement and irritation. The new system was opposed very generally by the Congregational clergy, and churches of Connecticut, and was never finally consummated until the election of Governor Wolcott in 1817, and the adoption of the State constitution in 1818. The vote of Durham on that constitution will be given elsewhere.

MINISTRY OF REV. HENRY GLEASON.

REV. HENRY GLEASON'S STATEMENT.

"I commenced preaching in Durham, on the first Sabbath in April, 1832, and continued until June 20th. I subsequently received the following communications:

DURHAM, July 3d, 1832.

"At a meeting of the Church of Christ in Durham *voted* unanimously that we give the Rev. Henry Gleason a call to take the pastoral charge of this church.

"Voted a committee; Miles Merwin, Jun., Dea. Samuel Newton, Alfred Camp.

Attest, SETH SEWARD, *Clerk.*"

"At a meeting of the Society held July 17th, 1832, *voted* that this society unite with the Church in giving the Rev. Henry Gleason a call to take the pastoral charge of this Church and Society; and the hireing committee are hereby authorized to offer him the sum of five hundred dollars per annum so long as he shall continue our minister.

A true copy.

Attest, JOHN WHITE, *Society's Clerk.*"

"*Voted*, That the conditions of the above call be such, that whereas a subscription of five hundred dollars has been received, for the purpose of paying the Rev. Henry Gleason for one year, ending on the 20th of June, 1833.

"Now if either the society or the Rev. Henry Gleason, at that time, viz. on the 20th of June, 1833, or at any time subsequent to that period, shall wish to discontinue the relation existing between them as minister and people, and shall have given ninety days previous notice of the same, then the said relation shall cease, by mutual consent, and no further obligation shall rest on either party, or further demands be made, and the hiring committee are hereby authorized to treat with the Rev. Henry Gleason accordingly.

Attest, JOHN WHITE, *Society's Clerk.*

Rev. Henry Gleason,

Dear Sir,

We the undersigned, a committee of the Church and first Ecclesiastical Society in Durham, being on sufficient grounds well satisfied of your ministerial qualifications, and having good hopes from our past experiences of your labors, that your ministrations in *the gospel* will be profitable to our spiritual interests, do earnestly call and desire you to undertake the *pastoral office* in said Church and society; and that you may be free from the worldly cares and avocations we do hereby promise to pay you the sum of five hundred dollars per annum by the first of May annually so long as you shall continue our minister.

Durham, July 18th, 1832.

Miles Merwin, Jun.
John White,
John S. Camp,
Samuel Newton, } Committee of Society.

Miles Merwin, Jun.
Samuel Newton,
Alfred Camp, } Committee of Church.

To which I returned the following answer.

To the Church and Society in Durham

I have received from your committee a communication dated July 18th, 1832, inviting me to take the "pastoral charge of your church and society." Influenced as I trust by a desire for the advancement of Christ's kingdom among men, and after a prayerful examination of the question, "What is duty?" I have concluded to comply with your request, should the authorized council approve the call by granting ordination. On these conditions I accept your invitation on the terms specified in the communication of your committee.

With the highest regard for the best interest of your Church and Society, I remain yours,

HENRY GLEASON.

Thompson, July 24th, 1832.

The Consociation met in Durham August 21st, 1832, at 11

o'clock A. M. for the purpose of ordaining Rev. Henry Gleason. See Records of Consociation.

DURHAM, March 20, 1838.

To the first Ecclesiastical Society of Durham:

Beloved Friends—

It has become my duty to notify you that the relation existing between us as pastor and people should be dissolved at the expiration of three months from this date, agreeably to the terms of my settlement. If the Society desire it, I will continue to supply them till the present year expires, which will be on the 20th of June next. If, however, they should prefer to have me discontinue my labors earlier, I will not stand in the way of the good of the Society, nor oppose their wishes in the matter. You will perhaps wish to know the reason of this step on my part. I would briefly say, therefore, that ill health and the necessity of being free from care and labor in order to my recovery, constitute the principal reason at present for my wishing to leave you. I entertain a high regard for this people, and I trust I never shall cease to desire and to pray for your prosperity, temporal and eternal.

With sentiments of high esteem,

I remain your friend,

HENRY GLEASON.

SAMUEL NEWTON, *Clerk*

LIFE OF REV. HENRY GLEASON.

"The Rev. HENRY GLEASON was born in Thompson, Connecticut, September 11, 1802. Soon after his conversion to Christ, his heart become fixed on the holy ministry as a profession. Under the instruction of the Rev. Dr. Dow, his pastor, he pursued a course of preparatory studies under formidable difficulties, employing only a small portion of each day over his books, while most of the time he spent in assisting his father in the labors of the farm.

"He graduated at Yale College with honor in 1828. The following year he passed in Sag Harbor as preceptor of the Academy in that place.

"After pursuing his Theological studies in the Seminary of Yale College, at the close of his third year of study, he was ordained pastor of the Congregational Church and Society in Durham, August 22, 1832. He was united in marriage with Cynthia S Vandervort, Sept. 29 of that year. During his ministry in Durham one hundred and thirty-six were added to the church. In June, 1838, he was obliged to suspend preaching on account of ill health. After spending the Summer and Autumn in journeying and relaxation, his health was so far restored, that he resumed his labors among his people, the following December. He preached his last sermons, on the second Sabbath of August, 1839. One of them was from the text, "Prepare to meet thy God" The following week he was attacked with a low sinking typhus fever which terminated his life on Monday morning, the 16th instant. He was very calm during his whole sickness, and met death with the composure of a true Christian

"He was a consistent, earnest, devoted Christian. The following lines from his pen, enclosed in a letter to a friend a year before his death, breathes his spirit.

Beyond the stormy sea of life,
  There is a land of glorious rest,
Where winds and waves in angry strife
  No more disturb the peaceful breast,
Though clouds and darkness now attend
  My weary way across the sea,
These scenes of darkness soon will end
  In an eternal cloudless day
On that far distant happy shore
  I soon shall stand forever bless'd,
Where sin and tears are known no more,
  Of heavenly peace my soul possessed.
O thought transporting! wondrous grace,
  That guides me safe through peril's way!
When shall I reach that happy place,
  And dwell in everlasting day?
Come! Jesus, come, and take me home,
  My spirit now would gladly rise,
I long to stand before thy throne,
  And join the chorus of the skies.

"He was a faithful husband and father. The following is found among the written rules which he adopted with reference to his own conduct and habits, viz: 'No efforts should be spared to render a family happy in themselves To this end there must be—1st. Subordination among its members to its divinely constituted head. 2d. There must be self-government among its members. 3d. There must be kindness and affection among its members and benevolence towards all; for a contracted selfish ness is hostile to domestic happiness. 4th. There must be subordination to God, or piety If there is rebellion against God, there will be against all authority, there can be no parental or self-government. All government depends on the Divine government. 5th There must be order and system, not too minute but definite. 6th. Home must be the most attractive place, and the society of each other the most desirable. The parent must be himself happy or he will not have a happy family.

"'In order to this he must—1st. Maintain his station in the family as its *head* and *governor.* 2d. He must govern himself *thoroughly.* 3d He must possess mingled dignity, gravity, cheerfulness, and affection He must make an exhibition of those tempers only which he would have his family cherish. 4th. He must be pious and consistently so. 5th. He must be at once the *companion*, the governor, and head of the family, and also the teacher and guide' These are words of wisdom, from a wise teacher.

"He was a good minister. He loved his work, and when want of strength obliged him to suspend it, he experienced a sore trial. He studied to adapt himself to his people. He was beloved as a pastor, the mourner valued him, and loved him for his kindness, faithfulness and consolation. He sought the spiritual interests of his people, and was deeply grieved, when he saw obstacles interposed in the way of his object."—From a notice in the *New Haven Record.*

As already stated, Mr. Gleason was united in marriage with Cynthia Vandervort. Their children were—1. William Henry, a lawyer in Sag Harbor; 2 Gabriel Havens; 3. Maria Waring, 4. Henry Vandervort, deceased.

After Mr. Gleason's separation from his people and before the resumption of his labors, the Church and Society, September, 1828, gave a call to the Rev. Arthur Grainger, which he declined.

On the 19th of October, 1839, a call was voted to Rev. William C. Fowler, which he declined.

On the 21st of March, 1840, a call was voted to James McDonald, to settle in the ministry, which he declined.

Rev. CHARLES LEWIS MILLS was graduated in Yale College, 1835, was installed April 28th, 1841, was dismissed in September, 1845. He was the last pastor settled over the church before its division.

The following have been Clerks of the Ecclesiastical Society. SIMEON PARSONS, WORTHINGTON G CHAUNCEY, ALFRED CAMP, JOHN WHITE, JOSEPH CHEDSEY, ALFRED CAMP again, SAMUEL NEWTON, ELISHA NEWTON, WOLCOTT P. STONE.

SINCE THE DIVISION OF THE SOCIETY.

Rev. JAMES BRADFORD CLEVELAND was graduated at Yale College in 1847, was installed pastor June 8th, 1852, was dismissed by vote of the church Sept. 10th, 1853.

Rev. ABRAHAM CHITTENDEN BALDWIN was installed Oct. 18th, 1857, dismissed April, 1861.

The following have supplied the pulpit for a longer or a shorter period: Rev. MERRILL RICHARDSON; Rev. L. H. PEASE; the Rev. BENJAMIN PAGE at two periods; Rev. WILLIAM C. FOWLER, the Rev. Mr. CROSMAN; Rev. Professor FOSS; the Rev. Mr. LOOMIS. The Clerks of the Society since the separation have been WILLIAM A. PARMELEE, ISRAEL C. NEWTON.

SOUTH CHURCH.

Rev. JAMES R MERSHON was ordained pastor April 27th, 1848; was dismissed April, 1849.

Rev. ROBERT G. WILLIAMS was ordained pastor Oct 11th, 1852; was dismissed April 20th, 1853.

Rev. IREM SMITH was ordained pastor August, 1858, was dismissed January 2d, 1861.

The following have supplied the pulpit for a longer or shorter term. Rev. L. H. PEASE; Rev E E. HILL; Rev. Mr. HOOKER; Rev. WILLIAM C FOWLER; Rev. Mr. DUTTON; Rev. E. BAILEY SMITH. Rev. I. W. SESSIONS has been employed as stated preacher.

The Clerks of the Ecclesiastical Society have been W. P. STONE, DAVID C. CAMP, E. B. MEIGS.

THE FOLLOWING HAVE BEEN DEACONS.

WILLIAM SEWARD was born at Guilford, March 25, 1688. He was the son of John Seward, who was born Feb. 14, 1653–4, and grandson of Lieut. William Seward, who was born in Bristol, England, 1627. He was an inhabitant of Durham until about 1730, when he removed to Guilford, where he was Deacon, and afterwards to Killingworth, where he died, May 31, 1764. His wife was Damaris Punderson, daughter of John Punderson, Jun., of New Haven. Their children were—1. William, born July 27, 1712; 2. David; 3. Damaris; 4 Mary.

THOMAS LYMAN, son of Richard Lyman, who was the son of Richard, the emigrant from England, was born in Windsor and removed with his Father to Northampton. With his children, Thomas, Mindwell, Ebenezer, Elizabeth, Noah and Enoch, he came to Durham before 1715, and died July 15, 1725, aged 75 years.

HENRY CRANE, son of Capt. Henry Crane, first of Guilford and afterwards of Killingworth, was born October 25, 1677, settled in that part of Durham which had been granted to Killingworth, on the place now occupied by Henry E. Nettleton, and was the progenitor of a large number of descendants, all of whom left Durham, some of them to reside in Oneida County, New York. He was a leading man in civil as well as in religious affairs. He died April, 1741, according to the grave stone, aged 64 years. His wife was Abigail Flood, daughter of Robert Flood.

ISRAEL BURRIT, from Stratford, was the son of Stephen, who was the son of William. He was born 1687. He died 1750 in his 63d year. He left three sons, Israel, Charles and William. His second wife was Sarah Chauncey, daughter of Rev. Nathaniel Chauncey. His children by his second wife were—1. Israel; 2. Charles; 3 William.

JOHN CAMP, from Milford, died 1754, in his 54th year. He may have been the son of Samuel Camp.

JOSEPH TIBBALS from Milford, died October 14, 1774, in his 88th year.

EZRA BALDWIN from Milford, died March 4, 1783, in his 76th year.

JAMES CURTIS from Stratford, elected Dec. 25, 1766, died 1790 in his 80th year.

DANIEL HALL of Guilford, born Feb. 16, 1718, was the son of William Hall, of Guilford, who was born Jan. 15, 1683, who was the son of Samuel, born 1650, who was the son of William, emigrant from England to Guilford He was elected Deacon, May 2, 1782. The children of Daniel Hall were—1. Daniel; 2. Martha; 3. Elizabeth. He died 1790, aged 72.

JOHN JOHNSON died Nov. 18, 1819, aged 78. One of his daughters married Deacon John Tibbals, another Charles Robinson, and another Dr. Fitch.

DAN PARMELEE, who was the son of Hezekiah Parmelee, who was the son of Joel Parmalee from Guilford, married Abigail Norton Jan. 11, 1776. Died Dec. 11, 1825, aged 78. His children were—1. Hannah; 2. Betsey; 3. Dan; 4. Mahetabel; 5. Abigail.

ABNER NEWTON, born Dec. 27, 1764; elected Sept. 1803, and died Sept. 9, 1852. He was the son of Burwell Newton, who was the son of Abner, who came from Milford His children were—1. Elisha; 2. Abner; 3 Horace; 4. Gaylord; 5. R. Watson; Content; Parnell.

OZIAS NORTON was the son of Stephen Norton, who was born in Durham, Jan. 7, 1724, and died Oct. 8, 1808, aged 84. The latter was the son of John Norton, who was born Oct. 3, 1686, who was the son of Thomas Norton, who was born in England about 1624, and came with his father Thomas in 1639, to Guilford, and removed to Saybrook, and died in Durham after 1712. His father Thomas and his wife Grace came from England 1639, and settled in Guilford. He was born about 1603 and died May, 1648. Deacon Ozias Norton was born Dec. 31, 1759, married Hannah Parmelee, March, 1790. Elected Deacon 1803, removed to Charleston, Portage County, Ohio, June, 1812, and died Jan. 25, 1842, aged 82. His wife died Sept. 12, 1841, aged 80. His children—1. Leveret, born Nov. 28, 1791; 2. Clarissa; 3. Alfred; 4. Ozias. The Nortons lived in the northwest part of the town.

JOSIAH JEWETT, elected Sept. 3, 1812, removed.

JOHN TIBBALS, son of Ebenezer Tibbals, grandson of Deacon Joseph Tibbals, elected Nov. 6, 1805, died March 9, aged 45 years He married Concurrence Johnson, daughter of Deacon John Johnson. Their children were—1. Angus; 2. John.

SAMUEL C. CAMP, son of Col. Samuel Camp, and a descendant of Samuel Camp of Milford, was elected Deacon July, 1819; lived in Hartford, Middletown, and afterwards in his native place,

Durham, and built the house now owned by William Canfield; died Sept. 24, 1823, aged 62 years.

SETH SEWARD, elected Jan. 22, 1824. Died January 3, 1846, aged 79 years and 9 months. He was descended from John Seward, one of the original proprietors of Durham. His children were—1. Orpha; 2. Maria; 3. Eliza; 4 Nancy; 5. Rev. Dwight, D. D.

TIMOTHY STONE, born in Guilford, May 2, 1773. He was the son of Nathaniel Stone, born Dec. 10, 1731, who was the son of Timothy Stone, born March 16, 1696; who was the son of Nathaniel Stone, born Sept. 15, 1648; who was the son of John Stone, who was the fifth son of Rev. Samuel Stone of Hertford, England, and brother of Rev. Samuel Stone of the first church of Hartford. Timothy Stone of Durham married Eunice Parmelee, daughter of Levi Parmelee Elected Nov. 6, 1815, died January 14, 1826. Their children are—1. Maria; 2. Eunice; 3. Phebe; 4. Wolcott Parmelee; 5. Collins; 6 Lavinia; 7 Adeline, and 8 Sherman Timothy.

HETH CAMP, son of Heth Camp, elected Feb 5, 1842, married Phebe Bates, daughter of Daniel Bates; removed to Pennsylvania; deceased.

ELAH CAMP, son of Nathan O. Camp, elected January, 1842, removed to Meriden; father of David N. Camp, A. M., Principal of the Normal School at New Britain.

JOEL PARMELEE son of Joel Parmelee, who was the son of Joel Parmelee, who was the son of Joel Parmelee, who was the son of John Parmelee of Guilford, who was the son of John the emigrant from England, elected January, 1842; died Nov. 2, 1842, aged 37.

SAMUEL NEWTON son of Burwell Newton, elected January 4, 1827, died April 24, 1864, aged sixty-seven years. He married Betsey Parmelee, daughter of Joel Parmelee. He left two children—1 John; 2. Elizabeth

WOLCOTT P. STONE, elected 1844.

GAYLORD NEWTON, elected 1846.

NATHAN PARSONS, elected June 11, 1864.

JULIUS S. AUGER, elected June 11, 1864.

SOUTH CHURCH.

WOLCOTT P. STONE, elected May 27, 1847, removed to New Haven.

ISAAC PARMELEE, elected May 22, 1847

WILLIAM HART, elected Nov. 26, 1853.

THE METHODIST EPISCOPAL CHURCH.

The METHODIST EPISCOPAL CHURCH in Durham was organized about the year 1815. Rev. Messrs. Barnes, Bussie, Knight, Lorenzo Dow, Ebenezer Washburn, and Elijah Hibbard, were among the first preachers of that denomination that visited and preached in this town The first Class or Society was formed about this time and connected with Middletown Circuit, and supplied with occasional preaching by preachers that traveled that Circuit. Abraham Scranton, Capt. Eliphaz Nettleton, Timothy Elliott, John Swathel, and Timothy Coe, were among the first that identified themselves with this Society. For several years they occupied the South District School House, for a place of worship, and were embraced in Middletown Circuit, and afterwards with Black Rock Circuit, and supplied with preaching half a day or at 5 o'clock P. M. on the Sabbath. The Society at one time, numbered about thirty. These early Methodists did not long enjoy prosperity. A difficulty occurred in the little Church, the result of which was their almost entire destruction. Some were expelled, others withdrew, and from a Society of about thirty they were reduced to ten or twelve; so that in 1828 the Methodists were but a name, and only had preaching at 5 o'clock P. M. on Sunday, and that but once in two weeks. Rev. Henry Hatfield traveled the Circuit at that time In 1829, Rev. Alden Cooper occasionally met the appointment and with youthful zeal preached the word of life, and a few united with the society. Prayer meetings were held in the school house in the absence of the minister. In 1830, Dr. Chauncey Andrews being in the practice of medicine in the town, secured a place for holding Methodist meetings, and at his own expense fitted up a room in the Academy on the Green and hired a Local Preacher from Middletown by the name of Isham, to preach six Sabbaths, incurring the responsibility of paying him without any orders from the Society or Class. From that time forward Methodist meetings were held regularly on the Sabbath, and the students and Professors from the Wesleyan University at Middletown, supplied the pulpit. Rev. D. D. Whedon and Joseph Holdich, D. D., of the Professors, Rev. David Patton, then a student, now at the head of the Concord Biblical Institute, and Rev. Osman C. Baker, now one of the Bishops, with many other young men, whose names now stand high on the records of the M. E. Church, ministered to the little flock that worshipped in that "Upper Room." The Society and congregation gradually increased until the place became too strait for those desiring to worship with the Methodists; and as several families had removed from North Madison, who were formerly members of the Methodist Church at Black Rock, transferring their membership to this Society, the subject of erecting a church building was agitated. Several men of wealth and prominence in the town, among whom was Worthington G. Chauncey and his brother William, Henry Lyman, Wedworth Wadsworth, Samuel Parsons, and others giving their influence and assistance, the result of which was, the building of the present respectable edifice now occupied by the Society.

Rev. Moses L. Scudder, then a student in the Wesleyan University was preacher in charge, during the building of the church, in the year 1836. In the Autumn of 1837 the Presiding Elder of the District sent the Rev. Walter W. Brewer to take charge of the Society, and on the 1st of January, 1838, he commenced a protracted meeting assisted by the Rev. J. S. Arnold, then a student in the Wesleyan University, which was indeed a *protracted* meeting, continuing day and evening for nearly three months. So great was the religious interest created by these meetings, that the whole community, young and old, flocked to the Church, and were alike convicted by the Spirit and led to embrace the religion of Christ. The fruits of that great revival were alike beneficial to all the churches in the town, many of whom are now worthy members of the Congregational Churches. The larger portion however united with the Methodists, and constitute much of the strength of the Church at the present time. The first regular Conference appointment of a minister to this Church was made in the Spring of 1838, at which time the Rev. Harvey Husted was appointed, who remained preacher in charge two years Since which time annual appointments have been made in the following order: In 1840, the Rev. Salmon C. Perry. In 1841, Rev. Orrin Howard, who remaining but a few months, the Rev. Luke Hitchcock supplied for the year. In 1842, Rev. McKendree Bangs. In 1843 and 4, Rev. William C. Hoyt. During his pastorate the Congregational Church was burned, destroying the bell attached to it. Through the personal efforts of Mr. Hoyt, the M. E. Church was provided with the bell now in use. In 1845, Rev Nathaniel Kellogg. In 1846 and 7, Rev. Aaron Hill. In 1848 and 9, Rev. John E. Searles. In 1850 and 1, Rev. William Lawrence. In 1852 and 3, Rev. George S. Hare. In 1854, Rev. George A. Hubbell. In 1855 and 6, Rev. George Stillman. In 1857 and 8, Rev. R. H. Loomis. During his ministration the Church in common with most of the churches of the land shared in a gracious outpouring of the Holy Spirit. In 1859 and 60, Rev. J. W. Leek. In 1861 and 2, Rev. Levi P. Perry. In 1863, Rev. Horatio N. Weed. In 1864, Rev. Edwin Warriner. In 1865, Rev. Isaac Sanford. Thus from a feeble beginning with a membership of less than fifteen, and extending through a period of only fifty years, the Church has increased to its present number, of over two hundred, unencumbered by debt and contributing to the various religious and benevolent objects at home and abroad, an annual amount of not less than nine hundred and fifty dollars.

In numbers, character, and wealth, it occupies at the present time an honorable position in the community, her members sharing equally with her sister churches in the business and offices of the town. Her success under the Divine Guidance has been the result of an ardent attachment to the peculiar doctrines and discipline of the Church, and the zealous and united labors of her members in the great work of evangelizing the world.

CHURCH OF THE EPIPHANY, DURHAM.

A parish, in communion with the Protestant Episcopal Church, appears to have been organized in Durham as early as 1802. It was never, however, placed under the charge of a resident Rector, and never seems to have reached any permanent existence.

It was represented by a lay-delegate in five Conventions of the

Diocese of Connecticut, those namely, of 1804, 1805, 1806, 1809, and 1819. It is mentioned, in 1818, as forming with Middletown and Berlin one Cure, then vacant. In 1818, the Rev. D. Burhaus, who is called "Rector of —— Church, Durham," reports 35 families, 9 baptisms, and 2 funerals. And on two occasions afterwards, Missionaries of the Christian Knowledge Society report services at Durham, and collections for the Society.

In 1848, the Rev. Frederick Sill, who was ordained Deacon June 12th, 1849, began public services in Durham, according to the rites of the Protestant Episcopal Church. These services were continued for about a year. No parish was organized; though Mr. Sill reports ten baptisms, and two funerals in 1850 and 1851.

In 1859, some of the students of the Berkeley Divinity School, at Middletown, began to officiate as Lay-Readers, in Durham, under the direction of Bishop Williams; and since that time services have been uninterruptedly continued. On the 28th of June, 1862, the Bishop laid the corner stone of a neat and commodious church, which was consecrated by him, as the Church of the Epiphany, Jan. 29th, 1863. In Easter week following, the parish was organized, and received into union with the Diocese in the Convention which sat in June of that year.

CHAPTER VI

MEETING HOUSES

First Meeting House.—"On the 17th of November, 1709, "The Town by voate did agree that ye place to build the Meeting-House upon should be upon the place commonly accounted for the Meeting-house Green, which green lyeth between Mr. Chauncey's home lot and Samuel Camp's home lot."

"At the same Town meeting the Town by voate did enact and agree that they would build a meeting house forty feet square, with a flat Ruff, and Turritt, and to be twenty feet between joynts."

"At the same meeting the Town made choyse of WILLIAM SEWARD, SAMUEL PARSONS and JAMES WADSWORTH, to be their committee to take care of building of the sd Meeting-House, that is to say, the framing and covering of said House as cheap as may be for the Town's advantage."

"At the same meeting the Town by voate made choyce of Serj. JOHN SUTLIFF to go to Guilford, Killingworth and elsewhere to gather what money ye Gentlemen that have farms within this Town will contribute towards the building of the Meeting-House."

"At a meeting Dec 25, 1711, the Town by voate did enact and agree, that ye pulpit be built the next summer or sooner, if may be, the £5 given by Mr. Chauncey towards the building of the pulpit to be improved thereon, so far as it will go."

This meeting-house was located on the "Meeting-House Green," on the crown of the hill in what is now the grave yard, about where stand the monuments of Edward P. Camp and Samuel Parsons. The site was an admirable one, where the House would be a conspicuous object in the landscape, and where it would afford a distinct view of the eastern and the western hills. In 1723 it was ordered by the Town "that the pulpit should be new-built, and a comely canopy to cover it."

SEATING THE MEETING-HOUSE.

"At a Town meeting, Durham, Oct. 8, 1714, voated by the Town, that the meeting-house should be seated; and also the Town by voate made choyse of JAMES WADSWORTH, CALEB SEWARD, Jun., NATHANIEL SUTLIFF, WILLIAM SEWARD and HENRY CRANE to be a committee to seate sd house, and for instructions to sd committee, the Town by voate ordered sd committee to seate all the inhabitants of this Town that are free holders therein, and are in the general list of estates; and in their so doing that the sd committee should have respect to the age of persons, and to the whole charge in general that hath been laid out or expended upon the Meeting-House, and also to the places that any persons do sustain, both civil and military."

It would seem to us, in these times, that it would be a difficult task for the committee to follow the instructions of the town in seating the House. They were enjoined to have respect to age, to the *amount* of the *contributions* furnished by the several tax payers; and to their *official rank.* But in those times, and indeed down to my own remembrance, clergymen and private Christians were accustomed to pray that all might perform their relative duties as "superiors, inferiors and equals," "to give honor when honor is due." It seemed reasonable to them that the aged, and those who were taxed largely in comparison with others, and those who had an official rank should have better seats than others. The doctrine of human equality had not made much progress.

The inhabitants continued to worship in this house twenty years, when they had increased so much in numbers that a new church became necessary.

THE SECOND MEETING HOUSE.

"At a Town meeting Dec. 31, 1734, the Town by a major vote did enact and agree that the new Meeting-House, agreed to be set up in this Town shall be sixtie-four feet in length, and forty-four in breadth, and twenty-five feet in height between joints." It was finished in 1737.

"Monday, May 10, 1736, the Town before, by agreement being divided into two parts, the southern part of the town began to raise the Meeting-House; on the next day the northern part of the Town went on with the raising; and on Wednesday the Town generally met, and completed the raising of said House—part of Monday it rained, and beat off the raisers, so that this said House was raised in less than three days."

"February 15, 1737-8, the above named Meeting-House being finished excepting the hanging of the windows, and some small trifles of trimming off the work, we had a lecture on sd day, there being a large concourse of people from the neighboring Towns, the House much crowded, and Mr. Chauncey preached from Haggai 2: 9th verse."

The first meeting-house was raised in April, 1710, and pulled down in the spring of the year 1738. What were the reasons for changing the location does not appear The precise spot where the new house was placed was probably determined by the building committe, as in the case of the other house, whether wisely or not. The records show that the town was consulted about the location It was erected on the north-east corner of the present green, in a range with the road running east. It was built in the common style of the times with narrow windows, the posts and other timbers projecting from the walls. The pulpit had some decorations, besides its sounding board, and hour-glass which the speaker often turned when he commenced his sermon. The pulpit stairs were on the Sabbath decorated with boys who could not conveniently find seats with their parents, and who were too young to be sent up into the gallery. There was a Deacon's Seat under and in front of the pulpit, where, in my own recollection, sat Deacon Johnson and Deacon Parmelee, with their solemn and cheerful faces, gazed at by the whole congregation, inspiring awe and respect, especially in the young. There were the galleries on three sides of the house, in which sat the young people, and one or more tything men. On the West side were the Bass singers; on the South fronting the pulpit were the Tenor and Counter singers; on the East were Treble singers, often the flower of Durham. The pews were fitted up with small swing tables, for taking notes of the sermon, or supporting the elbows. The practice of taking notes had nearly disappeared before my remembrance. The pews were square; and consequently a portion of the audience sat with their backs to the preacher. Hence arose the practice of rising during the sermon on the part of some of the men, which at once enabled them to see the minister, and relieve themselves from drowsiness or from an uncomfortable posture. This they often did in their shirt sleeves. There they stood with eager upturned eyes gazing at the minister in his lofty pulpit, or at the singers as they made the house ring with their strong voices, and animated melody. The women in the pews, solaced themselves, successively in the season, with caraway, dill and fennel, giving a sprig of it to a sleepy child, or hospitably offering a bunch of it to a stranger.

Dec. 2, 1721, "The Town by their voate ordered the Select men to have some suitable person to beate a drum upon the Town charge, upon the Sabbaths, and other public meetings."

THE THIRD MEETING HOUSE.

On the 17th of July, 1835, the corner stone of the third Meeting-house was laid, just a century after the building of the second House was commenced The address on the occasion was delivered by Rev. David Smith, D. D. It was erected on the site where now stands the South Congregational Church. Its size was sixty feet by forty. This building was consumed by fire November 28, 1844

The corner stone of the present M E. Church was laid July 1st, 1836. The address was by Rev Joseph Holdich, D. D. The dedication service was Jan. 7, 1837. The sermon was by the Rev Wilbur Fisk, D D., president of the Wesleyan University. The original cost of the building was about $4000.

The first Trustees were Dr. Chauncey Andrews, Curtis C. Camp, Zebulon Hale, L. W. Leach, Enos Rogers, Timothy Elliott, and Henry M. Coe. Alterations and repairs have since been made, and the church is now valued at $5000. The present Trustees, Jan. 7th, 1866, are Wm H Walkley, Alvin P., Roberts, Charles I Haywood, Alexander Camp, Asa Fowler Phineas Robinson, Edward A. Thayer, Judson E. Francis and Henry Page.

The North Congregational Church was dedicated in June, 1847. The Sermon was preached by the Rev. Merrill Richardson from the 77th psalm, 13. "Thy way, oh God, is in the Sanctuary."

The South Congregational Church was dedicated December 29, 1849 The Dedication Sermon was preached by Rev. William C. Fowler.

It may not be out of place to say that the two Congregational and the Methodist Churches have lately been repaired and are in good order. The Episcopal Church has been so recently built that it needs no repairs.

STABLES OR SHEDS ON THE GREEN.

Dec. 5, 1718, "Resolved by voate by the Town that all persons being inhabitants of the Town may have libertie to build stables for horses on the Meeting-House Green; always provided that the place be first measured out and assigned to them by the Select Men before any such stable be erected on the green."

SABBATH DAY HOUSES.

"Dec. 1721, The Town by their major voate gave liberty to Deacon William Seward, Serj. Joel Parmely, John Seaward,

Stephen Hickox and James Morris to build houses on the edge of the Meeting-House Green adjoyning Mr. Camp's North line, to be for the entertainment of sd persons and familys on Sabbath and other public days; and the Select men are to lay out convenient places for sd persons to build sd houses upon.

This meeting is adjourned untill Friday next at sunset, at Thomas Stanley's house." Mr. Stanley kept a public house at this time.

These houses were from twenty to twenty-five feet in length, and from ten to twelve feet in breadth, and one story high with a chimney in the middle dividing the whole space into two rooms with a partition between them, for the accommodation of two families, who united in building the house. The furniture consisted of a few chairs, a table, plates and dishes; some iron utensil, it may be, for warming food which had been cooked. Besides the Bible, there was sometimes a book on experimental religion, like Baxter's Saints' Rest, or Allein's Alarm. On the morning of the Sabbath the mother of the family with provident care, put up her store of comforts for the dinner, substantial or slight fare as most convenient, a bottle of cider almost of course. The family then set off from their home in a large two horse sleigh, or on saddles and pillions. They stopped at the Sabbath-day house, kindled a blazing fire, and then went forth "to shiver in the cold during the morning Services." At noon they hurried back to their warm room After they had taken their meal and by turns drank from the pewter mug, thanks were returned. Then the sermon came under review, from the notes taken by the father of the family, or a chapter was read from the Bible, or a paragraph from some favorite author, the service concluding with prayer or singing. After again visiting the sanctuary, the family would return to the Sabbath-day house if the cold was severe, before they sought their home. The fire was then extinguished, the door was locked, and the house remained undisturbed during the week.

In time the custom of repairing to these houses changed; the houses themselves became dilapidated or furnished a refuge for the poor. They were better suited to those times when so much was thought of private family religion, than they would be to ours, when religion has become more of a public and social concern. The last Sabbath-day house which I remember, stood on the land owned by the first minister. It was occupied by John King, a Hessian deserter from the British army. It was owned by one of the Nortons The present writer can recollect as many as half a dozen of these houses. They grew up out of the type of religion which existed at that time. It was a *family religion*, rather than a public one.

PEST HOUSE.

"April 14, 1760. The Town resolved by a major vote that some House be forthwith built and erected in some suitable place, for the reception of such persons as shall be taken with infectious diseases" A committee was chosen to carry that vote into execution This committee made their report Dec. 4, 1760, "that they had built the house according to the direction of the Town."

This house was used for a number of years to receive persons taken with small pox, as well as for those inoculated. It was built on the *Town lot*, so called to this day, which lies north of Parke's Ledges, and northwest from Pisgah. There are several graves there with head stones to mark the spot where some of the victims of the disease were buried. The terror inspired by the small pox can hardly be understood in these times when vaccination has been substituted for the original disease. The subjects of it were banished from the abodes of men while living, and from the public grave yards when dead. The trees are growing up around these graves and striking their roots into them, as these tenants lie "in this neglected spot" But though unvisited as they lie under the forest trees, and unthought of by men, God will remember them and take care of their dust, as precious in his sight Though, in that retired place, they will hear the voice of the Arch Angel and the trump of God, and will rise up as promptly as those who lie under marble monuments in the most popular grave yard. I have just visited the spot. The remnant of a cellar and of a chimney are there. The well is there. Five grave marks are there. One stone has the following inscription · "Timothy Hall died July 17, 1775, aged 50." In the "South West Side" near the Nathan Camp house, are three graves of victims of the same disease; John Jones, who died of the small pox, Nov. 25, 1759, in the 47th year of his age;

Hannah Jones, who died of the small pox, Dec. 4, 1759, in the 42d year of her age. Sarah, daughter of Mr. John and Mrs. Hannah Jones, Nov. 28, 1759, in her tenth year.

In the year 1795, the steeple of the second church was built. The following story was current when I was young:

Mr. Jesse Austin was painting the steeple, on a long ladder The ladder fell; he was not only not injured, but he carried the paint pot, through the quarter of a circle which he described in falling, without spilling the paint

On the 15th of December, 1793, at a Town Meeting, voted that the bell in the steeple, shall be rung on each day excepting Sabbaths at sunrise in the morning, at 12 o'clock in the day time, and at 9 o'clock at the night; and on the Sabbath an hour before the beginning of the exercise, and at the opening of Town and Freeman's meeting, and also in the night season when it shall so happen that any building be on fire This bell was presented to the town by Mr. Elias Camp.

The practice of ringing the bell at these hours, contributed to give regularity to household arrangements throughout the town

That bell at that time uttered a distinct voice, with a distinct meaning, to earnest listeners. It meant that all that were not up with the lark, should be up with the sun. It meant that the weary laborer in the field at mid-day should hasten home to his smoking board, ready to receive and refresh him. It meant that the evening visitors should hasten home to family prayers, and to sleep the sweet sleep of the laboring man with unbarred doors, and unshuttered windows, ready to receive his neighbor, or the sun.

SINGING SCHOOLS.

Before the year 1727 it appears that very little attention was paid to the art of singing. Those who sang in the House of God on the Sabbath, may have sung with the spirit, but not with the understanding. They learned the tunes by the ear and not from the notes. At that time Rev. Mr. Chauncey prepared a pamphlet, which was afterwards published, entitled "*Regular singing defended and proved to be the only true way of singing the songs of the Lord.*" By "regular singing" he meant singing by *rule.* With reference to this, the General Association of Connecticut passed the following: "At a General Association at Hartford, May 12, 1727. This Association having heard the Rev. Mr. Chauncey's Arguments for Regular Singing, do approve of them and vote them to be printed; Recommending them to the publick and hoping they may be of usefulness. As Attest, TIMOTHY WOODBRIDGE, *Moderator*."

The question stated by him is "Whether in singing the songs of the Lord, we ought to proceed by a certain Rule, or to do it in any Loose, Irregular way, that this or that people have accustomed themselves unto?" The "arguments" in favor of "regular singing, as the only true way of singing," he states with logical accuracy and convincing power. In the course of his remarks he states that "the difference among towns in singing is very great, scarcely any two towns sing perfectly alike; and yet each town or person asserts they are in the right, and their neighbor is in the wrong"

The following he says are the objections made to regular singing: "Objection 1. This practice leads to the Church of England and will bring in organs. Objection 2. The very original of this way was from the Papists. Objection 3. The way of singing we use in this country is more solemn, and therefore much more suitable and becoming. Objection 4. It looks very unlikely to be the right way because young people fall into it. Objection 5. It is the cause of sore and bitter contentions." These objections he answers in a very satisfactory manner.

This pamphlet of fifty-four pages, published in 1728, must have had great influence in correcting the false taste and the loose practice not only in Durham but elsewhere. The argumentation was conclusive. It settled the question.

Before this, each singer seemed, in a certain sense, to sing his own tune though he sang with others, just as a certain dancer who did not keep step to the music pleasantly said, "I always dance to my own tune"

In the first Meeting House it does not appear that any special accommodation was made for the singers. But in the second Meeting House they occupied the front slips on three sides of the Gallery. In this house for a hundred years singing was practiced as an art. It was taught as an art probably before the congregation left the first house, in singing schools, and it has continued thus to be taught ever since, with more or less success These singing schools were formerly popular with the young people. Besides furnishing them with instruction they furnished pleasant occasions for intercourse.

A chorister regularly appointed, named the tune after the psalm was read, sounded his pitch pipe, and uttered two or three notes immediately after. When he rose, the singers, forty or fifty sometimes in number, rose on the three sides of the house, and sang generally with great animation. Sometimes there was a break-down, and then there was a good natured smile on the faces of the congregation. For a long time there was an inherited dislike of instrumental music. A certain man in my own recollection, would go to the south door of the Meeting House and inquire, "Is the great fiddle there?" On being told that it (the Bass Viol) was there, he would depart to his home He was not willing to be present where there was such a "Dagon."

THE BURIAL GROUND.

The old Burying Ground, so called, which was given by the proprietors, was the only burying ground in the town until 1822, when the new one was laid out. The old burying ground was formerly much frequented. I have collected from it a number of striking epitaphs. But instead of printing them, I introduce the words of HOLMES

> "Go where the ancient pathway guides,
> See where our sires laid down
> Their smiling babes, their cherished brides,
> The patriarchs of the town,
> Hast thou a tear for buried love?
> A sigh for transient power?
> All that a century left above,
> Go read it in an hour"

CHAPTER VII.

EDUCATION.

COMMON SCHOOLS.

As in Connecticut generally the School Master has not been far off when the Minister has been settled, and the School House has been side by side with the Church, so in Durham, the very year that the first Minister was ordained, the town authorized the Selectmen to engage a School Master for six months, and soon after the Meeting House was finished, the Town appointed a Committee to build a School House on the Green. But one school appears to have been kept until December, 1737, when the people on the west side of Coginchaug swamp were allowed to have a School. One was set up soon after at the North end of the Town.

"At a Town meeting on the 25th of December, 1711, the Town by voate made choyse of the selectmen, who are now chosen, to hire a school-master as soon as may be (or the space of half a year) for the advantage of the children in the Town, that they may be instructed, to Write and Read, and the sd school-master to be paid as the law directs."

"At a Town meeting in Durham October 8, 1722. The town by their Major voate did agree to build a school-house, to be in length twentie six feet and in breadth eighteen feet, to be set upon the meeting-house Green; and the Town by their Major Voate made choyse of Ensign Joseph Coe, Serj Joseph Seaward, and Noah Lyman to be their committee to pitch upon the particular spot, where sd house should be sett, and also to sett up and finish sd house and chimley with all convenient speed."

I have understood that the *primer*, and the *psalter*, were for a time, the only reading books in the school. Afterwards the New Testament was introduced. Later, Dilworth's spelling book was used, and afterwards Webster's and his Third part

From the settlement of the Town to the year 1741 it appears that one half of the expense of the Schools was defrayed from the Town Treasury, and the other half was assessed on the pupils

In 1741 the General Assembly granted to the Town of Durham a certain sum derived from the Sale of five Townships of land. In 1765, certain sums of money from the excise on spirits, were appropriated to schooling, amounting to £30,14,4. These two sums now amount to $739.42, the interest upon which has been annually applied to schooling down to the present time. This is called the common bond money.

In 1775, Ebenezer Robinson deeded to Elihu Chauncey and his heirs in trust, a piece of land five rods square, on the "Corner of his Green lot," for any of the inhabitants to build a school house. The Centre School House now stands upon this ground.

In 1780, Ebenezer Robinson, willed to the Town of Durham, about three acres of land for a Burying Ground, the profits of which were to be applied to the centre school, both before and after it shall be used for a Burying Ground At the same time said Robinson willed to the inhabitants of the Town of Durham £100 lawful money for a school to be kept at the centre school house eleven months in the year

In 1787 a portion of the donation, namely £39, was vested in Ohio lands These lands were sold and the Report of the selling committee was made 1835, that the avails in their hands amounted to $892. This added to the other portions of the £100 makes the sum of $1152.18 the interest on which, $69.13, has been applied to the Centre School agreeably to the will.

The third source from which money is received for schooling is the state appropriation, on the first of October about $147.00, on the first of March $314.00.

There is also received on the first of October annually from the Town deposite fund $171.90. The aforesaid moneys, in all $746 39, are annually divided on the scholars between the age of four and sixteen, amounting to about three hundred and twenty

Select Schools have been kept in Durham from time to time in private houses, or in the Academy on the Green, and in the Academy in the north part of the town.

THE BOOK COMPANY.

The Book Company of Durham was instituted on the 30th day of October, Anno Domini 1733. This it is supposed, was the first established in the colony. The original founders were namely, Col. ELIHU CHAUNCEY, Capt. NATHANIEL SUTLIEF, Mr. HUIT STRONG, Mr. SAMUEL SEAWARD, Capt. EBENEZER GUERNSEY, Lieut. NATHANIEL SEAWARD, Mr. THOMAS ROBINSON, and Capt. ROBERT FAIRCHILD. The formation of the company was by the following agreement made and subscribed by the founders and afterwards by their associates

Articles of the Book Company of Durham, Oct. 30, 1733. "Forasmuch as the subscribers hereof, being desirous to improve our leisure hours, in enriching our minds in useful and profitable knowledge by reading, do find ourselves unable to so do, for the want of suitable and *proper books*. Therefore, that we may be the better able to furnish ourselves with a suitable, and proper collection of books for the above said end, we do each of us unite together, and agree to be coparcenors in company together by the name of The 'BOOK COMPANY of Durham,' 'united to buy books, and we do agree and covenant with each other; and it is hereby covenanted and agreed upon, by each of us, the subscribers hereof, that we ourselves and successors will be in future a society or company of coparcenors united for said end, viz. to buy books, and we will each of us so often as we shall agree by our major vote, bear our equal parts in advancing any sum or sums of money at any time as a common stock to be laid out for such books, as shall be agreed upon by the major vote of the company, to enlarge our Library, and in pursuance of said design, we have each of us put into one stock the sum of twenty shillings, which is already laid out according to our Direction in purchasing books, which books shall be kept as a common stock Literary for the use of said company, by some meet person, whom we shall choose, each member having one equal right in said Library, and the use of the same under such regulations, as we shall agree upon."

In addition to this were sixty by-laws, carefully and judiciously drawn up, which with the preamble was signed on the 30th of October, Anno Domini 1733, in the seventh reign of our sovereign Lord George second, King, &c In the order of subscription, the following names are signed."

1. Elihu Chauncey, 2 Nathaniel Sutliff, 3. Huit Strong, 4. Samuel Seaward, 5. Joseph Sanford, 6. Ebenezer Guernsey, 7. Nathaniel Seaward, 8. Thomas Robinson, 9. Robert Fairchild, 10.

Azariah Beach, 11. Ezra Baldwin, 12. John Parmalee, 13. William Johnson, 14. Samuel Fairchild, 15. James Curtis, Jun, 16. John Camp, Jun , 17. Job Wheeler, 18. Moses Parsons, 19. Ithamar Parsons, 20. Richard Spelman, 21. Abel Beach, 22. Joseph Coe, 23. Daniel Merwin, Jun, 24. John Camp 2d, 25. Bryan Rosseter

In 1747, new by-laws, and articles of agrement were made, and new names were added, among which were, Israel Burrit, Noah Lyman, Thomas Lyman, Israel Camp, Benjamin Wells, Abraham Bartlet, and Elnathan Chauncey as possessing the right of Robert Fairchild. Col Chauncey continued to be clerk and library keeper until 1782, when he resigned the office and Mr. Bridgman Guernsey was elected to that office. The number of rights at that time was sixty-three.

A standing Committee on the Library was appointed, namely, Rev Elizur Goodrich, Capt. Elnathan Chauncey, Mr. Benjamin Picket and Mr. Thomas Lyman.

In January, 1787, Mr Lemuel Guernsey was appointed Librarian in place of Bridgman Guernsey, resigned

Nov. 25, 1788. The New Library Company was formed in connection with the old A new constitution was formed under which Rev. Elizur Goodrich was chosen clerk, Elnathan Chauncey, Librarian; General James Wadsworth, the Rev. Elizur Goodrich, Mr Thomas Lyman, Capt. Medad Strong and Mr. John Curtis, Jun., were chosen standing committee.

In forming the New Library the rights of the Old were carefully respected, and half the money received for the purchase of books was appropriated to the Old Library.

Dec. 1, 1794, Capt Elnathan Chauncey resigned the office of Librarian, and Gen. James Wadsworth was appointed Librarian.

On Death of Rev. Elizur Goodrich, Mr Elnathan Camp was chosen clerk, Dec 4, 1797.

Dec. 2, 1799, Rev. David Smith was chosen clerk in place of Elnathan Camp, resigned.

Dec. 1816, Charles Camp was appointed Librarian.

Dec. 1839, Worthington Chauncey was appointed Librarian.

Feb. 1856, the Book Company was dissolved, and the books sold at vendue.

The Durham Book Company was, as stated to Dr. Goodrich

by Col. Chauncey, the *first of the kind* established in the Colony, though many were established afterwards. It was patronized by President Clapp and the Fellows of Yale College, by Rev. Samuel Johnson, D. D., President of King's College, New York, by Dr. Sherlock of London, through Rev Ichabod Camp. President Stiles was a member of the company. The most intelligent men in the town belonged to it. The number and character of the books reflected honor upon the town. For nearly a century the books were circulated extensively through the town, and being read in the families nourished, for two or three generations, strong men who understood important subjects, in the various elevated branches of human knowledge. It was this Library that helped to make the voice of Durham potent in the Legislature for sixty or eighty years. It was this Library that helped to make the two first clergymen eminent. It was this Library that helped to refine the manners of the people, and which gave their high character to the emigrants from Durham. It was this Library that gave a high character to the schools, and which created a taste of a liberal education, which for a long time characterized the town.

But for the last twenty or twenty-five years of its existence it ceased to be attractive to the mass of the people. Newspapers, light reading and party politics, took the place of solid books, so that the Library was neglected, and Durham lost in some degree its high standing among the other towns.

THE ETHOSIAN LIBRARY.

About the time of the formation of the Federal constitution, 1787, a society called the *Ethosian*, was organized by some of the young men, and middle aged people of Durham and Middlefield. "The object of it was to obtain knowledge, encourage industry, and the moral virtues, and to make good members of society."

This it proposed to do by discussing questions, and reading books which it embodied in the Library, for circulation among its members who owned rights in it. In the discussions, and in some of the books, there was a good deal of freedom of thought, so much so indeed, that some well meaning men in Durham became alarmed. I have never learned that Dr. Goodrich or any of the intelligent and liberal minded men in the town expressed any apprehension about it. Noah Talcott, afterwards a leading merchant in New York, was the secretary. The society was dissolved in 1793. The Library company continued to exist, and books for twenty or thirty years were drawn from it by the members. It was kept at Mr. Bridgman Guernsey's, one of the most respectable men in town, and was afterwards removed to Mr. Thomas Lyman's. I drew books from it not unfrequently, as from the other Library, and with advantage. The discussions in the society were sustained by speakers on both sides of important questions in morals and religion as in Colleges. Books, too, on both sides of important questions were in the Library, some of which were supposed to be of a dangerous tendency.

After party spirit in politics and religion began to run high in Durham and Middlefield, some odium was cast upon the society and the Library, as if they were infidel in their character. Public opinion was divided, as may be seen in the "Report of the case of JOSHUA STOW *vs.* Sherman Converse for Libel." Like the other Libraries the books in it long since ceased to be read. When Libraries were in fashion at one period, the boys of six or eight years of age established a library. It was kept at Mr. Gillum's by Anson Gillum. He resided in a house just east of Mrs. Blatchley's house.

MEN LIBERALLY EDUCATED.

The first who was liberally educated from the town of Durham, was the Rev. William Seward, son of Deacon William Seward and Damaris Seward. He was born July 27, 1712, and received his degree of Bachelor of Arts in Yale College in the class of 1734. He was ordained at North Killingworth, Jan. 18, 1738, and died 1782, after a ministry of 44 years. Possessing good natural talents, though he spent a portion of his time in manual labor, his acquisitions were respectable. As he preached without notes in the latter part of his life, his sermons may not have possessed all the correctness of written sermons. To all his people he was a father and a friend and from them he received continually the expressions of affection and esteem. And he had abundant reason to rejoice in the belief that the evangelical truth which he loved himself, took effect on the hearts and lives of the people of his charge, who in their turn remembered him with gratitude as their first minister, as one, too, who was a minister of God for good for many generations.

It is understood that all the early graduates from Durham fitted for college with Mr Chauncey.

Maj. Gen. PHINEHAS LYMAN was the son of Noah Lyman and Elizabeth — Lyman of Durham, grand son of Thomas Lyman and Ruth (Baker) Lyman of Northampton, who was widow of Joseph Baker and daughter of William Holten, gr. gr. son of Richard Lyman of Windsor, Conn., and Hepzibah (Ford) Lyman, daughter of Thomas Ford, gr. gr. gr. son of Richard Lyman, emigrant from High Ongar, England, in Rev'd John Elliot's company to Roxbury, Mass., with his wife Sarah.

Gen'l Phinehas Lyman was baptized at Durham, March 6th, 1615–16. At Yale College he was one of the Berkley scholars of the class of 1738, and remained at College, and the next year, 1739, he was appointed Tutor. During his Tutorship he studied law—probably with Daniel Edwards, Esq, and was admitted to the Bar. He settled at Suffield, then a new town, where he kept a law school. He was endowed with great abilities, and soon rose to distinguished eminence in his profession. Suffield was then reckoned as a part of Massachusetts, and Mr. Lyman was at the head of the bar of Hampshire County. Col. John Worthington, of Springfield, and Major Joseph Hawley, of Northampton, were his pupils. Through the instrumentality of Mr Lyman, Suffield, Enfield and Somers, were removed from the jurisdiction of Massachusetts and transferred to that of Connecticut In 1750, Mr. Lyman was chosen Representative to the General Assembly of Connecticut, and in 1753, Assistant In 1755, he was appointed Major General and Commander-in-chief of the 5,000 Connecticut forces, and the actual commander of the American forces raised and sent to the Canadian war In the important battle of Lake George, Sir William Johnson having received a slight wound early retired from the field, and General Lyman not only planned all the strategy of the battle but for five hours overlooked, comprehended and directed, with the consummate coolness and skill all the varying changes of that eventful fight, and guided it on to success and victory. For this Johnson was made a Baronet and received £5,000, while Lyman, who bore the burthen and heat of the day, and achieved the victory by his matchless coolness and skill, hardly received an empty fame.

Gen. Lyman was also with Lord Amherst at the capture of Crown Point, and in 1758, with Abercrombie and also with Lord Howe when he was killed. He commanded also the Provincial troops in the expedition to Havanna. He had so high a reputation for wisdom, bravery, integrity, military skill and daring, that he, most unfortunately, was induced by some persons high in office to visit England, in hopes of receiving some reward for the brilliant services which he had rendered his country. He went as the agent of a company styled Military adventurers, to obtain a tract of land on the Mississippi and the Yazoo rivers, which they proposed to colonize

He went confident of success, and danced attendance for many long, weary, unrequited years on the British ministry, which put him off from time to time till he learned how disastrous it was for a New England man to seek redress at an English court. He tasted the bitter and ruinous cup to the dregs, and after eleven long years of patient waiting, he returned wasted in health, spirit and fortune and deeply in debt. He returned in 1774 to find all that was beautiful and hopeful when he left for England withered and blasted with an irretrievable ruin.

He went down to the territory which he had obtained, broken in health and spirits and ready to die. He reached West Florida, where he ended his days at the beginning of the Revolutionry war, in 1775. See President Dwight's Travels.

He married Eleanor Dwight, aunt to President Dwight, and daughter of Timothy Dwight, of Northampton, Oct. 7th, 1742. Their children were Phinehas, born Sept. 21, 1743, Gamaliel Dwight, April 4, 1745, Thaddeus, March 16, 1746, Thompson, Nov 10, 1752, died Aug. 9, 1755; Oliver, Jan. 22, 1755; Eleanor, Dec. 13, 1756; Experience, Nov., 1758; Thompson, Dec. 22, 1760.

PHINEHAS LYMAN, who graduated 1763, holding the highest place in social position in his class, was the eldest son of Gen'l Phinehas Lyman of Suffield, Y. C., 1738, and Eleanor (Dwight) Lyman, daughter of Col. Timothy Dwight, of Northampton, Mass. Phinehas Lyman, Jun., was born at Suffield, Sept. 21st, 1743. The history of his father so disastrous in its latter years, is well known. Phinehas Lyman, Jr., while a youth, soon after taking his first degree at Yale, received a commission in the British army. That commission was given up for the study of the law, which he pursued waveringly under an expectation early entertained, that he was to remove to a distant country where he was to enjoy the rewards of the extraordinary services rendered by his father to the Mother Country. This irresolution, increased by long suspense resulting from the protracted absence of his father in England, and the weariness of hope deferred' in an ardent but irresolute mind, issued in a broken heart and confirmed delirium. He was carried by his father to West Florida, on his return, in hope of recovering his health, but he died soon after he landed in that country ; unmarried, in the year 1775.

NATHANIEL CHAUNCEY, Esq , second son of the Rev. Nathaniel Chauncey, born Jan. 26th, 1720, was graduated at Yale College, 1740. He resided at Middletown Upper Houses, where he was much respected as a gentleman of strong good sense, of much general information and strict integrity. He was in the Commission of the Peace when the county was formed, and continued to be so until his death, September 3, 1798, in the 78th year of his age. He married, 1st, Mary Stocking; 2d, Susannah Gilbert. His children by his first wife were, 1st, John Stocking, a Light horseman in the American Army; he was killed by British Cavalry after he had surrendered. 2d. Sarah; 3d, Mary; 4th, Abigail; 5th, Nathaniel, father of Henry Chauncey of New York, Michael Chauncey of Hartford, and John Chauncey of Western New York; 6th, Catharine.

ELNATHAN CHAUNCEY, the third and youngest son of Rev. Nathaniel Chauncey, was born September 10th, 1724. In company with his brother Nathaniel he pursued his studies under his father's instruction, and entered Yale College in 1739. He took his first degree in 1743. He studied Divinity until 1745, when he was licensed to preach the Gospel. He received a call to settle in North Guilford and in some other places, but he declined a settlement His father beginning to feel the infirmities of age, requested him to remove to Durham and take care of him, and as an inducement made him generous offers. "From his filial affection he gave up a settlement in his profession," and devoted himself to agriculture. Mr. Chauncey is spoken of as possessing much information, great equanimity of temper, and gentleness of feeling and fine social qualities. He was a good scholar and an acceptable preacher. He retained his license and preached occasionally until advanced age. Dr. Field remembers that he preached in East Guilford in 1791. He died May 4th, 1796.

His wife was Elizabeth, the daughter of Rev. William Worthington of Saybrook, and the widow of Col. Samuel Gale. They had four children. 1. Nathaniel William, born September 12th, 1761, died January 29, 1840. 2. Catharine, born August 6th, 1764, was married to Reuben Rose Fowler, the father of the writer; died April 12th, 1841. 3 Elnathan Elihu died when four years old. 4. Worthington Gallup. Asa Worthington Gale, the son of Mrs. Chauncey, died at Cape Francois, August 14th, 1772, aged about 16. Benjamin Gale, the second son, was in the Battle of Bunker Hill; commanded a vessel for some years, sailing to the West Indies; was washed overboard in a storm from a ship in which he had taken passage from the East Indies to New York, in 1796 or 7, aged about 39 years.

The Rev. ICHABOD CAMP, son of John Camp, was graduated at Yale College, 1743. He became an Episcopal minister, and divided his labors between Middletown and Wallingford, from 1753 to 1760, when he removed to Louisburg, Virginia. Some years afterwards he was murdered by his son-in-law. He was a man of excellent character and principles. His wife, Mrs Content Camp, died while he officiated in Middletown, and on a tablet in the church her name was placed.

DANIEL LYMAN, the son of ——, was born 1722. In college, he was one of the New Light associates of David Brainard, John Cleaveland and others. After taking his degree in 1745, from 1747 to 1752 he was the Steward of Yale College. He studied law and was a magistrate and Representative of New Haven. He was a member of the Common Council. He died at New Haven, Aug., 1788. He married first, June 6th, 1748, Sarah Whiting, daughter of Col. Joseph Whiting of New Haven. She died Aug. 1st, 1751. He married second, June 25th, 1752, Sarah Miles of New Haven; she died ——. He married third, Eleanor (Fairchild) Benedict, in 1768. She died March 23d, 1825, aged 95.

ELIHU LYMAN was graduated at Yale College in 1745. He

was a younger brother of Daniel Lyman the last mentioned, and they pursued their college course together. He was born 1728. He joined his brother at the New Light meetings at the rooms of David Brainard and John Cleveland, during the revival of 1742.

He was associated in business with his brother at New Haven, and he lived with him. It is supposed that he also studied law and was in company with his brother.

He died unmarried, leaving his brother his sole executor and legatee, at New Haven, August, 1758.

NOAH PARSONS, son of Simeon Parsons, graduated at Yale College, 1747. The following is his epitaph: "In memory of Noah Parsons, A. M. A gentleman of a sprightly mind improved by a liberal education at Yale College, at which he was sometime a Tutor. The fair prospects of his youth were soon clouded by disorder of body, which continuing several years, he took a voyage to West India for the recovery of his health, and died at the Island of Hispaniola, May, 1774, in the 37th year of his age.

EBENEZER GUERNSEY graduated in Yale College in 1757, was licensed to preach, and after preaching three months as a candidate in Pittsfield, Mass, received a call to settle, conditionally. This call he negatived but supplied the pulpit further on probation and was invited a second time to settle. This call he also declined in 1761. He returned to Durham and died in 1763. The following is his epitaph:

In memory of Ebenezer Guernsey, A. M. In literary accomplishments an honor to his education; constant and cheerful in all duty, benevolent to all mankind, a tender relative and faithful friend After a lingering sickness, in full hope of glory, he died October 24th, 1763, in the 26th year of his age, much beloved and lamented.

Rev. ROGER NEWTON, D. D., was born in Durham, May 23d, A. D., 1737. He was a descendant of the Rev. Roger Newton, minister, first of Farmington and afterwards of Milford, and he inherited the virtues of that excellent man. His parents were Mr. Abner and Mrs. Mary Newton. They were respected for their prudence and piety, and their discreet management of their domestic concerns, and the virtuous education of their children. The subject of this notice was the youngest of five sons. He received the advantages of a liberal education at Yale College in the class of 1758. His distinguished success in his studies prepared him for that long series of labors in which he served Christ and the Church more than fifty years.

He was ordained the pastor of the Church and congregation in Greenfield, Mass., on the 18th of November, 1761. He continued in the discharge of the duties of his office with much reputation and to the general acceptance of his people, until a few years before his death, when he was relieved from the more active duties of his profession by a colleague pastor, the Rev. Gamaliel Olds, afterwards a professor in Amherst College. He received the degree of Doctor of Divinity from Dartmouth College in 1804.

In 1762 he was united in marriage with Miss Abigail Hall of Middletown. They had five sons and three daughters. Roger, Isaac 1st, Isaac 2d, Abigail, married Rev. Mr. Lambert, Susannah 1st, Ozias Hall, Susannah 2d, married Proctor Pierce. Dr. Newton died December 10th, 1816, in the 80th year of his age and the 56th of his ministry. He was a man of uncommon strength of mind and of a pacific disposition, and was much employed as a counselor in cases of difficulty in churches. Few ministers have lived in more harmony with their people or have left behind them a more precious memory than this man of God. See Panoplist, Vol 13. p. 189.

Roger Newton, the eldest son of Dr. Newton was a graduate of Yale College in the class of 1785. When a Tutor in that Institution, he fell a victim to the consumption, at the age of twenty-six. From the Oration delivered at his death, by Barnabas Bidwell, a fellow Tutor, it appears that he was a gentleman of great excellence of character and of great promise in the profession of law which he had chosen.

Several excellent people removed from Durham to Greenfield about the time when Dr. Newton was settled. The Hon. Rejoice Newton, of Worcester, Mass., is the descendant of one of these. He was graduated at Dartmouth College, 1807. Another descendant of one of the Newton family, was the Hon. Daniel Wells, of Cambridge, Mass. He was Senator in the State Legislature; and District Attorney for the four western counties. He was Chief Justice of the Court of Common Pleas in Massachusetts. Another descendant of the same family was the Hon.

James Alvord. He was a graduate of Dartmouth College in the class of 1827; studied in the Law School in New Haven; was Senator in the State Legislature; died while he was a member of Congress elect, in 1838 or 9 He was regarded as a man of great promise His brother, Daniel Wells Alvord, graduated in Union College, 1835, and is now a lawyer in Greenfield. Jesse Newton, another descendant of an emigrant from Durham, entered Yale College, and died while a member of the Sophomore Class, not far from the year 1820. The emigrants from Durham to Greenfield and their descendants, have been the friends of order, education, and religion.

SAMUEL JOHNSON took the degree of Bachelor of Arts at Yale College in 1769. In his printed "testimony" signed by his own hand, he states that his parents were members of the Congregational church; that he studied Theology with Dr. Goodrich and others; was licensed to preach in Pittsfield, Mass.; was ordained at New Lebanon, Nov. 1772, and continued pastor of the church there three years and a half; was dismissed and removed to West Stockbridge, where he says he became acquainted with one Talmadge, a shaker; was pleased with his religion, and joined the shakers in 1780, with his wife, and took his children with them His wife by her "testimony," which she also signed, was as fully a shaker as he. Of his five children, one died in infancy before they joined the shakers, and one soon after, and three were brought up to be shakers. He died at New Lebanon, May 14th, 1835, aged 91 years and 8 months. Elizabeth, his wife, when 24 years of age was married to Mr Johnson after he was settled at New Lebanon. She died August 5th, 1829, in the 81st year of her age. These facts were obtained from a letter to Rev. David D. Field, D. D., dated June, 1847, by Rev. Silas Churchill.

The Hon. CHARLES CHAUNCEY, LL. D., son of Col. Elihu Chauncey, was born May 30th, O. S. 1747, and died April 28th, 1823. He early manifested a vigorous and rapid intellect, and intense application to the objects of his pursuit. His native powers were such, that without the advantages of a public education, he soon came forward to a commanding eminence in his profession. Having studied law, with James Abraham Hillhouse, Esq., he was admitted to the bar in November, 1768. In 1776, he was appointed Attorney for the State of Connecticut; and in

1789, was placed on the bench of the Superior Court. As an advocate and a Judge, he satisfied the public, that he possessed powers and attainments of no ordinary character. In 1793, he resigned his seat on the bench, and retired from the business of the courts. From this time, he devoted himself, principally, to reading, superintending the education of his family, and giving lectures to a class of students at Law. In testimony of respect for his talents, his acquirements, and his public services, the honorary degree of Master of Arts was conferred on him by Yale College in 1777, and the degree of Doctor of Laws by Middlebury College, in 1811. His mind had not been roused to activity, merely by the pressure of business, or the calls of ambition. He was excited to unceasing exertion by an intense ardor which continued with him through life. His thirst for knowledge was unbounded. Few men have read so extensively; or with so deep an interest. Scarcely any department of literature, of history, of civil policy, or of theology escaped his attention. The rich furniture of his mind, was manifest to all those who had the opportunity of hearing him converse. In legal science, his investigations were profound and original. He did not content himself with treasuring up a confused mass of forms and precedents. The practice of the law, he delighted to reduce to the invariable principles of justice The relations and connections of these, he traced in his lectures, with a kind of professional enthusiasm. This awakened the interest of his pupils, among whom are numbered some of our ablest advocates and statesmen On political subjects, he had enlarged and liberal views. While he considered all rightful authority as proceeding from the people; he saw the necessity of checks and balances, to give stability to government.

But that in which he felt his own highest interests and those of his fellow men, to be involved, was religion. His intellectual endowments which were of so high an order, he believed to be given by his Creator, for high and holy purposes; to be employed in obedience to the divine commands He had long been directing his views to that invisible state upon which he has now entered. But he did not consider his own unassisted understanding, as a sufficient guide, in preparing for the retributions of eternity. He sought for the light, which neither learning nor philosophy can bestow. He looked for a revelation from heaven, and he believed that he found this revelation, in the volume which claims to be a message from God. In so momentous a concern, he was not satisfied to rest upon the opinions of others. He examined the evidences of Christianity for himself. He consulted the records of antiquity. He weighed the cavils of unbelievers, with the arguments which are adduced, in support of the scriptures. The result of his investigations, was a settled conviction, that the Bible is indeed the word of God.

But he did not confine his attention to the outworks of Christianity. He was sensible that he was bound to inquire, not only whether God has made a revelation; but *what* he has revealed. Though he had read, extensively, the works of able theologians, he was not disposed to call any man master. The tenets which he believed to be of the greatest importance, and the most clearly supported by scripture, were those in which the great body of protestant churches, are nearly agreed. Nor did he think it sufficient, to hold a system of speculative opinions merely. He knew that religion was intended, not only to enlighten the understanding but to influence the heart, and appear in the life. He early made a public profession of his faith, and as he advanced in years, the effect of religious considerations, on his feelings, appeared to be more and more happy; inspiring him with grateful recollections of the past, and serene anticipations of the future. After he had reviewed, in his last sickness, with deep emotion, the kindness of Providence to himself and his family, the slumber of death came upon him gradually and gently, like the repose of the night, upon him who has faithfully performed and finished the labors of the day.

His wife, Abigal Darling, daughter of Thomas Darling of New Haven, was born November 9th, 1746; died December 24th, 1818. They had five children. Charles Chauncey, LL. D; Elihu Chauncey, Esq.; Nathaniel Chauncey, Esq , Sarah Chauncey, who was married to W. W. Woolsey, Esq., the father of President Woolsey; and Abigail Chauncey, who died many years since. His three sons were graduates of Yale College. From President Day's obituary notice, Christian Spectator, Vol. 5, 336 p.

SAMUEL SEWARD was graduated at Yale College 1762. The following is his epitaph:

"Mr. Samuel Seward, a gentleman of a liberal education and polite accomplishments, a kind relative, in friendship sincere, dear to his acquaintances, and benevolent to mankind, having acted an honorable part, in the instruction of youth, departed this life in the midst of public usefulness, on the 13 day of June, 1773, in the 33 year of his age.

Hope humbly then on trembling pinions soar,
Wait the great teacher death and God adore"

Hon. CHAUNCEY GOODRICH was the eldest child of Dr. Goodrich and was born at Durham, 1759. He was educated at Yale College of which he became a member in 1772, at the early age of thirteen; and although the youngest, it is recorded of him that "he shone foremost among his contemporaries." In 1779, he was chosen Tutor of the College, in which office he greatly endeared himself to his pupils, who in after years could well attest to the benefit of his able instructions. He left College for the Bar; fixing his residence in Hartford, where the advantages of protracted study in the University were strikingly exemplified in his early becoming eminent as a Counsellor and Advocate.

In 1793, he represented the town of Hartford in the Legislature of the State. The following year he was elected representative to the Congress of the United States, which office he continued to hold till 1800. The history of those times is well known. It was a period of turbulence and excitement; when great wisdom and prudence were needful in the councils of the nation. To what ends the energies of his mind were directed, and what station he held in the deliberative assembly of his country, the Journal of Debates sufficiently discloses.

On retiring from Congress he resumed his profession, which for several years he pursued with great industry and reputation. Few men possessed a more thorough knowledge of jurisprudence, and seldom if ever did a practitioner of the Bar, hold justice, truth, and integrity in higher estimation, or exert a happier influence to exact and improve the legal profession. In these respects he was a model. That was a high enconium, which was passed upon him some time after his decease "His judgment was so guided by rectitude," said one who well knew him, "that of all men living he was perhaps the only one to whom his worst enemy (if enemy he had) would confide the decision of a controversy sooner than to his best friend." In 1802, he was chosen an Assistant Counselor of the State, which office he retained until 1807; in which year, he was elected to the Senate of the United States. This was the station for which his learning, his wisdom, his political sagacity and integrity peculiarly fitted him. "By his moderation he checked the presumption of party power; the integrity of his soul gave efficacy to the powers of his understanding; while the amenity of his manners bowed the stubbornness of political will." Honored is that State which honors and exalts such men to public office.

In 1812, he accepted the Mayoralty of the city of Hartford; and the following year, having been elected Lieutenant Governor of his native State, he resigned his seat in the Senate of the United States. The two last named offices he sustained at the time of his death.

In the conjugal relation he was twice respectably connected, but those endearing ties were as often early broken.

His death occurred on Friday the 18th of August, 1815, and was the consequence of an affection of the heart under which he had been laboring for several months. On the day of his death, however, he rode and walked—"cheerful, dignified, wise and exalted in character, as at any period of his worthy life." On his return from a ride of several miles he retired to his room, soon after which he expressed a feeling of faintness, and expired with a single groan.

He was a firm believer in the truth and value of the Christian Religion. "Reasons of a peculiar nature," said the late venerable Dr. Strong in a discourse delivered on the occasion of his interment, "prevented him from making a public profession of his faith. These objections, however, were at length removed, and he died while an applicant for Christian privileges in the church" under the pastoral care of the above eminent divine. To the importance of vital piety, and to the value of the atoning sacrifice by Jesus Christ he bore full and solemn testimony. "A moral life, of itself," said he, "is nothing for the salvation of the soul. I have lived a moral life in the estimation of the world but in the sight of a holy God I feel myself to be full of moral defilement. If there were not an atonement I must be condemned and miserable forever. Here my hope is staid. Sometimes a sense of my own imperfections sinks my spirits but generally I have a hope that supports me; at times I have rejoiced in God without fear and wished only to be in his hands and serve him."

The Hon. Daniel Lyman, the son of Thomas Lyman and grandson of Deacon Thomas Lyman, and the brother of the late Thomas Lyman, was graduated in Yale College in the year 1776. In 1775, he with the class, or a large part of it, excited by the intelligence of the battle of Lexington, marched to Cambridge. Soon after his arrival an expedition was set on foot to take possession of Ticonderoga, Crown Point, and St. Johns. He received the commission of Captain for the occasion, and accompanied Arnold and Ethan Allen in the enterprise, which proved successful. After this, he returned to New Haven to finish his collegiate course. With Chauncey Goodrich, his classmate, he received the Berkley bounty, which in this instance was divided between equals. In 1776 he received the appointment of Brigade Major. In the campaign he was engaged in an action in White Plains, in which his horse was killed under him. In the Spring of 1777, he was appointed Captain in Colonel Lee's regiment, one of the sixteen Congress regiments which served during the war. In the Spring of 1778, he was invited by General Heath to join his family as Aid, which invitation he accepted. In the Spring of 1778, he also received the appointment of Adjutant General of the Eastern Department. On the arrival of the French troops at Rhode Island, General Heath was ordered to receive Count Rochambeau. Colonel Lyman was dispatched on board the ship of the Admiral to welcome the gallant strangers to our shores. He had the gratification of being the first American officer who visited that ship and of being there received with the strongest demonstrations of regard. After the treason of Arnold, General Heath was ordered to the North River where Colonel Lyman remained with him during the war.

Colonel Lyman commenced the practice of law in Newport, R. I., in which State he resided through a long and useful life. He sustained the character of an able advocate, and of a firm, intelligent, and high minded man. He was three years on the bench of the Superior Court. He retired from the practice of law many years before his death. He spent the latter part of his life at a pleasant seat, near Providence, where his youngest son, Henry B. Lyman resides. His wife was Mary Walton, by whom he had thirteen children, four sons and nine daughters. One of his daughters is the wife of Benjamin Hazard, another of Governor Arnold. In private life his deportment was the admiration of all who knew him His sufferings in his last sickness he bore with the firmness of a soldier and the resignation of a Christian. He died on the 16th of October, 1830, in the 75th year of his age.

Hon ELIZUR GOODRICH, LL. D., the second son of Dr. Goodrich, was born on the 24th of March, 1761. At the age of fourteen he entered college, and completed his academical education in 1779 Soon after, he received the appointment of Tutor, in which office he continued two years, and then entered upon the profession of law at New Haven, which has since continued the place of his residence.

Mr. Goodrich enjoyed the public confidence through a long life; and few upon whom office has been bestowed have sustained its honors and responsibilities with greater credit, or with more uniform fidelity. His knowledge is of the most useful, because of the most practical character. He successively held the office of Collector of the Port of New Haven—of representative in Congress—of Assistant Counselor of his native State—of Judge of the County Court—and of Mayor of the city of his residence. For several years he was a Fellow of Yale College; also Professor of Law, and the able and efficient Secretary of the Corporation of that Institution.

Mr. Goodrich was united in marriage with Miss Nancy W. Allen of Great Barrington, a lady of great intelligence and accomplished manners. Three children were the fruit of this union, two sons and a daughter. The daughter, Mrs. Nancy G. Ellsworth, died about a year since at Lafayette, Indiana, at the residence of her husband, the Hon. Henry L. Ellsworth.

The eldest son, Elizur Goodrich, Esq., is a much respected Attorney at Law in Hartford. The second son, Rev. Chauncey A. Goodrich, D. D., was for many years a distinguished Professor in Yale College.

LEMUEL GUERNSEY was graduated in Yale College in the class of 1782, and died soon after he had taken his degree. The inscription on his monument says, "by an unblemished reputation, and improved public education, he bade fair for usefulness."

SAMUEL GOODRICH, third son of Dr. Elizur Goodrich, was born

on the 12th of January, 1763. While a member of College, he became hopefully pious, and thus early decided upon the ministry as a profession. He graduated in 1783, and after a course of Theological study, was ordained at Ridgefield, Conn., on the 6th of July, 1786 Under his pastoral care the church and society of Ridgefield flourished, and he became an instrument of extensive good. He was often called to aid in the settlement of ecclesiastical difficulties, for which he was peculiarly fitted by his extensive knowledge of mankind, and by his plain, practical sense. On the 22d of January, 1811, he was dismissed from his charge at Ridgefield, at his own request, and on the 29th of May following he was installed at Worthington. Here he continued in the active and successful duties of the ministry for nearly twenty-four years. In 1831, Rev. Ambrose Edson was settled with him as a colleague; but the health of both not long after failing, they were at their mutual request dismissed. Mr. Goodrich, however, was able for sometime occasionally to preach, and which he did to several vacant churches to great acceptance.

In 1784, Mr. Goodrich married Elizabeth Ely, daughter of Col John Ely of Saybrook. She survived him about two years Their children were ten in number, eight of whom were living at the time of his death, and seven of whom were professors of religion. Two of his children died in infancy

For several years Mr Goodrich had been occasionally afflicted with gout; which in its attacks was more frequent and more serious as he advanced in life. His last sickness was short, and as the disease early affected his brain, he was favored with but few lucid intervals. But during these he manifested a full knowledge of his danger and a willingness to depart. A short period before his death, he revived so considerably as to distinguish his friends and to express his strong confidence in God. "My soul," said he, "is on the Rock of Ages, and my confidence in God is as firm as the everlasting mountains." "Yet," he continued after a short pause, "in myself I am a poor creature." On Sabbath evening, April 19th, 1835, he expired.

Mr. Goodrich lived and died a Christian. As a pastor he was greatly beloved; as a minister of Jesus Christ he was eminently successful. Several seasons of revival occurred under his ministry both during his residence at Ridgefield and Worthington.

16

Many still live to whom he was a spiritual Father, and who cherish his memory as "a good man," and a kind and faithful shepherd.

In the language of one who knew him well, "he possessed many excellent qualities as a man and a minister. His judgment was accurate, being founded on an extensive acquaintance with men and manners, and a long study of the human heart. He readily discerned the springs of action, and knew well how to approach his fellow men in regard to objects which he wished to accomplish. He did not misjudge in respect to means or ends. He was remarkable for his practical good sense and an acquaintance with common and therefore useful things. His understanding was rather solid than brilliant, and his knowledge seemed to be in wide and diversified surveys, and was gathered from many a field, rather than contracted to a point, or derived from prolonged investigation of particular subjects. Hence his sermons were plain, instructive exhibitions of truth and shared his varied information and practical good sense." "During the last few years of his life he preached with increased fervency, spirit and solemnity."

How highly he prized the Scriptures may be gathered from a memorandum in his family Bible as follows: "1806, began to read the Bible in course in the family and completed it the thirteenth time, Oct. 29th, 1833 The years are specified in which he each time completed the reading: "1809—12—14—16—21—23—25—27—28—30—32—33" Such a man we might well expect to hear say, as he said on the eve of his departure—adopting the language of the Psalmist—"Though I walk through the valley of the shadow of death I will fear no evil, for thou art with me,—thy rod and thy staff they comfort me."

His eldest son, the Rev. Charles A Goodrich, and the second son, Samuel G. Goodrich, Esq., are both extensively known as Authors, the latter wrote the works ascribed to Peter Parley. The eldest daughter, was married first to Amos Cook, Esq., of Danbury, and afterwards to the Hon Frederick Wolcott of Litchfield; the second to the Rev. Noah Coe; the third, known as the editor of the Mother's Magazine, was married to Rev. Samuel Whittlesey; the fourth, to Mr. Dunbar, a lawyer in Worthington; the fifth to Nathaniel Smith, Esq., of Woodbury; the sixth to the Rev. Mr. Mead.

ELIHU CHAUNCEY GOODRICH, Esq, a name derived from his maternal Grandfather, was the fourth child of Dr. Goodrich, and was born September 16th, 1764 He also received his education at Yale College, from which Institution he graduated in 1784, with the reputation of a sound scholar. He devoted himself to the profession of law, engaging at times, as interest and inclination prompted, in the purchase and sale of western lands. His residence was at Cleveland, N. Y. His death occurred in 1802, and was occasioned by fever induced by injudiciously bathing, during an excursion on the western lakes. He was never married.

EBENEZER BELKNAP, graduated at Yale College, 1785; spent the last years of his life in New York.

ROBERT SPELMAN graduated at Yale College, 1785.

CHARLES AUGUSTUS GOODRICH, the fifth son, was born March 2d, 1768. Like his brothers, he was liberally educated, and took his bachelors degree in 1786. In constitution he was less vigorous than the other sons, but to a fine taste and poetical genius he united a disposition the most affectionate, and manners the most persuasive. Before leaving College he had chosen the ministry as a profession, for which he was well fitted, both on account of his piety, his love of learning and the native kindness of his heart. Soon after, however, and by reason of too close application to study, his nervous system became seriously affected, and which in a few months induced a permanent derangement of his mental powers This prevented the further prosecution of his profession, and cast for the remainder of his life a cloud over his otherwise cheerful prospect. For several years he resided with his brother at Ridgefield, in whose family he was generally able to mingle, but at intervals was subject if not to protracted, to severe paroxisms of his malady With a constitution so delicately formed, and possessing a heart naturally full of the generous sympathies of our nature, his sufferings in the aggregate were by no means small. Yet he had, beside the uniform kindness and tender sympathy of friends, other sources of alleviation. He abounded in prayer, and often were his supplications couched in language most fervent and importunate. And in the midnight watches members of the family were not unfrequently awakened by his strains of music so sweet and so plaintive as to prevent sleeping for hours.

In the very conclusion of his life the divine goodness was conspicuous toward him and his friends. The cloud which had long enveloped his mind was withdrawn, and he was able to converse with calmness and composure of his approaching departure. The Sun of Righteousness now shone brightly and joyfully upon him—the pledge and presage to him of a residence in a world where reason is never dethroned, and the affections of the soul are never benumbed His death occurred in 1804

The Rev. JOSEPH E CAMP received his first degree in Yale College, 1787. Before the settlement of the Rev. John Elliott in East Guilford he was employed to preach to the people, some of whom became very much attached to him. He was subsequently settled in a parish in Litchfield, where he was pastor 42 years. He died in 1838. His son, the Rev. Albert B. Camp, is settled in Bristol.

JAMES WADSWORTH, Esq, the son of John Noyes Wadsworth, who was the brother of Gen James Wadsworth, was born the 20th of April, 1763, and received his degree of Bachelor of Arts in Yale College, 1787 The adoption of the Federal constitution, by creating confidence in the strength of the Government, opened new fields of enterprise. "Massachusetts and New York had compromised their claim to the country west of the Seneca lake; the former acquiring the right of soil and the latter that of jurisdiction; and Massachusetts in a happy hour for the prosperity of New York, had sold her wide territory to the Copartnership long known on the map of New York under the name of Gorham and Phelps." Col. Wadsworth of Hartford, having obtained large tracts under them proposed to James and his brother William, that they should take an interest in his purchase, by buying a part, and of becoming his agents for the management of the remainder. Their purchase of him was made in what is now known as the townships of Geneseo and Avon, on the eastern banks of the Genesee river.

In the year 1790 they commenced their enterprising journey for their future home In the language of professor Renwick, "Little Falls on the Mohawk formed the extreme limit of continuous cultivation in the State of New York. The Indian trade enabled two white families to earn a scanty support at each of the two places where Utica and Geneva now stand, and Canadaguia was the seat of the land office of Phelps and Gorham. With these exceptions the whole country was a wilderness, rendered more dreary by the excited minds of the Indians. With great energy and perseverance, with great address and good judgment they met the difficulties which they encountered in their journey and their first residence. The success which attended their operations in drawing settlers to their own lands and those of which they were agents, attracted the attention of other parties who held property of the same description, and from their confidence in the personal address and business talent of James, they requested him to undertake a mission to England in 1796, to interest capitalists in the lands in Western New York. This mission he successfully accomplished. From the increase of population, from the construction of the Erie canal, from the great good judgment in the investment of their gains chiefly in lands, they furnished as splendid an example of Agricultural success as our country has afforded.

Mr. Wadsworth married in the year 1804, Naomi Wolcott of East Windsor, Conn. By this marriage he had several children, three of whom survived him, namely, James, William, and Elizabeth. From the high intelligence and refinement of himself and family, his home was made attractive and delightful.

Mr. Wadsworth belonged to the Federal party while that had an existence, but he never was inclined to enter into political life. His great influence and his great wealth he employed successfully in promoting the cause of education. His influence was exerted in procuring the enactment of a law by which the Controller of the State of New York, was authorized to purchase and send to every school district a copy of Hall's Lectures on Teaching. It was stated that at his own expense he published and distributed, the book entitled, "The School and the Schoolmaster," to every school district in the State of New York. Religious forms and observances were "treated by him with marked respect, and he was punctual in his attendance upon the stated Sunday service of the Presbyterian church during the early years of his residence in Genesee, and towards the close of his life upon those of the Episcopal church. He died on the 7th of June, 1844.

General WILLIAM WADSWORTH was older than his brother James and died some years before him. He commanded a Brigade at the Battle of Queenstown, and honorable mention is made of him in Mansfield's life of General Scott, page 40, and in Armstrong's History of the War.

JOHN WADSWORTH, Esq., the son of Colonel John Noyes Wadsworth who was a brother of James and William, was graduated in Williams College in the class of 1802 Mr Wadsworth having studied the profession of law, entered upon its practice in the city of New York, where he spent several years. An injury received from a boom of a vessel striking against his chest, brought on a consumption which terminated his life either in 1815 or 1816, aged 35. He was intending to study for the ministry. He was calm and dignified in view of death and yielded up his spirit to God in firm reliance on the atoning blood of his Great Redeemer.

Mr. Wadsworth was united in marriage to Alice Colden Willet. They had three children. 1st, John W. Wadsworth, died in New York on the 6th of July, 1847. In the notice of his death in Michigan, where he had resided since 1835, he is mentioned as a man of great personal, and high intellectual endowments, that rendered him esteemed in life and in death much lamented. "He was a man of exemplary piety and died rejoicing in the hope of a blessed immortality." 2d, William Murray Wadsworth died in Savannah, Ga, April 13th, 1840, in the 27th year of his age. Having studied law in New Haven, "in the summer of 1835, he commenced the practice of law in Munroe, Michigan, with high hopes and aspirations." In the spring of 1839, he was forced by disease to leave Munroe and return to his mother and sister for their kind offices and sympathy, and then to spend the winter of 1839–40 in Augusta, whence he was returning to New York, when death overtook him. He is spoken of as a young man of great promise. 3d, Susan Wadsworth is the wife of Rev. E. G. Smith.

The Rev. NOAH COE, son of Charles Coe, Esq., was graduated in Yale College, 1808, and has been a pastor of a church in New

Hartford, N. Y , and in Greenwich, Conn. He now resides in New Haven.

Rev. TIMOTHY TUTTLE, was born in East Haven, Nov. 29th, 1781. His father was Joseph Tuttle of the fourth generation from William Tuttle, the Emigrant ancestor, who settled in New Haven, in 1638. His mother was Mary Granger, a daughter of Daniel Granger, a native of Suffield. With limited advantages in his early education and in his preparation for college, he graduated with honor in the class of 1808, in Yale College. He studied Theology with his pastor and classical preacher, Rev. Dr. Smith of Durham.

He was ordained over the churches in North Groton and South Groton, Aug. 14th, 1811. He preached in these churches alternately on the Sabbath, until April, 1834, since which time he has confined his labors to North Groton, now called Ledyard. When he first came to that place the Society had been without a minister thirty-nine years. The Church had become extinct. The present church was formed Dec 10th, 1810, consisting of four persons, with but one male member, and he died before another man was added. He was greatly blessed in his labors. During his ministry, there were five revivals of religion. He was a man of but few words, but he was a man of wisdom. He was wise to win souls, his words were fitly spoken, and they were like apples of gold. He lived to preach his fiftieth anniversary, sermon Aug. 14th, 1861, which was published, as were several sermons of his.

I once enjoyed the opportunity of seeing him at his home. Immediately after leaving the tutorship at Yale College I went with Dr Smith, who was one of the Corporation to collect funds for building the chapel for the College. On that excursion we spent a night at Mr. Tuttle's, who received us with great cordiality We were delighted with the interest which he manifested in the object of our mission, and generously, according to his means, contributed to it. His family presented a beautiful picture of domestic felicity. I have ever since considered him as a model minister of a certain type.

His wife was Mary Norton of Durham, daughter of Stephen Norton and Mary Merwin, his wife, and was born in Durham, Aug. 28th, 1783. She was married to Mr. Tuttle, Feb. 15th,

1810, and died Feb. 14th, 1856. She was a woman of great excellence of character, and contributed largely to her husband's usefulness, and respectability in his profession.

He died on the 7th of June, 1864. Their children were 1st, the wife of N. B. Cook. 2d, the wife of Leonard Smith.

The Rev. DAVID MARSH SMITH, graduated in Yale College in 1811, was a pastor of a church in Lewiston, N. Y., and a Teacher in a town on the Hudson, and is now in Princeton, N. J.

The Rev. ELIZUR GOODRICH SMITH, a graduate in Yale College, 1822, studied Theology in New Haven; was ordained in Ogdensburg, 1829; was editor of the Christian Spectator; and is now in the Patent office at Washington.

The Rev. TALCOTT BATES, son of Guernsey Bates, graduated at Yale College, 1823; studied Theology in New Haven, was settled in the ministry in Manlius, N. Y.; died Oct. 24th, 1832, aged 30. Mr. Bates was a highly acceptable preacher, an amiable, useful and promising man, much beloved by his church and congregation, and much lamented.

Rev. HENRY BATES CAMP, son of Dennis Camp and grandson of Elnathan Camp, graduated in Yale College, 1831, studied Theology and licensed to preach, was settled in Bradford, Mass., and has been employed as Teacher in the Asylum for the deaf and dumb in Hartford He is the father of Major Henry Ward Camp, the "Knightly Soldier," whose interesting biography was prepared by Rev. H Clay Trumbull.

The Rev. DWIGHT SEWARD, D. D, son of Col Seth Seward, graduated in Yale College, 1831; was settled in the ministry in New Britain, and West Hartford, and Yonkers, N. Y., where he now resides. His son ———, a very promising young man died not long after graduating with honor in Hamilton College.

COLLINS STONE, son of Deacon Timothy Stone, graduated in Yale College, 1832. He has been employed as a Teacher in the Asylum for the deaf and dumb in Hartford.

JAMES WADSWORTH, the son of Wedworth Wadsworth, and his wife Content (Scranton) Wadsworth, graduated in Yale College, 1845; studied law; practiced in Buffalo, N. Y., where he was Mayor of the city, and a member of the Senate of New York. He now resides in the city of New York.

WEBSTER ROGERS WALKLEY, son of William H. Walkley,

graduated at the Wesleyan University, 1860; principal of the Clinton Academy the two succeeding years; has since that period been principal of the Lewis Academy in Southington.

THE WILL OF EBENEZER ROBINSON

In the name of God, amen I, Ebenezer Robinson of Durham, in the County of New Haven, in the State of Connecticut, in New England, being in bodily health and of sound mind and memory, blessed be God therefor, considering my own frailty and mortality, and that it is appointed for all men once to die, do make this my last Will and Testament; and first of all, I commit my soul to God that made it; my body I commend to the earth, to be buried with decent Christian burial at the discretion of my Executor; and touching such worldly estate as it has pleased God to bless me with in this life, my just debts and funeral expenses being first paid and satisfied, I give, devise and dispose as follows: *Imprimis.* I give and bequeath to the inhabitants of said Durham the sum of one hundred pounds, lawful money, equal to silver at six shillings and eight pence per ounce for the use and support of the Center School in said town so called, to be loaned out and the interest thereof to be annually applied for said purpose, always provided that said Center School be kept in the School House lately erected on a piece of land I gave to the said town for that purpose near the meeting house in said town, at least eleven months in a year annually according to the laws of this State relating to Schools.

Item.—I give, bequeath and devise unto the inhabitants of said Durham, the land I bought of the heirs of Mr. Hezekiah Tallcott, deceased, lying near the meeting house, in said Durham, containing about Three Acres, be the same more or less, to be used and improved by said inhabitants for a burying ground or place to bury their dead in forever,—and with regard to the profits of said three acres, that may arise before the said inhabitants shall want to improve the same for a burying place and indeed all the profits that may at any time hereafter arise from the improvement of said land, my will is that all such profits shall forever hereafter be appropriated, used, and improved for the benefit and support of the said Center School annually, in the same manner and on the same conditions as the interest of the said One Hundred Pounds is to be improved and applied, reference thereto being had.

Item.—I give and bequeath unto the Church of Christ in said Durham, such sum as shall be sufficient in money to procure a silver cup for the use of the Lord's Table, to be paid to the Deacons of said Church for said purpose by my Executor.

Item.—I give and bequeath unto my Sister, Mary Parsons, the sum of Twenty Pounds lawful money as above said.

Item—I give and bequeath unto my cousins, children of my above said sister, that is to say, to Timothy Parsons, John Parsons, Hannah Marsh and Tabitha Arnold, the sum of Twenty Pounds, lawful money to each of them. Also to the heirs of Jemima Rowley, I give and bequeath the sum of Twenty Pounds lawful money, to be equally divided between them.

Item.—I give and bequeath unto my cousins Samuel Stow Hawley, Mary Wolcott, Hope Fowler, and Hannah Ward, the sum of Ten Pounds lawful money, to each of them.

Item—I give, bequeath, and devise unto Jacob Clark, of Durham, his heirs and assigns forever, my dwelling house, which was my Brother Thomas Robinson's, deceased, and Two acres of land adjoining said house.

Item—I give, bequeath, and devise to my cousin, Ebenezer Robinson, Jr., son of Capt. James Robinson, and to the heirs of his body, lawfully begotten, my old dwelling house and barn and twenty acres of land, and my will is that he have liberty to take said Twenty acres of land where he shall choose, excepting the land which was my brother Thomas Robinson's. Also I give and bequeath to him, the said Ebenezer, my cloak and my silver tankard.

Item.—All the residue of my estate, both real and personal, I give, bequeath, devise, and dispose of as follows, viz.: to my cousins, the children of my brother David Robinson, deceased, that is to say, to David, Dan, Timothy, Phineas, Noah, James, Asher, Rebecca, Mary and Abigail, I give, bequeath, and devise the one-third part of the said Residue of my said estate both real and personal, to them and their heirs and assigns forever to be equally divided between them share and share alike.

Item.—The one-third part of the Residue of my said estate I give, bequeath, and devise to my sister, Hannah Miller, her Heirs and assigns forever.

Item.—The other third part of the said Residue of my estate I give, bequeath, and devise to my cousins, children of my sister Abigail Coe, deceased, that is to say, to Joseph Coe, David Coe, Josiah Coe, Abel Coe, and Abigail Granger, to them and to their heirs and assigns forever, to be equally divided between them, share and share alike.

Finally—I nominate, constitute and appoint my cousin, Capt. James Robinson, of said Durham, Executor of this my last Will and Testament, and I do hereby declare this and no other to be my last Will and Testament.

In witness whereof I have hereunto set my hand and seal this 7th day of July, A. D. 1780.

N. B. by lawful money mentioned in my above will I mean silver at six shillings and eight pence per ounce or the value thereof.

EBENEZER ROBINSON. 

Signed, sealed, published, and declared by the said Ebenezer Robinson to be his last Will and Testament in presence of us.

ELIHU CHAUNCEY.
MARY CHAUNCEY.
SARAH CHAUNCEY.

CHAPTER VIII.

DURHAM IN THE WARS.

THE INDIAN WARS.

The war against the Pequots, under their Sachem, Sassacus, took place in 1637. The war against the Narragansets, under our former ally, Miontonimo, took place in 1643. The war against the Wampanoags, under Philip, aided by other tribes, took place in 1675. Durham was not settled until these wars were over. So that if the Town can claim none of the honor, if it be an honor, of exterminating the Indians, or selling them into slavery, in the West Indies, it did not incur any of the disgrace. Still, it should be confessed that many of the farms granted to individuals were bestowed upon men who had distinguished themselves in these wars; some of whose descendants afterwards resided in Durham. It should be confessed that some of the people of Durham were under the influence of a common hatred and horror against the race. In more than one instance when the hat, or contribution box was carried round in the meeting-house, on the Sabbath, for money to christianize the Indians, instead of a coin, a bullet was dropped in, as if it were the fittest Missionary. Even in my own recollection, children were sometimes quieted by the cry, "The Indians are coming."

THE FRENCH WAR.

Durham sympathized strongly with the Mother country in the French War; and, according to tradition, sent a considerable number of volunteers The circumstance that Colonel Elihu Chauncey, commanded a regiment, in the year 1755, and that Major General Phinehas Lyman, a native of Durham, was for a period commander in chief of the Connecticut troops during a portion of the war, would lead us to the conclusion, that the tradition is true. I have in my possession a journal kept by one of these volunteers during his campaign, and a cannon ball weighing twelve pounds which he brought in his knapsack, all the way from Ticonderoga, and which had been fired by the French. His name was Charles Squier. Ebenezer Squier distinguished himself in that war. On a certain occasion, a beech tree was to be cut down which obstructed our cannon balls, in an attempt to dislodge the enemy. It was a dangerous service to cut down that tree; for whoever did it, would be exposed to the fire of the enemy while going to and from the tree. Ebenezer Squier, volunteered to cut it down, when the commander called for a volunteer for this service He reached the tree in safety, though the bullets flew thick on each side of him. After he had cut down the tree he was exposed on his return to a still more dangerous fire from the enemy, which they were prepared to open upon him. Walking back with not a hurried pace, when the balls were flying past him he turned round, shook his axe at the enemy, and then resumed his walk. He was immediately raised to the rank of a sergeant. I once, when a boy, asked him if he ever killed a man. He replied "I do not certainly know, but I blew up a boat in which there were fifteen men." JOSEPH HINE, JOHN HINMAN, one or more of the SEWARDS, one of whom was killed, were in that war. A man whom I have seen, by the name of Dunn, resided here, who was in the battle in which General Wolf was killed. There was a good deal of dissatisfaction in Durham, because General Phinehas Lyman was not treated by the British Government according to his merits.

LETTER FROM GENERAL PHINEHAS LYMAN TO HIS WIFE.

LAKE GEORGE, OR ST. SACRAMENT, Sept. 9th, 1755.

My Dearest:

Since the finishing the enclosed, viz., yesterday morning, we sent out about 1000 men, and about 170 or 180 Indians tc intercept the French army, who marched out about three or four miles, and the Indians and French catched them in an ambush, and soon shot down Colonel Williams, who headed the party; and some of the men and Indians, being surprised got into disorder and fled, and the rest were forced to fight on a retreat to the Fort, but lost some considerable number by death and captivity. But when they came up to our camp, we had flung up a breast work of logs and though they came up 1800 of them, that is, 1200 French and 600 Indians, as confident of success as troops could be, headed by a Swiss General, who was a baron sent from old France for that purpose, and a fine gentleman he is. Yet I say, we gave them such a warm reception that we stopped them and fought them from a little before eleven o'clock till half after five, and then they retreated, and we issued out upon them, and took their General, killed his second officer, who was chief Commander of the party, who defeated General Braddock; and when he received his mortal wound, cried out to his men to fight, "for," says he, "you have not got Braddock to fight with." Our men brought in large numbers of French guns and wide laced hats, cartouch boxes, &c. Took a number of prisoners, and killed a great many. They made their first attack on Connecticut forces where we were posted. They were so warmly received that after two or three hours' fighting, they went and tried the other wing where the Province troops were posted, and found such a warm reception that they retired—and the fight in the woods was from about one-quarter before nine o'clock, till about one-quarter before eleven, when they retired. I believe there never was such a hot and incessant firing with cannon and small arms, in New England, and one that lasted so long. I was forced to command where I was more exposed than any one soldier in the army, to make them save their firing, and behave well; and I believe never any army exceeded them in valor, courage and bravery, in the world. The whole 1800 were repulsed and drove back, by our Connecticut forces in their first attack, and after that by the Province forces; for when they saw they could not fire, as they went to the other wing, where the Province forces were posted, and met with so very warm reception that they retreated. Gen. Johnson was wounded by a shot into his thigh, and the bullet lodged near the bone, in the fore part of the engagement, and he retired to his tent. Col. Titcomb, Col. Ephraim Williams, Major Ashley, are killed, and Captain Hawley very badly wounded. While we fought at the head of the encampment, we lost but two men, and two badly wounded, and a number more received wounds. I believe we have lost no officer. Captain Hitchcock, Doctor Bliss and friends, of Suffield are well. I am well, and so is Phine who went with the doctor to the Hospital and continued there.

Major Nichols is badly wounded. Thus you see how eminently God has covered our head in the day of battle, and given us a glorious victory, over his and our enemies, and though the bullets whistled by my ears and body, very near, yet not one so much as touched my clothes. Pray for us and trust in God, for who would not trust such a Friend? When we come to an exact number of the killed and wounded, I will inform you. The re-inforcements have none of them arrived, yet we are about 2300 strong. I have not lost one man in my company.

Sept 10th. After writing the above I am informed by a scout from the lower forts, that news is sent to New England that we were all defeated, but I hope that news will not reach you till this arrives; for I assure you there never was a more complete victory by God's goodness. The party we sent yesterday to bury our dead, think we have lost 100 men. How many we have killed of the French we cannot exactly tell, but doubtless a very great number. The French prisoners say we have ruined their army. Now, my dear, how often have you trusted me with God, and prayed him to cover my head in the day of battle, and how remarkably has God appeared for me; for the battle came on when our men were retreating, and dejected, which is dangerous, but we recovered our men, and forced those retreating, to face and defend the front, and for a long time there was nothing but one continued fire of cannon and small arms. I believe there was never a hotter battle. Phine, &c. Pray, bless and praise God for his wonderful goodness to us and our Country. I am in haste, your Loving Husband,

P. LYMAN.

Colls. Titcomb and Williams, Major Ashley, Capts. Porter, Hawley, Keyes, killed. Lieut. Burt killed.

SECOND LETTER OF GENERAL LYMAN TO HIS WIFE.

Sept. 11th, 1755.

My Letter of yesterday and day before will convince you, that God is on our side and fights our battles for us, and makes our enemies flee before us. I wrote long, but could not give all particular circumstances. But I can now add some circumstances of the battle not therein particularly set forth.

On Sabbath day last, being the 7th day of this month, the Indians brought us word that a large army marched along the South Bay towards Fort Lyman, as now called, at Lydia's House, on which General Johnson called a council in the afternoon, and we advised to send an express to the other fort, and one Adams, an officer to Indians offered to go. On which a letter was soon wrote, a horse prepared, and he set out and several more sent, one after another, so that if one was attacked the other might hear and send back word to us; and several others, disorderly, set out without leave. When they arrived within about one mile from that fort, the express, viz., Adams was shot down, and heard to cry to Jesus for help, though perhaps he never prayed before; he was killed and his horse, the wagoners all taken, and qr. wagons burnt, the news brought back to us by one behind.

The next morning we fitted out a party of 1000 men, and about 170 Indians after the enemy to cut off their retreat, under the command of Col. Williams, who marched out a little better than three miles in the road to Fort Lyman, and sat down and consulted together, and waited for some to come up till the French, who encamped the night before about thirty or forty rods below, perceived them and almost surrounded them, and so soon as they began to march, rose and fired on them and killed Col. Williams, Major Ashley, Captain Ingersol, and about seventeen or eighteen on the spot. Old Henderick was there and fought valiantly, and encouraged his men, but in fine was killed. The Indians first began to run, and some of the men after them, the rest fought valiantly on the retreat, from before nine o'clock till about half after ten, and killed a vast many more of the French in the retreat, as the French General owned, than they killed of our men. We heard all the fighting, and soon found they came near to us; we beat up to arms and all made ready at proper places, so as to be all round the encampment—to be ready on every side, and none to leave his post on pain of death, without order.

The enemy came close to our men, and drew up near. Their arms glistened like the sun, with their bayonets fixed, and as confident, I suppose, of coming straight into our camp and carrying all before them, as ever any army was. My great concern was for fear the retreating party by their dejection, would frighten our men, and make them run as Braddock's did, and therefore I spent my time encouraging them, by all arts I was master of, for there was no other officer by to help do the same, but in spite of all I could do, when our men came in in a body, all sank dejected, tired and choked almost to death with thirst; some had shot away all the powder, others the bullets. I was about four rods east of where they came in, encouraging and engaging the men. I saw them press right through our men, and our men began to run after them.

I called to some officers to stop them, for I saw the French would be in the camp in ten minutes, if they were not stopped, for our men would have run like Braddock's, but the officers' commands did not influence them any more than the trees. I run about ten rods to the foremost and told him to face to the front, and march up and defend it or I would kill him in one minute.

They told me they were choked and tired to death, no powder, no shot, &c. I told them I would send for powder, shot, water, &c, but if they did not march back and defend the front I would kill them in a moment.

They all marched back, and the fight came on right before me. There was in one minute, nothing but one continual clangor of cannon and small arms which held a long time, in which time, I saw our men shoot so fast, and some of them so carelessly that I was afraid the enemy intended to draw our shot and men, and break in upon us, for I saw that their army was very great and that they had a good commander.

I was forced to run from one end of the firing to the other, and halloo as loud as I could speak, to make them save their fire, and not to shoot unless they had a fair shot, for if the French would draw away our fire or make us shoot till our guns were foul, or so hot as to break, they would soon break in upon us. I sent the same order to others whom I expected they would engage if they found they could not find us; all readily obeyed, and I believe never men nor mortals fought better in the world.

The fight continued as hot as fire till past five, when the enemy slackened and retreated; our men sprang over the breast-works, and followed them like lions, and made terrible havoc, and soon brought in arms full of guns, laced hats, cartridge boxes, &c.; and brought in the General of the army, and many other prisoners The General is a Swiss gentleman, educated in France, and had the command of all the forces in Canada; has in his army 3117 men but part were left at Crown Point, and on this side he had but 1800 to fight us of his best chosen men, and we chastised them that about 300, of New Hampshire chiefly and some of them Yorkees, coming from the other fort, met about eight hundred of them, chiefly Indians, and tackled in, and fought and beat them off from their packs, killed many and took some, so that they never returned to take their packs. Thus, my dear, has God preserved us, thus miraculously has God covered our heads in day of battle, even the God of the armies of Israel in the hottest and most obstinate battle that was ever fought in North America Alas! who would not trust such a God! Can you think I can desert his cause, who has evidently surrounded us with mercies, and encompassed us with blessings ever since I left you Praise and bless his name, and forever remember the 8th day of September. This God did, with only the Province troops, about 1000 or little more, and Connecticut forces, about 100 of Rhode Island, and about 200 of the men raised in Connecticut for New York, but they had not much of the battle. The Connecticut forces sustained the whole of the first onset. The French intended to attack us next morning as soon as it was light, but how happy was it that God brought on the battle in open day-light.

But we always watch, set sentries at a distance to give notice, and sleep on our arms, all ready at first start. I was very tired, and faint for want of eating and drinking, when the battle was over I had lost my voice so that you could not hear me one rod, but was forced to be up all night, and all watched through the night. But my voice is almost come to, and I am as well as ever. Never one shot touched the hem of my garment, hat, or any thing about me, but they killed my saddle horse. Gen Johnson was wounded near the beginning of the battle, and repaired to his tent at the other end of the encampment. We can not yet tell the number we have lost, but few considering the violence of the battle, and the loss of the French The French General is as complete a man as the country affords; his second officer killed. They are terribly dressed off, and I hope the recruits will soon be here, and we shall soon be masters of Crown Point. I know you must think it terrible to appear before the mouths of guns, shots so plenty and thick, then so much plainer does God's preserving mercy appear.

P. LYMAN.

P. S.—There are some hopes the French General may recover.

N. B.—The Indians have all left us this day save one, and gone home, to mourn for their dead. I don't expect them again this fall, but they are well pleased with the noble victory.

These two letters of General Lyman were furnished to the author by Rev Henry Robinson, of Guilford, formerly a settled clergyman of the Church in Suffield of which General Lyman was a member.

THE VOLUNTEERS TO NOVA SCOTIA.

"DURHAM, April 2nd, 1760.

"At a meeting of the subscribers, petitioners for a Township in the province of Nova-Scotia, in Acadia, pursuant to a proclamation given by Charles Lawrence, Governor, in the year 1759, Jan. ye 11th, at the house of Elnathan Chauncey, in Durham, in the County of New Haven in the Colony of Connecticut, in New England

"At the incorporation Elnathan Chauncey was chosen Clerk to sd meeting, and proprietor.

"Samuel Dimock, Esq, was chosen Moderator to sd meeting.

"*Voted*, To be at the Charge and Expense of sending a Committee to inquire and inform themselves, and act as our directions are.

"*Voted*, That we send two Committee men to request our desire to the Governor of Halifax, and to act according to the directions

"*Voted*, That each signer shall be taxed one dollar and a half to support the Charge of the Committee.

"*Voted*, That Captain Samuel Dimock and James Pelton be the Committee.

"*Voted*, That the Committee as soon as possible go to Halifax, and wait upon the Governor at Halifax, and ascertain what lands he will dispose of to the settlers, and when they have taken a survey of the lands, and find the lands to be good, the title to be such as they may have a peaceable, quiet, and good settlement, then to apply to his Excellency, Charles Lawrence, for a grant to us, the subscribers, for the survey, with all the privileges and appurtenances to said Lands, and in all particulars, and know his Excellency's pleasure in sd lands and settlements, and that they return as speedily as possible, and call a meeting at such a time and place, as they shall think proper, and make a report to the proprietors of their expenses and doings.

"*Voted*, That Mr. James Bates be the Collector to gather that tax laid upon the polls as soon as may be possible.

"Then this meeting was dismissed by a regular vote.

ELNATHAN CHAUNCEY, *Clerk*."

A TRUE LIST OF THE GENTLEMEN WHO LISTED FOR NOVA SCOTIA.

Samuel Dimock,
James Pelton,
Thomas Stevens,
Benjamin Picket,
Michal Griswold,
David Wood,
Jeremiah Parmele,
John Bacon, Jun.,
David Blatchley,
Abner Kelsey,
David Baldwin,
Aaron Bacon,
Daniel Francis,
James Arnold,
Jonathan Mitchel,
Steven Post,
John Pelton,
Francis Clark,
John Marcy,
Robert Mackleve,
Evaight Plumb,
Isaiah Mackleve,
Elnathan Chauncey,
Israel Godard,
Gideon Warner,
Jonathan Walkley,
Sarah Chamberlain,
Richard Hayly,
Benjamin Royce,
Andrew Leet,
James Hill,
James Pelton, Jun.,
Samuel Squire,
Zachra Henman,
John Camp, Jun'r,
Israel Burrit,
Ezra Porter,
John Parmele,
Jonathan Basset,
Hezekiah Buckingham,
Gideon Buckingham,
Moses Sheldon,
Nehemiah Merwin,
Aaron Baldwin,
William Mitchel,
Daniel Dimock,
Barzillia Dudley,
Samuel Seaward,
Mark Parmely,
Joseph Blatchley,
John Norton, 3rd,
Charles Squire,
Elias Austin,
William Clark,
Jonas Bishop,
John Birdsey,
James Bates,
John Canfield,
Abraham Bishop,
Samuel Spelman,
William Bishop.

THE REVOLUTIONARY WAR.

The Second Continental Congress met at Philadelphia on the 5th of September, 1774 The several delegations came prepared to act in concert, in opposing the encroachments of the British Government upon the rights of the several colonies. In order to attain a restoration of their violated rights, "They, for themselves and their constituents, agreed and associated, under the sacred ties of virtue, honor and love of country, not to import after the first of December, 1774, from Great Britain or Ireland, any goods whatever, or from any other place, or any such goods as should have been imported from Great Britain or Ireland." This celebrated "Association" also sent forth very able and stirring addresses to the KING, and to the PEOPLE of GREAT BRITAIN, and to the PEOPLE of the COLONIES

In view of these doings of the Association, the inhabitants of Durham in Town meeting, Nov 17, 1774, passed the following vote: "The Association entered into and signed by the delegates of this colony in behalf of the colony, in the late Continental Conress, held at Philadelphia, and approved of and recommended to the several towns in this colony, by the Honorable House of Representatives in their session at New Haven, in October last, to be by the said towns faithfully observed and kept, being laid before the meeting for consideration, and this meeting having seriously and maturely considered,—*Voted* unanimously, that the meeting do accept and approve of the said Association, and will faithfully observe and keep the several articles therein contained according to the true intent and meaning thereof"

"The same meeting *voted*, that Col. Chauncey, Col. Wadsworth, Mr. Daniel Hall, Captain Israel Camp, and Mr John Newton be a committee to observe the conduct of all persons in this Town touching said Association, and deal with such persons as shall violate the same according to the eleventh article in said Association."

"The meeting being informed that the Honorable House of Representatives of this Colony in their session at New Haven, in October last did resolve that the several towns in this colony do contribute towards the relief of their distressed Brethren in the town of Boston, as their circumstances may call for—Therefore, *Voted* by this meeting, that Mr. Phinehas Spelman, Elnathan Camp, and Elias Camp be a Committee to receive all such contributions as shall be voluntarily offered by any of the inhabitants of this Town, for the purpose above mentioned, and cause the same by them to be improved for the relief and support of the poor of that Town suffering under the oppressive *Port Bill*."

These votes, showing the spirit of the people of Durham were passed the 5th of September, nearly two years before the Declaration of Independence.

"At a special Town Meeting March 25, 1777, Daniel Hall was chosen moderator; the following vote was passed: "This Town taking into consideration the slow progress made in filling up the Continental Battalions, the great importance of their being immediately completed, and the necessity of every possible exertion for that purpose, it is *voted* that the families of such soldiers belonging to this Town as shall engage in said service, on their reasonable request shall be supplied, in their absence, with necessaries at the prices stated by law, and that a committee be appointed for that purpose to see them provided for and supplied accordingly on such soldiers lodging, or from time to time remitting, money to said Committee for that purpose, and that without any additional expense, and the necessary expense to be borne by the Town."

"At the same meeting, and by a major vote, Messrs. Lemuel Guernsey, Samuel Parsons, and Caleb Fowler, were chosen a Committee for the purposes mentioned in the preceding vote."

"At a Town Meeting held in Durham by a special warning Sept. 16, 1777, " *Voted*, that the Select men purchase at the expense of the Town, 33 pair of shoes, 33 pair of stockings, 33 shirts either linen or flannel, 33 pair of overalls, 33 hunting shirts or frocks for the use of the non-commissioned officers and soldiers belonging to the Continental Army who went from this Town, and exhibit an account thereof to the General Assembly to be held at New Haven in October next, to obtain payment therefor, and lodge the moneys they shall receive of the State for the same in the Town Treasury for the use of the Town."

"At the same meeting *voted*, that Robert Smithson, Jesse Crane, Elah Camp, Timothy Parsons, Heth Camp, Elias Camp, and Abel Coe, were chosen a Committee for supplying the families of the officers and soldiers of the continental army belonging to this Town, with clothing and provisions."

"At the same meeting *voted*, that the salt belonging to this Town be divided to each family in proportion to the number of souls, and that to ascertain the number each head of a family shall return to a committee to be appointed for that purpose the name of each person in his family in writing on or before the 11th instant, and in case they shall fail to make such return, they shall forfeit their right to such salt; which division shall be made on the 15 day of instant December."

"At the same meeting by a major vote, Ebenezer Tibbals, Joseph Chedsey and Phinehas Spelman were chosen a committee for the purposes mentioned in the preceding vote."

"At a town meeting held in Durham by special warning of the Select men, the fifth day of January, 1778, Daniel Hall being chosen moderator. The Articles of Confederation and perpetual union between the States of New Hampshire, Massachusetts, Rhode Island, &c, proposed by Congress to the Legislatures of all the United States for their consideration and approbation at the desire of his Excellency the Governor having been communicated to this meeting; impressed with a deep sense of the necessity of speedily entering into a confederacy as well as the important advantages resulting therefrom, but not possessed of the means of knowledge of the differing habits, produce, commerce, or an internal police of the several States, yet rising superior to local attachment, willing with a candor and liberality becoming brethren and fellow citizens embarked in a Common cause to promote, to our utmost, the safety, happiness and glory of the general confederacy.

Therefore *voted*, that we will cheerfully adhere to and abide by what the Legislature of this State, (whose great wisdom and zeal for the public good we have long experienced) shall do in the premises, at the same time cannot but express our desire that some alteration may be made in the 8th article, and 8th paragraph of the 9th Article of Confederation."

The objections to these articles will be mentioned hereafter.

"Feb. 27, 1782. At a Town Meeting, *voted* that Capt. Simeon Parsons, Capt. Samuel Camp, Capt. Charles Norton, Mr. Elnathan Camp, Lieut Abraham Scranton, Lieut. Jeremiah Butler, Lieut. Joseph Smith, Ens. John Johnson, Ensign Medad Strong, Ens. David Scranton, were chosen a Committee to procure able bodied men to serve in a Regiment ordered by the General Assembly holden on the 10th day of Jan. 1782, to be raised for the defense of Horse Neck and the western frontier."

"At a Town meeting held by special warning, Aug. 25, 1783, Capt Simeon Parsons was chosen moderator. "*Voted* that General James Wadsworth, Capt. Simeon Parsons, Daniel Hall, Esq, Capt Wadsworth, and Mr. Elnathan Camp are appointed a Committee to report to this Meeting a proper vote expressing their disapprobation of the giving half pay for life to the officers of the Army or a commutation therefor. Then by a major vote this meeting was adjourned to Monday next at 3 o'clock in the afternoon."

"The meeting met according to adjournment.

"September 1, 1783 This Town, being advised by a late publication of General Washington's last official Address to the Legislatures of the United States and the papers thereto annexed, of the *Half pay and Commutation of half pay* given by Congress to the officers of the Army—Think it a duty they owe to the public, themselves, and posterity to show their disapprobation of the various arts and practices made use of to induce Congress to give the same, and also of the measures adopted by Congress to subject the citizens of the United States to the payment thereof—measures notwithstanding all the high colorings that have been put on them to render them tempting, we conceive are founded in injustice and impolicy, and which we are by no means convinced Congress are vested with competent power to adopt In the beginning of the late contest with Great Britain, it was the duty of every citizen of the States to lend his aid according to his ability to defend his country and just rights, some in one way and some in another, all equally necessary All these are justly entitled to a reward in proportion to their services, taking into consideration the dangers, hardships, risques, losses, &c. If then the officers of the army have sustained no greater losses in proportion to their mode of defending the country, exclusive of half pay or commutation, than the other citizens in proportion to theirs (as observation must clearly convince every one they have not) nothing but injustice will compel the citizens to yield up their property to be expended in half pay, or commutation of half pay. The impolicy of the measure is clearly evinced from the old and true proverb, that honesty is the best policy; for it cannot be honest to take the property of one citizen who has as essentially served his country as another and has received no greater reward for his services (ceteris paribus) and give it to the other. The experience of mankind shows the impolicy of such measures. We need look no further than Great Britain, where by paying their public officers far beyond a reasonable reward, they have so exhausted themselves of moneys, as to be obliged to deluge themselves in blood to obtain supplies. Will not the misfortunes of others teach us wisdom? We boast ourselves of having obtained independence and freedom from the arbitrary measures of Great Britain. But if a half pay establishment or commutation takes place, may we not say, we have only changed masters.—Thereupon *voted*, that we will, in every constitutional way, oppose the half pay establishment or commutation of half pay."

At the same meeting, Daniel Hall, Esq., and Simeon Parsons, Esq., were chosen Delegates to attend a convention in Middletown, on the first Wednesday of instant September, to consider what ought to be done upon the subject of commutation in order to some constitutional mode of redress, &c.

We have seen the zeal and patriotism with which Durham, as a Town, entered into the war of the Revolution. It is impossible to give the names of all those who were soldiers in that war. Almost every able bodied man in the town from the age of sixteen to that of sixty, at one time or another, was in the service. More than one volunteered when short of that age. One at least, exempt by law, furnished a soldier for the army. The following are the names of persons from Durham: Major General James Wadsworth, Col. Daniel Lyman, Col. James Arnold, Capt. Simeon Parsons, Capt. Samuel Camp, Capt. Charles Norton, Lieut. Abraham Scranton, Lieut Benjamin Sutliff, Ensign Jeremiah Butler, Ensign John Johnson, Benjamin Gale, Charles Coe, William N. Chauncey, three or four by the name of Brown, Phinehas Squier, John Strong, John Meeker, Eliakim Hull, John Hull, Jeduthan Bemus. Benjamin Gale distinguished himself in the Battle of Bunker Hill His Mother had written to him, "You may be called to lose your life, but save me from the mortification of knowing you were wounded in the back." He shot a British officer, took his purse and watch and other valuables to the tent of his commanding officer, who kept the property for his own use. He afterwards enlisted on board a privateer which was successful in capturing, and bringing prizes into the port of Boston.

The following is a list of soldiers which Durham had in the army, Dec. 9, 1777. I have no means of ascertaining precisely a list of the men which Durham furnished at any other time. Lieut. William Burritt, Serj. Eliakim Strong, Serj. Benjamin Sutliff, Cor. Huston Hinman, Cor. Samuel Lucas, Dr. Sweton Squire, Dr. Phinehas Squire, Dr. Reuben Brown, Dr. David Brown, Dr. John Bishop, Fif. Samuel Brown, Fif. Nathaniel Brown, Eliakim Hull, Timothy Dunn, Warren Murray, William Lucas, Simeon Mallory, Phinehas Meigs, Seth Strong, Samuel Seward, Enos Crane, John Meeker, Nathan Kelsey, William Carr, Jun., Bryan Rossiter, Schuyler Goddard, Gideon Chittenden, Thomas Cooke, Abiathan Squier, Amos Davis, Wm. Johnson, John Hancock, Sharp a negro, Cato a negro, Robert Neal, Gershom Brown, ——— Newton, Joseph Hickox. Five of these served the two following years, viz: Eliakim Strong, Abiathan Squire, Thomas Cook, William Johnson, Samuel Seward. There is no reason to suppose that there was a greater number of soldiers from Durham in the year 1777, than there was in other years.

The following is an interesting letter from General Andrew Ward, to General Wadsworth, and his letter to the officers of the Militia in Durham.

"Sir,

This moment I have received advice from Fairfield that the enemy have embarked after destroying the Town and are standing East-ward; have ordered all the companies near the coast, to march immediately to the shore; beg you will give notice to the several companies in Durham to be in readiness to march on the shortest notice, in case I should send the latter part of the night or in the morning—as the safety of our habitations depend on our united efforts.

I am, Dear General, your assured
friend and humble servant

Guilford, July 8, 1779.
Gen. Wadsworth. ANDREW WARD."

"8 of July, 11 O'clock P. M. 1779.

Gentlemen,

Have just received as above, by Express; I suppose this will meet you on your return; if so must advise the arms and ammunition of each company to be lodged in some place at which they may parade on some signal being given; but this I submit to your prudence.

I am, gentlemen, yours &c.,

J. WADSWORTH.

To the officers of the Militia
companies of Durham."

The events of the war formed the staple of conversation at the fireside, and in the field, and on the way, when I was a boy. Bunker Hill, Saratoga, Monmouth, and Yorktown were as familiar as household words. Washington and Lafayette, Burgoyne and Cornwallis, were constant topics of conversation. The old soldier would tell of his perils and privations, of his sufferings and his victories, would shoulder his hoe, or his staff and "show how fields were won." There were certain anecdotes which were current at the time but which derived their chief interest from the animation of the narrator.

Lieut. Samuel Hart was in the battle of Saratoga when Burgoyne was taken. Gen. Benedict Arnold was so excited in that battle that he was what was called "military mad." He urged the men into the fight in a furious manner, striking some of them and even the officers with the flat of his sword. Lieut. Hart, upon being asked whether Arnold struck him, replied "No, no, I was so near the enemy that he durst not come there." He was shot through the body, and though pensions were not readily granted, he obtained one for life.

Worthington G. Chauncey, in 1792, viewed the battle ground where Col. Baum was defeated, near Bennington, Vermont. The enemy were back of a stone wall upon which there were rails. These rails and a tree back of the fence bore many marks of the balls. There were an old man and his sons chopping wood, and when they heard the guns, they supposed there was a foraging party. Accordingly they hastened home, took their guns and plunged into the battle. A ball struck the old man and killed him. "I swear," said a son "they have killed Dad." He then turned his gun taking hold of the barrel, sprung over the fence and began to belabor the enemy with the breech of the gun. The American soldiers, encouraged by his example, followed him over the fence, attacked and defeated the enemy.

Deacon Abner Newton was in a company of which Charles Norton was Captain. He had been on guard all night in the cold; when the Captain met him in the morning, he said to him "You have had a cold time, you must now come and take a *knock in the jaw*," that is, a glass of bitters.

VOTE ON THE FEDERAL CONSTITUTION.

"At a Special Town Meeting legally warned by the Select Men by order of the General Assembly, at their Session October, 1787, and holden at Durham on the second Monday of November, being the 12 day of said November, A. D. 1787.

"At the same Meeting, by a Major vote, General James Wadsworth was chosen Moderator.

"At the same Meeting, the Question was put whether you will accept and approve of the Constitution made by the Convention holden at Philadelphia, in Sept. 1787, and recommended by Congress to this State, *voted* in the negative by 67, and 4 in the affirmative.

"At the same meeting, by a major vote, General James Wadsworth and Daniel Hall, Esquires, were chosen Delegates to attend a Convention to be holden at Hartford on the first Thursday of January next."

In taking the above vote, those opposed to the constitution and those in favor of it were arranged in two lines running south on the Green from the south door of the Meeting House. Four only were in one line and sixty-seven in the other. This vote was given in the negative, from the apprehension and fear felt by the people of the town, that the Federal Government to be created by it, would take advantage of the powers delegated to it, to assume other powers not delegated. So I was often told by those who knew.

THE WAR OF 1812.

The State of Connecticut was opposed to the war of 1812, and to the policy by which it was carried on. It placed itself on its constitutional rights, and refused to comply with the unconstitutional demands of the Administration of the Federal Government. Connecticut had always been a staunch supporter of the rights of the Colony against the usurpation of Great Britain. She had in the Federal convention which formed the Constitution of the United States, opposed the too great concentration of power in the Federal Government; and now, true to her traditions, she opposed the usurpation of power by the Federal Government. She refused to raise troops and place them under Federal officers, to be marched into Canada.

In this struggle between the State Government and the Federal Government, Durham by her votes in the Legislature, sustained the State in opposition to the Federal administration.

The following soldiers from Durham enlisted under Captain JOHN BUTLER, 1813–14, Captain of the 6th company of *State troops:* Joseph Tuttle, James Clarke, James Potter, Spencer Camp, Enos Camp, Miles Merwin, Jun., Florus Cook, Ichabod Curtiss, Aaron Baldwin, Dan. Baldwin, Elah Camp, 2d, Lyman Camp, Collins Hosmer, Norris Baker, William C. Butler, Charles Parsons, Samuel Curtiss.

In the cavalry, Parsons Coe, Charles Camp, Samuel Newton, Abner Newton, Jonathan Southmayd.

In the course of the war there were some bitter feelings and some bitter language. But when peace was declared in 1815, all parties were united in the common joy. At the Festival for celebrating the return of peace, the following toasts, which contained nothing that could be offensive to either political party, were drank with the entire approbation of all present. They were prepared by a committee composed of an equal number from both parties.

TOASTS AGREED UPON TO BE DRANK AT THE CELEBRATION OF PEACE.

1. *Peace.*—The harbinger of *good will towards men* ; may it continue until the sun shall rise and set no more, and may all nations be partakers of the blessing.

2. *The United States.*—May they never be disunited, *let their* motto be Union and *peace.*

3. *Great Britain.*—Our Parent Country—in war, enemies, in *peace*, friends. To forgive injuries is God-like.

4 *The President of the United States.*—In his exalted station may he enjoy *peace* of conscience.

5. *The Governor of the State of Connecticut.*—*Peace* to his government and wisdom to his councils.

6. *The Army and Navy of the United States.*—Able to command *peace*, and willing to receive it.

7. *The Memory of our departed Heroes* —May they live in memory to the latest posterity, *peace* to their manes.

8. *The State of Louisiana.*—The youngest sister in the Union has set a noble example for the family, namely, unity and *peace* among themselves.

9. *Agriculture, Commerce and Manufactures.*—May they *peaceably* go hand in hand.

10. *True Religion.*—That gives *peace* to the Soul, comfort in time and happiness in eternity.

11. *The different sectaries of Christians.*—May their difference in Opinion never disturb their *peace* in Society.

12. *Parties in Politics.*—Differing in local and personal matters, but agreeing in the great essentials to promote *peace* and happiness.

13. *Local prejudices and Party Animosities.*—May they be overcome and subdued by the reign of *peace.*

14. *Society.*—Happy only in *peace.*

15. *Solitude* for those who cannot live in *peace.*

16 *The Festive Board.*—Moderation in its enjoyment and *peace* among the partakers.

17. *Our own Fire Sides* —Never to be disturbed by a foreign foe, never to feel the gripes of necessity and never to loose the enjoyment of *peace.*

18. *The Female Sex.*—Powerful in opposition, lovely in submission, and essential to all our enjoyments, even in *peace.*

VOTE ON THE STATE CONSTITUTION.

"At a town meeting legally formed and held in Durham, on the 5th day of October, A. D. 1818, pursuant to a Resolve of the General Assembly of May last, and the Recommendation of the Convention of the 15th of September, 1818, for the purpose of Ratifying the Constitution recommended by the convention, begun and held in Hartford, on the 4th day of August last, James Robinson was chosen Moderator. *Voted*, that the presiding officer should call for the votes, for and against the constitution; which were as follows, viz: For the constitution, yeas 82; against the constitution, nays 74.

THE WAR WITH MEXICO, 1846.

In the war with Mexico, the State of Connecticut, by the action of the Legislature in 1847, opposed and censured the Administration of the Federal Government The yeas and nays were not taken in the vote referred to, so that it cannot, from them, be seen whether Durham, by her representatives, sustained or censured the Administration in that war. It has been stated that the vote of Durham was divided, yea 1, nay 1.

THE CIVIL WAR OF 1861.

The State of Connecticut and the Town of Durham sustained the Federal Administration in the war which commenced in 1861.

Copy of report rendered to the Provost Marshal on his application for the same, June 24th, 1865.

Amounts paid by the town of Durham and by individual subscription for Volunteers, Commutation Tax and Substitutes

By Town,	$1700 00	on call 1861 for 300,000 volunteers.
By Town,	$400 00	on draft of 1862, 9 months' men.
By Individuals,	$375 00	
By Town,	$850 00	on draft of 1863
By Individuals,	$850 00	
By Individuals,	$875 00	on call of 1863, October.
By Individuals,	$250 00	on call of 1864, February.
By Town,	$4000 00	on call of 1864, July
By Individuals for Substitutes,	$1675 00	on call of 1864, December
By Town,	$600 00	on call of 1864, December.
By Individuals,	$615 00	
	$12,890 00	

LIST OF VOLUNTEERS FROM DURHAM FROM 1861 TO 1864 INCLUSIVE.

Calvin Albee, killed.
Francis L Albee.
Wm. H. Augur, (Capt.)
Julius Augur
Michael Angly.
Curtiss C Atwell.
Seager S. Atwell, (Col.)
H. H Bishop.
Ezra E Bailey.
Henry Bemus, killed.
E. M. Brainard.
Whitney Brainard, died in serv'e.
Gilbert W. Blinn.
Heman Bailey.
George H. Barnes.
Samuel A. Camp.
Dallas Clark, killed.
Samuel G Camp.
Henry H Church.
Eli S. Camp.
Leonidas M Camp
Frederick Canfield
John B. Clark
Russell P. Clark.
William E. Camp.
Howard A Camp
Whitney D. Clark.
Frederick E. Camp, (Lt. Col.)
Wm H Davis, died in service.
William Eurle.
George W. Farnham, (Lieut)
Wadsworth Fowler.
Nelson Fowler
Friend H. Francis.
Thomas Francis, killed.
Thos. Francis, Jr., died in serv'e
William Francis.
Franklin F. Field.
W. R. Griswold, (Asst.Surgeon)
William H. Harrison.
Lewis W. Hart.
Charles E Hart, (Capt.)
Frederick J Hart, (2d Lieut.)
T. E. Hawley.
Samuel L. Hall.
Timothy Hickey.
Sylvanus A. Hull
John Hearne.
John Hickey
Albert P. Hull.
Charles A Justin.
James Lyden
Edwin J Merriam, (1st Lt. killed)
Augustus W. Morse.
Steven Mix
Robert M. Murdock
Eckford J Morse.
L. M Maynard.
Edgar Nettleton
George Olin.
Ira A. Graham, (1st Lieut)
Frederick Parmelee
Harry Parsons, killed
Frederick J Payne
Edwin W. Priest.
D W. Robinson
Philip Rheinhardt.
Henry P. Rich.
John Rich
James Rich.
Phineas L. Squares.
Guernsy B Smith
Edmond W. Shelley.
Talcott Strong.
Franklin S. Smith
Howard A Smith.
Albert M. Sizer, died in service.
Frederick Sizer.
George H Twitchell
Charles Tibballs
John E Vandervoort.
Luther White, died in service.
Seymour L. White, killed.
Henry A. White.
Wedworth Fowler.

Twenty-two volunteers were also furnished by the town.

Also, the following persons furnished substitutes. S. S Scranton, Andrew Hull, L. A. Stone, L M. Leach, Oscar Leach.

Durham, it is said, was represented in 17 regiments.

In the Summer of 1865, there was a large gathering of the people of Durham, who assembled in Lyman's Grove to welcome the returned soldiers.

CHAPTER IX.

OCCUPATIONS AND CUSTOMS.

AGRICULTURE.

At the first settlement of Durham, the principal occupations of the inhabitants were to open a place in the wilderness, each for himself; to build a log-house, and then to replace it by a better one, after saw mills were built; to cut down and burn the forest trees; to build fences, and establish boundary lines; to bring the land to good tilth; to lay it down to grass, to stock it with orchards, and furnish it with barns, and put cattle and sheep and horses upon it. Since these arrangements were made, agriculture has been the chief employment, to which the land is well adapted.

The soil in the Town Plat is excellent; some of it indeed lying on a hard pan, some of it requiring drainage, but all of it productive with good cultivation. The soil in the first range of hills, in the eastern part of the town, is with some exceptions sufficiently free from stone, is easily worked, and for many years after the first settlement of the town, produced good crops, first of Wheat, and Indian-corn, and afterwards of Rye, and Buckwheat. But by continual cropping for a long period, the soil, never the strongest, became in many localities exhausted; though with a good dressing of manure it will still produce good crops, with a moderate amount of labor.

In the west part of the town, the soil being on or near a trap formation, though rather hard and stony is strong, and well adapted to grass and apple orchards. Some of the western hills are excellent pasture lands.

The central range of land from the northern to the southern boundary, is sometimes called the swamp, is meadow land or prairie, which bears a coarse grass which has been, from the first settlement of the Town, of great value in furnishing hay for cattle; and thus manure for the upland; while the prairie or meadow itself is kept in a good condition of fertility, from the flooding to which it is subject. It was from this source of fertility, that Durham has had its high character, as an agricultural Town; a character which it is in danger of loosing, now that some of the farmers, instead of raising and feeding cattle, are selling off their upland hay at Middletown and Portland. Something may indeed be done by the purchase of artificial manures, but probably not enough to repair the fertility of the land, from which the hay is thus taken, and to which it is not returned in the shape of manure. Other farmers understand this, and adhere to the old mode of feeding out the hay with less immediate but more prospective profit, using artificial manure as auxiliary, but placing the most dependence on barn-yard manure.

It has long been a problem what should be done with the large tracts of the old worn out pasture land, on the eastern hills. Should they be permitted to lie as they now are, and let them grow up to wood, or should the bushes be cut off, or should they be plowed up, and laid down to timothy in the hope of improving the pasture? Different answers would be given correctly in different cases. It has been found on trial, in some cases, that there is not all the advantage expected from endeavoring to substitute timothy for the natural grasses and herbage. By plowing, the old grasses and herbage which are natural to the soil are destroyed, and the timothy, not being sustained by sufficient fertility in the soil, dies out, leaving the ground without verdure. In other cases, especially when the land is well manured, the experiment works well. Major Chedsey informs me that he has sown timothy on some of these pastures without plowing, and that it took root, and benefitted the pasture. Perhaps an improvement upon this would be, to sow mixed grass seed of various kinds, adapted to different varieties of soil, and to different portions of the season. In this way lawns in England are treated.

For many years the farmers of Durham not only made their own cheese, and raised their own breadstuff, wheat, rye, and Indian corn, but also, to some extent, sent these articles to market elsewhere. But this has not only ceased to be the case but the people depend largely on importing from the west all these articles, unless rye is an exception. The farmers, who seventy years ago used to kiln dry their Indian corn and send it to the West Indies, could hardly have believed that the farmers of Durham would ever depend largely on the Western states for this article.

"At a Town Meeting in Durham, Dec. 9, 1718—The Town taking into consideration, the great damage yt hath happened in the town in the increase and growth of a good breed of cattle, for want of a sufficient number of Good Bulls, do now enact and order yt they will annually pay out of the Town treasury, 15 shillings per year for Bulls three years old and upward, and ten shillings a year for two year old Bulls, the number of Bulls not to exceed seven, and the select men for the time, and so from time to time, shall take effectual care to have good bulls, by choosing likely, well grown calves to be kept for Bulls to be paid for as above sd and the selectmen shall take care, as near as may be, that sd Bulls be raised and kept by persons that may suite the Town for situation." Other acts like these at different times showed that the Town were in earnest in their endeavors to procure a good breed of cattle.

As a large number of the inhabitants came from Guilford, it is probable that they obtained from there cattle of the same fine breed, for which Guilford has been distinguished, and which were imported by Governor William Leete, from Devonshire, England. This breed have the same general characteristics as the Devons, but are larger, and better milkers. Whether this difference results from a change which they have undergone since they were originally imported, or whether the breed has changed in England in the two hundred years that have elapsed, it is difficult to say; perhaps it is owing to both causes. The Guilford breed of cattle, which are indeed found in Branford, Killingworth, Madison and Durham, are of a high red color, of a good size, larger than the imported Devons, very active, and hardy, excellent for farm work, and good milkers. Many of the farmers in these towns adhere persistently to this breed in preference to Durhams, Ayershires, Alderneys and Devons; but others kill their calves, and furnish themselves from the droves with cattle of all breeds, "ring streaked and speckled and spotted," so that there is danger that the taste of Jacob the patriarch may prevail, and the old breed run out, or become mixed.

It should be mentioned that Nathaniel W. Chauncey, Worthington G. Chauncey, Wedworth Wadsworth and Jared P. Kirtland, M. D., now a distinguished pomologist of Ohio, took pains to introduce into Durham the best of fruit from Burlington, New Jersey, Long Island and elsewhere. The two former had a large nursery and furnished the inhabitants with trees at reasonable prices, many of which are now bearing in the town. There is not as much cider made as formerly; and it is believed that cider made of grafted apples, for the table, is not as good as what is made of apples from wildings.

COMMERCE.

The commerce of ancient Durham consisted in the exchange of those articles of agricultural produce, which they sold in Boston, and in Middletown, and New Haven, or were by themselves sent to the West Indies, in the shape of private adventures. These private adventures were intrusted to ship-masters or mariners, sailing out of Connecticut river chiefly from Middletown, and were horses or cattle or fowls, or sometimes grain, or, it may be, kiln dried Indian corn. In return they obtained sugar, molasses, a cask of rum, or a young negro. In the early period, as their minister, Mr. Chauncey, was paid at least in part, in country produce, he, when disposing of it in Boston, would to some extent dispose of the agricultural products of his parishioners and receive in return such merchandise as was needed for family use. This has been alluded to elsewhere. The stores in Durham and Middletown render this inconvenient process unnecessary Shoes were largely sent to the South.

MANUFACTURES.

In some respects, Manufactures have fallen off in Durham. The present writer remembers the time when there were three gristmills in the town; and one fulling mill, and a clothier's shop, and one hatter's shop, and one watchmaker, and a malt house, and a corn kiln, and four blacksmith's shops, a manufacturer of grave stones. Every large farmer had his shop, in which on a rainy day yokes and bows, and hoe handles, &c., were manufactured. Besides the spinning wheel, many families had a loom for weaving linen and woolen and worsted. A stocking weaver found employment. A turning lathe found constant employment, where the boys could get tops, and the women chairs and bedsteads. There were two distilleries, several cooper shops; and there is now in the Town a gun, manufactured in Durham, and carried to the American Army in Boston by Capt Simeon Parsons. There were four tanneries.

In Durham as elsewhere, within the memory of some living, the spinning wheel, especially the one for flax, often made a part of the outfit when the bride left her father's house to dwell with her husband. A farmer said, that "he had rather see a bunch of skeins of yarn, than a bunch of Marygolds." A spinner who could annually count a goodly number of skeins of linen yarn and a goodly number of sheets and towels, bleached by herself, was sure of suitors. The spinning wheel made pleasant music in the house of the married pair; to which in the way of interlude, were added, in some families, the labors of the loom, with alternate notes of the treadle pressed by the foot, and the shuttle thrown by the hand. Nor was the voice wanting, to trill forth some old English ballad or some Puritan psalm. Music like this, coming in strong tones from healthy lungs and an animated heart, would ring in the ears and the soul of the listener, taking him captive, whether in the house, or walking in way side, or checking his horse as trotting by. The "great wheel" gave health and a graceful, ready step, and nimble fingers to the young maiden. The "little wheel," borne by a brother or a "neighbor lad," she would on a morning carry to the house of some young friend, as light hearted and as merry as herself, to spin in concert during the day.

And then annually, for a period, came the spinning bee, a donation party at the parson's, when the matrons and the maidens carried their run of yarn, and their husbands or their lovers some equivalent; and when all found it "good to be merry and wise," cheered on by their courteous and pious host and hostess.

But times have changed. Family employments have changed. The spinning wheel has given place to the cotton mill and the woolen mill. The hand shuttle has given place to the power-loom. A single machine, tended by a single person, will often do the work of twenty hands. Machinery has changed the manufacturing business of the country, and the family spinner's occupation is gone. Since the invention of the knitting loom and the sewing machine, knitting and sewing in families seem destined to the same fate as spinning. There are, therefore, in Durham as elsewhere, those who are like the lillies of the field in beauty, and who like them "toil not, neither do they spin" The good house wife no longer "seeketh wool and flax and worketh willingly with her hands." Flax is no longer seen in the summer field. The wool-bearing sheep that once adorned the hills of Durham have fled from the landscape.

FLAX.

Flax was formerly an important crop, requiring a large outlay of labor on the farm and in the house, and yielding remunerative returns. The plowing, the sowing, the pulling, the collecting of the seed, the rotting, the breaking, the dressing, the spinning, the weaving, the bleaching, demanded a great amount of labor. The dressing of flax was the great business of the winter. But labor was low at that season of the year, when there was not much else to do besides getting fire wood. Rev. Mr. Chauncey hired a man for a week to dress flax. On Saturday evening he came for his pay. The flax which he had dressed was weighed, and was offered to him for his labor He declined the offer with the question, "Rev. sir, how do you think a poor man can support his family at this rate?"

Drawing wood to market employed a good deal of labor, and often furnished a good remuneration. On a pleasant day in the winter time, when the roads were good, a dozen teams might sometimes be seen carrying wood to Middletown. But now coal has largely taken the place of wood.

SHEEP.

For very many years every farmer, almost, kept sheep for the wool and the carcass, putting them into a public flock in the summer. It was pleasant on a summer day to see the Town shepherd tending his sheep, himself reclining with his dog under a tree, or driving them to better pasture as they went bleating along the road, yarding them at night in pens enriched by them for turnips. That pleasant vision has passed away. There is no longer a sheep master, or a shepherd with his dog, or the town flock.

The following may be acceptable to some of our readers, as showing the enemies the farmers had to contend with, and the victories they won, as well as a specimen of town accounts:

The Town of Durham Deb'r to Sundry persons as allowed by the Selectmen in Decembr 1729.

To Benonie Hills for one Black bird	£0. 0. 1
To Noah Lymans Widow for 15 black birds & one crow	0. 1. 9
To Ebe. Lyman for 61 black birds & 6 crowes	0 8. 4
To Moses Parsons for 20 black birds & 4 crowes	0. 3. 8
To Eli. the widow of Deac. Tho. Lyman for 31 black birds	0 2. 7
To Simeon Parsons for 6 black birds	0. 0. 6
To Timothy Parsons for 17 black birds	0. 1. 5
To Capt. Jos Coe for 59 black birds	0. 4.11
and for laying the meeting house steps, and for 50 foot of boards for the meeting house, & for perambleating ag't Middletown, and for halfe a days work at the meeting house all.	0. 8.10
To Ensn. Hez. Talcott for 10 black birds & one crow	0. 1. 4
To Richd Beach for 16 black birds & one crow	0. 1.10
and a three yeare old Bull	0.15. 0
To Serj Jos. Norton for 32 black birds 2*s* 8*d*, & a bull 15*sh*, all	0 17. 8
To Lieut. Sam Fairchild 33 black birds & 2 crowes	0. 3. 9
To Serj Merwin 2 black birds 2*d*. & pream. & gainst Middletown	0. 2 10
To David Robinson for 25 black birds & one crow	0. 2. 5
To Jos. Tibbals for 28 black birds	0. 2. 4
To Jos. Hickcox for 23 black birds & 4 crowes	0. 3.11
and for a two yeare old Bull	0.10. 0
To Samuel Stanley for 11 black birds	0. 0.11
To Richard Spelman for one crow	0. 0. 6
To Sam. Roberts for 5 black birds	0. 0. 5
To John Norton for 33 black birds	0. 2. 9

To Jonathan Wells for 21 black birds	0. 1. 9
To Cornelius Hull for 30 black birds & one crow	0. 3. 0
To Silas Crane 23 black birds	0. 1.11
To Capt. Henry Crane for 32 black birds	0. 2. 8
and for a growen Bull	0.15. 0
To Albert Rossetter for 6 black birds	0. 0. 6
To Samuel Norton for 5 black birds and 2 crowes	0. 1. 5
To George Squire for 2 black birds *2d.* and sweeping the meeting house	1.10. 2
To Eliakim Strong for 7 black birds	0. 0 7
To Ser. John Camp for 6 black birds	0. 0. 6
and for work at the meeting house	0. 1. 8
To Ser. Nathaniel Sutlief for one black bird	0. 0. 1
To Ser. Josiah Avered for 26 black birds	0. 2. 2
To Nathan Camp for 14 black birds	0. 1. 2
To Noadiah Crane for 4 black birds *4d* & druming *13s 9d*	0.14. 1
To Curtis Fairchild for drumming	0.13.10
To Lieut. Joel Permele for 6 black birds & one crow	0. 1 0
and for two bulls	1. 5. 0
and for nails & work at the meeting house	0. 5. 8
To Jos. Wheeler 2 black birds	0. 0. 2
To Josiah Fowler for 3 black birds	0. 0. 3
To mr. Hez. Kilborn for nails used at the meeting house	0. 1. 6
To Daniel Squire for work at the meeting	0. 1. 8
To Theo. Morrison for mending the School masters chayre	0. 2. 0
To Zacha. Hinman for 5 black birds	0. 0. 5
To Constable Moses Parsons for crying & selling one shay	0 3. 0
To James Curtis for a 2 yeare old Bull	0.10. 0
To David Baldwin for a growen Bull	0.15. 0
To Deacon Wm Seward for a growen Bull	0.15. 0
To David Baldwin in part for waits for the Town Standard	0. 8.11
To Samuel Seward for a two yeare old Bull	0.10. 0
To Caleb Seward for 13 black birds	0. 1. 1
To Abraham Crittenden for three black birds	0. 0. 3
To David Johnson for 2 black birds & two Crowes	0. 1. 2
To Ser. Jos. Norton for halfe a loade of wood for the Town meeting	0. 1. 9
To Ezra Baldwin for carrying & returning the Tow[illegible] to Hartford to have them sealed	[illegible]. 6

To James Wadsworth for his services as Town Treas'r	1.10. 0
and for a growen Bull	0.15. 0
To Doctor Seaward for peram. agt. Kilingworth	0. 2. 8
To Samuel Camp for a grown Bull	0.15. 0
To Benj. Everest 3 black birds & a crow	0. 9. 0
To Ser. Murwin for the Servise of his Bull	0. 2. 0

SLAVERY IN DURHAM.

Like other towns in Connecticut, Durham owned slaves, who labored on farms, and in families. These slaves were some of them brought directly from Africa, or quite as often from the West Indies, with which a brisk commerce was carried on by the people of Connecticut. It was not uncommon for individuals to send out by ship-masters, adventures in the productions of their farms, to the West Indies, and to receive in return the productions of the West Indies, and negroes. Thus a man would sometimes send an order for a likely young negro. These negroes were more frequently obtained for Durham from the port of Middletown, which numbered, among its shipmasters, those who traded in the West Indies and dealt in negroes, for the supply of the country, that is the Colony.

In a letter on the 5th of July, 1773, his Majesty's secretary inquired of the Governor of Connecticut as to the population of the Colony. The answer of the Governor in 1774, was that the number of whites was 191,372, and the number of blacks 6,464. I have not consulted the tables, but taking the population of Durham as about 1,000 at that time, the average number for Durham would be 33. But the town had actually 44 slaves. Nearly all the blacks were slaves.

At that time family government was of a high type, active, vigilant, and effective. Slavery was regarded as a family institution. When slaves were married, it was done only with the consent of their masters, just as children in their minority were married with the consent of their parents. This consent was carefully recorded by the minister who married them. They were regarded as no better qualified to take care of themselves, than children during their minority. Like children, they were carefully [illegible]ht the catechism and the commandments, in the famil[illegible] infants were not unfrequently offered in baptism, by th[illegible]ving masters.

They had their holidays and amusements. They would statedly, or occasionally, appoint a King who was decorated with some of the emblems of royalty. One of these kings the present writer recollects to have seen. He had the appropriate name, Cæsar, and held his court in the west side of the town.

They had their balls, in imitation of the whites. One of these balls the present writer witnessed at the Wilkinson house, just south of the Goodrich house. Sawny Freeman, whom some now must remember, was their musician. He accompanied his violin with a sort of organ, which he played with his foot It was somewhat, in its effect, like the Aeolian attachment to the piano It added greatly to the volume of the music. At this ball besides contra dances they had jigs and reels. They danced with great agility and spirit, like the dancing pair in Goldsmith's *Deserted Village*, "who simply sought renown, by holding out, to tire each other down." About the year 1800, the number of the negroes had diminished, and most of the adults were either slaves or recently manumitted. Free negroes do not generally keep their numbers good in the successive generations. In Durham now, there are only five, without any prospect of increase. The diminution of negroes in comparison, with the increase of whites, since the emancipation of slaves in Connecticut, is greater than it is on an average, in the State at large. "Durham contained in 1756, 765 whites and 34 blacks, in 1774, 1074, white and 44 blacks." In 1776 every 24th person was a negro.

Among the names of those that owned slaves in Durham, are those of Chauncey, Wadsworth, Talcott, Parsons, Merwin, Coe, Bates, Lyman, Fowler, Parmelee, Camp, Newton, Baldwin, Guernsey, Sutliff, Burritt and others. To those who deem slavery wrong, these facts may seem strange. But it is to be remembered that every age has its own interpretation of the divine law, and its own favorite morality. In those days, slavery was not considered as sinful by many of the best men. Such men as Rev. John Davenport of New Haven, and Governor Theophilus Eaton, the founders of the Colony, Rev. Joseph Elliott of Guilford, the son of the Apostle John Elliott, Rev. Jared Elliott of Killingworth, Rev. Timothy Woodbridge of Hartford, the Rev. Noadiah Russell of Middletown, and Governor Joseph Talcott owned slaves. Rev. President Jonathan Edwards, the greatest divine of

New England, owned slaves, and wrote in defense of the slave trade. Governor Gurdon Saltonstall, a minister of the Church in New London, and owner of one of the farms granted by the General Assembly in Durham, addressed the Legislature in defense of slavery. Those who owned slaves in Durham and elsewhere in Connecticut were not considered as inferior to those who did not own slaves, in piety or in intellectual culture, or in social position. After the act of the Legislature for the gradual emancipation of the slaves of Connecticut, the aged ones were generally well taken care of by their owners, better than were the Town poor by the Town, better than were the free negroes.

A SPECIMEN BILL OF SALE OF A NEGRO.

Durham June 19th, 1759.

Know all men by this present: that I the subscriber, widow Mary Merwin, Executrix of the last will of Daniel Merwin Jun. do sell alien, and convey and confirm unto Elnathan Chauncey of Durham in the county of New Haven, to him and his heirs one certain Negro man, about 30 years of age named Ginne, for, and during his natural life, it being for the consideration of 13 pounds already received to my full satisfaction, in witness hereof I set my hand and seal; this 19th of June in the year of our Lord 1759.

In presence of MARY MERWIN.
JAMES TIBBALS.
ABNER NEWTON.

ANECDOTES OF DEVONSHIRE, A GUINEA NEGRO SLAVE OF REV. MR. CHAUNCEY.

Mr. Chauncey, on going into his hay field found his men raking hay at rather a rapid rate, said in a pleasant, familiar way, "Many hands make light work." Devonshire, (who was raking behind two others) answered quickly, *No, no* Massa, "*Not when you'r rakin' behind.*"

It being customary among the older part of the congregation to take notes of the heads of the sermon on the Sabbath, D. solicited of Mr. C. pen, ink and paper for that purpose. After service he produced a paper covered with all *manner* of *hieroglyphics*, and on viewing which the Rev. gentleman said, What is THIS,

Devonshire? I cannot read it at all. Devonshire (in astonishment, taking the paper.) *Not*, READ, THAT, Massa! Come out of your OWN MOUTH, every word of it.

On returning from Church, (after hearing a discourse from the text, "DEAD in tresspasses and sins," &c.) he found the barn door open and the "Old ram" on the hay satisfying the demands of nature. He returned immediately to the house exclaiming MASSA, MASSA, the Old RAM is DEAD! Mr. C. followed him to the barn and found as above stated, and then, in a reproving manner said, Devonshire! *how came you to say so?* D. replied quickly, DEAD in *tresspass* and SIN, I GUESS Massa.

Mr. Chauncey had a meadow (called the Burnham lot) the crop of hay on which, unfortunately, for a number of successive years was nearly ruined by rain. Devonshire, on seeing the Rev. gentleman preparing to attend a meeting appointed by the good people of the place on Thursday, in mid-summer of a severe drought, to invoke the blessing of Almighty God in sending the necessary showers to water the dry and thirsty earth, said to Mr. Chauncey, Is it Sabbath *day*, *to*-DAY, Massa? No, replied Mr. C. Dev. Then WHY go to meeting if it's not Sabbath day? Mr. C. in reply said earnestly, Devonshire, Don't you see all our fields, meadows and gardens are drying up for want of rain? God is the author of all our mercies, and we meet to pray that *He* would send down rain to water the earth. O-o, said Devonshire, with a curious twinkle of the eye. *Rain*, Massa, *rain*, THAT'S what you want. Better go and mow the Burnham lot, get RAIN quick enough THEN.

The anecdotes above were furnished by Leveret Norton, Esq.

TOWN AFFAIRS.

In ancient Durham, office, whether Town or Colony, was regarded as a duty to be performed, and not as a privilege to be enjoyed. If a man was elected to office, he paid his fine, unless he performed the duty; excepting in a few cases when he could show a good and sufficient reason for declining the appointment. Thus December, 1778, we have the following record, "Whereas, Col. James Arnold having excused himself from serving as selectman by paying his fine, Simeon Parsons was chosen selectman for the year ensuing." One reason why anciently office was regarded as a duty to be performed, and in modern times it is regarded as a privilege to be enjoyed, is, that anciently there was generally no emolument attached to Town offices, and in modern times there is.

There is a tradition that on one occasion so few were present at "Freemen's Meeting" that they waited for men who would go past with their team, and persuaded them to come in and elect delegates to the General Assembly So little party spirit was there and so much confidence that the right men would be elected.

The poor were disposed of at auction to individuals who would keep them at the lowest price, it being expected that the person so sold or disposed of, should work for those that bid them off. Thus in the town account for the year 1795, it is stated that "Sarah Allen was vendued by the week one month at a place, to certain persons named" for the twelve months commencing Dec. 15th, 1794. To Joel Parmalee one month, 2s. 5d., to Joel Parmalee the second month for 2s. 4d., to John Spencer the third for 2s. 5d. &c., to Eliphas Parmalee the last month for 1s. 4d.

In the town account for 1766, are the following items: Paid to Joseph Francis for perambulating Killingworth line, 2s.; to Benjamin Picket for perambulating Haddam line, 2s.; to Wm. ——— for keeping the middle school, £4,14.4; to Mr. Thomas Burgess for keeping the middle school, £12,13.2; Simeon Parsons for keeping the North School, £2,19.1½, Charles Chauncey for keeping the North school, £4,10.10½; Bryan Rosseter for keeping the south school, £3,19.6; Caleb Fowler for keeping the west side school, £5,5.8; Elihu Crane for a load of wood, 4s. 6d.

ARCHITECTURE.

After the inhabitants began to build commodious houses, the fashionable style for a time was the *Lean to* house, of which Frederick Parmelee's house is a type. This kind of house was two stories in front and one story in the rear, had at one end of the kitchen a bed-room, and at the other end a pantry. The next style that came into fashion was the *Gambrel Roofed house*, of which the house owned formerly by Dennis Camp, is a type. The next style that came into fashion was what was called the *Upright house*, sometimes with one chimney, and sometimes with two. The next style in order was the *Half house* so called, with one room in front, of which Mr. William Canfield's house is a type. The next style in order is that of the present time, which has in it a good deal of variety. Mr. Haywood's house may be taken as a type.

DOMESTIC CUSTOMS.

A characteristic of the houses built in the first half century after the settlement of Durham, was the large kitchen fire place, which in some cases was seven or eight feet in width, having sometimes one and sometimes two ovens in it, admitting back logs two or three feet in diameter, and three or four children into the "chimney corners." The large and steady fire on the hearth in such a fire place shone on faces of many a large family circle, gathered together on a winter's evening. To many a large family of eight or ten children the hearth-stone was a load-stone to draw them around it. There was knitting for the mother and the elder daughters. There were the slates for the older sons. There were apples and nuts for the younger children, or it may be a lesson in spelling. There were the two volumes from the Town Library for the father and others. There was story telling and song singing. There was the mug of cider enlivened by red pepper against cold. There was the family bible, and there was family prayer before retiring to rest. In short there were family government, family instruction, family amusement and family religion.

"In what Arcadian, what Utopian ground
Were warmer hearts or manlier feelings found,
More hospitable welcome, or more zeal
To make the curious "tarrying" stranger feel
That, next to home, here best may he abide,
To rest and cheer him by the chimney side,
Drink the hale farmer's cider, as he hears
From the gray dame the tales of other years;
Cracking his shag barks as the aged crone,
Mixing the true and doubtful into one,
Tells how the Indian scalped the helpless child,
And bore its shrieking mother to the wild—
Butchered the father hastening to his home,
Seeking his cottage,—finding but his tomb;
How drums and flags and troops were seen on high,
Wheeling and charging in the northern sky,
And that she knew what these wild tokens meant;
When to the old French war her husband went;
How by the thunder-blasted tree, was hid
The golden spoil of far-famed Robert Kidd;

And then the chubby grand-child wants to know
About the Ghosts and Witches long ago,
That haunted the old swamp—the clock strikes ten—
The prayer is said, nor unforgotten then
The stranger in their gates A decent rule
Of Elders in this puritanic school."—BRAINARD.

CLOTHING.

The inhabitants were generally clad in fabrics manufactured, that is made by hand, in the family. There was woolen cloth spun in the house but fulled and dressed at the clothier's shop. There was brown tow cloth, and streaked linen for the males, with bleached linen for shirts. In the summer they generally wore brown tow or linen trowsers and frock; the latter being a kind of over shirt. The fulled cloth worn in the winter time though often coarse was warm It was sometimes very decent in appearance when made of fine wool, well spun and well dressed. The females were clad in streaked linen or checked linen, on week days, and in chintzes and it may be muslins and silks on the Sabbath. The wedding gowns if not muslin were sometimes of brocade or lutestring. Near the close of the last century silk was reeled and woven in Durham. For a considerable time the women wore cloaks of scarlet broadcloth. In the year 1800 women might be seen on the Sabbath riding or walking in the street, or sitting at church having on these cloaks; a very comely and comfortable article of dress.

Chaises were introduced into Durham about 1775 or 80. For some years there were only three chaises in the town. The people went to meeting on horse-back, the women sitting behind the men on pillions. While this fashion continued every house had a horse-block.

DIET.

For diet, bread and milk was generally used before tea and coffee had been introduced. After the land had ceased to produce wheat, rye bread was commonly used. The present writer once heard an aged man say, that he remembered the time when turnips were the principal vegetable used, and that, generally, potatoes were planted in gardens, in such quantities as beets and carrots are now. Salt-meat broth was a standing dish in many families. This was made by soaking salt beef in water until sufficiently fresh and then boiling it and adding to the liquor fragrant herbs, with pieces of bread, and it may be onions. Besides hasty-pudding there was plain Indian pudding which was used almost every day, in some families at dinner, before the meat, with butter and molasses. This pudding was boiled in a bag; hence the proverb "the proof of the pudding is eating the bag" This does not mean that the bag itself is eaten, but only that the whole of the pudding in the bag is eaten, thus proving that the pudding is a good one. "A bag of meal," means the whole of the meal in the bag. Besides cider, beer was brewed in many families, after the fashion in England. This was done partly for the purpose of using the "emptyings" of the beer barrel, that is lees, for yeast Hence the proverb, "as you brew, so you must bake." If you make good beer, you can make good bread.

In many families meat was eaten three times a day, though it was sometimes in the shape of dried beef. But the most of the population of both sexes were accustomed to labor actively, either in the house or on the farm. Even the females were much in the open air, either in milking or drawing water with the old fashioned well-sweep, or riding on horse back, or gathering nuts or berries, or bleaching cloth, or in the case of an approaching thunder storm, raking or loading hay.

SOCIAL ENJOYMENTS.

The people of Durham like others of puritan descent in the towns of Connecticut, inherited the dislike of amusements of many kinds. Their ancestors in England had quarrelled with the king in their opposition to the book of sports, and it would therefore not be very consistent to engage in amusements like those mentioned in that book, after they came to this country. But they had their social enjoyments. The whole population here for several generations attended meeting together, where they felt that they had common interests and common enjoyment. Here they saw each other's faces every Sabbath, and in the intermission, heard of each other's welfare or misfortunes. Here they received impressions of each other which, not unfrequently, ripened into friendship or conjugal love.

They had small supper parties at first, and tea drinkings afterwards. There were weddings and quiltings, and huskings where the red ear had especial honor. There were sleigh-rides and barbecues sometimes, and plays in which the forfeits were paid with kisses; and balls which were considered as the school of good manners in opposition to clownishness and rowdyism.

The young men met together and appointed managers of the ball, usually four or six in number, who provided a room and refreshment, engaged music, sometimes sent out cards, sometimes assigned to the several gentlemen the duty of waiting on the several ladies, or assigning partners, preserved order, paid the bills by collecting the assessments on the gentlemen who attended. I do not certainly know whether there was an ordination ball when Rev. David Smith was ordained. When Rev. Aaron Dutton was ordained in Guilford there was an ordination ball. While dancing was fashionable, dancing masters taught dancing in schools from time to time, thus improving, as was generally believed, the manners of the young people. Besides hunting and fishing, there was the wrestling ring on training days, when the champions showed their strength and agility in "side-hold," "back-hold," and "at arms length." When the present writer was a boy, Samuel Wright was the acknowledged champion, though he was sometimes laid on his back by a young Robinson.

Sometimes, as now, men amused themselves in making bargains, which exercised the skill of both parties as much as a game of chess, while they differ from that game inasmuch as both parties are often winners. Still it should be said that the passion for making bargains has in the progress of time grown stronger rather than weaker.

A man by the name of Penfield used to buy apples of Gideon Leete, who owned the lot opposite Mr. John Hickox, where they grew, and to make parties and invite the young folks. He would give a particular kind of apple to each girl, kissing her at the same time, much to the amusement of the young fellows. The apple thus got the name of the "bussing apple." He became old and poor, and the young men made up a subscription for him, and clothed him well, and invited him to a party, for the fun of seeing him give an apple and a kiss to each girl.

A Mr. Tuttle in Whitestown, N. Y., was in the habit of holding a meeting every Sabbath in a barn and of asking each one to pray. William Handy, a loose, noisy man proposed to William Hinman and Asher Camp, two at least of the three being emigrants *from* Durham, that the first man that he asked to pray, should either pray or pay a bottle of rum. He was asked the first. He made a short, incoherent, hurried prayer, became thoughtful and serious, and afterwards a Christian, and Deacon of a church.

HOLIDAYS.

Election day, when the Governor, first of the Colony, then of the State, was inducted into office, was a holiday. The farmers endeavored to finish their planting of corn before this day, which came in the first part of May. This induction into office of the Governor and the meeting of the Legislature bore some faint resemblance to a coronation, or the meeting of Parliament in England. The men laid down their hoes, or left their work shops, to enjoy a respite from labor. There were little gatherings about the town, and sometimes a great gathering. The women made election cake—raised cake; the young ladies prepared for a ball in the evening.

The fourth of July for many years after 1776, was kept as a holiday—sometimes in the spirit of party, and sometimes in the spirit of '76. In 1859, it was kept in this latter spirit, and nothing was said or done at which any political party could take offense.

Thanksgiving was a holiday, as now, and on the day before Thanksgiving, the young men hunted game in the forest, or shot at hens and turkeys, tied to a stake, paying a fee for the shot; fourpence half penny a shot for hens, at the distance of eight rods, and ninepence a shot at a turkey at the distance of ten rods.

Owing to the old grudge against Episcopacy, not much was made of Christmas for many years, not so much as recently.

The children who attended school, had Saturday afternoon for a holiday. In the forenoon they recited the "Assembly's Catechism," and in the early part of the present century, after Episcopalianism had been introduced, a portion of them recited the "Church Catechism" as it was called.

Fast days appointed by the Governor of the Colony or the

State were for a long time honored, when "all servile labor and vain recreation on said day, were by law forbidden." In the preaching, for nearly a hundred years, on Fast days and Thanksgiving days, there may sometimes have been a little of the spice of politics, that all could relish; but this spice was not turned into the pepper of party politics until more recently.

The schools were taught by males for a long time. The precise time when females began to be employed in summer schools I have not been able to ascertain. A man by the name of Jones was a noted school master. He was a full believer in the doctrine that "the rod and reproof bring wisdom." When he whipped a boy, his language was, "it comes tough but it is for your own good." To encourage his pupils to behave well he would lisp, "Boys, boys, if you will be good to me, I will be good to you"

EXECUTION OF THE LAWS.

When the laws of the Colony or of the State were few and simple, and before they had been tampered with for party purposes, or degraded by the chicanery of lawyers, the authorities and people of Durham were strict to enforce the laws. Indeed they became somewhat famous in the region round about, for enforcing the laws, respecting the observance of the Sabbath, rivaling the Jews, or at least the primitive puritans. Travelers were stopped on the Sabbath and sometimes fined, and sometimes detained until Monday. The "*Whipping post*," which like Ex-Presidents, retains its title after its occupation is gone, was for a long time thought to be a valuable auxiliary to good morals. Instead of sending the criminal to the penitentiary, or letting him off without punishment for petty larcenies and crimes, he was sentenced to be whipped five or ten lashes or more. The present writer saw this punishment inflicted by the constable, both in Durham and in New Haven. In Durham the punishment was inflicted with a lash whip, with more parade and flourish than severity. In New Haven it was inflicted with a raw-hide whip, much to the satisfaction of the admiring students of the college who assembled to witness it.

The following will be sufficient to show the impressions formerly produced on the minds of intelligent travelers, by the appearance of Durham:

Extract from President Manning's diary during a journey from Providence to Philadelphia and back, April 29th—Sept. 29th, 1779.

"Wednesday, Sept. 22.—Set out (from New Haven) at seven o'clock, having taken breakfast. Took the road to Durham, crossed the bridge, and the long causeway one half mile over the marsh. The first six or seven miles very sandy, then a good soil and well improved to and through Paug, (Northford) a pleasant village, nine miles. Mr Williams, minister, invited me to his house, but we could only stop to oat. From thence to Durham, excellent land and husbandry. and the buildings uncommonly elegant. Durham, a considerable town, situated on a hill; the buildings good; distance nine miles. Dined at Landlord Camp's. The people agreeable. After setting out was stopped by General Wadsworth, and invited to call, but time would not admit." —GUILD'S "*Manning and Brown University*," page 285.

THE FIRST TEMPERANCE SOCIETY.

The first temperance organization in the town was formed, June 30th, 1828, with the following pledge or bond of Union:

"Believing that the use of intoxicating Liquors is for persons in health, not only unnecessary but hurtful; that it is the cause of forming intemperate appetites and habits; and that while it is continued the evils of intemperance cannot be prevented.

Therefore, we the subscribers for the purpose of promoting our own welfare and that of the community, agree that we will abstain from the use of distilled spirits except as a medicine in case of bodily infirmity; that we will not allow the use of them in our families nor provide them for the entertainment of our friends or for persons in our employment; and that in all suitable ways we will discountenance the use of them in the community."

The foregoing was first and originally signed by

Rev. David Smith,	Nathan S. Camp,
Wedworth Wadsworth,	Wm. A. Hart,
Abner Newton,	Silas Merriman,

Roger Newton,	Allen Shipman,
Seth Seward,	Alpheus W. Camp,
Talcott Bates,	Dennis Camp,
David Johnson,	Chs. Lyman,
Peres Sturtevant,	Horace Newton,
David Harrison, M. D.	Joseph Chedsey,
Alfred Camp,	Abner Newton, Jun
Wolcott P. Stone,	Samuel Newton.

After this society went into operation, additions were made to its members, meetings were held, addresses delivered, the pulpit spoke out, until the society in less than eight years numbered 377 members, many of them pledged to abstain from the use of all intoxicating liquors. Such was the success of this movement in favor of temperance, that the various temperance organizations that have existed in the town since 1828, have at times, embraced more than half the entire population pledged to abstain from all intoxicating liquors as a beverage. The good effects of these early movements in favor of temperance on the morals and health and prosperity of the town were strikingly manifest. But while to the honor of the town this early movement in favor of temperance, and this early success are recorded, it may be proper to confess that the number of tobacco growers, chewers, and smokers has increased.

THE MERRIAM MANUFACTURING COMPANY.

The Merriam Manufacturing Company of Durham was organized January 25th, 1851, with a capital of $15,000, for the manufacture of Japanned and Stamped Tin Ware, Tin Toys, &c. The first election for Directors was held February 14th, 1851, with the following result, Miles Merwin, Jr., L. T. Merriam, Samuel Newton, William Wadsworth and Enos Rogers.

MILES MERWIN, JR., President.
T. S. HUBBARD, Secretary and Treasurer.

The capital stock was increased Sept. 7th, 1853, to the amount of $25,000. The present board of Directors Dec. 25th, 1865, are Miles Merwin, Jos. H Parsons, David Lyman, E. L. Johnson, and Francis Hubbard.

MILES MERWIN, President.
F. HUBBARD, Sec'y and Treasurer.

The success of the enterprise has been somewhat varied. Its productions are well known and appreciated, and the present state of its affairs is such, as promises permanency, and, as is believed, will add to the prosperity of the village in which it is located.

THE DEATH OF MR. ISAAC PRENTISS AND OF MR. JOHN T. PALMER.

"In passing through the town of Durham, the stage coach crosses a stream called Allyn's brook, usually small but with high banks. Over this stream was a wooden bridge, 94 feet long and 21 feet high. On the *east*, or above the bridge, at the distance of 180 feet is a mill-dam. At the distance of 36 rods below, is a log for the convenience of foot passengers, supported at each end by a tree. The earth, at this time, February 21st, 1822, was covered with a large body of snow, and the streams were deeply frozen.

"Before the dawn of this memorable day, a warm and violent wind commenced from the south, accompanied by a heavy rain. The water did not however rise until about 10 o'clock A. M., or less than two hours before the stage arrived. But so rapid was the rise of the water, that, in one hour and a half, large cakes of ice were brought down against the trestles of the bridge, and one pier was carried away.

"A few minutes after this event, which was known to but very few, between the hours of 11 and 12, the great mail stage arrived, containing Isaac Prentiss, John T. Palmer, and Philip Gray, as passengers. In attempting to cross the bridge from the north, the southern part gave way, and with the exception of the lead horses, which had reached the abutment, the whole were precipitated into the torrent which carried them down together, till they struck the above mentioned log. Here the carriage was dashed in pieces. The driver seized the limb of a tree, and held till he was rescued. Mr. Gray swam for a fence, which extended into the water, which he hardly reached and from which he was taken with difficulty. The two other gentlemen were overwhelmed by the torrent.

"The alarm was instantly given, and many were soon present, who used every possible exertion, even at the risk of health and life, to save the unfortunate sufferers. But all in vain, they had sunk to rise no more! It was nearly four hours before the body of Mr. Palmer was found, which was then past resuscitation. The body of Mr. Prentiss was not found until early the next morning. Their remains were treated with marked respect by every class of citizens. On the day of their interment they were attended to the House of God, by a large concourse of people, from this and the adjoining towns, when the preceding discourse was delivered to a deeply affected and sympathizing audience."

The foregoing is from a note attached to the sermon delivered by Rev. David Smith, on the 24th, which was a very solemn and appropriate one, and which was printed. In that sermon the speaker said, "In regard to the elder, Mr. Isaac Prentiss, we know very little. Fróm information by a passenger yesterday, it appears that he was respectable, and has left a young family to deplore his exit."

"In respect to the younger, Mr. John Temple Palmer, more particular information has been obtained. If this information be correct, he was the son of Capt. John Palmer, a British officer in the Revolutionary war. His mother, Augusta, was grand daughter of the late Governor Bowdoin of Massachusetts, and daughter of Sir John Temple, Bart., who was, at the time of her marriage with Capt. Palmer, Consul General in the United States to the Court of Great Britain. The parents of the deceased removed from this country to Great Britain; but for some years past, have resided in the south of France. Having given their son a classical education in Europe, they sent him, about four years since, to pursue the study of the law in this country, in which he intended to settle. So far as I can learn, he has spent a part of this time in Harvard University, and part with Mr. Emmet, a distinguished attorney in the city of New York. He had many respectable connections in Boston, particularly the Bowdoin and Winthrop families. To these he had made a visit, expecting, on his return to New York, to embark for Europe on a visit to his parents and friends."

The following was written by JOHN G. C. BRAINARD, and entitled "LINES SUGGESTED BY A LATE OCCURRENCE"

" How slow we drive !—but the hour will come,
  When friends shall greet me with affection's kiss ;
When seated in my boyhood's happy home,
  I shall enjoy a mild contented bliss,
Not often met with in a world like this !
  Then shall I see that brother, youngest born,
I use to play with in my sportiveness ;
  And from a Mother's holiest look shall learn
  A parent's thanks to God ; for a loved son's return.

" And there is one, who, with a down cast eye
  Will be the last to welcome me ; but yet
My memory tells me of a parting sigh,
  And of a lid with tears of sorrow wet,
And how she bade me never to forget
  A friend—and blushed—O ! shall I see again
The same kind look I saw, when last we met,
  And parted. Tell me then that life is vain—
  That joy is met with once, is seldom met again

* * * * * * *
* * " See ye not the falling, fallen mass ?
  Hark ! hear ye not the drowning swimmer's cry ?
Look on the ruins of the desperate pass !
  Gaze at the hurried ice that rushes by
  Bearing a freight of woe and agony,
To that last haven where we all must go—
  Resistless as the stormy clouds that fly
Above our reach, is that dark stream below !—
May peace be in its ebb—there's ruin in its flow."

CHAPTER X.

CHARACTER OF THE EARLY INHABITANTS.

The early inhabitants of Durham were *enterprising and energetic*. In the year 1698, when Caleb Seward of Guilford, the first pioneer of the unbroken wilderness, moved into his log-house in the south part of Cogenchaug, he might have climbed to the mountain top on the southern border, and have looked northwardly, as Moses looked from Pisgah upon Canaan, upon hills rising into mountain ranges on the east and on the west part of the landscape, and between them upon that long swamp, Coginchaug, and the small stream working its sluggish way through it; but he would have seen very little like a land of promise. The Metabessct or Middletown Indians ranged through the forests and swamps, in pursuit of the wild deer and the beaver; but they seem never to have made a settlement. The long swamp in the midst of the territory and occupying a considerable space in it, not only could not be easily brought into use, but it interrupted the communication from the east to the west side of it. And there is a tradition, that when some men explored the territory in order to learn its capabilities, they reported, that on the belt of land between the swamp and the eastern hills on the one side, and the bass tree hills on the other, there was space for about *six* farms. Think of that unbroken pathless wilderness, the abode of the wolf and the panther on the hills, a possession of the "bittern and the pools of water" in the swamps, guarded by the rattlesnake and the copperhead.

They must have been men of enterprise and energy, men of bold hearts and strong hands, who could undertake the task of planting their institutions, domestic and religious, social and civil, on this forbidding ground. But they performed their task nobly and well.

Think, for a moment, of what Durham is, in contrast to what Coginchaug was. Think of this glorious amphitheater of cultivated hills rising in successive ranges from the midland prairie as from an arena; these farms, long the abode of comfort, intelligence and religion; this beautiful and quiet village; and "these steeple towers and spires, whose silent finger points to Heaven." When you look around upon the beauty of your summer landscape, on which the "power of cultivation lies," or as you sit in a stormy winter evening, in your warm houses, call to mind what Durham was when that solitary family, near the southern border, were in their rude cabin of logs, listening it may be to the howl of the gaunt wolf, or to the stealthy step of the Indian. And gratefully call to mind the privations and toil, the virtues and wisdom of your forefathers, which procured for you the public privileges, and private advantages, which you now enjoy.

The early inhabitants of Durham *were strongly attached to the institutions of religion.* As early as April 29th, 1699, in the original petition to the legislature, that the "tract of land called Coginchaug, may be granted and settled for a township," the petitioners represent the settlement of the place as entirely depending on the fact whether the inhabitants could, with "convenient speed," enjoy "the ordinances of God," "the comfortable attainment of which they declare should be the greatest thing we should have regard to in our settling here in this wilderness." And having obtained the object of their petition on this ground, they proceeded to make allotments of land to the "first minister," and also to the "ministry" in perpetuity. Before the patent for the town was issued, and before a church was formed, while their members were limited, and their means scanty, they laid a generous tax for the support of the "ministerial charge." And they not only like David had it in their "hearts to build the house of the Lord," but they actually contributed of their poverty and privations to build a house that for their means and numbers was a large and respectable one.

And in twenty years from the time the first was completed, they were ready to build a larger house, commensurate with the increase of the population. And that they might be at the house of God on the Sabbath, they erected "stables," as they were then called, for their horses, and "Sabbath-day houses," in which they might at once be comfortable, and spend the intermission in an appropriate manner. They were careful to obtain learned, and able, and devoted ministers, and then to pay them generously, and especially to attend regularly upon their ministrations. The Sabbath with them was the great day of the week, for which the evening before furnished a preparation; and like God himself, they loved the place of worship better than any private habitation. Looking through more than a century of years, methinks I see the patriarchs of Durham, on a Sabbath morning, with their families leaving their habitations in the "West-Side," in the "South-End," in the "Quarter," "Up-Street," in the "Green," coming together at the beat of the drum, in that first meeting-house. Methinks I see them with devoted hearts and composed faces, taking their seats in their plain house, in which they could worship God in quietness in their own way, and with their own minister, as the puritans could not in the mother country. And as in their joy they were ready to cry out, "How amiable are thy tabernacles, O thou Lord of hosts," methinks they hung upon the lips of their first minister, as upon the lips of a man of God, who was wont to bring into the sanctuary on the Sabbath the fruits of his patient toil during the six days of the week. Methinks I see some with pen in hand, writing out for future use the divisions and subdivisions of a logical discourse.

And when they returned to their homes with hearts warmed and faces radiant, they were prepared to go six days in the strength of that spiritual food which they had received. And when severe disease confined them to their beds on the Sabbath, the prayers of the sanctuary went up for them from hearts in which they had often been in communion at the table of the Lord. And when they died, they died in the hopes which had been cherished and strengthened, and it may be originated in the house of God. And when they were buried, their children whom they had offered to God in baptism, and their kindred, on the next Sabbath repaired in their bereavement to the same house where the public prayer would be made on their behalf. Their consolations, their enjoyments, their rest from labor, their spiritual culture were found in the house of God; and why should they not be strongly attached to the institution of public worship, and those other religious institutions connected with it, and sustained by it, such as family prayer, and the religious education of children?

2. The early inhabitants of Durham *were men of deep reflection.* The range of their investigations was not a wide one, but they thought closely upon the subjects which engaged their attention, such as the doctrines of religion, and the external duties of morality, such as education and the laws of the land, such as the civil government of the town and its ecclesiastical concerns. These subjects of prime importance employed the earnest activity of their minds in their intercourse with each other and in their solitary hours. The weekly and daily press did not as now bring before the public a vast variety of subjects to furnish at least a superficial knowledge. The eloquent lecturer before Ly-

ceums, and the eloquent agent of some voluntary association before assembled congregations, did not as now exalt the claims of his favorite subject or society, calling in the aid of ridicule or fun Conventions, and clubs, and mass meetings did not as now interest and agitate the public mind. The post office system had then no existence The magnetic telegraph, which now communicates intelligence with the speed of lightning to electrify us at times with its startling telegrams, was not dreamed of. They were comparatively isolated from the world. The newspaper press was not then a power to enlighten or deceive. But though the helps for moral and intellectual cultivation were not as great as we of this generation enjoy, still they most judiciously and perseveringly, used their scantier means. How careful were they to provide for the education of their children in common schools, thus laying the foundation of the institutions which we now enjoy! In their civil affairs how careful were they to select the men best qualified for office! The most available candidate then was generally the one best qualified. How enlarged were their views in the early establishment of a Town Library, which was done by the "Durham Book Company," as it was styled, October 30th, 1733, before any other Library was formed in the Colony. The books thus collected were in those times *read.* Furnishing as they did solid nutriment to the mind, and not that trash which stimulates the appetite, while it impairs the digestion, what strong men they made! The great principles of Civil and Ecclesiastical Government, the great doctrines of the Gospel, the great duties of morality, the cardinal virtues, the chief end of man, became, in their elements, so familiar to the leading minds of the town, that superficial views of truth or of duty would not satify them.

3. The early inhabitants of Durham *were devoted to the public welfare.* Closely connected by descent with the Puritan Fathers of Connecticut, they inherited their spirit. They came to this place not to enjoy the fruits of the labors of their ancestors, but to labor themselves for the benefit of those who should come after them. Forests were to be cut down, and the land brought into cultivation. Roads were to be made across the swamp, and elsewhere. A church was to be erected. Schools were to be established, not with money given by the State, or devised by

some public benefactor. The ministry was to be supported. A burying-ground was to be set off, cleared and protected by a fence. These burdens they cheerfully bore. The love of money had not so seized upon them, that they were willing to neglect the public good for their private gain. The love of office had not so taken possession of them that each was inclined to have it in rapid rotation, rather than to confer it upon the one best qualified to serve the public. Witness their generous contributions of men and means in the French war, and in the war of the Revolution; read their patriotic resolutions adopted in Town meeting, followed by patriotic actions on the field of battle; and you may have proof that the early inhabitants of Durham were devoted to the public welfare.

4. The early inhabitants of Durham *were in their actions governed by fixed principles.* They were not driven about by every wind of doctrine, whether in civil or ecclesiastical concerns. They were not of the number of those who are ever learning, and never able to come to the knowledge of the truth; but having by the patient use of the means they enjoyed adopted their opinions, they retained them. We are now speaking of the leading men in the Town. Errors in opinion they may have adopted. Faults in conduct they may have committed. Imperfections and sins they must have had, but instability in their opinions on important subjects was not one of them.

Of the first settlers of Durham, a considerable number came from under the preaching of such men, as the Rev. Joseph Elliot, of Guilford, son of the Apostle John Elliot; the Rev. Mr. Andrew of Milford, and the Rev. Israel Chauncey of Stratford; to both of whom was offered the presidency of Yale College; the Rev. Solomon Stoddard of Northampton; the Rev. Abraham Pierson of Killingworth, president of Yale College. The enlightened principles derived from such men, they manifested in their own conduct, and transmitted to their immediate descendants. The same confession of faith, they used, it is believed, for nearly a century. They continued faithfully attached to their ministers the same length of time. They were also true to their public servants; sending some of them many years in succession to the Legislature.

INDIVIDUAL MEN.

Having described the general characters of the early inhabitants of Durham, would that I could bring out into distinct view each individual from the first to the present time who is entitled to our gratitude. But no. They are sleeping in their graves, some of them nameless, and forgotten or uncared for. But thanks to the omnipresent care of God, their names and their works are recorded in his book of remembrance.

Of the few that I can notice, CALEB SEWARD has the first claim, as the first inhabitant of Durham. He was the son of William Seward the emigrant, and was born March 14th, 1662–3 He was the uncle of John and brother of Joseph, both of whom came for a residence to Durham. He married Lydia Bushnell July 14th, 1686. He seems to have spent the winter, at least a portion of it, in 1698–9 in Durham, and he and his wife settled in Durham May 4th, 1699. He had seven children, Daniel, Lydia, Caleb, Thomas, Noadiah. After he removed to Durham, he had Ephraim, Aug. 6th, 1700, the first born white child of Durham, and Ebenezer the second white child born June 7th, 1703. He was the first Town Clerk; was a man in whom confidence was universally reposed. He was representative of the Town fifteen sessions of the Legislature. He died August 1st, 1728, aged 65. His wife died August, 1753.

Colonel JAMES WADSWORTH, born July 6th, 1675, in Farmington, was the son of John of the same place, who was born in England, and came to this country with his father William, in 1632. He was bred a lawyer, though it does not appear that he ever practised law extensively. The people of Durham gave him almost all the offices at their disposal; and when his abilities and moral worth came to be generally known, he was honored by appointments from the Colony. He was the first Justice of the Peace, and he had the command of the first military company at its formation. Upon the organization of the Militia in 1735, he was constituted Colonel of the 10th regiment. For a time he was Justice of the Quorum for the County of New Haven. He was Speaker of the House in the Colonial Legislature, 1717, and Assistant from 1718 to 1752. The election to that office was by a general ticket; and such was the confidence of the people of the Colony in his ability and integrity, at a period when ability and integrity were the indispensable qualifications for office, that on the returns for the year 1732, he had the highest vote of any one in the Colony. In May, 1724, he was appointed with several other gentlemen, to hear and determine all matters of error and equity brought on petition to the Grand Assembly; and from 1725 until he left the council, was one of the Judges of the Superior Court. At the October session of the General Assembly, 1726, a grant of 300 acres of land in the town of Goshen, was made to James Wadsworth, Esq., of Durham, John Hall, Esq., of Wallingford, and Hezekiah Brainard, Esq., of Haddam, father of the missionary David Brainard, for public services. It was called the Esquires' Farm, from its being given to these individuals, each of whom had the title of Esq. In fulfilling the public duties assigned him, ability and integrity were alike conspicuous; while an exemplary attendance upon the worship and the ordinances of the Lord, gave a dignity to his character. He exerted a salutary influence upon the Town, more so indeed than any one, except his "personal friend the minister." He died Jan 10th, 1756, aged 79. His wife was Ruth Noyes. They had one son, James, who died July 21st, 1770, aged 87, whose wife's name was Penfield. He was the father of General James Wadsworth, and John Noyes Wadsworth.

Colonel ELIHU CHAUNCEY, the eldest son of Rev. Nathaniel Chauncey, was born at Durham, March 24th, 1710. He married Mary Griswold, daughter of Samuel Griswold, of Killingworth. He died April 10th, 1791.

He was a gentleman of a strong mind, of extensive reading and of much influence in the Town and the State. He acted as Colonel in the French war and was stationed on the Northern frontier; and such was the confidence reposed in him, that he was always invited to sit with the officers of the regular army, in the councils of war with the British officers.

He was elected to the Legislature continuously, thirty-nine years, with the exception of the year when he was in the northern army; in all seventy-six sessions. It is believed that there are some omissions in the record. Besides acting as the Chief Justice of the County Court, he was, in the early part of the Revolutionary war, one of the Committee who sat for the trial of persons suspected of being tories. He himself was suspected of favoring the tories, and as from a regard to his oath of allegiance to the British Government, which he was unwilling to violate, he would not take the "oath of fidelity" to Connecticut, he resigned his place on that committee. During the war he held no public office, but lived respected as heretofore by the people. They knew that he was governed by high moral principle, and not by the love of popularity or by self interest. His children were, 1, Charles who died young; 2, Catharine the wife of Rev. Elizur Goodrich; 3, Sarah who died young; 4, Sarah who married first, Lemuel Guernsey; second, Simeon Parsons. She died March 19th, 1723; 5, Charles, who has been mentioned elsewhere.

General JAMES WADSWORTH, the son of James Wadsworth, Esq., and grandson of Colonel James Wadsworth, was born July 6th, 1730, and received his degree of Bachelor of Arts in Yale College, 1748, studying law and settling in Durham, he was soon promoted to office in civil and in military life. On the death of his grandfather in 1756, he was elected Town Clerk, some of the duties of which office he had performed for his grandfather. In this office he continued until 1786. In 1775, being at that time a Colonel in the Militia, he was appointed with Erastus Wolcott and others a committee to provide for the officers and soldiers and their families, who were prisoners of war.

In January, 1776, he was Colonel of the first regiment of the Militia of Connecticut in the army of the United Colonies, when the regiment marched to Boston. Under his command were Comfort Tays, Lieut. Col.; Dyer Troop, Major; Samuel Johnson, Adjutant; Thomas Lyman, Quarter Master; Robert Usher, Surgeon; Elias Norton, Surgeon's Mate; Capt. John Willey and Company; Capt. John Couch and Company; Capt. Eliphlet Buckley and Company; Capt. Joseph ——— and Company; Capt. Jeremiah Mason and Company; Capt. Jared Shepherd and Company; Capt. Jesse Moss and Company; Capt. Benjamin Richards and Company.

In 1776 he was appointed Brigadier General of the battalion raised to reinforce the Continental army in New York. In 1777 he was appointed second Major General, in the place of Major General Huntington. He was one session a member of the Continental Congress. In 1777 he was a member of an important Committee appointed to revise the militia laws of the State for the more effectual defense of the country. In March, 1777, General Wadsworth was ordered to march one-fourth of his brigade to New Haven, to defend the coast. In April, 1778, the Council of Safety directed him to inquire into the state of the guards at New Haven, and to dismiss the militia there, in whole or in part, at his discretion. For a time he was member of the Committee of Safety in the State.

For some time, he was Justice of the Quorum, and then Judge of the Court of Common Pleas in New Haven County. In 1786 and 7, he was Controller of Public Accounts in the State, and from 1785 to 1789, he was member of the Council.

Between him and Colonel Chauncey, there was a strong and generous friendship. They were both men of the highest moral principle, which no office could bribe them to desert Both of these were, to some extent, martyrs to their principles. When the Revolutionary war was impending, Col. Chauncey refused to violate his oath of allegiance to Great Britain. He, therefore, from high moral consideration, gave up public office. In his retirement from public life he enjoyed the confidence of his fellow men, because they considered him true to his principles of honor and moral obligation. When the new Federal Constitution was brought before the State Convention in Hartford, for adoption or rejection, General Wadsworth made the great speech against it. He thought that though the Convention that formed it, supposed that they had guarded the rights of the States, advantage would be taken of it, in times of popular excitement, to encroach on the rights of the States. And afterwards he always refused, on high moral grounds, to take an oath to support the Federal Constitution. His oath of fidelity to Connecticut he thought would be violated by taking that oath. He was offered office, even, it was said, the office of Governor of the State. But no, he must remain true to his "oath of fidelity" to the State of Connecticut. What would he say now with the experience of seventy-five years? Would he consider himself a true, or a false prophet?

In the year 1794, the General Assembly, notwithstanding he refused to take the oath to support the Constitution of the United States, appointed him "to settle the accounts between the State of New York and the State of Connecticut, and to receive the balance which may be due this State on such settlement."

The Library of the Durham Book Company was kept at his house for many years. He was very dignified but very courteous in his manners as I well remember. He sometimes had a word of encouragement in regard to reading certain books which I drew from the Library.

I remember too, that the boys of the Center School, often when they saw General Wadsworth coming, on his Narraganset pacer, with his large, erect military figure, with his broad brimmed hat, with his Olympian locks, would run across the Green to the road, to take off their hats and make a low bow. This courtesy he returned to each of us, taking his hat quite off, and bowing to each one. Thus he encouraged good manners, of which he was a model.

By invitation from his nephews, William Wadsworth and James, he spent a year or more at Geneseo, N. Y. But though surrounded with every thing that he could desire, his heart still yearned for Durham. He died Sept 22d, 1797, aged 87. His wife was Catharine Guernsey. She died Dec. 13th, 1813. Their two daughters Abigail and Catharine, died in childhood The high position which General Wadsworth occupied, as well as the intrinsic excellence of his character, both intellectual and moral, render it desirable that a full history of his life should be given to the public.

"LEBANON, 10th December, 1777.

Sir,

In reply to yours respecting Major Williams of the Royal British Artillery, I have thought proper, in consideration of the ill state of health of said Williams, that you grant him a Flag to go into New York, together with Doctor Graham, and the other persons mentioned, upon condition that he procure an exchange for himself, namely, Major Otho Holland Williams of Maryland, or Lieut. Col. Selah Hart, of this State, and for the other persons an equal number of equal standing; or in case of failure of exchange, his giving parole to return immediately in person.

You will please to cause some proper vessel to be procured at New Haven, with some suitable intelligent person to go with her, and do every other necessary requisite to effectuate this purpose. I am,

Sir, your most obedient

humble servant,

JONATHAN TRUMBULL.

P. S.—If Major Williams is obliged to return, there is no doubt that he may bring out a physician of his choice.

Major General Wadsworth."

DANIEL HALL, Esq, was for a long time a leading man in the town of Durham. He was often Moderator at Town Meetings; was often sent as a representative to the General Assembly; was a delegate to the Convention that adopted the Federal Constitution; often acted on trials as a Justice of the Peace; was a Deacon of the Church, and is represented as exemplary in religion, strict in morals, and faithful in office. He was the son of William Hall and Elizabeth Johnson his wife, who was the daughter of Deacon William Johnson of Guilford, to whom the General Court gave a farm in Durham, and sister of Samuel Johnson the father of the Samuel Johnson, President of King's College, New York. Deacon Daniel Hall died December 17th, 1790. He lived in the house now occupied by John S. Camp. He previously lived at the Tuttle place in the West side.

SIMEON PARSONS was born in Durham, and was the son of Simeon Parsons, who was born in 1701 in Northampton, who was the son of Joseph Parsons, who married a daughter of Elder John Strong. This Joseph was the son of Joseph the brother of Benjamin, both of whom emigrated from England. Simeon Parsons was well educated, was the brother of Noah Parsons, who was educated at Yale College. He was for a long period held in high public estimation; represented the Town for many sessions in the Legislature; was a justice of the peace; was Captain in the Revolutionary army; was Town Clerk from 1786 to 1810. He died July 12th, 1819, in his 87th year.

DAN PARMELEE was the son of Hezekiah Parmelee, who was the son of Joel Parmelee, who came from Guilford to Durham. This latter was the son of John Parmelee, who was the son of John Parmelee, who came from England with his son John as early as 1656; for he was at Guilford at that time. Dan Parmelee, Esq, represented the town of Durham many sessions in the Legislature where he was much respected as a useful member; was a Justice of the Peace; and a Deacon in the Church. He was a man of pleasant and bland manners, full of anecdotes, very sprightly in conversation, and was acceptable wherever he went. He died December 11th, 1825, aged 78. His wife was Abigail Norton, sister of Dr Lyman Norton. Their children were, 1, Hannah, who married Abraham Camp; 2, Betsey, who married Mr. Everest, a lawyer; 3, Dan; 4, Mehetabel, who married Rev. Mr. Eells; 5, Abigail, who married Mr. Enos.

WORTHINGTON GALLUP CHAUNCEY, the son of Elnathan, and grandson of Rev. Nathaniel Chauncey, was born March 22d, 1772. He died on Tuesday, 4 o'clock A. M, June 15th, 1858, in the 87th year of his age. In his early youth he went to Whitestown and took up land, made a clearing, and sold his land with improvements advantageously. He then acted three years as a private tutor in the family of Major Van Rensellaer in Claverack. Afterwards he was, for a time, a merchant in the same place, and was engaged in speculations in wild lands in the State of New York and elsewhere. After his return to Durham he was extensively engaged in public business. From a notice of him published at the time of his death the following is an extract:

"In the performance of his public and private duties he was distinguished for his strict integrity, and honesty of purpose; while he was courteous in his manners, and kind in his feelings, and generous in his services. Those who knew him gave him their confidence and good will, and though he outlived his generation, who could best appreciate his worth, there are still those among the living who will cherish his memory in their hearts, as their counselor, friend and benefactor.

"For many years Esquire Chauncey transacted a large part of the public business of the Town, as Justice of the Peace, as Town Clerk, as a member of the General Assembly, as executor or administrator on estates. He was always a supporter of law and order, and the institutions of education and religion."

He preserved the freshness of his feelings, and his ready sympathy with others, in their welfare and their affliction, and his interest in human affairs generally, to the last days of his life. "And as he drew near the close of his long life, he said, with deep feeling, 'I have arrived at that point, when all that remains to me is to say, 'Father, not my will, but thine be done.' He died apparently without disease, without pain, but simply of old age, retaining his mental faculties to the last. He had always been temperate in his habits, and to this fact must be attributed, his long life, and the remarkable preservation of his mental faculties. When a young man in the family of Major Van Rensellaer, he declined drinking wine, which was every day on the table, at dinner. The Major asked him one day why he declined drinking the wine offered to him. He replied, "I do not like the taste of it, and it does not do me any good." The Major pleasantly said, "these, are sufficient reasons."

As a magistrate, Squire Chauncey united something of the old regime, with something of the new. He was born under the King of Great Britain, when sovereignty, or the rights of command, was vested in one man. In Durham, as in many other towns, this sovereignty was exercised, to some extent by one, two, or more, as magistrates, who acted in the King's name, and by his authority. But when sovereignty, by the Declaration of Independence, and by the treaty with Great Britain, became vested in the State, that is, in the people of the State, the magistrates derived their authority from the people. This transfer of sovereignty to the people exerted a modifying influence on the character of the magistrates, who received their offices indirectly or directly from the people; it placed them more under the influence of popular feeling, whether that feeling happened to be right or wrong. Esquire Chauncey, in his judicial decisions, and in the duties of his office, generally united, in a good degree, the advantages of both systems; preserving the majesty of the laws on the one hand, while he conciliated and satisfied public opinion on the other.

In his conversation there was a fine vein of social feeling, which made him an interesting companion, while his intelligence and good sense made him an instructive one. He spoke and wrote, with precision and energy, sometimes playfully, and poetically. There was a good deal of life and spirit in his poetry. His public and private virtues endeared him to his fellow-men, who made his acquaintance, so that in the last years of his life, wherever he went, he was hailed as a good man, or a benefactor, or a personal friend. He had that "which should accompany old age, as love, honor, troops of friends."

In his relations to the Divine Government, such was his sense of religious obligations, and such was his consciensclous discharge of them, that he realized in his own experience the truth of the declaration, "great peace have they which love thy laws." His native qualities, improved by Christian culture, were such that he put one in mind of the young man that Jesus loved, and and also of the beloved disciple. He never made a public profession of religion, though he was a constant worshipper in the house of God. Beside these, many others might be mentioned, who served the town in their generation. Among them were Moses Parsons, Benjamin Picket, Elnathan Camp, Thomas Lyman, Abraham Scranton, Charles Coe, Daniel Bates, Bridgman Guernsey, Nathaniel William Chauncey, Richard Robinson, John Swathel.

THOMAS LYMAN, son of Thomas, and grandson of Deacon Thomas Lyman, who emigrated to Durham with his family, was a man of great intelligence, of extensive reading. He was dignified in his manners and impressive in his conversation. It is not impossible that he and some others were influenced in their opinions by the writings of Priestly and Price So much pleased with him was Mr. Jefferson, that he gave him an invitation to spend a week with him at Monticello, which he accepted very much to his satisfaction. He was with General Phinehas Lyman in one of his expeditions to the South. He and Lemuel Guernsey were delegates to the Convention that formed the State Constitution. He died, June 6, 1832, aged 86. He left three children—George, Henry and Betsey.

NATHANIEL WILLIAM CHAUNCEY, the elder Brother of Worthington G. Chauncey, was in the war of the Revolution and drew a pension for his services. He was with Colonel John Ely, his uncle, and Colonel Webb, when with their regiment they attempted a landing on Long Island. Both of those officers were made prisoners. Captain Collins with about two hundred men effected a landing; N. W. Chauncey being of the number They burnt their vessel and commenced a retreat of about seventy miles, to the east end of the Island, the enemy being in full pursuit. On their arrival in the evening, the enemy believing there were more troops, stationed there, made regular approaches, with a view to a general attack in the morning; but in the night the Americans procured boats and made their escape. Mr. Chauncey had read many of the standard works in the English language, especially in history and political economy, and possessing a strong memory he had treasured up large stores of information. Though he sought not for office, he represented the town in the General Assembly. He also had his share of town offices. He had great readiness of mind and fine powers of conversation and genial feelings. In his old age some well dressed youth in the stage, as it was passing, called out to him, seemingly as if they were candidates for the penitentiary, "how far is it to home old daddy?" With perfect composure he answered, in his clear, strong voice, "It is just twenty miles to Wethersfield." After a long, healthy, cheerful, useful life, beloved by his friends and the delight of the social circle, a lover of his Bible and his God, he died in the hopes of the Gospel, January 29, 1840, in the 79th year of his age. It may not be improper to say that the present writer was named after him, and now lives on the place where he lived.

PHYSICIANS.

JOSEPH SEWARD, son of William, and brother of Caleb, the first inhabitant of Durham, and uncle of John, born 1655, in Guilford; died February 14, 1732, aged 77 He is spoken of in the proprietors' book and the town records as a leading man in civil matters He had nine children. Joseph, Judith, Mary, Samuel, Patience, Nathaniel, Anna. Patience married Stephen Bates, December 29, 1715.

SAMUEL ELY came to Durham about 1745. Then being absent for a time, he returned again in 1748. In 1752 the town allowed him £6, 4, 9 for services. In 1755 he was appointed, with Dr. Collins, of Litchfield, Dr. Marsh, of Norwich, to attend the expedition fitted out by the colony against the French on the Northern frontier. Each surgeon was furnished with a complete set of implements, and a box of medicines, at the expense of the colony, and each was to receive £7 per month for his services. At this time Connecticut had two or three thousand men in the field. I have in my possession two or three of the letters of Dr. Ely. They bear the marks of a sprightly mind.

AMOS HUBBARD practiced in Durham after Dr. Ely left for the army, until his death, November 15, 1767, aged 43. His residence was on the "west side," half a mile from Quarry Hill, on the north side of the road, where the house of A. Jackson now stands

JESSE COLE succeeded Dr. Hubbard. He was born at Kensington, 1739, and was the son of Mathew Cole, and Ruth Hubbard. He came to Durham in 1765, and practiced here until 1793, when he removed to Southington, and from thence to Wolcott in 1803, and died February 25, 1811, in the 72d year of his age, and was buried in Plantville. During the early part of his residence in Durham, he resided on Meeting House Hill, in the south part of the town, between "South End," and the New Haven road; on the north side of the way. Afterwards he removed to the house formerly occupied by Dr. Hubbard. He was, for a time assisted by his nephew, Matthew Cole, who graduated in Yale College, 1783. Dr. Moses Gaylord, who was a student in Durham with Dr. Cole, settled in Wallingford and became a distinguished surgeon. Dr. Cole was considered to be a man of skill. When a boy, I heard it remarked, that he relied in difficult cases, on two pills, one of which he called the black dog, and the other, the white dog. When the one was not strong enough, he sent the other down into the stomach of the patient. His children were 1, Ruth, who married Sherman Merril; 2, Sarah, married David Langdon; 3, Polly, married Roswell Langdon; 4, Phebe, married—5, Samuel—6, Nancy—7, Sophia—8, Jessie, died in Kensington.

EBENEZER GUERNSEY, son of Lemuel Guernsey, of Durham, studied medicine with Dr. Jared Potter; died in Upper Canada, September 21, 1794, aged 31 years. He was a man of considerable talent, but violent in temper. On one occasion he threw a shovel full of hot coals from the hearth at some one or two, who, he thought, intruded upon him. His betrothed, Miss Camp, was asked what she would do if he should throw fire? "Why, I will throw water." He left one child, Lemuel, who died in North Carolina.

NATHANIEL THAYER, born in Boston, married Anna Fowler, November 6, 1791; removed to Lee, Massachusetts, about 1800, where he practiced many years. He died in Westfield, Massachusetts, June 24, 1824, aged sixty-five years. He left two sons, William and Lucius, and a daughter.

LYMAN NORTON, the son of Stephen and Abigail, was born June 1st, 1763, about two miles from Quarry Hill on the north side of Wallingford road He studied medicine with Dr. Jared Potter of Wallingford; purchased the house immediately north of Mr Samuel Parsons' house. Commenced practice before 1797. Died April 13th, 1814, aged 54 He was a man of agreeable manners, and was generally beloved He married Olive Wells, and left two children, Delia and Stephen.

WILLIAM FOOTE was born in Northford, studied medicine with his brother, Dr. Malica Foote, in Rye, New York, and with Dr. Benjamin Rockwell of New York, came to Durham in 1802; resided on the south corner nearly opposite the North Church; removed to Goshen in 1807, and practiced there two years, returned to Durham and resided in Haddam Quarter until his death, January 30th, 1842 He was cotemporary with Dr. Norton, had a better education than he, but less tact as a physician. He married Catharine Picket, only child of James Picket. Their children were, 1, James P ; 2, Katharine H.; 3, Rebecca R.; 4, William R.

WILLIAM SEWARD PIERSON, the son of Abraham Pierson, was born in Killingworth, graduated in Yale College, 1808, studied medicine with the celebrated Dr. Nathan Smith, at Dartmouth College, took his medical degree there in August, 1813, came to Durham on a formal invitation of the inhabitants upon the death of Dr. Norton, purchased the house occupied by Dr. Foot, remained four years in Durham, and then, upon the invitation of the people of Windsor, removed to that place, where he resided until his death, July 16th, 1860. He did a large business, and was successful in making his collections.

JARED POTTER KIRTLAND, born Nov. 10th, 1793, was the son of Turhand and Mary (Potter) Kirtland, and grandson of the late Dr. Jared Potter, a distinguished physician of Wallingford. He received his classical education, chiefly in Cheshire and Wallingford Academies, and he was, for a time, a private pupil and a member of the family of Rev. Dr Bronson, the President of Cheshire Academy. In the Autumn of 1810, he entered as student of medicine the office of Dr. John Andrews in Wallingford, and in 1812 that of Dr Sylvester Wells, of Hartford; and afterwards, was a private pupil of Dr. Eli Ives, and Dr. Nathan Smith, of New Haven. In the Autumn of 1812, he entered the first class in the medical department of Yale College, and was the first who signed the Matriculating Book, in the charge of Prof Knight. At the close of the medical term, in company with Lyman Foot, Selah Kirby, and Solon C H Smith, he formed a class for the study of Botany and Mineralogy; and they pursued these studies, as well as their medical studies, under Profs. Eli Ives and Benjamin Silliman.

In 1814, he entered the medical department of the University of Pennsylvania, under the instruction of Wistar, Physic Dorsey, Chapman, James, and Benjamin Smith Barton. He soon after passed an examination for a medical degree, before the Medical Faculty of Yale College, and the State Medical Censors The subject of his Thesis was, "Our Indigenous Vegetable Materia Medica," a favorite subject of his teacher, Dr. Barton.

In May, 1814, he was united in marriage with Caroline, daughter of Joshua Atwater; and practiced, for a time, in Wallingford. In 1817, a town meeting was held in Durham and a resolution was passed inviting him to locate there, as a physician. This invitation he accepted. Here he soon had a great amount of business.

In 1822, on the death of his wife and daughter, and the failure of his health, he removed to Poland, Ohio. Here he engaged in agricultural and horticultural pursuits, and in the study of Natural History and Natural Science, and made some important discoveries. He also resumed the practice of medicine.

He was elected Representative to the State Legislature three alternate sessions. He acted as Chairman of the Committee on the Penitentiary in the House. In 1836, was elected Professor of the Theory and Practice of Medicine in the "Medical College of Ohio." In 1839 he received the appointment of second Assistant Geologist, and entered earnestly and successfully on the duties of his office. In 1841 he discharged the duties of Professor of the "Theory and Practice of Medicine" in "Willoughby Medical School," one year; having resigned his position in the Medical College of Ohio. When the medical department was established in Western Reserve College, he accepted of a similar station in that College, where he continued until 1864. He has also successfully investigated the habits of the honey bee, and the characteristics of the fresh water naiads He was President of the Ohio State Medical Society, and member of many different societies. He received the degree of LL. D. at Williams in 1861. He owes his eminent success in life to his untiring industry, and his inextinguishable thirst for knowledge.

CHAUNCEY ANDRUS, born in Southington, Conn.; studied medicine with James Percival, of Kensington, the father of the celebrated James Gales Percival; settled in Durham, 1823, died October, 1863.

JOHN T. CATLIN was born in New Marlborough, Mass, and was the son of Rev. Dr. Catlin, who was the teacher of Dr. David Smith; attended a course of lectures at the College of Physicians and Surgeons at New York City in 1816 and 1817; was licensed to practise by the New York State Medical Society; practised several years in Salisbury, and removed to Durham, when Dr. Kirtland left. He died July 28th, 1825 He married Hannah Hall, daughter of John Hall of Durham, and left two children, a son and a daughter.

DAVID HARRISON was born in North Branford, graduated M. D. at Yale College, 1825; soon after came to Durham at the death of Dr. Catlin, removed to Middletown in 1831; practiced in Cuba; returned to Middletown and died, December, 1856, at Fair Haven, of heart disease.

HENRY HOLMES, son of Uriah Holmes of Litchfield, took his medical degree at Yale College, 1825; came to Durham about the same time with Harrison; boarded with Rev. Dr. Smith; spent the winter of 1830–31 at the College of Physicians and Surgeons in New York, taking another degree from the University of New York; returned to Durham where he resided until 1833, when he went to Hartford, where he now resides.

WILLIAM HAYDEN ROCKWELL, graduated at Yale College, 1824; studied medicine with Dr. Thomas Hubbard of Pomfret, who was afterwards Professor at Yale, and with Dr. Eli Todd of Hartford; took his medical degree at Yale College, 1831; came to Durham soon after and remained in Durham until the following year, is now Superintendent of the Insane Retreat, Brattleboro, Vermont.

ERASMUS D. NORTH was a son of Dr. Elisha North of New London; was graduated at Chapel Hill College, N. C., took his medical degree in New Haven, 1833; same year removed to Durham; married a daughter of John Swathel; practiced four years in Durham, left to be an instructor of Elocution in Yale College; was made wealthy by the death of a brother lost in the Arctic, died in 185 .

"We regret to learn that Erasmus D. North, M D, formerly teacher of Elocution in Yale College, died yesterday at Westfield, Mass. He was an excellent teacher and will be long remembered by those who received instruction from him for his eccentricities and his genuine worth."—*New Haven Palladium*, 18*th.*

SETH H. CHILD was born in Barnston, C E.; studied medicine at Fort Covington, New York; graduated at Woodstock, Vt.; came to Durham, 1838; was a member of the State Senate in 1845; built the house opposite the North Academy, which he sold to Dr. Fowler in 1845, and in Spring of 1846 removed to East Hartford, where he now resides He had three children born in Durham 1, Henry Theodoric; 2, Mary Taylor; 3, Henry Edwards. The two oldest are not living His daughter Julia, the wife of Rev. E. C. Baldwin, died in 1857.

BENJAMIN L. FOWLER was born in Northford; studied medicine with Dr. Stanton, of Amenia, New York, and N. B. Ives, of New Haven; graduated at Yale Medical School, 1845; same year came to Durham; married Harriet Jewet of Durham, and afterwards Mary Payne of Amenia, New York, sister of Dr. Stanton's wife, left Durham, 1856, for Poughkeepsie, N. Y, and there died September, 1858, of pneumonia, leaving three children by his second wife, born in Durham 1, William Stanton; 2, Benjamin M ; 3, Harriet Jewet.

RUFUS W MATHEWSON, born in Coventry, R. I , studied medicine in Norwich with W Hooker, now Professor of Practice of Medicine in Yale College, S. Johnson and with N B. Ives, New Haven; attended lectures at the College of Physicians and Surgeons in 1834 and 5, then the only medical school in New York, took his degree from the University of the State of New York at the Commencement of 1835; remained in Norwich till 1846; then attended another course of lectures in New York; removed to Gales Ferry in Ledyard, where he remained till he came to Durham, May, 1856, and purchased the house of Dr. Fowler; married Susan E. Williams of Ledyard, who died in Durham, April, 1865, leaving six children, Earl, Rufus, Mary, and Amelia, born in Ledyard; Randolph, Susan, and Ellen, born in Durham.

E DARWIN ANDREWS, studied medicine with his Father, settled in Durham, 1857.

WAIT R. GRISWOLD, born in Wethersfield, graduate of Yale College, 1844, studied medicine with Dr. Mathewson, attended lectures at the College of Physicians and Surgeons, New York, taking his medical degree from Columbia College, the two institutions having been recently united; was Surgeon 22d Regiment C. V, and 86th United States Colored Regiment; now Physician in Easton, Ct.

SAMUEL H. CATLIN, son of Dr. S. T Catlin, born in Durham; studied medicine with Dr. Fowler; took his medical degree at Yale College, 1848; practised for some years in Brooklyn, New York; has been for three years Surgeon U. S Army, Department of the Gulf

---

CHAPTER XI.

EMIGRANTS FROM DURHAM

CHANGE OF POPULATION.

In looking over the thirty-four names on the twenty-first page, borne by the patentees of Durham, we find only a few of them borne by the present inhabitants The two brothers, Caleb Seward and Joseph Seward, who had numerous families, have no posterity in Durham bearing their name. The same is true of Nathaniel Chauncey, Isaac Chauncey, Samuel Fairchild, James Curtis, Ezekiel Hawley, Benjamin Baldwin, Richard Beach and Benjamin Beach, James Baldwin, William Roberts, Samuel Sanford, Thomas Wheeler, Joseph Gaylord, Joseph Gaylord, Jr,

Stephen Hickox, Joseph Norton, Samuel Norton, John Sutliff, Nathaniel Sutliff, Jonathan Wells, Henry Crane, Ezekiel Buck, and Hezekiah Talcott.

But while twenty-six have no posterity in Durham bearing their name, the following seven or eight have: David Robinson, the second settler, Joseph Coe, and perhaps, Robert Coe, Joseph Hickox, Joel Parmelee, Samuel Camp, James Wadsworth, and John Seward, nephew of Caleb, who is supposed to be ancestor of William H. Seward, now Secretary of State. Besides descendants in Durham, these have numerous descendants elsewhere The same law of change has prevailed with respect to families that came in at a later period. The Guernseys, the Pickets, the Nortons, the Bateses, the Halls, the Goodriches, the Spelmans, the Morrises, the Bartletts, the Meekers, are no longer found here.

The first settlers generally had large families. Joseph Seward had 9 children, Caleb 7, Henry Crane 16, Nathaniel Chauncey 6, Joseph Coe 5, his son Joseph 10. I have somewhere seen it stated that in some of the towns in Massachusetts, at their first settlement, the average number of children, for every married couple, was between 7 and 8. The number in Durham was probably about the same. The rapid increase of population in Durham during the first fifty years furnished emigrants to other towns

CHANGES ON THE HOMESTEADS.

We are still more struck with the change by looking at the several homesteads, and their former and their present occupants. The following is from a memorandum by Worthington G. Chauncey, made out not long before his death, and enlarged and continued to the present time by William Wadsworth, as compared with 1783. Beginning at the Meeting House on the Green and passing south in 1783, Doct. Elizur Goodrich, and wife and children, Chauncey, Elizur, Samuel, Elihu, Charles, Nathan, and Catharine; now belonging to Zebulon Hale and Watson Davis. West side of Green about 1790, John Loveland, wife and children; house pulled down, a new house built on site by Oliver Knowles; now owned by William C. Ives. Next south, Elias B. Meigs; next, John Jones, pulled down, rebuilt by Chas. Camp, now owned by Horace Newton; next, William H Canfield. West end of Lane, west of Canfield's house, built by Elijah Addice, pulled down. Next, Phineas L. Squires. Next, house built by Col Samuel Camp; then Ozias Camp, now Phinehas Meigs. Next south of Doct. Goodrich, Widow Wilkinson and her son John, pulled down; new house built and occupied by William H. Harris, then Henry Williams, then Alfred Camp, now his heirs. Next, Alanson P. Brainard. Next, David W Robinson. Next, Parsonage. Next, David C Camp Next, Bela Davis Next, formerly James Hickox, now pulled down. Next, 1790, Daniel Dimock, then Anson Meigs, then Morris Stevens, now Samuel C. Camp Next south, formerly James Wadsworth the first Town Clerk after the Patent was issued, then James Wadsworth, Jr, then Gen James Wadsworth, then Wedworth Wadsworth, now James Wadsworth,—the oldest house in Durham. Next south, William Wadsworth, present Town Clerk, opposite, formerly John Noyes Wadsworth, and his three sons, John Noyes, William and James, then the said John Noyes Wadsworth. Jr., and his two sons, John and Wedworth, house pulled down, rebuilt by Wedworth Wadsworth, Jr., and consumed by fire. There was a house on New Haven road about fifty rods west of the above, owned by Southard, then Job Wheeler, now pulled down. Next south of Wadsworth's, formerly Kelsey, then Curtiss Parsons, now William Shelley. Next south on Madison Turnpike, Job Wheeler. Next, on old road, Henry Strong. Next, Phineas Robinson. Next, Henry E Norton. Opposite that, Jedediah Bemus, now pulled down. Next, formerly Daniel Hickox, then Daniel Hickox, Jr., now Almer Roberts. Next, east side, formerly Seward's, then Abraham Scranton, then Hamlet Hickox, then Capt. Charles Robinson, now Lyman C. Robinson. Next, Widow Phebe A. Robinson. Opposite, formerly Benjamin Gillum, pulled down, rebuilt, occupied by Elizabeth and Hannah Gillum; now Walter J. Chalker. Next south, George Atwell. Next, formerly Lieut Abraham Scranton, who went with Ethan Allen and the Connecticut troops and surprised Ticonderoga; and also in several battles in the Revolutionary war, fought Burgoyne three times, and was present when he surrendered and saw him deliver up his sword. Israel Scranton and family occupied the same house, removed to Michigan, the house pulled down, new one built by Curtis C. Camp, now owned by Widow A. M. Sizer. West of this, on Guilford Turnpike, house owned by Charles Keyser, and one by Henry E. Bailey. Next south, formerly Deac. Johnson, then Seth Tibbals, then Fairchild Camp. Next, Nathan Kelsey, now pulled down. Next, formerly Eliphaz Nettletown, pulled down, new house built by H. E. Nettleton. Next, Harvey Hubbard, then Smith Birdsey, then E. M. Hawley. On old road, first house, David Cone, now his widow and son Noyes. Opposite, Harvey Hull. Next formerly, house pulled down Next, Nathan Crane, then Hamlet Hickox, now Henry E Nettleton. Returning to the road leading to the South School House, where the house stands on the Rositer Lot, so called, near the Mill, was a house now pulled down, occupied by Caleb Seward, and where his first child was born, before he removed to the spot just north of George Atwell's On the hill east, formerly Jonas Bishop, then Jesse Atwell, now Bishop Atwell Next east, formerly Abraham Scranton, then Hamlet Scranton who removed to Rochester, New York, and built the first frame house on the site of that city. Next east, formerly Jabez Chalker, then Edmund Shelley, house pulled down, new house built by Charles Robinson, Jr. Next east, formerly Henry Hull's, pulled down Next south, Jabez Chalker, now Ozias Chalker. Next, Joseph Nettleton Next, Judson Francis, formerly Thomas Francis. Next, —— Fowler. Next, formerly Nathan Fowler. On the road east, formerly Jeremiah Nettleton, now Sherman J Nettleton Next, formerly Simeon Pratt, now Hubbard S Johnson and son, Charles B Johnson Next, formerly Sylvanus Hull, now Widow Levi Bailey. Returning on the east road, first Leonard Hull Next, formerly Eliakim Hull, dead. Next, Eliakim W. Hull, now Hinksman Roberts Next north, formerly Samuel Meeker, then James Mueket. Next, on east side, formerly Isaac Loveland, then Seth Tibbals, now Arnold Umbah. Next, formerly Titus Loveland Next east, formerly Titus Loveland, then Benjamin Chalker, now Widow Polly Chalker. Next west, formerly Crane, house burnt down, new one built by Ezra Loveland, now owned by Bela Davis, rented Opposite, formerly Joseph Hull, then Amos Smith, pulled down. Next west, new house built by Samuel C Nettleton Next north, formerly Simeon Scranton, pulled down Next west, in cross road, William

Wadsworth's, rented. Following road north and east, first house, formerly Eliakim Strong, then Lyman C. Camp, then Moses Stevens, now Albert Sanderson. Next east, formerly Chas. Thompson, now Ichabod Avery. Next, near Haddam line, formerly David Lynn, then Birdseye, then Ebenezer Clark, Jr., now John Hickey. Near south end of back road, east of Wadsworth's, formerly Widow Burrett, and Israel, Charles and William, house pulled down, another built by S. Johnson, then owned by Thomas S. Camp, then W. G. Chauncey, burnt down. Next north, formerly Charles White, now his widow, Hannah White. Next, formerly William Y. Bailey, then Harvey Robinson, then Anson Meigs and his son John Opposite, formerly, Widow Wells, and Jonathan, Rachel and Mahitabel, also occupied by Elihu Hinman, pulled down. Next north, east side, Russell Scranton, now his widow. Next, west side, formerly Zachara Hinman, also James Hinman, pulled down, new house built and formerly occupied by James Hickox, now by John Hickox. Next north in 1780, Jonathan Squire, in 1783 Husted Hinman, pulled down. Opposite, formerly James Clark, now his widow. Next north, formerly Asher Coe, now George W. Strong, from 1720 house owned and occupied by Rev. Nathaniel Chauncey, from 1756 by Col. Elihu Chauncey, house consumed by fire, new house built by Charles Chauncey. Next west, formerly David Squires and family on south side, now pulled down Next west, Widow Sutliff and her son Ebenezer, pulled down, north side, house built by Asahel Strong, now Asa Fowler, next W. C. Fowler, rented, next from 1755 Elnathan Chauncey and wife and Nathaniel, William, Catharine, Elihu, Elnathan, and Worthington Gallup, Town Clerk, now owned and occupied by W. C. Fowler. Next west on Main street, M. E. Church. Next, south F. J. Coe. Next, Dency Parsons. Next, George H. Davis and store. On the west side of the Green, Congregational Church. Next north, Academy and Centre School House Next north, formerly Stephen Spencer and family, pulled down. New house formerly owned and occupied by Rev. David Smith and now by his heirs. Next, from 1790 Gideon Chittenden, pulled down Next, on east side 1775, Jesse Cook, 1790 Thomas Cook, recently by Erastus Jones, now owned by W. C. Fowler, rented. Next north, 1760, Israel Godard, a Tory, property confiscated, bought of the State and rebuilt by Gen. James Wadsworth, now owned by W C. Fowler, occupied by Charles Fowler. On west side, Daniel Hall and family, then Israel Camp, then William S. Camp, now John S. Camp. Next north, formerly tannery, now a dwelling, sorgo mill and T J. Coe's store. East side, Mill. Next north, formerly Timothy Hall, wife and family, then Joel Blatchley, now his widow. East, Widow Hall and Asher Gillum, pulled down North, Ebenezer Guernsey and family, then Lemuel Guernsey and family, then Bridgman Guernsey, now owned by Eli Hubbard and Brother. Next north, formerly Benjamin Picket and family, pulled down. Next, formerly Lemuel Camp and family, now occupied by the family of Edward P. Camp dec'd, and by Sophronia Camp. Next north, formerly Robert Smithson, then Heth F. Camp, then Doct. Jared Kirtland, then Seth Strong, now Seth B. Cooper and family. Next, formerly Capt. Job Camp and family, then by Manoah Camp, house pulled down, new house built by F. Hubbard. Next, house built by Benjamin H. Coe, then owned by Samuel Parsons, Town Clerk, now by his widow. Next, Ambrose Field and family, then by Doct. Lyman Norton, then Harriet Butler. Next, formerly Jerry Shaddock, then James Robinson, then Charles Miller, now B. B. Beecher. Next, formerly Moses Austin, now Joseph P. Camp, next north on the north corner, formerly Elnathan Camp, then Dennis Camp, now owned by Simeon S. Scranton, rented. Next, Academy. Next, formerly Phineas Camp, then Col. Seth Seward, now John Hull. Next, Nancy Johnson. Next, formerly Samuel Fenn Parsons, then John White, now owned by Merriam Manufacturing Company. Next, Merriam Manufacturing Company's Factory. Next, H. M. Coe, new house. Next, formerly Job Merwin, then Mary Ann Bowers, now John Clark. Next, Timothy Parsons, then Giles Rose, pulled down, rebuilt and owned by R. H. Shelley. Next, formerly, Perez Sturtevant, now Oscar Leach. Next, William A. Parmelee, Town Clerk. Next, Alpheus W. Camp. Next, formerly Reuben Baldwin, now Alanson Nettleton. Next, north District School House, burnt down and rebuilt. Next, Elias Miller. Next, formerly, Abial Camp, then Jabez Bailey, now owned by Daniel Southmayd, rented. Next, formerly Daniel Johnson, now Daniel Coakley. West side Main street, north house, formerly William Butler, pulled down, rebuilt, then Quartus Smith, now his heirs. Next south, Samuel Wells, house pulled down. Next south, Abiel Coe, then John Swathel's Tavern, now John Turner. Next south, Boston Samuel Parsons, pulled down. Next south, formerly Noah Baldwin, house pulled down, rebuilt by James Parmelee, then owned by Farron & Parmelee, then Meigs Hand, then Henry W. Bailey, now S. N. Deming. Next, formerly, Phineas Squires, then James Rose, then Abner Newton, then Enos Rogers, now Simeon S. Scranton. Next, formerly Capt. Atwell, then Phineas Parmelee, now his widow. Next, L. M. Leach. Next, formerly James Bishop, dec'd. Next, house built by Elem L. Johnson, now owned by C. J. Haywood. Next, formerly Moffet, then Hall, now Mrs. Catlin, widow of Doct. Catlin, dec'd. Next, S. F. Leet. Next, formerly Parsonage, then Guernsey Bates, Phineas Squires, Parsons Coe, Warren Walkley, now L. L. Parsons. Next south, built by Doct Seth L Childs, then owned by Doct. Benjamin M Fowler, now Doct. R. W. Matthewson. Next, formerly, Jeremiah Butler, then Guernsey Bates, then L. W. Leach, now Clement M. Parsons, Next, built by Henry Tucker, then owned by Guernsey Bates, now Parsonage. Next, formerly Joseph P. Camp's store, now L. W. Leach's dwelling house. Next, Fairchild's house, pulled down. Next, L. W. Leach & Son's store. Next south, formerly Guernsey Bates, house pulled down, now North Congregational Church. Next south, formerly Sherman and Phineas Spellman, then Daniel Bates, now Parsons Coe. Next south, formerly Elizur Hall, now owned by Nathan H. Parsons and Perez Sturtevant. Next south, formerly T. W. Baldwin's store, now Asher Robinson. Next, formerly, Munson Strong, now Alexander Camp. Next, built by Henry Robinson, then occupied by Doct. Chauncey Andrews, and now owned by his heirs. Next, Episcopal Church. Next, Sophronia Camp, rented. Next, formerly the north, Asa Chamberlain's house, then Curtis Parson's, then L. C. Hickox, dec'd. Next, Asa Chamberlain's shop, now house, owned by Thomas C. Camp Next, formerly Robert Smithson, then Asa Chamberlain, now Erwin White, and T. J. Coe. Next south, formerly Charles White, in the south east corner of Grave Yard, now pulled down—north of new Grave Yard on Back Lane, house owned by John King, pulled down. Next north, south of Mill Brook, Moses Robinson, pulled down. Next north of Brook, formerly David Robinson, then Ebenezer Robinson 1783, then Ebenezer Robinson, Jr., now Charles Hickox. Next north, Andrew Robinson. Next, Doct. Ebenezer Guernsey, house pulled down. Next, formerly Lemuel Guernsey, now Parsons Coe, rented. Nearly opposite, James Hinman, dec'd. Next south, Elias Camp. Next, formerly Jehial Hull, pulled down. Next, south west of Grave Yard, Timothy Dunn, pulled down. On the corner north, the Quarry District School House. Next, on north west corner, house built by Joel Blatchley, now owned by Harrison Church. Next, east side, formerly William Lyman, then L. W. Leach, burnt down Next, Doct. R. W. Mathewson, rented. Next, formerly Israel Merwin, occupied by Jonathan Simons, negro, now pulled down. Next, formerly Hezekiah Talcott in 1783, pulled down, rebuilt by John Swathel, now H. N. Fowler. Next, on east side, Giles Rose, pulled down. Next, on west side, formerly Josiah Coe, then Abel Lyman, then James Lyman, then Alpheus Tibbals, now Elizur Camp. Next east, Asa Chamberlain, then Asher Coe, then Jesse Smith, then David S. Smith. Next north and west, formerly Abel Coe, then James Parmelee, Silver Smith, now Alvin P. Roberts. Opposite, house pulled down. Next, Aaron Parsons, then Marcus Parsons, now the estate of Thomas W. Lyman, dec'd. Next east, Michael Frain. Next, George Galpin, now, 1866, the oldest man in Durham. Next north, Simeon Parsons, Town Clerk, now Joseph Chedsey. Next north, formerly Thomas Lyman, 1st, then Thomas Lyman, 2d, house pulled down, new house built, occupied by Thomas Lyman and Henry Lyman, then Thomas W. and Frederick, now by Frederick Lyman. Next north, Noah Lyman, house pulled down. Next north, Joseph and Charles Parsons, on west side, pulled down They built on east side, pulled down and rebuilt and now owned by Jonathan Thayer. Next north, John W. Miller and son Charles. Next, Ithamer Parsons, pulled down. Opposite, Capt. Southmayd, pulled down. Next north, Charles Coe, then Parsons Coe, now Anson Squires. Commencing at Quarry School House, going west—first house near the bottom of the hill north side, formerly negro house, pulled down. Next west of crossway, Asher Robinson, house pulled down, rebuilt by Asher

Robinson, now owned by L. A. Stone. Opposite, Job Canfield, pulled down, rebuilt by Gaylord Newton. Next, south side, James Robinson, then Richard Robinson, then F. S. Field, now D. L. Davis. Next, Doct. Coles, then Stephen Robinson, then Noah Robinson, then Henry E. Robinson, now Alfred Jackson. Next, James Tibbals the 1st, then James the 2d, then David Tibbals, now pulled down. Next, Joseph Tibbals, and Ebenezer Tibbals, pulled down, rebuilt by Samuel Tibbals, and now occupied by Samuel G. Tibbals. Next, Nathaniel Clark, pulled down. Next, Chittenden house, pulled down. Next, Alfred Burr on east side, rented. In same lot farther south, formerly Seth Strong, pulled down. On north side, Noah Norton, pulled down, rebuilt by Sylvester Ward, now Thomas Clingan. Opposite, Chauncey Burr, burnt down, then rebuilt, now Jerome Shelley. Next, Alfred Burr. Next west, Joseph Morse. Next, Dinah Freeman, negro. Next, formerly Dea. Ozias Norton, then Samuel Tibbals, pulled down, rebuilt by Charles Cypherman. Next, Samuel Reed, then Thomas Smith, negro, pulled down. Next on north side, Reuben Brown, pulled down. South side, built by Joseph Mattoon, then owned by Alanson Nettleton, now John Assman. Next, David P. Reed. Next, John C. Reed, pulled down. Next north, Salmon Reed. On new road, house built by Richard Hotchkiss, then owned by New York and Boston Railroad Company, now Jeremiah Kenedy. East on old saw mill road, formerly Bartholomew Bailey, now David Tibbals, rented. Following round easterly and south, formerly Timothy Dunn, then Daniel Bates, pulled down. Thence south, first house south of the old Seth Strong place,—Medad Norton, pulled down. Next on east side, Lewis Norton, removed to the west, pulled down. Next west side, Stephen Norton, pulled down. Next, Daniel Hall, then Joseph Tuttle, 1st, then Joseph Tuttle, 2d, now Stephen Bailey On swamp lane road east, Blatchley house, pulled down. House south of Tuttles (Sabaday house drawn from the Green) pulled down. Next south, formerly Levi Parmelee, then Dea. Timothy Stone, then Dea. Dan Parmelee, than Alfred Camp, now Widow Thomas Miller. East on south side, Asher Canfield, then owned by Timothy Coe, pulled down. Next east, Levi Parmelee, then Dea. Timothy Stone, then Dea. W. P. Stone, house pulled down and rebuilt, now occupied by

Senaca Barnes. South over the bridge, formerly James Wright, then James Wheton, owned by Timothy Coe, then Isaac Parmelee, then Samuel G. Stevens, now Newel E Nettleton. Next east of Barnes, north side, formerly Selden Hall, now Henry Williams. Next east, Dea Isaac Parmelee. Next, Timothy D. Camp—first house west of Widow Thomas Miller, formerly Joel Parmelee, then Horace Parmelee, now Frederick Parmelee Next, west side School House. Next, Josiah Fowler, then Caleb Fowler, then Reuben Fowler, burnt down, rebuilt—then owned by Ezra Camp, then Colonel Osias Camp, then Abram Camp, now John K. Burr. South, was a House owned by Graves, pulled down—west, Elah Camp, now Eli S. Camp. Next, formerly Ezra Camp, pulled down, rebuilt and occupied by Ozias and Lyman Camp, then Elijah Coe, now J. B. Bailey. Next, on the mountain road was a house occupied by Thomas Smith, Negro, pulled down. Next south of Bailey's formerly Jefferson Ives, now Augustus Seward. Next, formerly Elias Camp, rebuilt by Elias and John S. Camp, now Joel Austin. Next west, formerly Joseph Camp, then David Graves, then Caleb Ives, then Joel Ives, now Heber G. Ives. Next south, Thaddeus Camp, now Dana Coe's widow. Next, William Strong, removed to New Connecticut, then James Potter, then Albert Munson, then Isaac Page, now Henry Page. Next, Joseph Bartholemew, pulled down. Next, Ransom Doolittle, uow Levi Allen. Next, formerly Brister, Negro, now James Brainard. Next, Joel Austin, rented. Next, at north end of Pistapaug Pond, formerly Enos Austin, then Captain Joel Curtis, then Daniel Thompson, house burnt down, rebuilt by Obediah Smith, house blew down. House on Howd road, owned by Stephen Mix. Going east on New Haven Turnpike,—south-west District School House, first house South, Abram Coe, then Merrick R. Coe. Next, Buel Strong, pulled down. Next, Abram Coe, now his daughter, Widow Peck. Next, Leman Bartholemew, now Lucius Foot. Next William A. Hart. On old road, just south of the line in Guilford, near the Lime Kiln, was a house owned and occupied by Timothy Elliott, Sen.,—his children were Timothy Elliot, Jr., William R. Elliott, both born in this house, also Willis Elliott and Henry Elliott, all deceased. Next north, Samuel Hart, Sen , pulled down, rebuilt by Samuel Hart, Jr Next north, Daniel Hart, now Henry Maltby. Next, John Hart, now Catharine Hart. Next, Samuel Coe; house pulled down. Next Timothy Coe, pulled down, rebuilt by William C. Coe. Next east, Eliphaz Parmelee, rebuilt by Eli Parmelee, pulled down and rebuilt by F T. Elliott. On Pent road south, David Pardee, house drawn to Guilford. North of F. T. Elliott, formerly Timothy Stow, pulled down. Next, formerly Jerry Norton, then Joseph Andrus, pulled down, rebuilt by Sherman Camp Next, formerly Nathan Ozias Camp, now Nathan S. Camp. East on old highway, Thomas Spencer, pulled down. North of N. S. Camp, School House, burnt down. Next, Thomas, Log House pulled down. Next north, formerly Harvey Seward, pulled down. North of School House on Turnpike, formerly Enos S. Camp, now his widow. Next north, Medad Hocum, then Orin Bartholemew, then Elah Camp, 2d, removed to Meriden, then William H. Maltby, now Simeon S Camp. Next north, formerly Union District School House, pulled down. Next, Timothy Elliott, now Luserne Elliott. Next, formerly Deacon Seth Seward, then Deacon Dan Parmelee and his son Dan Parmelee, Jr., then Samuel Birdseye, moved to Middlefield, then Augustus Howd, now Samuel G. Stevens. Next, formerly Noah Parmelee, removed to Guilford, house pulled down, rebuilt by Enoch F. Camp. Next, Selden Stevens, now Eleazur Bailey. On the Saw-Mill road, formerly Timothy Coe, then Abram Camp, now F. S. Smith. Next north, Ransom Prout. ·On old road west of Meeting-house hill, Samuel Bartlett, moved away. On the road south of Wilkinson Hill was Doctor Cole's house and four others, all pulled down, the occupants moved to the Black River country.

Now beginning at the North School House, first house east, formerly Jesse Austin, then James Bates, then Captain Dan Southmayd, now his son Daniel North, Daniel Smith, house pulled down. East, Miles Merwin, Sen. Next east, formerly Samuel Fairchild, then Abial Baldwin, then Aaron Baldwin, now Miles Merwin, Jr. Next, on south side, Henry S. Merwin, Next, Bridgman Guernsey, house pulled down, rebuilt by Elisha Southmayd, now Huntington Southmayd. Next, Oliver Coe, Sen., then Oliver Coe, Jr, then Oliver and William Coe.

Next east, William Bishop, pulled down. Next, David Brooks, then Joseph Southmayd, now John Southmayd's barn. Next, Edmund Fairchild, pulled down, rebuilt by Huntington Southmayd, now John Southmayd. Next, Samuel Bates, then John Coe, now William Coe. Opposite, James Bates, then Daniel Bates, then Isaac Newton, removed to Lenox, Mass., then Joseph Southmayd, then William Southmayd, house pulled down and new one built, now occupied by Samuel B. Southmayd. Next east, Burwell Newton, Sen., pulled down, new house built by Roger and Elisha Newton, now occupied by Elisha and his son, Israel C Newton. Next east, south side, Curtiss Bates, then Abner Newton, now Roger W. Newton. Nearly opposite, new house, John B. Newton. Next east, formerly John Newton, removed to Greenfield, Mass., one of the first settlers in that town, then Daniel Southmayd, Sen., then Abner Newton 2d, now a resident of Union Centre, N. Y., then Elisha Newton, then Dea. Samuel Newton, house rebuilt by Deacon Samuel Newton, now occupied by his widow and daughter. Next east, Daniel Smith, then Guernsey, pulled down. Next, on the hill, formerly, Thomas Stevens, then Burwell Newton, Jun , now deceased. Next, Picket, then James Picket, then Deacon William Foot, then James P. Foot, now Edwin Priest. Opposite, formerly Samuel Squires, then Deacon William Foot, now Admiral Clark Next east, house owned by Walkley, now pulled down. Next north, near Middletown line, formerly Oliver Clark, then Hezekiah Clark, known *as the specie* Counterfeit Money Factory. Now going south on south road towards Durham, first house, John Camp, then Thomas C Camp, now Henry Parsons. Next, south-east of Saw-Mill Brook, M. T. Merwin, rented. Next east, formerly Leander White, now Talcott Parsons. Next, house built by Guernsey Camp, then owned by Asahel Harvey, now Seth R. Parsons. Next south, formerly Selden Stevens, then owned by Elizur Goodrich, rented, now Richard Payne. Next house, west of Saw-Mill Brook, Theodore Blim. Next, Leander White. Next, formerly Joseph Smith, then Joseph Smith, Jr., then Ichabod Avery, now owned by Henry Tucker, rented. Next, on north side, formerly Rejoice Camp, and his brother Hezekiah, then Anson Squires, then Henry Tucker, pulled down and new house built. Next west, on south side, new house,

Miles T. Merwin. Next west, formerly Isaac Baldwin, then Jehiel Hull, then Russell Scranton, now owned by Henry Tucker, rented. Next north, in Brick lane, Abijah Curtiss and son, Samuel Curtiss, then Seymour White, then Noah Merwin, now his widow. Opposite, west side, formerly John White, now Sophronia Camp, rented. On the corner, south end of Brick Lane was a distillery on west corner, and tannery on the east corner, both pulled down. Next west, first house on south side, James Curtiss, then James Picket, now William H. Walkley. Opposite, John Curtiss, then Benjamin H Coe, then Doctor W. R. Griswold, a Surgeon in the army in the last war, removed to Easton, house now owned by Henry H. Newton. Next west, south side, the heirs of John Johnson, deceased. He was the maker of nearly all the free stone grave stones, in the Old Grave Yard. The stones were quarried in Durham.

PLACES TO WHICH THE EMIGRANTS WENT.

As early as 1737, Ebenezer Lyman went to Torrington, followed by Jonathan Coe. About 1750 a number of families emigrated to Granville, Massachusetts. Emigrants also went to Hartland, Connecticut. About 1786, others went to West Stockbridge and Richmond, Massachusetts. In 1788 several families emigrated to Durham, New York, and others since 1800. About 1790, the Wadsworths, went to Geneseo, New York. In 1796, several went to Whitestown, Oneida County, New York, among whom were Henry Crane, Camp Parmelee, Kirtland Griffin, Abraham Camp The Pickets and others, went to Greenfield, Massachusetts. Some, as early as 1761. June 12, 1812, Deacon Ozias Norton and his son Leveret went to Carleston, Ohio; and Jerry Norton to Atwater. Later than this, Lewis Norton, Ozias Camp, Samuel Johnson, Ichabod Curtis, and others settled in Ashtabula County, Ohio. Samuel Curtis settled in Medina, in the same State, and became a deacon there. Elah Camp went to Meriden, Thomas Spencer Camp removed to Michigan, and Ozias Camp to the city of New York, and others elsewhere.

Besides these, many enterprising and intelligent men of business, have at different times left Durham, to find a home elsewhere, who have adhered to the principles and habits which they formed here in early life. There was Noah Talcott, the son of David, the son of Hezekiah, who went to New York, and who is mentioned in the book entitled "The Old Merchants of New York," as having been extensively engaged in business as a large cotton broker and merchant. There was Reuben Rose Fowler, who was first a successful merchant in New Haven, and in Newbern, North Carolina, and then engaged in land operations, in New York, Pennsylvania, Vermont, and Upper Canada. There was Samuel Parsons, who, after being a successful merchant in New York, returned to Durham to spend his last years. In addition to these might be mentioned Henry Lyman, Charles A. Fowler, Parsons Rose, William S. Camp, Abner Newton, and men bearing the name of Strong and of Parsons, who have done a successful business in the south.

Moses Austin, and Moses Bates, who married the sister of Mr. Austin, left Durham near the close of the last century, and went to the lead mines of Virginia, near Louisburg, if I read the letter right. I have before me an original letter from Moses Bates to the wife of Captain John Johnson of Durham, in which he describes the journey of Mr. Austin and himself from Louisburg, down the Great Kenhawa, two hundred miles, then down the Ohio and up the Mississippi to St. Geneveive in New Spain, as it was then called. They left their residence in Virginia on the 6th of June, 1798, and arrived at St. Genevieve on the 8th of September, being just three months on their journey. Mr. Bates was called to suffer the loss of his wife, which Dr. Aaron Elliott, formerly of Killingworth, describes in an interesting and affecting manner, he himself having married her sister.

Mr. Bates was successful in obtaining of the Spanish Government a thousand acres of land, only for the expense of surveying it, for which he paid twelve dollars. He and his family seem to have prospered greatly in this wild region of country.

After the death of his wife, he married a daughter of Rev. Ichabod Camp, a native of Durham, mentioned on a previous page. He married her some years after the death of her father. She, too, he was called to lose. Her death was a triumphant one. Not long before it occurred, she often said, "Death hath lost its sting, and the grave its victory." A few minutes before she died, she said, "I am going to Jesus my Redeemer; I shall soon be in the paradise of my God; come Jesus, come quickly. There is now no doubt. I know that my Redeemer liveth. Farewell world, farewell terrestrial things;" and in a few minutes expired. "These dying declarations," remarked Mr. Bates, in his letter, communicating the intelligence of her death, "in addition to the course of life invariably pursued by her for many years, afford incontrovertible evidence of the power and reality of the religion of Jesus, and that her soul winged its way to the sublime regions of eternal felicity." Mr. Bates and his wife seem to have carried with them or inherited the religion which sustained them in their trials in that distant region.

The history of Mr. Austin is more remarkable. He obtained a grant of a league square, about sixty miles south of St. Louis, in the lead region, engaged in mining operations, laid out the city of Potosi, the present capital of Washington County. He was at one time considered wealthy, but in the general wreck of prosperity in 1819–20 he lost all his property. His attention then was turned to Texas whither he went and obtained a large grant of land from the Mexican Government, in order to establish a colony on it. He returned to Missouri in 1821 or 2 for the purpose of removing his family to Texas, when he was taken sick and died in May, 1822. Stephen F. Austin went to Texas and took possession of the grant made to his father, led on a colony to the river Brazos, and laid out and commenced the town of Austin, which was afterwards the seat of Government in Texas, and obtained the patronage of the Mexican Government. Iturbide, in 1822, and Victoria, in 1824, passed laws to encourage emigration, made generous donations of land, and granted exemption from taxes for ten years, and allowed immigrants' property to the amount of two thousand dollars to be admitted free of duty. In 1832, Stephen F. Austin also carried a petition to Mexico for a separate Government, and after waiting several months wrote back to his constituents and recommended the formation of a separate Government without waiting for the action of Congress; for which he was cruelly imprisoned, and did not reach home for upwards of two years.

When he returned he was appointed Commander-in-Chief of the Army, and was for a period at the head of affairs. He died in 1835. His sister, Emily M., the wife of Mr. James F. Perry, lives near Brazoria, owning as her brother's heir, a large amount of land. Mr. Moses Austin was regarded as a worthy man of great enterprise and talent. Had it not been for this enterprise and talent, the large grant of land would not have been obtained from the Mexican Government, the colony would not have been established on the Brazos, and the independence of the province would not have been obtained. *It is owing to the enterprise and talent of Moses Austin and his son, Stephen F. Austin, that Texas now is an integral part of the United States* It has been stated that the place of Moses Austin in Texas was called Durham Hall in memory of his native town. Some of the facts mentioned above are from a letter dated St. Louis, Dec. 27, 1845, to one of the connections of Mr. Austin, still residing in Durham, and written by Charles D. Drake, a lawyer in St. Louis, who married a daughter of James Austin, who went from Durham to reside with his kinsman, Moses Austin, first in Virginia, and then in Missouri.

MR. DRAKE'S LETTER.

"St. Louis, Dec. 27th, 1845.

Mr. Enos S. Camp, Durham, Ct.

Dear Sir:

I will very briefly explain to you, why I, who am a stranger to you, address this letter to you. My wife, a native of this State, while it was the Territory of Louisiana, born in 1812, is the daughter of James Austin, who was a native of Connecticut, and removed from Virginia to the Territory of Louisiana, about the year 1804, and died in this State, Oct., 1823. She learned from her father, that he left four sisters and one brother, (then follows James' connections, uninteresting)—he then observes, "I will briefly give you the history of the Austin family in this region.

"Moses Austin of Durham, Ct., emigrated thence to Virginia, and thence in 1796 to Upper Louisiana, then under the Spanish Government; he was cousin to my wife's father. Obtaining a grant of land from the Government of a league square, about sixty miles south of this city in the lead region, he engaged in mining operations, and laid off the township of Potosi, the present capital of Washington County. He was a very enterprising man, and was at one time considered wealthy, but in the general wreck of prosperity in 1819–20 he lost all his property. His attention was attracted to Texas, whither he went and obtained a large grant of land from the Mexican Government. He returned to this State in 1821 or 2 for the purpose of removing his family to Texas, when he was taken sick and died, leaving two children—Stephen I., who went to Texas and took possession of the grant to his father and died there about the year 1835—and Emily M., who now is the wife of Mr. James F. Perry, and who lives near Brazoria, Texas, owning as her brother's heir a very large amount of land."

(Then follows a long list of James Austin's family, uninteresting. The letter established the fact that Moses Austin went from Durham—and history established the fact, that Austin was the pioneer of Texas, and had Austin remained at Durham, Texas would have remained a part of Mexico, and Taylor and Scott would have remained in their towns.)

The letter is signed,

CHARLES D. DRAKE.

REV. MR. WILLISTON'S LETTER.

DURHAM, NEW YORK, 26th Jan., 1848.

Dear Sir:

My father being absent, and not having with him the necessary *materiel* (a-la-the French) for answering your letter, I have hunted up, and will now communicate the desired information myself. I will adopt the *tabular* form, as being the best both for you and me. Here is what I have been able to gather.

EMIGRANTS FROM DURHAM, CONN TO DURHAM, NEW YORK.	No of Children.	No Hopefully Pious.	No. Ed'ted at Colleges	Do. & that became Ministers	Min't is but not col Ed
Dea. Jonathan Baldwin,	6	6		1	
Eliab Baldwin,	8	8		1	
Curtis Baldwin,	8	8	1		
Dea. David Baldwin,	0				
Aaron Baldwin,	6 or 7	1 (or more)			
Seth Baldwin,	12	7 (or 8)		1	
Mrs. Eunice (Baldwin) Strong,	8	4		1	
Mrs. Mehitabel (Baldwin) Torrey,	8	4 (or 5)			
Mrs. Ruth (Baldwin) Chittenden,	8	8		1	
Dea. Noah Baldwin,	10	6			
James Baldwin,	5	4			
Mrs —— (Baldwin) Hays,	11	8 (or 9)			
Mrs (B'n) Post, and Mrs. (Bates) Bushnell					
John Hull,	5	5			
Silas Hull,					
Stephen Tibbals,	8	5			
Ebenezer Tibbals,					
Walter Field and Cyrus Field,	8	0			
Daniel Coe,	6	6			
Daniel Merwin,	6	6			3
David Merwin,	8	8			
Phinehas Canfield,	6 or 7	1 (or 2)			
William Hinman,	5 or 6	2			
Mrs Eunice (Merwin) Cooley,	7	5			
Mrs. —— (Merwin) Smith,	7	7			
Mrs. —— (Merwin) Smith,	7	7			
Mrs. —— (Merwin) Lamphier,	7	2			
Mrs. —— (Merwin) Jewell,	2	0			

Mrs. John Hull and Mrs. Stephen Tibbals, who were sisters of Noah and Jas Baldwin.

Of the 30 emigrants whose names are in the table, all but 3, I believe, were professors. Those 3 were Ebe'r Tibballs, Phin's Canfield and Wm Hinman. The most, if not all, of the pious 27, became so, it is believed, *after* removing to this place. Some 3 or 4 of them remained here but a few years; and much is not known of them now. In addition to the 5 college educated ministers, add, if you please, the Rev. Orlando Kirtland, of Morristown, N. J., who is a *grandson* of Daniel Coe. Of the 5 down in my table, one (the Rev. Elihu W. Baldwin, D. D.) became the president of a College,—Wabash College, Indiana. Another of the 5 is now a missionary at the Sandwich Islands,—Rev. Dwight Baldwin.

I can learn little of the *history* of Rev. Sam. Merwin. He was brought up here, a son of Dan'l Merwin; who, as the table shows, had two other sons become Methodist preachers, though not so noted ones as Samuel.

I have carried the tabular information no further than to the first generation after the Durham emigrants. If extended to the *grand* children, it would serve still further to confirm and illustrate that great *principle* of God's word—that God causes *piety* in progenitors to descend to their posterity like an inheritance. "Choose life, that both thou *and thy seed* may live." "I'll be a God to thee *and to thy seed after thee.*" "Visiting the iniquities of the fathers upon the children."

Yours, dear sir, in Christian and Ministerial bonds,
TIMOTHY WILLISTON.

REV. MR. MERWIN'S LETTER.

HEMPSTEAD, L. I., Nov. 21st.

Mr. Fowler,

Dear Sir: My brother has sent to me your letter addressed to Dr. Childs, as he had not the dates you requested. Dr. Sprague's Biography of Methodist Preachers would furnish, probably, all the information you desire.

I will copy from a biographical sketch that I have, what may furnish the material you want.

Rev. Samuel Merwin was born in Durham, Conn., Sept. 13th, 1777. His ancestry who came from North of Wales, to this country, settled in Milford, Conn. One branch of the family soon afterwards went to New Milford. His great-grandfather, Daniel Merwin, moved to Durham, Conn. Here his grandfather, Miles Merwin, was born and buried. His own father, Daniel Merwin, was born here, and married the sister of the late Thomas Lyman of Durham. When the subject of this sketch was seven years old, on November 4th, 1784, his father with five other families, moved into the State of New York and formed a town settlement, which in honor of their nativity, they called New Durham.

In his boyhood his soul fired with a laudable ambition for an honorable distinction in society. With such advantages as he could command he gave himself studiously to the acquisition of knowledge.

In his 18th year he was teacher of the District School where many of the scholars were older than himself, two of them his brothers.

In his 20th year he became a decided Christian. His conversion was clear, his feelings ardent. He was gifted with the highest qualities of an orator, in appearance, voice, manner, skill in commanding words and swaying the passions at will.

Thrust out by the voice of the Church and his own convictions, he commenced his labors as a preacher of the gospel in the M. E. Church. In 1803 he was ordained Elder, and appointed Missionary to Quebec and Montreal.

Subsequently his appointments were to the most important places in the Church, either as Presiding Elder over large districts, or stationed in our principal cities, Boston, Providence, New York, Albany, Philadelphia, Baltimore.

In 1807 he married Mrs. Sarah Janes, widow of Rev. Peter Janes, daughter of Nehemiah Clark of Salisbury, a woman of rare excellence, possessed of a beauty of person which is scarcely the gift of an age; a mind richly endowed and a most devoted Christian. They had five sons and two daughters. All but the oldest son are still living. He closed his life and labors in Rhinebeck, after a few weeks illness, on Sunday, January 13th, 1839. His remains sleep in Greenwood Cemetery.

In person he was full six feet in height and of portly proportions His voice was clear, musical and of great volume, which was perfectly at his command. His manner was in such suitability it always seemed in wondrous grace. His graphic and scenic powers were such that many are the incidents of astonishing effect upon large and cultured audiences that are narrated of him.

His Catholic and philanthropic spirit associated him with the various benevolent and religious institutions of the day. He was selected and often occupied the platform of the Bible, Seaman's Friend, Colonization and Missionary Anniversaries. He was capable as an executive officer, as he was able and gifted as an orator. So if there was any special difficulty of administration he was appointed to undertake it. This was the reason sometimes of his removal to distant cities.

There is one fact in reference to the Merwin family which I

believe is still true, that in each branch there has been a Minister of the Gospel.

I hope these items will afford you sufficient material for your purpose.

Yours truly,

J. B. MERWIN.

REV. DR. COOLEY'S LETTER.

GRANVILLE, January 17th, 1848.

Rev. and Dear Sir:

In the early settlement of this town, the emigrants from Durham aided much to give it a good name which it has not lost even to this day. The Church was strengthened by the following additions by letter:

Ezra Baldwin, Jun., 1764.
Lydia, wife of Stephen Hitchcock, 1757
Isaac and Susanna Bartlett, 1758.
David and Rebekah Parsons, 1760.
Wife of Roswell Graves.
Mary, wife of Benjamin Barnes, 1763.
Thomas Spelman and wife, 1756.
John Bates, 1757.

Names of emigrants from Durham to Granville:

Ezra Baldwin,
Ebenezer Baldwin,
Amos Baldwin,
John Bates,
John Bates, Jun.,
Jacob Bates,
Nathaniel Bates,
David Bates,
Noah Robinson,
Dan Robinson,
Phinehas Robins,
Timothy Robinson,
David Curtis,
Aaron Curtis,
Ebenezer Curtis,
Samuel Coe,
Aaron Coe,
Enoch Coe,
John Seward, (doubtful,)
Stephen Hitchcock,
Isaac Bartlett,
David Parsons,
Roswell Graves,
Benjamin Parsons.

Among their descendants are the following educated men: Elijah Bates, Esq., son of Nathaniel; Hon. W. G. Bates, son of Elijah; Isaac C. Bates, son of Col. Jacob Bates; Charles F. Bates, Attorney, son of Nathaniel; and Edward B. Gillet, a distinguished attorney in Westfield, grandson of Col. Jacob Bates;

28

David B. Curtis, died in the army in 1813; Rev. John Seward, son of John Seward; Rev. Harvey Coe, grandson of Samuel Coe; Rev. David L. Coe, grandson of Samuel Coe; Gurdon S. Stebbins, grandson of John Bates; Rev. Truman Baldwin, son of Amos B.; Rev. Benson Baldwin, grandson of Amos; Rev. Charles F. Robinson, who died at St. Charles, at the confluence of the Missouri and Mississippi.

In addition to educated men I may add: Hon. *Anson V. Parsons*, self educated, grandson of David Parsons, now Chief Justice in Pennsylvania. The emigrants from Durham, *generally* were strong men. The above facts and statistics speak their commendation.

Col. Jacob Bates was a Lieutenant in the army, and crossed the Delaware on Christmas Eve, in the celebrated attack on Princeton.

Col. *Timothy Robinson* was Justice of the Peace, Representative, Deacon in the Church, and for years a Father of the Town. He possessed native talents equal to any in his day. He was truly a *great* and *good man.* In the time of Shay's Rebellion, he and a company of the "Court Party," on their way to Springfield, were met by a party of the mob, and after a skirmish near the great rock in Granville, were taken prisoners. The Colonel, as being the most obnoxious, was confined under a strong guard. Next day was Sabbath, and he read and prayed with them, and discoursed on State affairs, setting forth the moral wrong of resisting law by arms, especially when the people have all the power at the ballot box, of redressing their wrongs, by changing their rulers. They listened to their prisoner, for *he* wept and *they* wept. The result was, the guard became *politically converted*, and the next day he and his guard proceeded to Springfield in the cause of "*law and order.*"

ANOTHER FACT.—He was the father of a brilliant family, all but one being daughters. A favorite daughter was connected with a clergyman in Vermont. Having taken leave and gone to her new home, scarcely had she laid aside her bridal dress, when news flew back, as if the winds had given it speed, that their daughter had died suddenly, and *that by poison from her own hand.* The mother and the daughters shrieked and cried aloud for grief and agony. The father entered the room, at the moment, and with sternness of rebuke characteristic of great minds, stamped upon the floor and hushed the tumult; and then sitting down, with great parental kindness, commenced a train of remarks, to soothe the anguish of broken hearts, and to vindicate the sovereignty, goodness and tender mercy of God. The effect was most happy.

You know the character and standing of Senator I. C. Bates. Perhaps I have given you nothing to your purpose.

I remain very truly,

Your Friend and Brother in the Lord Jesus,

TIMOTHY M. COOLEY.

Rev. W. C. Fowler.

PRINCIPLES OF THE EMIGRANTS.

We have seen, in a previous chapter, what were the characteristics and principles of the people of Durham. In this we have seen that when they sought habitations elsewhere they carried with them their principles. They carried them to their new homes in Hartland and Torringford in Connecticut, among the hills of Berkshire and old Hampshire in Massachusetts. They carried them beyond the Catskill Mountains to New Durham, to Oneida County, to the Genesee River, in the State of New-York; and into New Connecticut in Ohio. They carried the same attachment to the institutions of law and order, to education and family government, the same public spirit and habits of reflection, into the camp and the halls of legislation, to the work-shop and the farm, to the bench, the bar, and the pulpit. Those same principles carried from Durham and transmitted from father to son live still in the hearts of their descendants.

If we follow the emigrants, we shall find the same love of education transmitted to their children. In proof of this, I would cite the family of Daniel Lyman of Newport and afterwards of Providence, and the family of James Wadsworth of Genessco, whose son General James S. Wadsworth, fell in the late war at the battle of the Wilderness. John W. Wadsworth, the son of John Wadsworth of Monroe, Michigan, and Maria (Chedsey) Wadsworth, graduated at Princeton, in 1857. Charles Chauncey, the son of Judge Chauncey of New Haven, graduated in Yale College, 1792, and his son Charles graduated there in 1828.

Elihu Chauncey, another son of Judge Chauncey, graduated there in 1796; and Nathaniel, another son, graduated there in 1806; and his two sons are recent graduates of Harvard College. Henry Chauncey, a graduate of Harvard College, is a descendant of Nathaniel Chauncey, who removed from Durham to Middletown. William C. Fowler, the present writer, son of Reuben Rose Fowler, and Catharine (Chauncey) Fowler, is a graduate of Yale College. His two sons Charles C. Fowler and William W. Fowler, graduated at Amherst College. Chauncey M. Hand and Charles F. Hand, sons of Catharine (Fowler) Hand, graduated the one at Yale and the other at Williams College. Chauncey A. Goodrich, son of Elizur Goodrich of New Haven, graduated at New Haven where he was a distinguished Professor. His two sons, Chauncey and William, are graduates of Yale, and a son of the former, Edward, is now a member of Yale College. Elizur Goodrich of Hartford, son of Elizur of New Haven, is a graduate of Williams. Henry Ellsworth, grandson of Elizur Goodrich of New Haven, was a graduate of Yale. Rev. Charles A. Goodrich the son of Rev. Samuel, graduated at Yale College in 1812. Samuel G. Goodrich was the celebrated Peter Parley, whose son Francis B. Goodrich, the author of the "Court of Napoleon," is a graduate of Harvard College. Rev. Noah Coe, son of Charles, who was the son of Abel, who was a son of Joseph and a descendant of Robert Coe, the magistrate, has two sons who are graduates of Yale, Frederick A. Coe and Samuel G. Coe. Samuel G. Whittlesey, grandson of Rev. Samuel Goodrich, was a graduate of Yale College, and a Missionary; and his son Samuel has recently graduated at the same college. Henry Lyle, the son of Simeon Smith, has lately received a medical degree in New York. Besides these should be mentioned Joseph Hull, author of a Spelling Book, and David N. Camp, the distinguished Principal of the Normal School of Connecticut.

DEED OF CAWGINCHAUG FROM TARRAMUGGUS, &C.

This writting made the twenty-fowerth of January, 1672, Between Tarramugus, Wesumpsha, Wannoe, Mackize, Sachamas mother, Tom alias Negannoc, Neshcheag squa, Taccumhuit, Wamphunch, Puccacun, spunno, Sarah Kembosh squa, Marragans mother and Tabhows squa of the one part, and Mr Sam'll Willys, Capt John Talcott, Mr. James Richards and Mr. John Allyn of the other part, witnesseth that the sayd Tarramugus, Weshumpsa, Wannoe Mackize, Sachamas mother, Tom Mesehegens, Squa Tacumhuit, Wamphunck Puccacun spunno Sarah Marragans mother, and Tabhow's Squae for themselves and in behalfe of the rest of the proprietors of Cawginchaug, and the lands adjoining, for a valuable consideration to them in hand, payd by the sd Mr. Sam'll Wyllys, Capt. John Talcott, Mr. James Richards and John Allyn, haue giuen, granted, Bargained and sold, and by these presents doe fully deed & absolutely giue, grant, bargain, sell, enfeoffe & confirm unto the sayd Mr. Sam'll Wyllys, Capt. John Talcott, Mr. James Richards and John Allyn, their heirs & assignes, one Tract of land comonly known by the name of Cawginchaug, a butting on midle Town bownds north, Haddam Bownds east, and to runne towards the west Two miles at least or so farre as may take in all those lands granted by the Generall Court of Conecticutt, to the afoarsayd Gent'n, and on the South on Guilford bounds together with all the Timber, Trees, brush, Rivers, waters, stones, mines or mineralls, being in the afoarsayd Tract of land, to have & to hold the afoarsd Tract of land as it is bownded with all the profitts comodities & appurtenances whatsoever, belonging thereto, unto the afoarsayd Gen'n, their heirs & assigns, & to the onely proper use & behoofe of the sayd Mr. Sam'll Willys, Capt. John Tallcott and John Allyn, theire heirs and assignes forever, and the sayd Tarramugus, Wesumpsha, & the first aboue mentioned Natiues for themselues & in behalfe of the rest, doe couenant & with the sd Mr. Willys, Capt. Talcott, Mr. Richards & John Allyn, that they onely haue full power & Good right & lawfull Authority to grant, Bargain & sell the aforesad Tract of land with its appurtenances, unto the sayd Mr. Willys, Capt. John Talcott, Mr. James Richards & John Allyn, their heirs & assignes for euer, & that they the sayd Gentm, there heirs & assignes, shall and may by force & vertue of these presents from time to time, & at all times for euer hereafter, lawfully, peaceably & quietly, haue, hold, use, occupy, possess, & enjoy the aforesd Tract of land with all its rights, members, & appurtenances, & haue receiue & take the rents, Issues and proffits thereof to their own proper use and behoofe for euer with out any lawfull lett, suit, trouble, or dissturbance whatsoeuer, from the said Tarramugus, Wesumpsha, wannoe Machize, Sachamas mother, Tom allas Negannoe, nesehegen Squa, Taccumhuit wamphanch, Puccacun Spunno, Sarah Kemhosh squa, Marragons mother and Tabhows squa, their heirs or assignes, or of any other person or persons claymeing right by from or under them or any of them or by their means, act, consent, priuity or procurement, & that free & clear & freely & clearly acquitted, exonerated & discharged or otherwise, well and sufficiently saued and kept Harmless by the sayd Tarramugus, Wesumpsha, Wannoe, Machize, &c., their heirs, executors or Administrators of & from all former & other grants, gifts, bargains, titles, troubles, demands and incumbrances whatsoeuer, had made' committed, Suffered or done by the afoaresayd Tarramugus, Wesumpsha, Wannoe, Machize, Sachamas mother, Tom alias Negannoe, neschey squa, Taccumhuit, namphanch, puccacuw, spunnoe, sarah Kembosh squa, marraguns mother, and Talhows squa, in witness whereof of the afoarementioned natives have signed, sealed & deliuered this writing, the day & yeare first above written with their own hands.

Sighned and delivered
in presence of
Joseph Nash,
Georg Groue,

Sepannamoe her marke.

Neshegen his marke.

Thomas Edwards.

Neganno his marke and seale.

Neschegens squa her marke and seale.

Taccumhuits marke and seale.

wamphanch his marke and seale.

puccacun his marke and seale.

Spunnoes his marke and seale.

Marragans mother her marke and seale.

Tarramuggus his marke and seale.

wesumpsha his marke and seale.

Wannoe his marke and seale.

machize his marke and seale.

Sachamas mother her marke and seale.

Tubhous squa her marke and seale.

Sarah her marke and seale.

Alice being lame and not able at the writing hereof to be present, and haveing received a coate towards the purchass of cawginchauge, I, under written in her behalfe doe assent to the agreement & deed herein written, & as her agent doe in her behalfe testify her assent by subscribeing my hand, January 24, 1672.

one peny his marke and seale.

The aboue written is a True coppy of the originall, being ex amined & compared therewith, April 5, 1673, pr me.

JOHN ALLYN, *Secretey.*

The original is left with Capt. John Talcott for the use of the proprietors.

ADDITIONAL STATEMENTS.

The Township of Durham is from five and a half to six and a half miles long from east to west; and four miles broad from north to south. The principal stream is called Coginchaug, or Aramamit. It rises in a spring near Bluff Head, eight or ten rods in circumference, and, running nearly north through the meadows, assumes the name of West River, and forms a junction in Middletown with Little River. It receives Wheeler's brook from the south-west, and Malt brook from the south-east, and Allyn's brook from the east. The meadows at different times have been partially drained by deepening and broadening the Aramamit, much to their advantage. A further outlay would, it is believed, be attended with a further corresponding advantage. There is another brook in the west part of the town, called Saw-mill brook, remarkable for its sudden rise into a swollen torrent in case of rains; and also another still, called Potash brook, from the potash works near it, formerly carried on by Dr. Cole.

The New Haven and Middletown Turnpike, and the Durham and Haddam Turnpike, and the Durham and Madison Turnpike, and the Durham and Guilford Turnpike, have all been given up to the public by the several companies.

There are several pleasant drives, as to Pistapaug Pond, to Quonapaug Pond, and to Middlefield, and to Middletown. Pistapaug is remarkable for containing in its limits a single monument, the corner boundary of four towns, Durham, Guilford, Wallingford and Branford.

The Town gave a call to the first minister before the Church was formed, and invited a Council of ministers who settled him. The Town gave a call to the second and third ministers. The Church, after an interval of some weeks, seconded these calls by its action. The Town was recognized by the laws of the colony and of the State as a religious parish, and permission was given to it, by the Legislature to embody themselves as a church.

The three first ministers, at their settlement asserted their official rights. See pages 41, 43 and page 55, and page 66. At the settlement of Mr. Smith, it was agreed that he should take the pastoral charge of the church, "to teach, guide and direct" them.

The ministers then settled had great influence in the town for more than a hundred years. Macauley, in his history of England, Vol. III, page 89, speaking of dissenting ministers, in England, says: "His influence over his flock was immense. Scarcely any member of a *congregation of Separatists* entered into a partnership, married a daughter, put out a son as an apprentice, or gave his vote at an election, without consulting his spiritual guide. On all political and literary questions the minister was the oracle of his circle." The same was true of many of their brethren in New England, and of the three first ministers of Durham.

According to one theory of Congregationalism, the principal officers of each church were a ruling elder, a teaching elder, pastor and deacons; to say nothing of deaconesses. When from one cause and another the three offices of ruling elder, teaching elder and pastor became merged in the one office of minister, it was very natural that his people should concentrate on him the respect, and affection, and confidence which had been distributed upon the three. He enjoyed the affection and respect, which in given cases in the Episcopal Church, were shared by the bishop, priest and deacon.

In the New Haven Colony, there was virtually a union of Church and State, the Church taking the lead. In the Connecticut Colony there was virtually a union of Church and State, the State taking the lead. In Durham, which was incorporated after the union of the two colonies, the civil power seems to have taken the lead.

In Durham, the Congregational denomination, for more than a century, enjoyed the advantage of belonging to the "standing order," the privileged denomination of the colony and of the State. In common with other Congregationalists in the State, they lost this advantage, especially after the adoption of the State Constitution. In Durham, as elsewhere, many of the Congregationalists took ground against the Constitution; as did the Congregational clergy generally, even those who had carefully eschewed political preaching, and political intrigues. For instance, the Rev. John Elliott, D. D., who had carefully avoided political preaching, rose in the Town Meeting in Guilford, which was about to vote on the adoption of the Constitution, and said,

29

"I have been reported to be in favor of the constitution. I rise to contradict this report, and to say that I shall give it *my entire negative.*" In Durham, as in some other towns, this opposition to the State Constitution operated unfavorably upon the Congregational denomination.

For a long period, Durham, like many other towns in the Commonwealth, was somewhat isolated, so far as frequent intercourse with other towns was concerned, and hence, like them, had a character of its own, shaped by influences largely within itself. For more than a century, religion and education were the two great interests very ably set forth, and strikingly illustrated by three distinguished clergymen. The influence of these three men, and of other leading minds, and the powerful impression which they made, were distinctly seen in the character and tastes of the people of the town, in creating an interest in these two great interests, religion and education.

SANITARY.

The geological formation, and geographical position of Durham serves to render it a very healthy town. This is proved by comparing the registration statistics with those of the State at large, with those of the United States, as proved by the last census, and with the statistics of the State of Massachusetts, where they have attained great perfection, extending over a range of more than twenty years. That State seems to be divided into two great sections, the Atlantic coast, where consumption is found to greatly predominate, and the inland, where Zymotic diseases take the lead and bring up the balance of mortality. That division is found to extend through this State; the sea coast, with its predominence of consumption, and the inland and northern section, with its predominance of Zymotic diseases. In Durham, located on the confines of these great divisions, sheltered in a measure from each by the beautiful hills which mark its boundaries, these opposing causes of disease seem to be so nicely balanced that neither obtains predominance, and the minimum of diseases of each division seem to be obtained.

The fevers which were so prevalent and fatal a half century ago in this vicinity, have changed to a mild form of Typhoid, rarely fatal, and which by its renovating effect on the system, warding off consumption, is, no doubt, conducive to long life in the masses. There have been but two deaths from fever registered for several years. These were both in the army. One died there, and the other a few hours after his arrival in Durham. There have been two hundred and fourteen deaths regis tered in Durham the last eleven years. Of these, one male and seven females were over ninety years of age, fifteen males and fifteen females were over eighty, nineteen males and twelve females were over seventy. Of one hundred persons, nearly one-half of the whole number of deaths, the average age was 75 9 Of the whole number, the average age at death was 32 1-2, males 28 1-2, females 36 1-2. In Massachusetts, average age 30, males 29, females 31.

In this State the returns are not sufficiently complete to ascertain the average age, or the number of inhabitants to each death. In Durham, it is 1 death to 59 of the inhabitants yearly. In Massachusetts, 1 to 52; United States, 1 to 45; in Boston, 1 to 41; in New York City, 1 to 36. There have been 10 cases of consumption in Durham during the last five years; average per cent. 8; in this State, for the same years, 15 per cent.; in Massachusetts, for a term of years, 16.7 per cent.; United States 14 per cent. Of Zymotic diseases, which more clearly indicates the healthfulness of a section, there are 20 deaths, average per cent., 17 1-2; average in this State, 30 per cent.; Massachusetts, 29, United States, 32 per cent.

Of Births during 10 years, there were, 121 males, 109 females. About this proportion holds good in all statistics; average per year, 23. Of these the average foreign births were about 5 1-2 per annum and no material increase during the 10 years.

EXTRACT FROM A LETTER OF JARED POTTER KIRTLAND, LL.D.

"In that town (Durham,) at this period (1817), an intelligent, kind and social set of manners prevailed through the whole population; the imprint of one or more past generations. More wealth, splendor and show, as well as vice, could be found in other Connecticut towns; but here were order, civility, and the very essence of good breeding—the art of making every one comfortable and happy

"General Wadsworth, who died about this time, was the type of a generation whose living representatives were the Chaunceys, Wadsworths, Chedseys, Bateses, Lymans and others that should be enumerated.

"The young and middle-aged formed and made one social circle. Its meetings were frequent, and into it little that was frivolous found its way, and less that was malevolent and scandalizing. Its influence soon become manifest in my own manners, and expressions. Hitherto retired, cold, melancholic, I became cheerful and social, with an entire change of deportment.

"Two individuals exerted great and favorable influence over me. The first was Worthington G. Chauncey. At our first acquaintance we neither looked, thought, nor acted alike: except we both had similar and congenial tastes for pomology and agriculture. Soon, however, the kind ways, industrious habits and strict integrity of Esquire Chauncey commanded my respect and ensured my confidence. Here an intimate acquaintance sprung up between us; and every perplexing matter, even medical cases were submitted confidentially to him, and his advice solicited.

"In recent years I have been heard to assert, that Worthington G. Chauncey was the best balanced man with whom I was ever acquainted. A highly cultivated moral faculty was united with kindness and benevolence. He was industrious and persevering, ever reliable, ever ready to aid the feeble and distressed, and to advance the public good.

"The other individual, to whom I referred, was the Rev. David Smith. His example and precepts corrected my skeptical views of religion, which I had formed early in life, and through life confirmed me in the truth of the Christian religion.

"Soon after my locating in Durham, the population in different localities were, from time to time, attacked with the lowest form of that malignant Typhus Fever which, for the first 30 years of this century, swept with such virulence the valley of the Connecticut River. During the progress of that epidemic, I was often thrown in communication with Drs. Miner and Tully and an intimate acquaintance sprung up among us. It was almost a daily practice for the three to arrange our business so as to meet, consult and compare our views; a course not always followed among medical men."

CHAPTER XII.

RECORDS.

TOWN CLERKS.

Caleb Seward from 1706 to 1707.
Col. James Wadsworth from 1707 to 1756.
Gen. James Wadsworth from 1756 to 1786.
Simeon Parsons from 1786 to 1810.
Worthington G. Chauncey from 1810 to 1830.
Asher Robinson from 1830 to 1843.
Samuel Parsons from 1843 to 1846.
William Wadsworth from 1846 to 1859.
William Parmelee from 1859 to 1860.
William Wadsworth from 1860.

JUSTICES OF THE PEACE.

1710.—James Wadsworth, who was annually re-appointed until he was elected to the Council in 1718, by virtue of which and of being a justice of the quorum, he was a justice of the peace until 1752, (when probably having retired from the Council and the County Court,) he was re-appointed a justice of the peace, also in '53 and '54.

1728.—Capt. Henry Crane, annually re-appointed—the last time was May, 1740.

1741.—Elihu Chauncey. This name disappears from the list of annual appointments after May, 1752.

1750.—James Wadsworth, Jr., continues to 1761, when the appointments having been confined to him solely for several years are two, viz.: James Wadsworth, James Wadsworth, Jr.

1762.—James Wadsworth, Jr., was re-appointed as usual and continued sole justice to 1774.

1774.—Elihu Chauncey sole justice until May, 1778.

1778.—James Wadsworth and Daniel Hall, who were each re-appointed in 1779, 1780, 1781 and 1782.

1783.—James Wadsworth, Simeon Parsons, Daniel Hall.

1784.—James Wadsworth, Daniel Hall, Simeon Parsons.

1785.—James Wadsworth, Daniel Hall, Simeon Parsons.

1786.—Daniel Hall, Simeon Parsons.

1787.—Daniel Hall, Simeon Parsons.

1788.—James Wadsworth, Daniel Hall, Simeon Parsons.

1789.—James Wadsworth, Daniel Hall, Simeon Parsons.

1790.—Daniel Hall, Simeon Parsons.

1791.—Simeon Parsons, Dan Parmelee.

1792.—Simeon Parsons, Dan Parmelee.

1793.—Simeon Parsons, Dan Parmelee.

1794.—Simeon Parsons, Dan Parmelee.

1795.—Simeon Parsons, Dan Parmelee.

1796.—Simeon Parsons, Dan Parmelee.

1797.—Simeon Parsons, Dan Parmelee.

1798.—Simeon Parsons, Dan Parmelee.

1799.*—Simeon Parsons, Dan Parmelee.

1800.—Simeon Parsons, Dan Parmelee.

1801.—Simeon Parsons, Dan Parmelee.

1802.—Simeon Parsons, Dan Parmelee, Charles Coe.

1803.—Simeon Parsons, Dan Parmelee, Charles Coe.

1804.—Simeon Parsons, Dan Parmelee, Charles Coe.

1805.—Simeon Parsons, Dan Parmelee, Charles Coe.

1806.—Simeon Parsons, Dan Parmelee, Charles Coe.

1807.—Simeon Parsons, Dan Parmelee.

1808.—Simeon Parsons, Dan Parmelee, Charles Coe, Guernsey Bates.

1809.—Simeon Parsons, Dan Parmelee, Charles Coe, Guernsey Bates.

1810.—Simeon Parsons, Dan Parmelee, Charles Coe, Guernsey Bates.

1811.—Simeon Parsons, Dan Parmelee, Charles Coe, Guernsey Bates.

1812.—Simeon Parsons, Worthington G. Chauncey, Dan Parmelee, Job Merwin, Charles Coe, Isaac Newton, Guernsey Bates

1813.—Simeon Parsons, Dan Parmelee, Charles Coe, Guernsey Bates, Worthington G. Chauncey, Isaac Newton, Job Merwin.

---

* From 1799 to 1843, the list is taken from Green's Register The records not showing the town.

1814.—Dan Parmelee, Charles Coe, Guernsey Bates, Worthington G. Chauncey, Isaac Newton, Job Merwin.

1815 —Dan Parmelee, Charles Coe, Guernsey Bates, Job Merwin, Isaac Newton, Worthington G. Chauncey.

1816.—Dan Parmelee, Charles Coe, Guernsey Bates, Job Merwin, Isaac Newton, Worthington G. Chauncey.

1817.—Dan Parmelee, Charles Coe, Guernsey Bates, Job Merwin, Worthington G. Chauncey, Bridgman Guernsey.

1818.—Guernsey Bates, Worthington G. Chauncey, Bridgman Guernsey, James Robinson, Lemuel Camp.

1819.—The same as in 1818.

1820.—Guernsey Bates, Worthington G. Chauncey, James Robinson, Lemuel Camp.

1821 —Worthington G. Chauncey, Guernsey Bates, Lemuel Camp, Bridgman Guernsey.

1822.—Worthington G. Chauncey, Samuel Tibbals, Jesse Atwell, Timothy Coe, Jr , William S. Camp.

1823.—Worthington G. Chauncey, Lemuel Camp, Samuel Tibbals, William S. Camp, Jesse Atwell, Timothy Coe, Jr., Asahel Strong.

1824.—The same as in 1823.

1825.—Worthington G. Chauncey, Lemuel Camp, Samuel Tibbals, William S. Camp, Timothy Coe, Jr., Asahel Strong.

1826 —Worthington G. Chauncey, Lemuel Camp, Samuel Tibbals, William S. Camp, Timothy Coe, Asahel Strong, John White.

1827.—Worthington G. Chauncey, Lemuel Camp, Samuel Tibbals, Timothy Coe, Asahel Strong, John White.

1828.—The same as in 1827.

1829.—The same as in 1827 and 1828.

1830.—Worthington G. Chauncey, Asahel Strong, Samuel Tibbals, John White, Lemuel Camp, Timothy Coe.

1831 —Worthington G. Chauncey, Lemuel Camp, Samuel Tibbals, Asahel Strong, John White, Timothy Coe.

1832.—Worthington G. Chauncey, Lemuel Camp, Samuel Tibbals, Asahel Strong, John White, Timothy Coe, Parsons Coe, Asher Robinson.

1833.—Worthington G Chauncey, Lemuel Camp, Samuel Tibbals, Asahel Strong, John White, Timothy Coe, Asher Robinson

1834.—Worthington G. Chauncey, Lemuel Camp, Samuel Tibbals, Asahel Strong, John White, Timothy Coe, Asher Robinson, Joseph Chedsey, Gaylord Newton, Alexander M. G. Elliott.

1835.—Worthington G. Chauncey, Samuel Tibbals, Asahel Strong, Asher Robinson, Alexander M. G. Elliott.

1836.—Worthington G. Chauncey, Samuel Tibbals, Asahel Strong, Asher Robinson, Lucius Foote, Erastus Jones.

1837.—Worthington G. Chauncey, Samuel Tibbals, Asahel Strong, Asher Robinson, Lucius Foot, Erastus Jones, Ebenezer Cook.

1838.—Worthington G. Chauncey, John White, Asher Robinson, Enos Rogers, Alfred Camp, Munson Strong.

1839.—Worthington G. Chauncey, John White, Alfred Camp, Zebulon Hale, Erastus Jones, William C. Coe.

1840.—Worthington G. Chauncey, John White, Lemuel Camp, Zebulon Hale, Alfred Camp, Charles Hickox, Munson Strong.

1841.—Worthington G. Chauncey, John White, Asher Robinson, Zebulon Hale, Wedworth Wadsworth, Jr., Alfred Camp, Charles Hickox.

1842.—John White, Asher Robinson, Wedworth Wadsworth, Jr., Timothy Coe, Charles Hickox, Miles Merwin, Jr., Alfred Camp, Benjamin Chalker, Lucius Foot.

1843.—Asher Robinson, Timothy Coe, Erastus Jones, Wedworth Wadsworth, Jr, Miles Merwin, Jr., John White.

1844.—John White, Alfred Camp, Miles Merwin, Jr, Zebulon Hale, Samuel Newton, Charles Hickox, Clement M. Parsons.

1845.—John White, Alfred Camp, Miles Merwin, Jr., Samuel Newton, Charles Hickox, Enos Rogers, Clement M. Parsons, Asher Robinson.

1846.—Asher Robinson, William Wadsworth, Erastus Jones, Charles Hickox, Frederick T. Elliott, Miles Merwin, Jr., Isaac Parmelee, John White.

1847.—Miles Merwin, Jr., Enos Rogers, John White, Samuel G. Tibbals, Asher Robinson, Charles Hickox, William Wadsworth, Alfred Camp, Frederick T. Elliott, Samuel Newton.

1848.—Benjamin B. Beecher, Alfred Camp, Frederick T. Elliott, Charles Hickox, Miles Merwin, Jr., Samuel Newton, Asher Robinson, Enos Rogers, Charles Thompson, William Wadsworth.

1849.—Alfred Camp, Henry Canfield, Frederick T. Elliott,

Miles Merwin, Jr., Samuel Newton, Asher Robinson, Enos Rogers, William Wadsworth.

1850.—Lucius Foot, Erastus Jones, Miles Merwin, Jr., Samuel Newton, Asher Robinson, Wolcott P. Stone, William Wadsworth.

1852.—Alfred Camp, Henry Canfield, Zebulon Hale, Erastus Jones, Miles Merwin, Jr., Samuel Newton, William Wadsworth.

1854.—Henry Canfield, Timothy J. Coe, Frederick T. Elliott, L. M. Leach, Miles Merwin, Jr., Samuel Newton, William Wadsworth.

1856.—Joseph Chedsey, Frederick T. Elliott, Frederick S. Field, Erastus Jones, Miles Merwin, Jr., Samuel Newton, William Wadsworth.

1858.—James E. Bailey, Henry Canfield, Frederick T. Elliott, Frederick S. Field, Miles Merwin, Jr., Israel C. Newton, William Wadsworth.

1860.—Frederick S. Field, Miles Merwin, Samuel Newton, James E. Bailey, William H. Maltby, Alfred Camp, William Wadsworth.

1862.—Samuel Newton, Frederick S. Field, John K. Burr, William Wadsworth, David C. Camp, William C. Ives, Miles T. Merwin.

1864.—Samuel Newton, William Wadsworth, Bishop Atwell, Miles Merwin, E. B. Meigs, Frederick S. Field, Joel Austin, Oscar Leach.

REPRESENTATIVES IN THE GENERAL ASSEMBLY.

1710. May—James Wadsworth, Caleb Seward. Oct.—James Wadsworth, John Russell.

1711. May—[none recorded.] Oct.—Caleb Seward.

1712. May—James Wadsworth. Oct.—James Wadsworth.

1713. May—James Wadsworth. Oct.—[none recorded.]

1714. May—James Wadsworth. Oct.—James Wadsworth, Caleb Seward.

1715. May—James Wadsworth, Caleb Seward. Oct.—James Wadsworth, Caleb Seward.

1716. May—James Wadsworth, Caleb Seward. Oct.—Caleb Seward, John Sutliff.

1717. May—James Wadsworth, (Clerk,) Caleb Seward. Oct.—James Wadsworth (Speaker,) Samuel Fairchild.

1718 May—Henry Crane, [one vacancy.] Probably Mr. Wadsworth was elected, but went into the Council Oct.—Caleb Seward, Henry Crane.

1719. May—Caleb Seward, Samuel Fairchild. Oct.—William Seward, Thomas Lyman.

1720. May—Caleb Seward, Thomas Lyman. Oct.—Samuel Parsons, Henry Crane.

1721. May—Caleb Seward, Thomas Lyman. Oct.—Caleb Seward, Thomas Lyman.

1722. May—Caleb Seward, Thomas Lyman. Oct.—Samuel Parsons, Henry Crane.

1723. May—Caleb Seward, Samuel Parsons Oct.—Henry Crane, Thomas Lyman.

1724. May—Henry Crane, Samuel Parsons. Oct.—Henry Crane, Thomas Lyman

1725. May—Henry Crane, William Seward. Oct.—Henry Crane, Thomas Lyman.

1726. May—Henry Crane, Thomas Lyman. Oct.—William Seward, Thomas Lyman.

1727. May—Henry Crane, Thomas Lyman. Oct.—Henry Crane, William Seward.

1728. May—Henry Crane, Joseph Coe. Oct.—Henry Crane, Nathaniel Sutliff.

1729. May—Henry Crane, Nathaniel Sutliff Oct.—Henry Crane, Nathaniel Sutliff.

1730. May—Henry Crane, Nathaniel Sutliff. Oct.—Henry Crane, Nathaniel Sutliff.

1731. May—Henry Crane, Nathaniel Sutliff. Oct.—Nathaniel Sutliff, Nathan Camp.

1732. May—Henry Crane, Moses Parsons. Oct.—Henry Crane, Moses Parsons.

1733. May—Henry Crane, Moses Parsons. Oct.—Henry Crane, Moses Parsons.

1734. May—Henry Crane, Elihu Chauncey. Oct.—Moses Parsons, Elihu Chauncey.

1735. May—Henry Crane, Nathan Camp. Oct.—Henry Crane, Nathan Camp.

1736. May—Henry Crane, Nathan Camp. Oct.—Elihu Chauncey, Nathan Camp.

1737. May—Nathan Camp, Elihu Chauncey. Oct.—Ebenezer Lyman, Elihu Chauncey.

1738. May—Elihu Chauncey, Moses Parsons. Oct.—Elihu Chauncey, James Wadsworth, Jr.

1739. May—Elihu Chauncey, Robert Fairchild. Oct —Henry Crane, Nathan Camp.

1740. May—Elihu Chauncey, Robert Fairchild. Oct.—Elihu Chauncey, Nathan Camp.

1741. May—Elihu Chauncey, Robert Fairchild. Oct.—Nathan Camp, Elihu Chauncey.

1742. May—Elihu Chauncey, Nathan Camp. Oct.—Elihu Chauncey, Robert Fairchild.

1743. May—Elihu Chauncey, Robert Fairchild. Oct.—Elihu Chauncey, Nathan Camp.

1744. May—Elihu Chauncey, Nathan Camp. Oct.—Elihu Chauncey, Robert Fairchild.

1745. May—Elihu Chauncey, Nathan Camp. Oct.—Elihu Chauncey, Nathan Camp.

1746. May—Elihu Chauncey, James Wadsworth. Oct.—Elihu Chauncey, James Wadsworth, Jr.

1747. May—Elihu Chauncey, James Wadsworth Oct.—Nathan Camp, Abram Bartlett.

1748. May—Nathan Camp, James Wadsworth. Oct.—Elihu Chauncey, James Wadsworth, Jr.

1749. May—Elihu Chauncey, James Wadsworth. Oct.—Elihu Chauncey, James Wadsworth.

1750. May—Elihu Chauncey, James Wadsworth. Oct.—Elihu Chauncey, James Wadsworth.

1751. May—Elihu Chauncey, James Wadsworth. Oct.—Elihu Chauncey, James Wadsworth.

1752. May—Elihu Chauncey, James Wadsworth. Oct.—Elihu Chauncey, James Wadsworth.

1753. May—Elihu Chauncey, James Curtiss. Oct.—Elihu Chauncey, Nathaniel Seward.

1754. May—Elihu Chauncey, John Camp, 3d. Oct —Elihu Chauncey, Ezra Baldwin

1755. May—Elihu Chauncey, James Wadsworth, Jr Oct.—James Wadsworth, Jr., John Curtiss.

1756. May—Nathan Camp, Elihu Chauncey. Oct.—Elihu Chauncey, James Wadsworth.

1757. May—James Wadsworth, Elihu Chauncey. Oct.—Elihu Chauncey, [one vacancy.]

1758. May—James Wadsworth, Nathan Camp. Oct.—Elihu Chauncey, John Camp.

1759. May—Mr. James Wadsworth, Elihu Chauncey. Oct.—Mr. James Wadsworth, Capt. James Wadsworth.

1760. May—Elihu Chauncey, Capt. James Wadsworth. Oct.—Elihu Chauncey, Capt. James Wadsworth.

1761. May—Elihu Chauncey, [one vacancy.] Oct.—Elihu Chauncey, Capt. James Wadsworth.

1762. May—Elihu Chauncey, Capt. James Wadsworth. Oct.—Capt. James Wadsworth, Elihu Chauncey.

1763. May—Elihu Chauncey, Capt. James Wadsworth. Oct.—Elihu Chauncey, Capt. James Wadsworth.

1764. May—Elihu Chauncey, Capt. James Wadsworth. Oct.—Elihu Chauncey, Capt. James Wadsworth.

1765. May—Elihu Chauncey, Capt. James Wadsworth. Oct.—Capt. James Wadsworth, Ebenezer Guernsey.

1766. May—Capt. James Wadsworth, Nathan Camp. Oct.—Capt. James Wadsworth, Elihu Chauncey.

1767. May—Elihu Chauncey, Capt. James Wadsworth. Oct.—Elihu Chauncey, James Curtiss.

1768. May—Elihu Chauncey, James Curtiss. Oct.—Elihu Chauncey, Capt. James Wadsworth.

1769. May—Elihu Chauncey, Capt. James Wadsworth. Oct.—Elihu Chauncey, Capt. James Wadsworth.

1770. May—Elihu Chauncey, Capt. James Wadsworth. Oct.—Elihu Chauncey, Capt. James Wadsworth.

1771. May—Elihu Chauncey, Capt. James Wadsworth. Oct.—Elihu Chauncey, Capt. James Wadsworth.

1772. May—Elihu Chauncey, Capt. James Wadsworth. Oct.—Elihu Chauncey, Capt. James Wadsworth.

1773. May—Elihu Chauncey, Capt. James Wadsworth. Oct.—Elihu Chauncey, Capt. James Wadsworth.

1774. May—Elihu Chauncey, Capt. James Wadsworth. Oct.—Elihu Chauncey, Capt. James Wadsworth.

1775. May—Col. James Wadsworth, Daniel Hall. Oct.—Col. James Wadsworth, Daniel Hall.

1776 May—Elihu Chauncey, Col. James Wadsworth, Jr. Oct.—Elihu Chauncey, Benjamin Pickett.

1777. May—Gen. James Wadsworth, Jr., Elnathan Camp. Oct.—Elnathan Camp, Isaac Miles.

1778. May—Gen. James Wadsworth, Elnathan Camp. Oct. —Gen. James Wadsworth, Elnathan Camp.

1779. May—Gen. James Wadsworth, Stephen Norton. Oct. —Gen. James Wadsworth, Phineas Spelman.

1780. May—Gen. James Wadsworth, Simeon Parsons. Oct. —Simeon Parsons Benjamin Pickett.

1781. May—James Wadsworth, Simeon Parsons. Oct.—James Wadsworth, Simeon Parsons.

1782. May—James Wadsworth, Simeon Parsons. Oct.—James Wadsworth, Simeon Parsons.

1783. May—James Wadsworth, Daniel Hall. Oct.—James Wadsworth, Daniel Hall.

1784. May—Daniel Hall, Simeon Parsons. Oct.—James Wadsworth, Simeon Parsons.

1785. May—James Wadsworth, Simeon Parsons. Oct.—Simeon Parsons, Daniel Hall.

1786. May—Simeon Parsons, Daniel Hall. Oct.—Simeon Parsons, Daniel Hall.

1787. May—James Robinson, Simeon Parsons. Oct.—Simeon Parsons, Benjamin Pickett.

1788. May—Simeon Parsons, Daniel Hall. Oct.—James Wadsworth, Daniel Hall.

1789. May— Simeon Parsons. Oct.—Simeon Parsons, Dan Parmely.

1790. May—Simeon Parsons, Dan Parmely. Oct.—Simeon Parsons, Dan Parmely.

1791. May—Simeon Parsons, Dan Parmely. Oct.—Simeon Parsons, Dan Parmely.

1792. May—Simeon Parsons, Dan Parmely. Oct.—Simeon Parsons, Dan Parmely.

1793. May—Simeon Parsons, Dan Parmely. Oct.—Simeon Parsons, Dan Parmely.

1794. May—Simeon Parsons, Dan Parmely. Oct.—Simeon Parsons, Dan Parmely.

1795. May—Simeon Parsons, Dan Parmely. Oct.—Simeon Parsons, Dan Parmely.

1796. May—Benjamin Pickett, James Hickox. Oct.—Simeon Parsons, Abraham Scranton.

1797. May—Elnathan Camp, Abraham Scranton. Oct.—Elnathan Camp, Levi Parmelee.

1798. May—Elnathan Camp, Dan Parmelee. Oct.—Elnathan Camp, Dan Parmelee.

1799. May—Elnathan Camp, Dan Parmelee. Oct.—Dan Parmelee, Bridgman Guernsey.

1800. May—Dan Parmelee, Elnathan Camp. Oct.—Dan Parmelee, Elnathan Camp.

1801. May—Dan Parmelee, Elnathan Camp. Oct.—Dan Parmelee, Charles Coe.

1802 May—Dan Parmelee, Charles Coe. Oct.—Dan Parmelee, Charles Coe.

1803. May—Dan Parmelee, Charles Coe. Oct.—Charles Coe, Abraham Scranton.

1804. May—Dan Parmelee, Charles Coe. Oct.—Charles Coe, Nathaniel W. Chauncey.

1805. May—Jeremiah Butler, Nathaniel W. Chauncey. Oct.—Jeremiah Butler, Joseph Parsons.

1806. May—Joseph Parsons, Dan Parmelee. Oct.—Dan Parmelee, Daniel Bates.

1807. May—Dan Parmelee, Daniel Bates. Oct.—Dan Parmelee, Charles Coe.

1808. May—Dan Parmelee, Charles Coe Oct.—Job Merwin, Charles Coe.

1809. May—Charles Coe, Benjamin Merwin. Oct.—Guernsey Bates, Seth Seward.

1810. May—Bridgman Guernsey, Asher Canfield. Oct.—Bridgman Guernsey, James Pickett.

1811. May—Bridgman Guernsey, James Pickett Oct.—Worthington G. Chauncey, Isaac Newton.

1812. May—Worthington G. Chauncey, Isaac Newton. Oct.—Abner Newton, John Butler.

1813. May—Abner Newton, John Butler. Oct.—Dan Parmelee, Guernsey Bates.

1814. May—Dan Parmelee, Guernsey Bates. Oct.—Nathan O. Camp, Worthington G. Chauncey.

1815. May—Guernsey Bates, Nathan O. Camp. Oct.—Dan Parmelee, Abner Newton

1816. May—Dan Parmelee, Worthington G. Chauncey. Oct—Charles Coe, Worthington G. Chauncey.

1817. May—Charles Coe, Worthington G. Chauncey. Oct.—Bridgman Guernsey, Asahel Strong.

1818. May—Bridgman Guernsey, Asahel Strong. Oct.—Abel Lyman, Manoah Camp.

1819—Thomas Lyman, John Swathel

1820.—Richard Robinson, Samuel Tibbals.

1821.—Bridgman Guernsey, Dennis Camp

1822.—Richard Robinson, Samuel Tibbals.

1823.—Daniel Bates, Samuel Camp.

1824.—John Swathel, Asahel Strong.

1825.—John Swathel, Eliphaz Nettleton.

1826.—Richard Robinson, Asahel Strong

1827.—Richard Robinson, Jabez Chalker.

1828.—John Swathel, Samuel Tibbals

1829.—Charles Robinson, John Swathel.

1830.—Richard Robinson, Jesse Atwell.

1831—Richard Robinson, Timothy Coe.

1832.—John Swathel, Asahel Strong.

1833.—Samuel Tibbals, Charles Robinson.

1834.—Richard Robinson, Charles Thompson.

1835.—Samuel Tibbals, Munson Strong.

1836.—Munson Strong, Lucius Foote

1837.—Richard Robinson, Samuel Tibbals.

1838.—Leverett W. Leach, Joseph Chedsey.

1839.—Joseph Chedsey, Munson Strong.

1840.—Nathan Parsons, Samuel G. Tibbals.

1841.—John S. Camp. [one vacancy.]

1842.—Zebulon Hale, Alfred Camp.

1843.—Asher Robinson. No choice of 2d representative.

1844—Perez Sturtevant, Bennett B. Beecher.

1845.—Zebulon Hale, Curtis C. Camp.

1846.—Elisha Newton, Enos Rogers.

1847.—Clement M. Parsons, Wolcott P. Stone

1848.—Henry Lyman, Watson Davis.

1849.—Frederick T. Elliott, L. M. Leach.

1850.—Asher Robinson, Henry E. Robinson

1851.—Clement M. Parsons, Henry Strong.

1852.—W. P. Stone, B. B Beecher.
1853 —William Wadsworth, Russell H Shelley.
1854.—Phineas Robinson, Clement M. Parsons.
1855 —Bishop Atwell, William H. Walkley.
1856.—Samuel Newton, Thomas Francis.
1857.—Samuel G. Tibbals, David C. Camp
1858.—Luzerne Elliott, Leander C. Hickox.
1859.—William A. Parmelee, Joel Ives
1860.—Leverett M. Leach, Watson Davis.
1861.—Horatio N. Fowler, Joel Austin.
1862.—B. B. Beecher, David C. Camp.
1863 —Edward P. Camp, William C. Ives.
1864.—Roger W. Newton, William H. Canfield.
1865 —S. S. Scranton, Isaac Parmelee

SENATORS FROM THE EIGHTEENTH DISTRICT.

1842.—Wedworth Wadsworth, Jr
1845 —Seth L. Childs.
1852.—Asher Robinson.
1859.—Henry Canfield.
1862.—Leverett M. Leach.
1864.—William C Fowler.

DELEGATES TO THE CONVENTION WHICH ADOPTED THE FEDERAL CONSTITUTION, 1788.

Gen. James Wadsworth, Daniel Hall.

DELEGATES TO THE CONVENTION WHICH ADOPTED THE STATE CONSTITUTION, 1818.

Thomas Lyman, Lemuel Guernsey.

THOSE WHO TOOK THE OATH OF FIDELITY.

"A Roll of the Names of those Inhabitants of Durham who have taken the oath of Fidelity to the State of Connecticut, with the time of their taking said oath, kept in the Town Clerk's Office in said Durham."

August 26th, 1777.—Gen'l James Wadsworth, Mr. Elnathan

Camp, Daniel Hall, Esqr., Capt. Israel Camp, Capt. Stephen Norton, Capt. Job Camp, Capt. James Robinson, Capt. Samuel Camp, Capt. Charles Norton, Benj'n Picket, Phinehas Spelman, Thomas Strong, Thomas Lyman, Simeon Parsons, Jun., John Coe, Abial Baldwin, Abram Baldwin, Elihu Crane, John Johnson, Jr., Joseph Smith, Israel Burritt, Ephram Coe, Joseph Parsons, Lemuel Parsons, Samuel Bates, Moses Bates, Asher Robinson, Jon'n Wackly, Dan Parmelee, Phinehas Parmelee, Jeremiah Butler, Ithamar Parsons, Jun., John Coe, Jun., Eliphaz Parmelee.

August 27th, 1777.—Samuel Hart.

September 15th, 1777.—Jesse Austin.

September 16th, 1777.—Rev. Elizur Goodrich, David Robinson, Capt. Ebenezer Gurnsey, Ithamar Parsons, Elah Camp, Bryan Rossetter, John Canfield, Elias Camp, Noah Norton, Samuel Guernsey, Jabez Chalker, Joseph Chedsey, Ezra Baldwin, Phineas Baldwin, Lemuel Johnson, John Curtiss, Ephram Norton, Josiah Parsons, Eben'r Robinson, Reuben Bishop, Thomas Strong, Ju'r., James Bates, Abijah Curtiss, Henry Crane, Joseph Wheeler, Jesse Cook, Daniel Hall, Jun., David Talcott, Nathan Hickox, Joseph Wright, Jun., Robert Smithson, Noah Lyman, Jacob Clark, Timothy Parsons, Moses Seward, John Crane, Gideon Canfield, Ebenezer Tibbals, Joseph Southworth, Samuel Moffitt, Joseph Hall, Caleb Fowler, Jesse Crane, Dan'l Meeker, Hezekiah Parmelee.

Nov. 3d, 1777.—Capt. John Noyes Wadsworth.

December 8th, 1777.—Charles Burrit, William Burrit, Capt. James Curtiss, Sam'l Picket, Abra'm Scranton, Jr, Simeon Coe, Ju'r., John Johnson, Noadiah Grave, Wm. Bishop, John Norton, Titus Loveland, Dan'l Wright, Sam'l Bartlet, Phin's Camp, Abraham Scranton, Morris Coe, John Jones, Eli Crane, Abel Coe, Simeon Coe, Heth Camp.

November 24th, 1777.—Abel Tibbals.

January 5th, 1778.—Jared Whiton.

January 6th, 1778.—Medad Strong, Col. James Arnold, Samuel Parsons.

February 9th, 1778.—Abel Lyman.

April 8th, 1778.—Stephen Richardson, Samuel Squire.

June 15th, 1778.—Ambrose Field.

December 8th, 1778.—Reubin Baldwin, Frederick Crane, Daniel Coe

December 12th, 1778.—Eliakim Strong, Timothy Coe.

December 28th, 1778.—Benj. Ames.

January 5th, 1779.—Samuel Fenn Parsons.

January 11th, 1779.—Josiah Coe, Thomas Stevens, Daniel Dimock, Curtiss Bates, Phineas Canfield.

September 5th, 1779.—Giles Rose.

April 10th, 1780.—Sam'l Seward, Levi Parmelee, Jas. Hickox.

May 1st, 1780.—Ashur Canfield, Joseph Tibbals, John Robinson, Elnathan Norton, Ozias Norton, Ebenezer Tibbals.

May 8th, 1780.—Daniel Smith.

September 19th, 1780.—Charles Parmelee, Stephen Norton, Jr.

December 21st, 1780.—Joseph Camp.

April 9th, 1781.—David Scranton, Thomas Cook.

May 10th, 1781.—John Newton.

August, 1781.—Jonathan Wells.

September 18th, 1781.—Gad Camp, Rejoice Camp, John Curtiss, Jun., David Parsons, Timothy Coe, Jun.

September 1st, 1782.—Richard Spelman.

October 7th, 1782.—Charles Coe, James Robinson, Jun

October 7th, 1782.—Bille Torry.

April 9th, 1783.—Stephen Kiley.

May 2d, 1783.—Bridgman Gurnsey.

June 12th, 1783.—Eliakim Strong, Jun.

September 9th, 1783.—Job Merwin.

December 10th, 1783.—Miles Merwin, Jun., Daniel Merwin.

January 28th, 1784.—Miles Merwin.

April 12th, 1784.—Abraham Stowe, Nathan Camp.

September 21st, 1784.—Abr'm Bartlett, Jun., Sam'l Camp, Ju'r.

December 12th, 1786.—William Wadsworth.

January 7th, 1787.—Elnathan Stevens, David Parsons, David Merwin, Job Canfield, Joseph Hull

January 15th, 1787.—Jacob Brooks.

January 16th, 1787.—John Hall.

January 17th, 1787.—Asher Coe, Daniel Southmayd, Silvenus Hull, Phinehas Squire, Samuel Weld.

March 23d, 1787.—John Hull, Josiah Hull, Abiather Crane.

September 10th, 1787.—Elias Camp, Jun.

November 12th, 1787.—Benjamin Gillim, James Picket, Jabaz Chalker, Jun.

September 21st, 1790.—Joel Coe, Abel Coe, Ju'r

May 23d, 1791.—Stephen Robinson.

FREEMEN.

A Roll of the names of the Freemen in the Town of Durham, with the time of their taking the oath by law provided, kept in the Town Clerk's Office in said Durham.

September 16th, 1777.—Rev'rd Elizur Goodrich, Gen'l James Wadsworth, Dan'l Hall, Esqr, David Robinson, Capt. Eben'r Garnsey, Capt. Israel Camp, Capt Stephen Norton, Bryan Rossetter, Elah Camp, Ithamar Parsons, John Coe, Gideon Canfield, Benj'm'n Picket, Capt. Samuel Camp, John Canfield, Elias Camp, Noah Norton, Lemue Garnsey, Elnathan Camp, Jabez Chalker, Joseph Chidsey, Noah Baldwin, Capt. Job Camp, John Crane, John Curtiss, Ephram Coe, Lemuel Johnson, Moses Seward, Thomas Strong, Simeon Parsons, Jr., Josiah Parsons, Abial Baldwin, Thomas Lyman, Eben'r Robinson, Reuben Bishop, Phinehas Spelman, Thomas Strong, Jr, James Bates, Abijah Curtiss, John Coe, Ju'r., John Johnson, Ju'r., Ithamar Parsons, Henry Crane, Joseph Wheeler, Jesse Cook, Dan'l Hall, Ju'r., Noah Parsons, Jeremiah Butler, Moses Bates, Phineas Parmelee, David Talcott, Capt. James Robinson, Jonathan Wackley, Nathaniel Hickox, Joseph Wright, Ju'r., Capt. Charles Norton, Eliphuz Parmelee, Joseph Smith, Jacob Clark, Noah Lyman, Timothy Parsons, Lemuel Moffit, Ezra Baldwin, Ephraim Norton, Joseph Southworth, Samuel Pickett, Samuel Hart, Eli Crane, Phinehas Camp, Abraham Butler, Israel Burrit, Robert Smithson, Ebe'r Tibbals.

April 13th, 1778.—Samuel Bates, Daniel Wright, Amos Fowler, Hezekiah Parmelee, Jun, Jared Whedon, John Johnson, Jesse Crane, John Camp.

September 15th, 1778.—Capt. Elnathan Chauncey, Dan Parmelee, Hezekiah Camp, Hezekiah Parmelee, Joel Parmelee, Samuel Parsons, Caleb Fowler, Titus Loveland, John Jones, Abel Lyman.

September 21st, 1779.—Medad Strong, Charles Burrit, Samuel Seward, Levi Parmelee, James Hickox.

April 10th, 1780.—Giles Rose, Ruben Baldwin, Thomas Stevins, Frederick Crane, Samuel Fenn Parsons, Samuel Parsons, Jr., Sam'l Squier, Abel Tibbals, Tim. Hall, Tim. Coe, Simeon Coe, Jun., Morris Coe, Abraham Scranton, Curtiss Bates.

April 19th, 1780.—Ashur Canfield, John Coe, Abraham Fowler, Charles Parmelee, Stephen Norton, Jun.

April 9th, 1781.—David Scranton, Thomas Cook, James Talcott, Gad Camp, Rejoice Camp.

August 18th, 1781 —John Curtiss, Jun., Aaron Parsons, Timothy Coe, Jun.

September 7th, 1782.—Richard Spelman.

April 7th, 1783.—Stephen Kelsey.

September 16th, 1783.—Eliakim Strong, Jun., Asher Wright.

April 12th, 1784.—Jesse Austin, Abraham Stowe, Samuel Wright, Nathan Camp.

September 21st, 1784.—John Noyes Wadsworth, Jun., Samuel Camp, Jun., Abraham Bartlett, Jun.

April 11th, 1785.—Bridgman Gurnsey, Beriah Chittenden.

September 20th, 1785.—Charles Coe.

April 10th, 1786.—Eliakim Strong.

April 9th, 1787.—Job Merwin, John Hall, David Robinson, William Wadsworth.

September 18th, 1787.—Elias Camp, Jun., Phinehas Squire.

April 7th, 1788.—David Merwin.

September 13th, 1789 —Israel Camp,. Samuel Camp, Jun., Abiather Crane, John Wilkinson, Luther Hall, Elah Camp.

April 12th, 1790.—Joseph Hull.

September 21st, 1790.—Joel Coe, Job Canfield, Abel Coe, Jun.

April 9th, 1792.—Nathaniel W. Chauncey.

April 8th, 1793.—Doct. Ebenezer Gurnsey.

September 16th, 1793.—Manoah Camp, James Robinson, Jun., Oziah Norton, Samuel Meaker.

September 15th, 1794.—Ebenezer Robinson, James Tibbals, Jun , Noah Talcott.

April 13th, 1795.—Burwell Newton, Jun., Jabez Chalker, Jun , Isaac Newton.

September 21st, 1795.—Thaddeus Squire, Daniel Bates, Gurnsey Bates.

April 11th, 1796.—Joel Parmelee, Ezra Camp, Samuel Weld, Seth Strong, Lemuel Camp.

September 19th, 1796.—Miles Merwin, Richard Robinson, Luke Camp, Stephen Robinson, Hezekiah Baldwin, Elisha Austin.

April 10th, 1797.—Daniel Southmayd, Jun., James Rose.

September 18th, 1797.—Jesse Atwell.

April, 1798.—Seth Seward.

September 7th, 1798.—James Parmelee.

September 16th, 1799.—David Camp, Dennis Camp, Vester Camp, Hamlet Scranton, Samuel Tibbals, John Tibbals, Charles Robinson, Morris Johnson, Nathan Kelsey, Eliphaz Nettleton.

April 7th, 1800.—Rev. David Smith, Nathan Crane, Eliakim Hull, Jun., Nathan Spelman, Titus Loveland, Jun., Ezra Loveland.

September 15th, 1800.—Burwell Newton, Julius Fowler, Daniel Hickox, Reuben Fowler, John Spencer, Henry Stevens, John Camp, Roger Newton, Noah Cone, Daniel Hart, Lyman Norton, George Lyman, Worthington G. Chauncey, Nathaniel Seaward, Aaron Baldwin, Seth Baldwin.

April 13th, 1801.—David Cone.

September 21st, 1801.—Samuel Hart, Jun., John Hart, Selah Parker, Asher Robinson, Jun., Jesse Coe, Samuel Coe, John Butler, Charles Parsons, Timothy Elliot, Jeremiah Butler, Jun.

April 12th, 1802.—Ozias Camp, Jesse Smith, Oliver Coe, Joseph Southmayd, Thaddeus Camp.

September 20th, 1802.—Josiah Jewett, Joseph Tuttle, Jun., Ramoe Butler.

April 11th, 1803.—William Augustus Strong.

September 19th, 1803.—George Galpin, Henry Lyman, Timothy Tuttle, Eli Parmelee, Russell Strong, Isaac Loveland.

April 9th, 1804.—Ebenezer Robinson, Jun., Dan Parmelee, Jr.

September 17th, 1804.—Abner Newton, Richard Loveland, Joy Scranton, John Loveland, Gideon Canfield, Lemuel Norton, James Arnold, Jun., Curtiss Parsons, Sylvanus Hull, Richard Barret, Elizur Spelman, Henry Hall, James Bishop, Asa Chamberlin, Jr.

April 8th, 1805.—James Clarke, Ichabod Camp, Charles White, Jun., Asher Gillim, William Foote, Timothy Stowe, Wait C. Francis, Allen Clarke.

September 15th, 1806.—Josiah Parsons, Hamlet Coe.

April 13th, 1807.—Lewis Norton.

September 21st, 1807.—Samuel Robinson, Noah Coe.

April 11th, 1808.—David Grave.

September 19th, 1808.—Seth Tibbals, Jesse Squire, Timothy Coe, Jun , James Hickox, Samuel Curtiss, Nathan Parsons.

April 9th, 1810.—Asahel Strong, Lynus Butler.

September 17th, 1810.—Lemuel Guernsey, Seth R. Strong, John White, Daniel Dimmock, Jun.

April 8th, 1811.—Ozias Fowler, Joseph Smith, Hezekiah Clarke, David Lynn.

September 10th, 1811.—Samuel Hall, Dennis Robinson, Joseph P. Camp, Enos S. Camp, William Smith, Joseph Hull, 2d, Moses Robinson, Zerry Norton.

April 13th, 1812.—Ozias Camp, 2d, Thomas Spencer Camp, Medad Strong, Benjamin Chalker, David C. Hull, Aaron Hosmer, James Potter, Ezra Dennison, Morris Bailey, Jabez Bailey, Elizur Hall, Joseph Andrews.

September 21st, 1812.—Horris Parmelee, Edmund Shelley, Edmund Avery, Abraham Coe, David Clarke, Charles Camp, James Parmelee, Phinehas Parmelee, Richard Hubbard.

April 12th, 1813.—Parsons Coe, Ichabod Curtiss, Noah Parmelee.

September 20th, 1813.—Elah Camp, 2d.

April 11th, 1814.—Abner Newton, 2d.

September 19th, 1814.—Elisha Newton, Henry Hickox, Caleb Ives.

April 8th, 1816.—Marcus Parsons.

September 15th, 1816.—David Curtiss, Miles Merwin, Jun., Heth Camp, Lyman Camp.

April 7th, 1817.—David Lymn, Joseph Nettleton

September 15th, 1817.—David Robinson, Timothy Scranton, Jun., Elias Camp, 2d, Harry Camp, Harry Atwell, Simeon Scranton, Jun , David Scranton, John Loveland, Jun., Seldon Stowe, Josiah Hull, Reuben Hickox, Ransom Doolittle, William Hickox, Asher Robinson.

April 13th, 1818.—Dwight Lyman, Henry Strong, Noah Robinson, Daniel Hickox, Jun., George Butler, Elisha Crowell, Quartus Smith, Ebenezer Graham.

July 4th, 1818.—James Robinson, Jun., James Hinman, Jun., Daniel Meeker, Robert Fowler, Augustus Foote, Jehiel Hull,

Amasa Tuttle, Harvey Robinson, Samuel Newton, Jonathan Southmayd.

Sept. 21st, 1818.—Henry Scranton, Samuel C Johnson, Saymour White, Thomas C Camp, Martin Morgan, John S. Camp.

April 5th, 1819—Henry A. Hubbell, Albert Munson, Lyman Bemies, John Johnson 3rd, Alfred Camp, Asher Lyman.

April 3rd, 1820.—William S Camp, Rufus Hine, George Camp, Horace Newton, Oliver Coe, Jun., Timothy Baldwin, Phinehas Robinson.

April 3rd, 1820.—Shulock Rogers, Sheldon Ransom, Stephen Robinson, Jun., Nathan F. Basset, Herschal Camp, William Foster

April 2nd, 1821.—John Swathel Jun., Jabez Chalker, Jun., Samuel Lynn, Benjamin Camp, Sylvestar Hart.

April 1st, 1822.—Eliakim W. Hull, Jefferson Ives, Guernsey Camp, Ervine Lee, Isaac Parmalee, Darius Cone, Abraham Camp, John Graves, Heman Cone, Marvin Riley.

April 7th, 1823.—Jeremiah Bradley, Isaac Baldwin, Ashael Harvey, Selden Stevens, Salmon Reed, Truman Southmayd, William Coe, David Tibbals, Steven L. Norton, Ebenezer Brown, Charles Hickox, Lyman Butler, David Johnson, Lyman Dowd.

April 5th, 1824.—Elias Miller, Egbert Alt, McGilvery Elliott, Eli Cone, Horace Loveland, Henry Camp, 2nd, Frederick Camp, Timothy W. Baldwin, Lewis I. Davis.

April 4th, 1825—George W. Jewett, Samuel Camp, John Robinson, Giles H. Robinson, Munson Strong, George Crustenden, Edwin H. Coe, William Southmayd, Henry L. Camp, Bartholomew Bailey.

• April 3rd, 1826.—Elias Pratt, Henry Hull, Joel Thomas, Elizur Camp, John Camp, Jun, Gaylord Newton, Benjamin Spencer.

April 2nd, 1827.—Israel Scranton, Clement M Parsons, Morris Stevens, Samuel G. Tibbals, Orren Camp, William Thomas, Charles Robinson, 3rd, Benjamin Thomas, Dennis Gillum, Huntington Southmayd, Elias B. Meigs.

April 7th, 1828.—David E. Leach, Hosmer Fowler, Chauncey Swathel, Andrew I. Norton, Alpheus W. Camp, Albert Camp, Phinehas Meigs, Ezekiel W. Lynn, George Atwell,

Talemacus N. Scranton, Henry Nettleton, Samuel Camp, Leander C. Hickox, William Robinson, Ozias Chalker, Edwin Hubbard, Talcott Camp, James C. Francis, Nathan S. Camp, Abner Rutty.

April 6th, 1829.—Lucius Cook, Leonard Hull, Curtiss C. Camp, Silas Merriman, Julius Rich, David S. Smith, Alexander Buel.

April 3d, 1830.—Seth R. Parsons, John C. Buel, Henry Williams, Noah Merwin, Joel Ives, Edward P. Camp, Hobert S Beach, Rodman E. Church, James P. Foote, Henry Coe Camp, Nathaniel D. Fowler, Ozias Parmelee, James Curtiss, William A. Hart, William C. Coe, George W. Goram, Sylvester Bates.

April 4th, 1831.—Leander White, Watson Newton, Elisha Southmayd, Francis N. Chamberlain, James H. Bishop, Lewis P. Strong, Edward Hart, Alba B. Strong, Harvey Hull, James Nettleton, Osmer Beamis, Eli S. Camp.

April 2nd, 1832 —Noyes Cone, Henry Thomas, Beriah Scranton, Lyman C. Robinson, Israel Camp, Henry Parsons, Daniel Thompson, George Hart, Albert Ward, Wolcott P. Stone.

April 1st, 1833.—Joel Blatchley, Talcott Parsons, Erwin White, David P. Camp, Edward P. Church, John Hull.

1834 —Joel Parmele, Henry Canfield, Samuel Southmayd, Henry Robinson, Thomas Francis, Isaac H. Hurman, Bishop Atwell, Isaac Hull, Albert M. Sizer, John C. Clarke, Isaac C. Loveland, Alpheus Tibbals, Henry M. Coe, George Sizer, Benjamin H. Coe, Phineas Camp.

April 6th, 1835.—William Thompson, Charles Kirtland, Luzerne Elliott, Richard M. Nary, Russel Shelley, James M Tibbals.

April 4th, 1836.—William H. Harris, Jihial C. Hull, Phinehas P. Swathel, Moses Norton, Henry Francis, Andrew J. Robinson, Horace B. Lucas.

Oct. 3rd, 1836.—John Bailey.

April 3rd, 1837 —Benjamin W. Field, George Paubgraff, Calvin Albee, James M. Chamberlain, Wedworth Wadsworth, Jun., Blynn Brainard, Daniel Southmayd, Stephen Bailey.

April 2nd, 1838.—Samuel Parsons, Anson Squire, Ebenezer Farrand, Merrick R. Coe, Samuel Hart, Jun., Henry Tucker.

April 1st, 1839.—Eliakim S. Hull, Charles Stevens, John T. Camp, Alexander Camp, William Ives, William Lyman, Gilbert Hale, Josiah Camp, Ichabod Avery, Josiah F. Leete, William Smith, Charles Chedsey, John Parmelee, Phinehas Ward, Samuel Maynard, Jun., Henry Gleason, Comfort Prout, Hiram Bishop, Joel Austin.

April 5th, 1840.—John Buryhardt, Israel S. Burr, Henry E. Bailey, Edward Canfield, Seth L. Child, Hezekiah Dickerman, William Parmalee, John Smith, Augustus Seward, Jonathan Wells, Albert Wheeler, John Wingood, William Wadsworth

Oct. 26th, 1840.—Timothy J. Coe, William P. Chamberlain, Benjamin Curtiss, Henry E. Robinson.

April 3rd, 1841.—Chauncey Bartholemew, John H. Elliott, Harry A. Griffing, Samuel Hull, William A. Parmalee, Samuel Stevens, Bridgman White.

April, 1842 —Timothy G. Stone, David N. Camp, James Wadsworth.

March 25th, 1843.—Jerome Shelley, Andrew I. Thompson, Seldon Hall, Sherman J. Nettleton, Leverett M. Leach, Daniel B. Coe, James W. Lynn, Edwin Brown, Elijah C Tuttle.

April 3rd, 1843.—Alfred Fairchild, John Jackson, William E. Graham, Leander R. Parsons, Israel C Newton, George R. Finley, Sylvanus Hull, Stephen Mix, Nathan A Chedsey.

March 25th, 1844 —Horace Howd, Sereno F. Leete, Jared Robinson, Worthington Scranton, Miles T Merwin, Daniel Camp.

April 1st, 1844.—Isaac D. Loomis, Henry P. Robinson.

October 28th, 1844.—John Shelly, Henry E. Johnson, Harry Camp, Lucius J. Cook, Nathan H. Parsons.

November 2d, 1844.—Seth B. Cooper, Leonidas Maynard, Bartholomew Bailey.

March 31st, 1845.—Samuel H. Catlin.

April 5th, 1845.—Justus I. Bailey.

March 30th, 1846.—James Bailey, Timothy Dwight Camp, Frederick Jackson, Alfred White, William Prout, Abel Nettleton, Henry Merwin.

April 4th, 1846.—Andrew Hull, Henry A. Howd.

March 29th, 1847.—Henry G. Fowler, John E. Hickox, Enoch F. Camp.

April 3d, 1847.—Walter J. Chalker.

32

March 2d, 1848.—David W. Robinson, Franklin Shelley, Franklin S. Smith.

April 3d, 1848.—Alfred S. Curtiss, David P. Reed, Samuel G. Camp, Henry H. Wright, John K. Burr.

October 30th, 1848.—Charles B. Sturtevant.

November 7th, 1848.—David C. Camp, William A. Robinson, Samuel R. Fairchild, Diodet K. Brainard.

March 26th, 1849.—Lyman Norton.

April 2d, 1849.—Jeremiah Chalker, Asahel Nettleton.

March 25th, 1850.—Jeremiah B. Bailey, Jr., Leonard Bailey, Ransom Prout.

March 30th, 1850.—Erwin S. Davis, George W. Strong, Elias Miller, Jr., Phineas L. Squires.

April 1st, 1850.—Andrew Jackson, Bennet Dyer, Patrick Kelley.

March 31st, 1851.—Alvin P. Roberts.

April 7th, 1851.—Henry H. Tibbals, William S. Myers, James H. Parsons, Isaac Farnham, Chauncey A. Smith, Joseph P. Camp, Jr., John A. Marsh, Edward A. Thayer.

March 29th, 1852.—Joseph H. Parsons.

April 5th, 1852.—Nicholas Hess, Jr., Abner B. Severance, Lumas H. Pease, Denis A. Burr, Henry G. Hotchkiss, Henry J. Burdick, Richard Hotchkiss, Frederick Parmelee, Oscar Leach, Ezra Dowd, Charles J. Haywood, Joseph Skinner.

October 25th, 1852.—Alfonso L. Chalker, Henry Page, Charles D. Reed, Joseph Sharratt.

November 2d, 1852.—Zolva W. Frisba, Charles E. Camp, John Marshal, Charles C. Hickox, Jonathan Dolph, Jerome H. Johnson, Richard Fox.

March 27th, 1854.—Zebulon Wilbur Davis, Henry W. Coe.

April 3d, 1854.—George W. Farnham, Henry E. Bemus, Thomas W. Lyman, Frederick Lyman.

March 26th, 1855.—Noyes F. Camp, Frederick H. Parmelee.

April 2d, 1855.—Charles C. Johnson, Thomas F. Fuller, Franklin Pierce, George A. Hubbell, James M. Williams, Talcott Parsons, Oliver W. Lyman, Guernsey L. Strong, Joseph R. Adams.

April 7th, 1856.—Francis K. Finley, Edward B. Severance John B. Burr, John G. Davenport, Edward Volmiller, Benj S.

J. Page, Samuel B. Southmayd, Milton Lewis, John A. Johnson, Henry M. Pratt, William H. Wright, Augustus Morse, Albert C. Griswold, Henry P. Rich.

October 27th, 1856 —Daniel Coakley

November 4th, 1856 —John Southmayd, Charles W. Camp.

April 4th, 1853.—Evlyn Jackson, David O. Camp, Michael Horan.

March 30th, 1857.—John S. Chalker.

April 6th, 1857.—Martin Fuderer, William Coets, Charles H. Kaiser, Charles L. Robinson, George H. Davis, Almer J. Roberts, Charles Leonard, Arthur Strong.

April 5th, 1858.—Frederick Selser, Frans. Hilbert, Frederick Reinhardt, Samuel A. Camp, Theodore Blynn, Sherman E. Camp, Edgar L. Meigs, Nelson J. Tuttle, Thomas Miller, Henry Maltby, A. M. Bond, A. E. Haskell

March 28th, 1859.—William A. Camp, Francis O. Bidwell, Dennis Coakley.

April 4th, 1859.—Albert J. Cooley, Dwight L. Hickox, Jacob Holden, John O. Connell, James Connell, Joseph Miller, George J. Hall, Segar S. Atwell, Nelson D. Fowler, D. W. Fields, R. B. Dunham, Valentine Soure, James H. Utter.

April 2d, 1860 —William Lewis Hart, Jared E. Clarke, William C Fowler, Wadsworth Fowler, Wedworth Fowler, Mathew Hersivs, Wendelin Meister, William Glover, George W. Davis, Frederic J. Hull, Curtiss C. Atwell, William H. Harrison, Charles Snfernman, Heber G. Ives.

October 29th, 1860.—Seymour L. White, George W. Taylor.

October 31st, 1860 —John B. Meigs, John B. Newton.

March 25th, 1861.—Newel E. Nettleton, Dennis H. Peck, William H. Francis, Freeman Southmayd.

March 27th, 1861.—Engellbert Vogelfonger, William Marshall, Michael Frien, George A. Hills

March 31st, 1862.—Henry H. Newton, William E. Camp, George Ashendon, Charles Harrington, William H. Davis, Frederick J. Coe, Gilbert G. Tibbals, Gottlieb Enesle, Henry S. Jewett

April 2d, 1862.—Simeon S. Camp, Levi P. Perry.

April 7th, 1862.—Richard Payne.

March 30th, 1863.—William N. Beecher, Guernsey, B. Smith,

Theodore F. Barnes, John E. Vandervoort, James W. Wadsworth, Edgar T. Elliott, William M. Austin, Morelle Francis.

April 1st, 1863.—Daniel C. Southmayd, Henry V. Tucker, Joel W. Wells.

March 28th, 1864.—Leonidas M. Camp, George L. Camp, Judson E. Francis, L. L. Parsons.

March 30th, 1864.—Stillman N. Deming, John B. Clarke, Joseph W. Sessions, Daniel M. Spencer, Talcott P. Strong.

October 31st, 1864.—Henry A Parmalee, William H. Augur, Edwin Warriner, Stephen A. Seward, Luman A. Stone, Carroll L. Dudley, Henry G. Newton, Timothy E. Hull, George Miller.

November 2d, 1864.—Joseph Ferry, Frederick M. Sizer, John C. Atwell.

March 27th, 1865.—Charles C. Fowler, Sidney H. Olin, Gilbert E. Blinn.

March 29th, 1865.—Edgar A. Nettleton, Charles G. Tucker.

REV. NATHANIEL CHAUNCEY'S RECORD.

In ye 2d year these children were baptized. Feb. 17th, 1711–12, Abel Beach, son of Ben. and Dinah Beach; Sarah and Mary Wells, daughters of Jonathan and Mehetabel Wells.

March 2d, 1711–12.—Sarah Chauncey, daughter of N. Chauncey and Sarah. Sd. Sarah Chauncey was born Feb. 24th, 1711–12, on the Sabbath day, and baptized the next Sabbath.

May 18th, 1712.—Jonathan Norton, the son of John and Eliz. Norton; Dinah Munger the daughter of John Munger.

May 24th.—Martha Sutlief, daughter of John and Hannah Sutlif.

June 1st.—Phebe Wheeler, the daughter of Tho. and Phebe Wheeler; Abigail Crane, daughter of Henry and Abigail Crane.

July 6th.—John, the son of Moses and Abigail Parsons.

July 6th.—Mary, ye daughter of Sam'l and Mary Fairchild.

July 27th.—Joseph, the son of Nath. and Sarah Sutlif, and William, the son of William and Damaris Seaward; Sam. Haycox, the son of Stephen and Ruth Haycox.

Nov. last, 1712.—John Talcott, the son of Hez. and Jemima Talcott was born.

Dec. 14, 1712.—Jonathan Wells, the son of Jonathan and

Mehitabel Wells was baptized. Feb. 2d, 1712–13, Samuel, ye son James and Abigail Bates.

March 15th, 1712–13.—Joel, the son of Joel and Abigail Parmelee was baptized.

March 22d, 1712–13.—Martha, ye daughter Robert and Barbara Coe; Sarah, the daughter of James and Hannah Curtis

April 5th, 1713.—Elizabeth, ye daughter of Thomas and Elizabeth Liman.

June 28th, 1713.—John, the son of Samuel and Mary Parsons.

Sept. 5th.—Joseph Coe, son of Joseph and Abigail Coe.

Luie Mungar, the daughter of John A. Mungar; Joseph, the son of James Wright, Nov. 1st, 1713.

Jan. 24th, 1713–14.—Noah Lyman, the son of Noah and Eliz. Lyman.

Feb. 7th, 1713–14.—Matthew, ye son of Eph. and Phebe Hawley, was baptized. Feb. 14th, Abigail, ye daughter of Moses and Abigail Parsons.

March 7th.—Ruth, the daughter of Joseph and Mary Gaylord.

March 20th.—John, ye son of John and Hannah Sutlief, and on ye same day, Samuel, the son of Samuel and Dinah Norton. Apr. Abigail Squire, ye daughter of George and Jane Squire.

May 16th, 1714.—Hannah, ye daughter of Richard and Hannah Beech.

June —David, ye son of William and Damaris Seward.

July 18th.—Stephen, the son of Stephen and Ruth Hickox.

Aug. 14th.—From Middletown, Alice, the daughter of Dan. and Alice White.

Aug. 15th, 1714.—Edmund Fairchild, the son of Samuel and Mary Fairchild.

Sept. 12th.—Mary, the daughter of Jehiel and Hope Hawley.

Sept. 26th.—Katherine, ye daughter of Nath'll and Sarah Chauncey.

Nov 21st.—John, ye son of John and Eliza Gaylord.

Jan. 9th, 1714–15.—Sarah, the daughter of Caleb Seaward, Jun., and Sarah his wife.

Feb. 13th, 1714–15.—Thomas, the son of Thomas and Eliz. Lyman.

Feb. 20th.—John, the son of John and Eliz. Norton.

March 6th.—Phinehas, the son of Noah and Elizabeth Lyman.

May 8th, 1715.—John, the son of John and Lydia Howe of N. Haven.

May 15th.—Thomas Norton, the son of Joseph and Deborah Norton, and Sarah, the daughter of Abraham and Sarah Crittenden.

May 22d.—James, the son of James and Abigail Bates.

June 5th.—Anna, the daughter of Nath'll and Sarah Sutlief.

June 25th.—Abigail, the daughter of Jonathan and Mehetabel Wells.

July 17th.—Helena, the daughter of Joseph and Helena Seaward.

Aug. 21st, 1715.—Eben, the son of Robert and Barbarra Coe.

Item.—Abigail, the daughter of Joel and Abigail Parmelee.

Aug 28th.—Esther, the daughter of James and Hannah Curtis.

Jan. 1st, 1715-16.—Ebenezer, the son of Samuel and Dinah Norton.

Jan. 15th —Josiah, the son of George Squire and Jane Squire.

Feb. 11th, 1715-16.—Margery, the daughter of Abraham Gillot.

March 18th, 1715-16.—Eben. Right, the son of James and —— Right, the next Sabbath after ye death of his Mother.

Apr. 15th, 1716.—Damaris, the daughter of W. Seaward and Damaris his wife, the same day, Sarah, the daughter of Stephen and Ruth Heycox.

May 6th, 1716.—Joseph Hull, the son of Cornelius and Mahetabel Hull.

Aug. 5th, 1716.—Abraham, the son of Abraham and Sarah Crittenden.

Sept. 2d —Dinah, the daughter of John and Hannah Sutlief.

Sept. 9th, 1716.—Joseph, the son of Joseph and Mary Gaylord.

October, beg.—Martha, the daughter of Moses and Abigail Parsons.

Jan. 13th, 1716-17.—Daniel, the son of Jonathan and Abigail Rose.

Jan. 20th, 1716-17.—David, the son of John and Eliz. Gaylor.

March 24th, 1716-17.—David Coe, the son of Joseph and Abigail Coe

March 31st, 1717 —Eunice Beach, the daughter of Richard and Hannah Beach.

April 7th, 1717.—John Bates, the son of James and Abigail Bates.

April 14th, 1717.—Mary Coe, the daughter of Robert and Barbarah Coe.

Apr. 21st, 1717.—Jonathan, the son of Noah and Elizabeth Lyman.

Apr. 28th, 1717.—Samuel, the son of Samuel and Mary Meeker.

May 5th, 1717.—Patience, the daughter of Stephen and Patience Bates.

May 12th, 1717.—Jeromy Leeman, the son of Jeromy and Abigail Leeman.

July 31st.—Mary, the daughter of James and Hannah Curtiss.

Sept. 1st, 1717.—Hannah, the daughter of Joel and Abigail Parmelee.

Sept. 22d, 1717.—Mary, the daughter of William and Damaris Seaward.

Abigail Chauncey, the daughter of Nathaniel and Sarah Chauncey, was baptized Oct. 23d, 1717. Amos, the son of Amos and Anna Camp.

Elias, the son of Nathan and Rhoda Camp, Feb. 2d, 1717–18.

Feb. 9th, 1717–18.—Ruth, the daughter of George and Jane Squire.

March 2d, 1718.—John Hull, the son of Cornelius and Mahetabel Hull.

Mar. 9th, 1718.—Samuel, the son of Samuel and Dinah Norton.

May 19th, 1718.—Eliphelet Gillot, the son of Abraham Gillot.

June 22d.—Elizabeth Meeker, the daughter of Samuel and Mary Meeker.

July 13, following.—Samuel, ye son of James and Bethiah Right.

Aug. 4th.—John, the son of Jonathan and Mehetabel Wells.

Sept 15th, 1718.—Mindwell, the daughter of Eben. & Exp Lyman, and the same day, Sarah, the daughter of Abraham and Sarah Crittenden.

Oct. 1718.—Phinehas, the son of Joseph and Abigail Coe.

Jan. 11th, 1718–19 —John Coe, ye son of John and Hannah Coe.

Feb. 8th, 1718–19.—Elisha Rose, the son of Jonathan and Abigail Rose; the same day, Daniel Camp, the son of Amos and Ann Camp; and Anna Bates, the daughter of Stephen and Patience Bates, the same day.

March 1st, 1718–19.—Samuel Parsons ye son of Moses and Abigail Parsons, being ye same day in which was born and on ye same day Elisha Rose was bury'd.

March, 1719.—Mary Gaylour, ye daughter of John and Eliz. Gaylour.

Apr. 12th, 1719.—Mary Seaward, the daughter of Caleb and Sarah Seaward. Susanna, the daughter of Benj. Leet.

June 7th, 1719.—Ruth, the daughter of John and Ruth Seaward, and on ye same day, Mathias, the son of Jeromy Leeman.

June 14th, 1719.—Robert Coe, the son of Robert and Barbara Coe.

July 11th, 1719.—Benjamin Norton, the son of John and Eliza Norton.

July 18th, 1719.—Hope, the daughter of Jehiel and Hope Hawley.

October Ruth Heycox, ye daughter of Stephen and Ruth Heycox, and Phebe, ye daughter of James and Hannah Curtiss.

Nov. 8th, 1719.—Cornelious Hull, the sun of Cornelious and Mehetabel Hull.

Nov. 22d.—Jemima Talcott, the daughter of Hezekiah and Jemima Talcott.

Jan. 17th, 1719–20.—Esther Squire, daughter of George and Jane Squire.

Feb. 18th, 1719–20.—John Rose, the son of Jonathan and Rose. The same day, Anne Clark, the daughter of Joseph Clark.

Apr. 10th, 1720.—Abijah Gillot, ye son of Abraham Gillot.

May 1st, 1720.—Sarah Grave, the daughter of Noadiah and Sarah Grave.

May 8th.—Benjamin Beech, the son of Richard and Hannah Beech.

August 15th.—Hannah, the daughter of John and Sarah Parrish.

Sept. 4th.—John, the son of John and Mary Hiccox.

Sept. 11th.—Susanna, the daughter of Abraham and Sarah Crittenden.

Sept. 18th, 1720.—Benjamin, ye son of Samuel and Mary Meeker.

Sept. 25th.—Mary, the daughter of John and Eliz. Gaylord.

Nov. 20th.—Hannah, ye daughter of Nathan and Rhoda Camp

Dec. 4th, 1720.—Abigail, the daughter of John and Ruth Seaward.

Dec. 11th, 1720 —Anne, the daughter of David and Rebecca Robinson.

Jan 21st, 1720-1.—Nathaniel Chauncey, ye son of Nath'll and Sarah Chauncey, having been born in ye night going before ye Sabbath, about midnight.

On ye same 21st Jan., Salmon Seaward, the son of Thomas and Sarah Seaward was baptized.

Feb. 5th, 1720-1.—Daniel Leete, the son of Benjamin Leete.

Feb. 12th, 1720-1.—Stephen and Lucy Bates, the twin children of Stephen and Patience Bates.

Dec. 26th, 1720.—Joel Camp, the son of Amos Camp and Abigail Right, ye daughter of James and Bathiah Right.

March 26th, 1721 —Simeon Coe, ye son of John and Hannah Coe.

Apr. 16th, 1721.—Joseph Seaward, the son of Joseph and Hannah Seaward, and the same day Jerusha, the daughter of Joel and Abigail Parmalee.

Apr. ult., 1721 —Hannah Coe, ye daughter of Ensigne Robert and Barbara Coe, and ye same day, Elizabeth, ye daughter of Cornel and Mehetabel Hull.

May 21st, 1721.—Rowland Rosseter, ye son of Timothy Rosseter.

June 11th, 1721.—Eleazar Gaylor, son of Joseph and Mary Gaylor was baptized.

June 25th, 1721.—Noadiah Grave, the son of Noadiah and Sarah Grave.

David, ye son of Sam'l and Dinah Norton, Aug. 20th, 1721.

Ephraim, son of John and Eliz. Norton, Aug. 27th, 1721.

Abraham Seaward, the son of Caleb and Sarah Seaward.

Nov. 19th —Abigail Leeman, ye daughter of Jeremiah and Abigail Leeman.

Nov. 21st, 1721.—John Curtis, the son of James and Hannah Curtis.

Jan 21st, 1721-2.—James Morris, son of James Morris.

33

March 4th, 1721–22.—David Robinson, the son of David and Rebecca Robinson. Sometime before ye last mentioned, was Damaris S. Rose, daughter of Jon'th and Abigail Rose baptized

March 25th, 1722.—Eliza Hickox, daughter of Stephen and Ruth Hickox, and David Levet, son of David Levet.

May 16th, 1722.—Baptized Mary Meekoe, ye daughter of Samuel and Mary Meekoe, in their own dwelling house

June 3d.—Deborah Seaward, the daughter of John and Ruth Seaward.

June 10th, 1722.—Samuel Stone Hawley, the son of Jehiel and Hope Hawley.

Sept 9th.—John Smith, ye son of Stephen Smith.

Sept. 23d, 1722.—Mary Crittenden, the daughter of Abraham and Sarah Crittenden.

Sept ult —Thomas Tibbals, the son of Joseph and Abigail Tibbals.

Oct 7th, 1722 —Eliphalet Clarke, ye son of Joseph Clarke

Oct. 28th, 1722.—Rachel Roberts was taken into Covenant, received baptism, and her children Sam. and Eliz. Roberts were baptized.

Nov. 4th —Rebeckah Gillot, the daughter of Abigail Gillot, and Mary Parsons, the daughter of Simeon and Mary Parsons.

Nov. 25th, 1722.—Leah Hill was taken into Covenant, received baptism, and her child, Sarah Hill, was baptized, and ye same day, Eunice Welton was taken into the Covenant and received baptism.

Dec. 2d, 1722.—Hepzibah Seaward, daughter of Joseph Seaward.

Jan. 20th, 1722–3.—Rhoda Camp, daughter of Nathan and Rhoda Camp. Lydia Seaward, daughter of Noadiah Seaward.

Feb. 17th, 1722–3.—Eliz. Merwin, the daughter of Daniel and Mary Merwin, and Mary Talcott, ye daughter of Hezekiah and Jemima Talcott.

March 20th, 1722–3.—Stephen Bates, the son of Stephen and Patience Bates

March 17th, 1722–3.—Elizabeth Parsons, daughter of Moses and Abigail Parsons, and ye same day, Anna Roberts, daughter of Samuel and Rachel Roberts.

March 24th, 1723.—Mary Baldwin, daughter of David Baldwin and Hannah Stephens, daughter of Thomas Stevens.

March ult.—Jehiel, ye son of Judith Sutlief and Thankful ye daughter of John and Mary Hickox.

Apr. 21st, 1723.—Susanna, ye daughter of Dan. and Leah Hill

May 5th.—Sybylla Coe, the daughter of John Coe.

June 23d.—Daniel Right, the son of James Right and Elizabeth Grave, daughter of Noahdiah Grave.

June ult., 1723.—John Robinson, son of David and Rebecca Robinson. Hannah Lyman, ye daughter Eben. & Exp Lyman. Robert Coe, ye son of Robert and Barbara Coe.

October 25th.—Aaron Parmalee, the son of Joel and Abigail Parmalee, whom I baptized in Joel Parmalee's house, the child being in hazard of dying.

Oct. 27th.—Jerushah Hickox, the daughter of Joseph and Sarah Hickox, Jun., was baptized.

Nov. 3d, 1723.—Cornelious Hull, the son of Cornelious and Mehetabel Hull.

Nov. 24th, 1723.—Dinah Norton, daughter of Sam'll Norton.

Dec. 8th, 1723.—Ann Burritt, daughter of James Burritt.

Dec. 29th, 1723.—Adonijah Morris, son of Adonijah Morris

Jan 4th, 1723-4.—Martha, ye daughter of Caleb and Sarah Seaward

Feb. 9th, 1723-4.—Phebe, the daughter of Thomas and Sarah Seaward.

Feb. 16th, 1723-4.—Israel Camp, son of J—— Camp

March 8th, 1723-4.—Sarah Beach, daughter of Richard and —— Beach

March 22d, 1723-4.—Justice Rose, the son of Jonathan Rose.

1724, Apr. 5th.—Josiah Fowler, son of Josiah and Hannah Fowler.

Apr. 12th, 1724.—John Squire, son of George Squire.

May 10th, 1724.—Sybilla Sutlief, ye daughter of Eunice Sutlief.

June 7th.—Stephen Norton, son of John and Eliz. Norton.

June 14th.—Joseph Frances, son of Dan. and Eliz Frances.

July 5th—David Curtiss, son of James and Hannah Curtiss

July 26th.—Ephraim Coe, son of Eph. and Hannah Coe.

Aug. 2d.—Brotherton Seaward, son of Joseph and Hannah Seaward.

Aug. 16th —Ezekiel Leete, son of Ben. Leete.

Sept 13th, 1724.—Elnathan Chauncey, son of Nathaniel and Sarah Chauncey.

Sept. 20th —Phinehas Parmalee, son of Joel Parmalee.

Oct. 4th.—Nath'll Meeker, son of Samuel and Mary Meeker

Oct. 11th, 1724.—Sarah Smith, daughter of Stephen Smith.

Nov. 22d, 1724.—Ruth Lyman, daughter of Eben Lyman, and Eliz. Seaward, daughter of Noahdiah Seaward.

Feb. 21st.—Mary Seaward, daughter of John and Ruth Seaward.

March 14th, 1724–5.—Jonathan Hickock, son of Stephen Hickock

Apr 4th.—Lucy Bates, the daughter of Stephen Bates.

April.—Hannah, ye daughter of Josiah Fowler.

May 16th.—Daniel Robinson, son of Robinson.

May 30th, 1725.—Elizabeth Hiccox, daughter of Joseph Hiccox, Jun.

June 13th.—Timothy Roster, son of Timothy Roster, born 4 months after ye death of his father.

June 22d.—The twins of Theophilus and Elizabeth Morrison, viz : Theophilus and Sarah.

July 4th, 1725 —Samuel Right, the son of James and Bethiah Right; the same day, Samuel Parsons, son of Timothy and Mary Parsons; and Abigail, the daughter of Joseph and Abigail Theobalds, commonly called Tibbals.

July 19th, 1725 —Daniel Hill, son of Daniel and Leah Hill; and ye same day, James, the son of Daniel and Elizabeth Francis.

Aug. penult.—Katharine Hickox, the daughter of James and Katharine Hickox, born after ye death of James Hickox.

Sept., 1725.—Annes Talcott, the daughter of Hezekiah and Jemima Tallcot.

Sept. penult.—Abigail the daughter of Noahdiah and Sarah Grave; and ye same day, Sarah, the daughter of Samuel and Rachel House.

October 3.—Mehetabel, the daughter of Cornelius and Mehetabel Hull.

Nov. 21st.—Hannah, the daughter of Jehiel and Hope Howley.

Dec. 12th, 1725.—John, the son of Adonijah Morris.

Dec. 19th, 1725.—Zimni Hills, son of Benoni Hills; and the same day, Sarah Coe, daughter of John Coe.

Jan 9th.—Ann Meeker, the daughter of Joseph Meeker.

Jan. 30th, 1725–6.—David Norton, son of Sam'l and Dinah Norton.

Feb. 20th, 1725.—Ichabod Camp, son of John Camp; the same day, Elizabeth Rose, the daughter of Jonathan Rose.

March 27th, 1726.—Amos Seaward, son of Thomas and Sarah Seaward.

April 24th, 1726.—Eli Camp, son of Nathan and Rhoda Camp.

May 28th, 1726.—Abner, the son of David Baldwin.

June 19th, 1726.—John Seaward, son of John and Ruth Seaward

June 26th.—Ebenezer Guernsey, daughter of Eben. Guernsey.

July 10th, 1726.—Theophilus, son of Theophilus and Elizabeth Morrison.

July 23d, 1726—John Sutlif, son of John and Mehetabel Sutlif.

Aug. 7th, 1727.—Samuel Coe, the son of Ephraim and Hannah Coe.

Sept. 4th.—Sylvanus Seaward, son of Noadiah Seaward.

Sept. 11th, 1726.—Asa and Tamar Leete, twin children of Benjamin Leete.

Oct. 23d, 1726.—Abner and John Newton, sons of Abner Newton; Elisha Kilbourn, son of Mr. Hez. Kilbourn, and Sam'l Smith, son of Stephen Smith.

Dec. 18th, 1726.—Rebeckah, daughter of David and Rebeckah Robinson

Dec. 25th, 1726.—Anna, the daughter of Abraham and Sarah Crittenden.

Jan. 15th, 1726–7.—Caleb Fowler, son of Josiah Fowler.

Jan 15th, 1726–7.— , daughter of Sam'l and Mary Meeker.

March 12th, 1726–7.—Miles, son of David and Mary Fowler.

May 21st, 1727.—Beulah, daughter of Joseph and Hannah Seaward.

May 23d.—Catharine, daughter of Joseph Hiccox.

June 25th, 1727.—Thomas, son of Robert and Barbara Coe.

July 23d, 1727.—Elias Leete and Ann Leete, children of John Leete.

July 30th —Abel Coe, son of Lieut. Joseph Coe.

Aug. 6th, 1727.—Jared Everest, son of Benjamin Everest.

Aug. 20th, 1727.—Rachel Strong, daughter of Huit and Dinah Strong.

Sept. 3d, 1727.—Thomas Francis, son of Daniel and Elizabeth Francis, and Beriah Hills, son of Benoni Hills.

Sept. 10th.—Manus Griswold, child of Sam'l Griswold.

Sept. 17th, 1727 —Hannah Parsons, daughter of Timothy and Mary Parsons.

Oct. 8th, 1727.—Hannah Curtis, daughter of James and Hannah Curtiss.

Oct. 22d, 1727 —Sarah Morrison, daughter of Theophilis and Elizabeth Morrison.

Oct. 29th, 1727.—John Tibbals, son of Joseph and Abigail Tibbals.

Nov., 1727.—Moses Seaward, son of John Seaward.

Dec. 10th, 1727.—Hannah and Sarah Right, twins of James Right.

Dec. 31st, 1727.—Katharine Seaward, daughter of Tho. Seaward.

Jan. 7th, 1727–8 —Holland, Negro servant of Capt. Crane.

Jan. 21st, 1727–8.—Elizabeth, ye daughter of John and Elizabeth Norton.

Jan. 28th, 1727–8 —Moses Hill, son of Dan'l and Leah Hill, and John Sutlif, son of John and Mehetabel Sutlif.

March 3d, 1727–8.—Mercy Johnson, daughter of David and Ruth Johnson.

Apr. 7th, 1728 —Anna Morris, daughter of Adonijah Morris.

Apr. 21st, 1728 —Elizabeth Kilbourn, daughter of Mr. Hezekiah Kilbourn; and on ye same day, David Leete, son of John and Eliz. Leete.

May.—Timothy Robinson, son of David and Rebeckah Robinson.

May 19th.—Job Camp, son of John Camp

June, 1728.—Elisha Rose, son of Jonathan Rose.

July 14th, 1728.—Hannah Thomas, daughter of Abraham and Hannah Thomas.

Sept. 1728.—John Smith, son of Stephen Smith.

Oct. 6th, 1728.—David Grave, son of Noadiah Grave; and Rachel Talcott, the daughter of Hez. Talcott.

Oct 13th, 1728.—Allen Leet, son of Gideon Leet, and Elizabeth Fowler, daughter of Josiah Fowler.

Oct. 20th.—Rhoda Guernsey, daughter of Eben. and Rhoda Guernsey.

Nov. 24th, 1728—Timothy Coe, son of Ephraim Coe.

Dec 8th, 1728.—Phinehas Meeker, son of Joseph Meeker, and Rachel Roberts, daughter of Samuel Roberts.

Dec. 22d, 1728.—Reuben Coe, son of Robert and Barbara Coe.

Dec. 29th—Martha Baldwin, daughter of David Baldwin.

Jan 26th, 1728–9—Noah Norton, son of Sam. C and Dinah Norton, and David Fowler, son of David and Mary Fowler

Feb. 16th, 1728–9.—John Fairchild, son of Curtiss and Mercy Fairchild

Feb. 23d, 1728–9.—Jared Seaward, son of Joseph Seaward

March 2d, 1728–9.—Samuel Roberts and Jehiel Hull, son of Cornelius Hull.

March 16th, 1728–9.—Margaret, the daughter of Theophilus Morrison and Elizabeth Morrison.

March 23d.—Mindwell Seaward, daughter of John and Ruth Seaward.

Apr 6th, 1729.—Aaron Griswold, son of Sam'l Griswold; Joseph Hiccox, son of Joseph Hiccox; Lucy Strong, daughter of Huit and Dinah Strong.

May 18th, 1729.—Aaron Meeker, son of Sam'l Meeker; and Temperance Leet, daughter of Benj. Leet.

May 25th, 1729.—Elah Camp, son of Nathan Camp, and Abigail Everest, daughter of Benjamin Everest.

July 6th, 1729.—Ephraim Camp, son of John and Hannah Camp.

July 20th, 1729.—Burwell Newton, son of Abner Newton

July 27th, 1729.—Phinehas Robinson, son of David Robinson, and Hannah Sanford, daughter of Joseph Sanford

Aug. 3d, 1729.—Eph. Bates, son of Stephen and Patience Bates.

Aug. 24th.—Dan'l Francis, ye son of Daniel Francis.

Oct. 26th, 1729.—Tamar Coe, daughter of John and Hannah Coe.

Dec. 14th, 1729.—Amy Spelman, daughter of Richard and Margery Spelman.

Dec. 28th, 1729.—Catharine Right, daughter of Jonathan and Phebe Right.

Jan. 11th, 1729-30.—John Ferguson, son of Sam'l and Isabel Ferguson.

Jan. 25th, 1729-30.—Ebenezer Tibbals, son of Joseph and Abigail Tibbals; Aaron Baldwin, son of Moses and Abigail Baldwin; William Clarke, son of William and Judith Clarke; Cloe Leet, daughter of John and Eliz. Leet, all the same day.

Feb. 22d, 1729.—Esther Parsons, daughter of Timothy and Mary Parsons.

March 8th, 1729-30.—Timothy Morris, son of Adonijah Morris.

March 22d, 1729-30.—Mary Kilbourn, daughter of Mr. Hez. Kilbourn.

Apr. 5th, 1730.—Nath. Crittenden, son of Abraham Crittenden, and Mary Camp, daughter of Mr. John Camp.

May 3d, 1730.—Jerushah Thomas, daughter of Abraham and Hannah Thomas, and Abiel Baldwin, son of Ezra and Ruth Baldwin.

May 24th, 1730.—Ephraim Howe, son of John and Lydia Howe.

June 7th, 1730.—William Coe, son of Ensign Robert Coe.

June 14th, 1730.—Nathan Seaward, son of Thomas Seaward, and David Johnson, son of David Johnson.

June 21st, 1730.—Esther Seaward, daughter of John and Ruth Seaward.

July 12th, 1730.—James Wadsworth, son of James and Abigail Wadsworth.

July 26th, 1730.—Nathan Smith, son of Stephen Smith.

Aug. 23d, 1730.—Jonathan Fowler, son of Josiah and Hannah Fowler; and Mehetabel Norton, daughter of Joseph Norton.

Sept. 13th, 1730.—Abigail Crane, daughter of Silas and Mercy Crane.

Sept. 20th, 1730.—Jenny, Negro, my own Servant girl.

Oct. 10th, 1730.—James Hinman, son of David and Hannah Hinman.

Dec. 17th, 1730.—Catherine Fairchild, daughter of Thomas and Thankful Fairchild.

Jan. 3d, 1730–1.—Experience Strong, daughter of Eliakim Strong, and Mary Hills, daughter of Benoni Hills.

Jan 10th, 1730–1.—Elizabeth Francis, daughter of Daniel and Elizabeth Francis.

Jan. 1730.—Dan. Squire, son of Dan and Patience Squire

Feb. 14th, 1730–1.—Mary Fowler, daughter of David and Mary Fowler.

Feb. 21st, 1730–1.—Aaron Coe, son of Ephraim Coe, and Hannah Seaward, daughter of Joseph and Hannah Seaward

Feb. ult., 1730–1.—Lemuel Gurnsey, son of Eben and Rhoda Gurnsey.

March 21st, 1730–1.—Sharon Rose, son of Jonathan Rose

Apr. 18th, 1731.—Sarah Hiccox, daughter of Joseph Hiccox

May 2d, 1731.—Levi Leete, son of Benj. Leete.

May 9th, 1731.—Gideon Leet, son of Gideon and Abigail Leet; Lewis Fairchild, son of Curtis and Mercy Fairchild.

June 7th.—Aaron Hill, son of Daniel and Leah Hill.

June 17th.—James Robinson, son of David and Rebecca Robinson.

June 22d, 1731.—Sarah Griswold, daughter of Samuel Griswold, of Black Rock.

July 11th, 1731.—Josiah Meeker, son of Samuel and Mary Meeker.

July 25th, 1731.—Nathaniel Crittenden, son of Abraham and Barbara Crittenden.

July 30th, 1731.—Sarah Sanford, whom I baptized in the dwelling house of Joseph Sanford, her father, she being threatened with convulsions, and she dyed the night after

Aug 1st.—Mindwell Beech, daughter of Azariah and Lydia Beech.

34

Aug 8th, 1731—Sarah Smith, wife of John Smith; Mary Roberts, daughter of Samuel and Rachel Roberts; and Elisha, Negro servant of Dea. Burrit.

Aug 22d.—Submit Seaward, daughter of John and Ruth Seaward.

Sept 5th, 1731.—Ozias Camp, son of Nathan and Rhoda Camp.

Sept.—Elizabeth Smith, daughter of John Smith.

Oct 3d, 1731.—Phinehas Camp, son of John and Damaris Camp, and Sarah Hinman, daughter of Samuel and Abigail Hinman.

Oct. 24th, 1731.—Phillis Leet, daughter of John and Elizabeth Leet.

October ult, 1731.—Rosamon Pamerly, daughter of John and ——— Pamerly.

Nov. 7th, 1731.—Elizabeth Lyman, ye daughter of Aaron and Rebecca Lyman.

Nov. 21st, 1731—Cloe Seaward, daughter of Eben and Sarah Seaward.

Nov. 28th, 1731.—Jemimah Meeker, daughter of Joseph and Ann Meeker.

Dec. 6th, 1731.—Eben. Ferguson, son of Sam'l Ferguson, whom I baptized privately.

Jan 9th, 1731-2.—Abraham Thomas, son of Abraham and Hannah Thomas.

Jan. 16th, 1731-2.—Roswell Grave, son of Noahdiah Grave, and Elihu Norton, son of Joseph Norton, Jun.

Jan. 22d, 1731-2—Phebe Baker, the wife of Samuel Baker, whom I baptized in their dwelling house, she being in great danger of death, who received much comfort that morning and died in two days

Feb. 6th.—Rhoda Talcott, daughter of Mr. Hezekiah and Jemima Talcott.

Feb. 20th, 1731-2.—Abigail Coe, the daughter of Capt. Coe, and Jane Wheeler, the daughter of Job and Jane Wheeler.

March 12th, 1731-2.—Hannah Right, daughter of Jonathan and Phebe Right.

March 26th, 1732.—Ruth Baker.

May 7th, 1732.—Abigail Kilbourn, daughter of Mr. Hezekiah Kilbourn.

May 14th, 1732.—Mary Griswold, daughter of Hezekiah Griswold, of Black Rock.

June 11th, 1732.—Jesse Crane, son of Silas and Mercy Crane, and Mary Bates, daughter of Stephen and Patience Bates.

July 2d, 1732.—Israel Squire, son of Daniel and Patience Squire.

July 9th, 1732.—Sarah Smith, the daughter of Stephen Smith.

July 16th, 1732.—Huldah Spelman, daughter of Richard and Margery Spelman.

July 26th, 1732.—I baptized John Noyes Wadsworth, son of James and Abigail Wadsworth, whom I baptized privately.

Aug. 6th, 1732.—Bela Strong, son of Huit Strong

Aug. 20th, 1732.—Lois Coe, daughter of John and Hannah Coe

Aug 21st.—Michal Avored, daughter of James and Abigail Avored.

Sept. 3d, 1732.—Charles Squire, son of Samuel and Abigail Squire.

Sept 10th.—Hazael Hinman, son of Zec and Hannah Hinman, and Peter, Negro servant of Capt. Nathaniel Sutlief

Sept. 17th, 1732.—Abigail Curtiss, daughter of James and Hannah Curtiss.

Sept. 24th, 1732.—Oliver Sanford, son of Joseph and ——— Sanford.

Oct. 1st, 1732.—Phebe Baldwin, daughter of Ezra and Ruth Baldwin, and Phebe Parsons, daughter of Ithamar and Sarah Parsons.

Oct. 22d, 1732.—Elihu Fowler, son of Josiah and Hannah Fowler, and Rachel, daughter of Robert and Barbara Coe.

Oct 29th, 1732.—Enos Fairchild, son of Thomas and Thankful Fairchild.

Nov. 5th, 1732.—Samuel Newton, son of Abner Newton.

Nov. 19th, 1732.—Abiathar Camp, son of John Camp, 3d.

Nov. 19th, 1732.—Eunice Parsons, daughter of Moses and Elizabeth Parsons.

Nov. 26th, 1732.—Simeon Parsons, son of Simion Parsons.

Dec. 3d, 1732.—Mary Theobald, daughter of Joseph and Abigail Theobald.

Dec. 10th.—Mary Fenn, daughter of John Fenn.

Dec 17th, 1732.—John Hills, son of Benoni and Hannah Hills, was baptized, and Peter, negro servant of Dea. Burrit.

Dec. 24th.—Daniel Coe, son of Ephraim and Hannah Coe.

Jan. 6th, 1732–3.—Zipporah Fairchild, daughter of Curtis and Mercy Fairchild, and Ann Parmalee, daughter of John Parmalee.

Jan. 21st, 1732–3.—Timothy, son of Timothy and Mary Parsons, Lucretia, daughter of Joseph and Hannah Seaward, and Catharine, daughter of Eben and Rhoda Gurnsey.

Jan. 28th, 1732–3.—Hannah, daughter of Joseph Johnson.

Feb. 24th, 1732–3.—Aaron Seaward, son of John and Ruth Seaward.

March 11th, 1732–3.—Huldah Francis, daughter of Daniel and Elizabeth Francis

Apr. 1st, 1733—Joel Robinson, son of David and Rebeckah Robinson, and John Crane, son of Henry and Mercy Crane.

Apr 22d, 1733.—Rachel Alfred, daughter of Thomas Alfred, Jun

Apr. 28 or 29th.—James Right and Sarah, wife of Noadiah Grave, were baptized, and by baptism admitted into full communion; also, Lucy, daughter of Nathaniel and Concurrence Seaward, Sarah, daughter of Joseph and Prudence Wheeler, and Lydia, daughter of Azariah and Lydia Beech, were all baptized.

May 20th, 1733.—James Hiccox, son of Joseph and Sarah Hiccox.

June 10th, 1733—Wilkinson Henman, son of Samuel and Abigail Henman.

June 17th, 1733.—Samuel Stent Squire, son of Ephraim and Mahetable Squire.

Aug 10th, 1733.—Sarah Thomas, daughter of Abraham and Hannah Thomas.

Sept 16th, 1733.—Nathan Osborn, son of Samuel and Hannah Osborn, and Mary Smith, daughter of John Smith.

Sept 23d, 1733.—Eunice Johnson, daughter of Benjamin and Eunice Johnson.

Sept. 30th.—Mary Wheeler, daughter of Job and Jane Wheeler.

Oct. 14th, 1733—Ruth Camp, daughter of John and Hannah Camp.

Oct. 28th, 1733.—Mary Meeker, daughter of Samuel and Mary Meeker, Ann Parsons, daughter of Aaron and Abigail Parsons.

Nov 25th, 1733—Joel Seaward, son of Eben and Dorothy Seaward; Adah, daughter of Nathan and Rhoda Camp

Feb 20th, 1733-4.—Samuel Crittenden, son of Abraham and Sarah Crittenden.

March 3d, 1733-4—Mary, daughter of David and Ruth Johnson.

March 17th, 1733-4—Phineas Parsons, son of Simeon Parsons, and Ann Latimer, daughter of David and Mary Lattimer.

March ult., 1734—Ann Graves, daughter of Joseph and Ann Graves.

Apr. 7th, 1734.—David Smith, son of Stephen Smith of Haddam.

Aug. 14th, 1734—Eleazar Squire, son of Daniel and Patience Squire; Abiathar Squire, son of Samuel and Abigail Squire

May 5th, 1734—Laurana Seaward, daughter of Noahdiah and M. Seaward, and Prudence, the negro child of Reuben and Dinah, negro servants of Dea. Burrit.

May 19th, 1734.—Hephzibah Hill, daughter of Dan. and Leah Hill.

June 3d, 1734.—Jonas, the son, and Mary, the daughter of Timothy Bishop.

June 23d, 1734.—Eunice, the daughter of James and Hannah Curtis.

June 30th, 1734.—John Norton, son of John and Deborah Norton of Saybrook, his mother Deborah, having owned the covenant that day.

July 7th, 1734.—Amy Spelman, daughter of Richard and Margery Spelman.

July 14th, 1734.—Sarah Fowler, daughter of Serj. Josiah Fowler and Hannah his wife.

Aug. 21st, 1734.—Enos Seaward, son of Nathaniel and Currence Seaward.

Aug. 28th.—John Roberts, son of Samuel and Rachel Roberts, 1734.

Sept. 1st, 1734.—Oliver Bates, son of Stephen and Patience Bates; and Abiel Camp, son of Edward and Mary Camp; and

Mary, daughter of Thomas and Thankful Fairchild, all in the same day.

Sept 8th, 1734 —Mary Strong, daughter of Eliakim and Mehetabel Strong

Sept. 21st, 1734.—Mary Hills, daughter of Benoni and H.—— Hills, and Amy Wetmore, daughter of Jabez and Abigail Wetmore.

Oct 13th, 1734.—Mary Guernsey, daughter of Eben and Rhoda Gurnsey; and Israel Rose, son of Jonathan Rose.

Oct 20th, 1734 —Phinehas Parmalee, son of John Parmalee; and Timothy Osborn, son of Samuel and Hannah Osborn.

Oct. 27th, 1734.—David and Daniel, twin sons of Joseph and Ann Meeker, were baptized.

Nov. 3d, 1734.—Sarah Burrit, daughter of Israel and Sarah Burrit, born Nov. 2d.

Nov 24th, 1734.—Mehetabel Johnson, daughter of Benjamin and Eunice Johnson

Dec. 7th, 1734.—Isabel, daughter of Jonathan and Phebe Right; also, Elizabeth, daughter of John and Ruth Seaward.

Dec. 7th, 1734 —Mary, daughter of David and Rebecca Robinson.

Dec. 22d, 1734.—Reuben Fairchild, son of Curtis and Mercy Fairchild.

Dec. 29th, 1744 —Elihu Hinman, son of Zachariah and Hannah Hinman.

Jan. 5th, 1734–5.—Seth Coe, son of Ephraim Coe.

Jan. 26th, 1734–5.—Elnathan Camp, son of John and Damaris Camp; and Aaron Spelman, son of Thomas and Sarah Spelman.

Feb. 2d, 1734–5.—Samuel Seward, son of Joseph and Hannah Seward; and Mercy Francis, daughter of Daniel and Elizabeth Francis.

Feb. 16th, 1734–5.—Hood Crane, son of Silas and Mercy Crane; and Miriam Beech, daughter of Joseph and Exp Beech.

March 2d, 1734–5.—Heth Camp, son of Eleazer and —— Camp; and Daniel Norton, son of Joseph and Prudence Norton.

March 9th, 1734–5 —Eben Baldwin, son of Ezra and Ruth Baldwin; and Hannah Bishop, daughter of Timothy and —— Bishop.

March 30th, 1735.—Samuel Parsons, son of John and Esther Parsons; and Dorathy and Deborah, the twin daughters of Hezekiah Griswold, of Black Rock.

Apr. 6th, 1735—Joel Right, son of John and Lucy Right was baptized; and Mercy Parsons, sd. daughter of Moses Parsons, Jun., was baptized.

Apr. 27th, 1735.—Jemima Parsons, daughter of Timothy and Mary Parsons.

May 18th, 1735.—Ann Wheeler, daughter of Joseph and Ann Wheeler.

May 25th, 1735.—Sarah, sd. daughter of Ben. Leete, and Prudence, negro child of —— and Dinah, the servants of Dea. Burrit.

June 1st, 1735.—Sam Tibbals, son of Joseph and Abigail Tibbals; David Parsons, son of Ithimar Parsons and Sarah his wife

June 15th, 1735.—Silvanus Ashur Fairchild, son of Samuel and Phebe Fairchild; and Aaron Parsons, son of Aaron and Abigail Parsons

June 29th, 1735.—Nathan Curtis, son of James and Hannah Curtis, Jun.; and Elihu Crane, son of Henry Crane, Jun. and Mercy his wife.

July 13th.—Enos Seaward, son of Eben and Dorothy Seaward.

July 27th, 1735.—Ruth Hiccox, daughter of Joseph and Sarah Hiccox.

Sept. 7th.—Jonah Sanford, son of Joseph and —— Sanford.

Sept. 21st, 1735.—Phebe Fowler, daughter of Joseph and Ruth Fowler.

Oct. 26th, 1735—Rebekah Picket, daughter of Samuel and Mary Picket.

Nov. 2d, 1735.—Lois Strong, daughter of Huit and Dinah Strong; and Lucy Right, daughter of John and Lucy Right.

Nov. 16th, 1735.—Sam. Camp, son of John and Hannah Camp.

Nov. 23d.—Mary Gullony, daughter of John and Abigail Gullony.

Nov. 30th, 1735.—Ruth Lyman, daughter of Eben Lyman. Jun. by his 2d wife; and Jacob Watrous.

Jan. 11th, 1735–6.—Mary, ye daughter of Noadiah and —— Seward.

Jan. 25th, 1735.—Phebe Coe, daughter of John and Hannah Coe.

Feb. 8th, 1735.—Eunice Talcot, daughter of Hezekiah and Jemima Talcot.

Feb 22d, 1735.—Daniel Smith, son of William Smith.

March 21st, 1735.—Samuel Squire, son of Samuel and Abigail Squire.

Apr. 4th, 1736.—David Rose, son of David Rose.

May 16th, 1736.—Elisha Fairchild, son of Samuel and Phebe Fairchild.

May 30th, 1736.—Noah Robinson, son of David and Rebekah Robinson.

July 4th, 1736.—Ashael Spelman, son of John Spelman; and Hannah Beech, the daughter of Joseph and Exp. Beech.

July 11th, 1736.—Henry Seaward, son of Nathaniel and Currence Seaward

July 25th, 1736.—Katharine Camp, daughter of Edward and Mary Camp; and Katharine Wetmore, the daughter of Jabez and Abig'l Wetmore.

Aug. 1st, 1736.—Samuel and Mary Henman, twin children of Samuel and Mary Henman.

Aug. 15th, 1736.—Israel Burrit, son of Dea. Israel and Sarah Burrit, having been born on the day before, viz: on Saturday, near night.

Aug. 22d, 1736.—Benjamin Hiccox, son of Joseph and S. Hiccox; and Mary Spelman, daughter of Thomas and Sarah Spelman.

Aug. 29th, 1736.—John Smith, son of John Smith, at Haddam, Conn.

Sept. 12th, 1736.—Elizabeth Griswold, daughter of Samuel and —— Griswold, at Black Rock.

Sept. 19th, 1736.—Seth Hills, son of Benoni and H—— Hills; and Aaron Parmalee, son of John Parmalee.

Oct. 3d, 1736—Submit Johnson, daughter of Benj. and Eunice Johnson.

Oct. 24th, 1736—Joel Roberts, son of Sam'l and Rachel Roberts; and Desire Squire, daughter of Daniel and Patience Squire.

Oct. 31st, 1736.—Abigail Norton, daughter of Isaac and —— Norton, and Judith, negro woman servant of Mr. Fowler, baptized and received into communion.

Nov. 7th, 1736.—Lois Hill, daughter of Daniel Hill and Leah Hill.

Nov 14th, 1736—Enoch Coe, son of Ephraim and Hannah Coe, and Pelor, negro boy, son of Judith, negro serv't of Mr. Josiah Fowler.

Dec. 26th.—Dinah Fairchild, daughter of Tho and Thankful Fairchild.

Jan 2d, 1736-7.—Mary Rose, daughter of Jonathan and ——, Rose, his wife.

Jan. 16th, 1736-7—I baptized Abraham Fairchild, son of Edmund and Mary Fairchild, privately, which child dyed the next day.

Feb. 5th, 1736-7.—Noah Fowler, son of Joseph and Ruth Fowler.

Feb 13th, 1736-7—Aaron Fowler, son of Joseph and Hannah Fowler; Alexander Fairchild, son of Curtis and Mary Fairchild; and Phineas Spelman, son of Richard and Margery Spelman

March 1st, 1736—In the night following the last of Feb. I baptized Ebenezer Gurnsey in the house of Eben Gurnsey, having been born before due time and not likely to live, and dyed that same night.

March 28th, 1737.—Susanna Fenn, daughter of Samuel Fenn.

Apr. 3d, 1737.—Reuben Henman, son of Ruben and Hannah Henman.

Apr. 17th, 1737.—Ann Right, daughter of John and Lucy Right.

May 1st, 1737.—Jonathan Right, son of Jonathan and Phebe Right; and Daniel Francis, son of Daniel and Elizabeth Francis.

May 8th, 1737.—Ezra Baldwin, twin son of Ezra and Ruth Baldwin, the other twin having been born dead.

May 15th, 1737.—John Seaward, son of Joseph Seaward; and Roger Newton, son of Abner Newton.

May 22d, 1737.—Lucy Bishop, daughter of Tim. Bishop.

May 29th, 1737.—Samuel Squire, son of Samuel and Abigail Squire.

35

June 5th, 1737.—Oliver Fowler, son of David Fowler.

June 26th, 1737.—Mary Camp, daughter of Eleazar Camp, and Mary Thomas, daughter of Abr. and Hannah Thomas.

July 3d, 1737.—Lucy Parsons, daughter of Moses Parsons, Jun.

Aug. 14th, 1737.—Urania Camp, daughter of John Camp ye 3d and Damaris his wife, was baptized.

Sept. 11th, 1737.—Aaron Curtis, son of James and Hannah Curtis, Jun.

Nov. 13th, 1737.—Silas Crane, son of Mercy and Silas Crane; and Katharine Rosseter, daughter of Bryan and Kate Rosseter; and Titan, negro son of Peter and Dinah, servants of Dea Burrit.

Nov. 27th, 1737.—Rhoda Parsons, daughter of Ithamar Parsons and Sarah.

Dec. 4th, 1737.—Katharine Rose, daughter of David Rose.

Jan. 1st, 1737–8 —John Parsons, son of Timothy and Mary Parsons; and Ruthamah Seaward, daughter of Noahdiah and Mary Seaward.

Jan. 8th, 1737–8 —Phineas Coe, son of Joseph and Hannah Coe; Submit Leete, daughter of John and Eliz. Leete

Jan. 29th, 1737.—Caleb Fairchild, son of Edmund and Mary Fairchild.

Feb. 5th, 1737–8.—Jonathan Norton and his wife, and Josiah Squire and his wife, owned the Cov.; and Sarah Squire, daughter of Josiah and Sarah Squire, and Sarah Wells, daughter of Jonathan and Mary Wells were baptized.

Jan 12th, 1737–8.—Phebe, the daughter of Henry and Mercy Crane, and Sarah, the daughter of Sumner and Sarah Stone, the last child was baptized in ye old Meeting House, baptized the last Sabbath of that year.

Feb. 19th, 1737–8.—Noah Parsons, son of Simeon and —— Parsons, the first child baptized in ye new Meeting House

Feb 26th, 1737–8.—Eben Guernsey, son of Eben and Rhoda Guernsey.

March 5th, 1737–8.—Ephraim Guthrie, son of John and Abigail Guthrie; John Camp, son of John and Hannah Camp; Jonathan, the son of Jonathan and Ruth Norton.

March 12th, 1737–8.—Abigail Robinson, daughter of David and Rebekah Robinson.

April 2d, 1738.—Phebe, daughter of Joseph and Experience Beech.

April 16th, 1738.—Aaron Smith, son of Steph. Smith, Hannah Pamely, daughter of Hezekiah Pamely.

May 1st, 1738.—John Meeker, son of Joseph and Ann Meeker.

May 14th, 1738.—Thankful Johnson, daughter of Benj and Eunice Johnson.

May 21st, 1738.—Sarah Fairchild, daughter of Samuel and Phebe Fairchild.

June 3d, 1738.—Mary Norton, daughter of Isaac Norton.

July 15th, 1738.—Daniel Spelman, son of Thomas and Sarah Spelman.

July 22d, 1738.—Sylvanus Bishop, son of William and Patience Bishop.

August 6th, 1738.—Mary Wheeler, daughter of Joseph and Prudence Wheeler; and Hannah Hiccox, daughter of Joseph and Sarah Hiccox.

Sept. 17th, 1738.—Elizabeth Hiccox, daughter of Samuel and —— Hiccox.

Sept. 24th, 1738.—William Smith, son of Dan'l and —— Smith; and Jerusha Parsons, daughter of Aaron and —— Parsons.

October 5th, 1738.—I baptized Benjamin Beech, son of Abel and Margaret Beech, privately in ye house Mr. Picket, it being very small and not likely to live, born within the space of half year and wanting two days of half a year from yr marriage.

Oct. 15th, 1738.—Sarah Stevens, daughter of Allen and Hannah Stevens.

Oct. 22d.—Nathan Seaward, son of Nathaniel and Currence Seaward; and Ann Griswold, daughter of Samuel and —— Griswold.

Nov. 5th, 1738.—Ann Fairchild, daughter of Thomas and Thankful Fairchild; and Lydia Griswold, daughter of Jer. and Bashua Griswold, and Zilpah, negro daughter of my servant negro maid, Jenny.

Dec. 3d, 1738.—Titus Fowler, son of David Fowler.

Dec. 24th, 1738.—Esther Norton, daughter of Joseph and Prudence Norton.

Jan. 7th, 1738-9.—Robert Fairchild, son of Curtis and Mercy

Fairchild, and Dinah Camp, daughter of Edward and Mary Camp.

Jan. 14th, 1738-9.—Eliphaz Parsons, son of Moses Parsons.

Feb 4th, 1738-9.—Aaron Right, son of John and Lucy Right.

Feb. 18th, 1738-9 —David Squire, son of Samuel and Abigail Squire.

Feb. 25th, 1738-9.—Oliver Spelman, son of John and —— Spelman.

March 4th, 1738-9.—Elihu Fowler, son of Joseph and Hannah Fowler, and John Parmalee, son of John Parmalee.

March 18th, 1738-9.—Eben Seaward, son of Eben and Dorathy Seaward, and Sarah Bates, daughter of James and Mary Bates.

March 25th, 1738-9 —Ruth, daughter of Joseph and Ruth Fowler.

Apr 29th, 1739.—Soloman Rose, son of Jonathan and Mary Rose.

June 24th, 1739.—Hezekiah Talcott, son of John and Sarah Talcott.

July 15th, 1739.—Rachel Hills, daughter of Benoni and Hannah Hills.

Aug. 5th, 1739.—John Johnson, son of Benjamin and Eunice Johnson.

Aug 12th, 1739 —Caroline Seaward, daughter of Lieut. Joseph and Hannah Seaward

Aug. 26th, 1739 —The widow Bethiah Barnes owned the Covenant, and her two children were baptized, viz: Mehetabel and John Barnes.

Sept 2d, 1739 —Noah Baldwin, son of Ezra and Ruth Baldwin

Sept. 23d, 1739.—Lucy Smith, daughter of Stephen Smith.

Oct. 21st, 1739.—James Merwin, son of Daniel and Elizabeth Merwin, and Noah Roberts, son of Samuel and Rachel Roberts.

Oct. 28th, 1739.—Hannah Leete, daughter of John and Elizabeth Leete.

Nov. 25th, 1739.—Daniel Barnes, son of John Barnes, deceased before he was born, and Bethiah Barnes; and Mary Crane, daughter of Henry and Mercy Crane.

Dec. 2d, 1739 —Hagar, negro' daughter of Relor and Dinah, negro servants of Dea. Burrit.

Dec. 9th, 1739.—Susanna Rossedor, daughter of Bryan and Kate Rossedor

Dec. 23d, 1739.—Ann Smith, daughter of Stephen Smith.

Dec. 24th.—In ye evening or night, I baptized Ruth Squire, daughter of Josiah and Sarah Squire, in ye own house, it not being likely to live, which died.

Dec. 30th, 1739 —Charles Chauncey, son of Elihu and Mary Chauncey.

Jan 20th, 1739–40.—Aaron Hinman, son of Zec. and Hannah Hinman.

Feb. 17th, 1739–40.—Hannah Camp, thus mis-baptized, called Anna, daughter of Sergt. John and Hannah Camp.

Feb. 24th, 1739–40.—Josiah Parsons, son of Timothy and Mary Parsons; and Robert G. Crane, son of Sergt. Silas and Mary Crane.

March 9th, 1739–40.—Lydia Norton, daughter of Isaac Norton; and Abraham Stowe, son of Sumner and Sarah Stowe.

March 23d, 1739–40.—Mary Wells, daughter of Jonathan and Mary Wells.

March 30th, 1740.—Mary Coe, daughter of Ephraim and Hannah Coe.

Apr. 6th, 1740.—Ira Wetmore, son of Jabez and Abigail Wetmore.

Apr. 13th, 1740.—Jonathan Mitchel and Lydia his wife, owned the covenant, and yr two children, Abner and Sarah were baptized.

May 4th, 1740.—I baptized John Lyman, son of John and Hope Lyman privately, who died immediately.

May 4th, 1740.—Helena Right, daughter of Joseph and Helena Right.

May 11th, 1740.—Asher Robinson, son of David and Rebeckah Robinson; and John Fowler, son of David Fowler.

May 18th, 1740.—Pelu, negro child belonging to James Curtis, Sen., and on the same day Silvanus Chipman.

May 25th, 1740.—Phebe Fairchild, daughter of Samuel and Phebe Fairchild.

June 15th, 1740.—Rhoda Griswold, daughter of Samuel and —— Griswold of Black Rock.

June 20th, 1740.—Prudence Wheeler, daughter of Joseph and Prudence Wheeler.

July 3d, 1740.—Lucretia and Lucena Smith, twin daughters of John and —— Smith, baptized privately and both died.

July 18th, 1740.—Rachel Glayde, daughter of James and Mabel Glayde, privately.

July 20th, 1740—Ebenezer Guthry, son of John and Abigail Guthry; and Damaris Seward, daughter of Ebenezer and Dorathy Seward.

Aug. 3d.—Simeon Parmalee, son of Hezekiah Parmalee; and Oliver Burton, son of Simeon and Hannah Burton

Aug. 10th—Elizabeth Spelman, ye daughter of Thomas and Sarah Spelman; and Abigail, ye daughter of Benjamin Cook of Black Rock; and on ye same day, Thomas Lyman and Ann his wife, made confession of the sin of fornication and received Remission.

August 14th, 1740—I baptized Sarah, the daughter of Thomas and Ann Lyman, in yr own house.

Oct. 5th, 1740.—Thomas Phillips, son of Thomas Phillips; and Sarah daughter of Daniel Smith.

Oct. 12th, 1740.—Ann Fairchild, daughter of Curtis Fairchild.

Oct. 19th.—James, the son of James and Mary Bates; and Hannah Hickox, daughter of Samuel Hickox

Oct. 26th, 1740.—Samuel Parmalee, son of John Parmalee.

Nov. 16th.—Abiathar Squire, son of Samuel and Abigail Squire.

Nov. 23d, 1740.—Benjamin Fairchild, son of Tho. and Thankful Fairchild.

Nov. 23d, 1740.—James Coe, son of Joseph Coe, Jun.

Dec. 7th, 1740.—Joseph Sutlief and Sarah his wife's children, Joseph, Sarah and Nathaniel, were baptized.

Dec. 14th.—Rebeckah, the daughter of Joseph and Ann Meeker.

Dec. 21st, 1740.—Mary Fowler, daughter of Joseph and Ruth Fowler.

Jan. 18th, 1740.—Paul Chapman, son of Sylvanus and Elizabeth Chapman; and Ann Avered, daughter of Israel and Abigail Avered.

Feb. 22d, 1740.—Josiah Squire, son of Josiah and Sarah

Squire; and Ann Thomas, daughter of Abraham and Hannah Thomas.

March 1st, 1740.—I baptized Ashael Camp, son of Edward and Mary Camp, at ye meeting of the Middletown Farms, to whom Mr. Baldwin preached.

March 8th, 1740.—John Spelman, son of John Spelman

March 15th.—Sarah Parsons, daughter of Ithamar and Sarah Parsons.

Apr. 12th.—Katharine Chauncey, daughter of Elihu and Mary Chauncey.

May 3d.—Hannah Burrit, daughter of James and Sarah Burrit, and Sarah Bishop, daughter of Timothy Bishop.

May ult.—Sarah Lyman, daughter of Thomas and Ann Lyman.

June 7th, 1741.—Naomi Parsons, daughter of Moses Parsons.

June 21st, 1741.—Hannah Coe, daughter of David and Hannah Coe.

June 28th, 1741.—Nathan Francis, son of Daniel and Eliz. Francis; and Stephen Norton, son of Jonathan and Ruth Norton.

July 5th, 1741.—John Crane, son of Henry and Marcy Crane.

July 26th, 1741.—Jonathan Griswold, son of Hez. Griswold; and Abigail Camp, daughter of Eleazar Camp; and Mary Rose, daughter of Jonathan Rose, all the same day.

Aug. 2d, 1741.—Moses Griswold, son of Jonathan and Bashia Griswold; and Desire Smith, daughter of Stephen Smith, Jun

Sept. 6th, 1741.—Bela Alverd, son of Aaron and Mabel Alverd; and Sarah Talcot, daughter of John and Sarah Talcot.

Sept. 20th.—Israel Canfield, son of Gideon and Ann Canfield.

October 25th, 1741.—Ruth Baldwin, daughter of Ezra and Ruth Baldwin.

Nov. 1st, 1741.—Hannah Stevens, daughter of Allen and Hannah Stevens.

Nov. 8th.—John Johnson, son of Benjamin and Eunice Johnson; Camp Mitchel, son of Jonathan and Bashua Mitchel; and Katharine Lyman, daughter of John and Hope Lyman, 1741

Nov. 22d, 1741.—Elisha Morton, son of Thomas and —— Morton

Dec. 6th.—Rachel Fairchild, daughter of Edmund and Mary Fairchild.

Dec. 13th, 1741 —Jonathan Smith, son of Stephen Smith, Jun.

Dec. 20th, 1741.—John Roberts and Jerusha his wife, and Elizabeth, the wife of Sam'l Roberts, owned ye covenant

Dec. 27th, 1741.—Joel, son of John and —— Right was baptized.

Jan 10th, 1741-2 —Zipporah Coe, daughter of John and Hannah Coe.

Jan. 17th, 1741-2 —Eliphaz Alverd, son of Jonathan Alverd; and Sarah Roberts, daughter of John and Jerushah Roberts

Jan. 24th, 1741-2.—Margery Right, the daughter of Joseph and Helen Right.

Feb. 7th, 1741-2.—Martha Morgan, an adult person who was baptized and received to Communion.

Phebe Camp, daughter of John and Hannah Camp; Elizabeth Merwin, daughter of Daniel and Mary Merwin; Elizabeth Roberts, daughter of Samuel and Eliz Roberts.

Feb. 21st. 1741-2 —Asahel Alvord owned the Covenant.

Feb. 21st, 1741-2.—Noahdiah Seward, son of Eben and Dorothy Seward, was baptized.

March 7th, 1741-2.—Benjamin Coe, son of Eph. and Hannah Coe, and Thomas Gold Alverd, son of Asahel and Mary Alverd.

March 28th, 1742.—Martha Spelman, daughter of Thomas and Sarah Spelman

Apr. 4th, 1742 —Jonathan Wells, son of Jonathan and Mary Wells.

Apr 24th, 1742.—Timothy Stowe, son of Sumner and Sarah Stowe, whom I baptized privately in ye dwelling house of D—— Stowe.

May 3d, 1742.—Abigail Guthy, daughter of John and Abigail Guthy.

May 23d, 1742.—Nathan Coe, son of David and Hannah Coe.

Sarah Guernsey, daughter of Eben and Rhoda Guernsey; and Hannah Griswold, daughter of Sam. and Hannah Griswold.

May 30th, 1712.—Rebeckah Hawley, daughter of John Hawley.

June 20th, 1742.—Ceazar, negro child belonging to Noahdiah Grave.

June 27th —Sarah Parmalee, daughter of John Parmalee; and Huldah Bishop, daughter of William and Patience Bishop.

July 18th, 1742.—Sylvanus Norton, son of Isaac Norton; and Rebecca, daughter of Susannah Hull.

Aug. 4th, 1742.—Hannah Bates, daughter of John Bates.

Aug. 8th, 1742.—Bryan Rosseter, son of Bryan and Kate Rosseter.

August 24th, 1742.—Prudence Norton, daughter of Joseph Norton, Jun., and Prudence Norton, his wife.

Sept. 9th, 1742.—Mehetabel Parmalee, daughter of Hezekiah Parmalee.

Sept. 12th, 1742 —Azubah Edee.

Sept. 17th, 1742.—Josiah Squire, son of Josiah and Sarah Squire.

Oct. 10th, 1742.—John Phillips, son of Mr. Thomas Phillips.

Oct. 24th, 1742.—Ambrose Hickox, son of Samuel Hickox.

Nov 14th, 1742.—Joseph Ingham, son of Joseph and Abigail Ingham; and Zipporah Fairchild, ye daughter of Curtis and Mercy Fairchild.

Nov. 28th, 1742.—Eli Crane, son of Silas and Mercy Crane.

Dec. 5th, 1742.—Samuel Fen, son of Sam'l Fen; Asenath Fairchild, daughter of Tho. and Thankful Fairchild.

Dec. 5th, 1742.—Phebe Roberts, daughter of Samuel and Elizabeth Roberts; and Sarah Lucas, daughter of Patience Lucas.

Dec. 19th, 1742.—Samuel Higgins, the son of Capt. Higgins, a mariner yt come from Eastham.

Dec. 26th, 1742.—Sarah Chauncey, daughter of Elihu and Mary Chauncey, having been born on Wednesday the week before in the forenoon.

Feb. 13th, 1742-3.—Lucy Fairchild, daughter of Samuel and Phebe Fairchild.

Feb. 20th, 1742-3.—Sarah Chapman, daughter of Sylvanus and Eliz. Chapman; John, son of William and Ann Smithson; and Mary Camp, daughter of David and Mary Camp.

Feb. 27th, 1742-3 —Eunice Coe, daughter of John and Hannah Coe; and Elizabeth, daugter of David Fowler and his wife.

March 20th, 1742-3.—Lois, daughter of Edmund Fairchild and Mary.

March 27th, 1743.—Selah Alverd, son of Aaron and Mehitabel Alverd

Apr. 3d, 1743.—Benjamin Young Smith, son of Daniel and —— Smith.

Apr. 17th.—Phebe Thomas, daughter of Abraham and Hannah Thomas.

Apr. 24th, 1743 —Samuel Bates, son of Samuel and Abigail Bates.

May 8th, 1743.—Sarah Bates, daughter of James and Mary Bates.

May 22d, 1743.—Ruth Wadsworth, daughter of James and Abigail Wadsworth.

June 12th, 1743.—Hannah Coe, daughter of Joseph Coe.

June 19th, 1743.—Elizabeth Fairchild, daughter of Capt. Robert Fairchild and Ann his wife; and on ye same day, Samuel Dane Cook, son of John Cook; and Hannah Lyman, daughter of John and Hope Lyman.

Aug. 1st, 1743.—Edward Hinman, son of Zechariah and Hannah Hinman.

Aug. 8th, 1743.—Sarah Merwin, daughter of Daniel and Mary Merwin

Aug. 20th, 1743.—Ruth Norton, daughter of Jonathan and Ruth Norton.

Sept 4th, 1743.—Samuel Johnson, son of Benjamin and Eunice Johnson.

Sept. 25th, 1743.—David Tibbals, son of Joseph and Esther Tibbals.

Oct. 2d, 1743.—Ebenezer Norton, son of Thomas Norton.

Oct. 9th, 1743.—Sarah Hickox, daughter of Stephen and Lydia Hickox.

Oct. 16th, 1743.—Ann Burrit, daughter of Dea. and Sarah Burrit, and Rebeckah Canfield, daughter of Gideon and Ann Canfield.

Nov. 20th, 1743.—Jesse Coe, son of Davie and Hannah Coe; and John Bates, son of John and —— Bates

Dec. 11th, 1743 —Abigail Smith, daughter of Stephen Smith.

Dec. 18th.—Aaron Griswold, son of Jeremy and Bathsheba Griswold.

Dec. 25th, 1743.—Charles Spelman, son of Thomas and Sarah Spelman; Elizabeth Parsons, daughter of Moses and —— Parsons; and Lois Camp, daughter of Abraham and Martha Camp.

Jan. 1st, 1743-4.—Eliphaz Parmalee, son of Joel and Rhoda Parmalee.

Jan. 22d, 1743-4.—Mary Jones, daughter of John Jones; and Gideon Allen, son of Mabel Gloyde by Gideon Leete.

March 4th, 1743-4.—Phinehas Spelman, son of John and —— his wife Spelman; and Rachel Parsons, daughter of Aaron and Abigail Parsons; on the same day John Norton and Mary his wife, owned ye cov.

March 11th, 1743-4.—Eliz. Lyman, daughter of Tho. and Ann Lyman.

Mary Norton, daughter of John and Mary Norton, of Black Rock, Apr. 15th, 1744.

Apr. 22d, 1744.—Amos Baldwin, son of Ezra and Ruth Baldwin.

May 6th, 1744.—Joseph Right, son of Joseph and Helen Right.

Miles Merwin, son of Miles and Mary Merwin; and Sarah Averd, daughter of Samuel and Abigail Averd.

May 27th, 1744.—Ruth Squire, daughter of Josiah and Sarah Squire.

June 3d, 1744.—Nathan Rose, son of Jonathan Rose; and Rachel Right, daughter of John and Lucy Right.

June 10th, 1744.—Mary Bowles, daughter of David Bowles.

June 25th, 1744.—Samuel Griswold, son of Samuel and —— Griswold

June 25th, 1744.—Elizabeth Wells, daughter of Jonathan and Mary Wells

July 1st, 1744.—Robert Smithson, son of William and Ann Smithson.

July 8th, 1744.—Joseph Wheeler, son of Joseph and Prudence Wheeler.

July 22d, 1744.—Ann Stephens, daughter of Allen and Hannah Stephens.

July 29th, 1744.—Charles Bishop, son of William and Patience Bishop.

August 19th, 1744.—John Roberts, son of John and Jerushah Roberts; offered by Ephraim Coe and his wife.

August 26th, 1744.—James and Martha Tybbals made confession of yr sin of fornication, had remission and they then owned the Covenant.

Sept. 23d, 1744.—Ebenezer Seward, son of Ebenezer and Dorothy Seward, after yy wr removed to Bedford.

Sarah Fowler, daughter of Joseph and Ruth Fowler.

Sept. 30th, 1744.—Nathan Parsons, son of Ithamar and Sarah Parsons.

Oct. 21st, 1744.—James Seaward, son of Ephraim and Abigail Seaward; and David Talcot, son of John and Sarah Talcot.

Nov. 18th, 1744.—Concurrence Crane, daughter of Henry and Mercy Crane; and Rachel Hiccox, daughter of Samuel Hiccox. Anna Bates, daughter of Sam'l and Abigail Bates.

Nov. 25th, 1744.—Lydia Mitchel, daughter of Jonathan and Lydia Mitchel; Abigail Rossiter, daughter of Bryan and Katharine Rossiter

December 23d, 1744.—Ann Norton, daughter of Isaac and Mary Norton.

Jan. 6th, 1744-5.—Seth Fowler son of David Fowler.

Jan. 13th, 1744-5.—Phineas Camp, son of John and Jerushah Camp; John Lyman, son of John and Hope Lyman; and Zipporah Camp, daughter of Edward and Mary Camp.

Jan. 20th, 1744-5.—Tabitha Parsons, daughter of Timothy and Mary Parsons, and Katharine Camp, daughter of John and Hannah Camp; and Martha Hawley, daughter of John and —— Hawley.

Feb. 10th, 1744-5.—Lois Hiccox, daughter of Stephen and Lydia Hiccox; and Ruth Griswold, daughter of Jeremiah and Bathsheba Griswold.

March 3d, 1744-5.— —— Crane, son of Silas and Mercy Crane.

March 10th, 1744-5.—Landon Smith, son of Daniel Smith.

March 24th, 1744-5.—Miles Lyman, son of Noah and Sarah Lyman; and Nathaniel Bates, son of John Bates.

April 29th, 1745.—Hannah and Abigail Fairchild, twin daughters of Thomas and Thankful Fairchild, which I baptized privately, and being sick

May 12th, 1745.—Sarah Chauncey, daughter of Elihu and Mary Chauncey, it having born in the night following ye 7th May, about break of day.

May 19th, 1745.—Abigail Ingham, daughter of Joseph and Abigail Ingham.

June 9th, 1745.—Prudence, negro child, daughter of Peter and Dinah, servants of Deacon Burrit.

June 23d, 1745 —Hezekiah Pamely, son of Hezekiah Pamely; and Levi Pamely, son of Joel and Rhoda Pamely.

July 28th, 1745.—Mary Bates, daughter of James and Mary Bates.

August 11th, 1745.—Alexander Pamely, son of John Pamely.

Sept. 1st, 1745.—Elnathan Merwin, son of Daniel and Mary Merwin; and Sarah Tybbals, the daughter of James and Martha Tybbals.

Sept. 22d, 1745.—Joel Norton, son of John and Deborah Norton; and Elizabeth Fairchild, daughter of Sam'l and Phebe Fairchild; and Eunice Fairchild, daughter of Edmond and Mary Fairchild, all the same day.

Sept. 29th, 1745.—Elizabeth Tybbals, daughter of Joseph and Esther Tybbals.

October 6th, 1745.—Mehitabel Alverd, the daughter of Aaron and Mehitabel Alverd.

October 13th, 1745.—Eunice Camp, daughter of Abraham and Martha Camp.

October 27th, 1745.—Mary Coe, daughter of David and Hannah Coe.

Nov. 10th, 1745.—Hannah Ball, daughter of David and Elizabeth Ball.

December 1st, 1745.—Rhoda Squire, daughter of Josiah and Sarah Squire.

December 8th, 1745.—Stephen Spelman, son of Thomas Spelman and Sarah.

Jan. 12th, 1745-6.—Abigail Coe, daughter of Joseph Coe, Jun. and —— Coe

Feb. 16th, 1745-6.—Thomas Lyman, son of Thomas and Ann Lyman.

March 22d, 1745-6.—Sam'l Rockwell, son of Ezra and Jemima Rockwell of Scantick.

March 29th, 1746.—Sarah Norton, daughter of Thomas Norton.

April 6th, 1746.—Ann Canfield, daughter of Gideon and Ann Canfield.

April 20th, 1746.—Hannah Johnes, daughter of John Johnes, and Hannah Coe, daughter of John Coe, Junior and Anna his wife. This child should have been Anna.

April 21st, 1746.—David Lyman, son of John and Hope Lyman, whom I baptized in their own house by reason of sickness of mother and child.

May 18th, 1746.—Abijah Stow, son of Sumner and Sarah Stow.

May 25th, 1746.—Elnathan Baldwin, son of Ezra and Ruth Baldwin; and Enoch Henman, son of Zecariah and Hannah Henman.

June first, 1746.—Daniel Merwin, son of Daniel and Mary Merwin.

June 8th, 1746.—Nathan Spelman, son of John and —— Spelman.

June 29th, 1746.—Abigail Alverd, daughter of Elisha and Hannah Alverd.

June 29th, 1746.—Benjamin Norton and Elizabeth his wife, own the covenant.

July 13th, 1746.—Benjamin Norton, son of Benjamin and Elizabeth Norton.

July 20th, 1746.—Abigail Parsons, daughter of Aaron and Abigail Parsons; and Rhoda Wells, daughter of Jonathan and Mary Wells.

August 3d, 1746.—Ann Smithson, daughter of Lieut. William and Ann Smithson; Sarah Right, daughter of John and —— Right.

August 10th, 1746.—Martha Austin, daughter of Elias and Eunice Austin.

August 31st, 1746.—Charles Burrit, son of Deacon Israel and Sarah Burrit, born on Thursday evening, before about 10 of ye clock.

October 12th, 1746.—Daniel Squire, son of Sam'l and Sarah Squire; and Ann Crane, daughter of Henry and Mercy Crane.

October 19th, 1746.—Sylvanus Hull, son of Cornelious and Abigail Hull.

October 26th, 1746.—Timothy Coe, son of S —— and Anna Coe.

Nov. 2d, 1746.—Jacob Bates, son of John and —— Bates.

Nov. 9th, 1746.—Job Seaward, son of Ephraim and Abigail Seaward.

Dec. 1st, 1746.—Sam'l Graves, son of Samuel Graves.

Jan. 4th, 1716-7.—Moses Norton, son of John and —— Norton.

Jan. 11th, 1746–7.—Eunice Tybbals, daughter of James and —— Tybbals

Jan. 18th, 1746.—Reuben Hiccox son of Stephen and Lydia Hiccox, and Zebulon Rose, son of Jonathan Rose.

Feb 22d, 1746–7.—Sarah Strong, daughter of Thos. and Phebe Strong.

March 1st, 1746 —Lois Camp, daughter of John and Hannah Camp, who died within 16 days.

March 28th, 1747.—Katharine Alverd, daughter of Aaron and Mehitable Alverd, whom I baptized in yr own house.

March 29th, 1747.—Isaac Norton, son of Isaac and —— Norton; David Right, son of Joseph and Hellena Right; Rebekah Picket, daughter of Sam'l and Hephzebah Picket; and Shem ——, son of

April 5th, 1747.—James Dorey, son of James and Jane Dorey.

May 31st, 1747.—Charles Chauncey, son of Elihu and Mary Chauncey, and Mary Pamely, daughter of Joel and Rhode Pamely.

June 7th, 1747.—Huldah Crane, daughter of Silas and Mercy Crane.

June 21st, 1747.—Noah Lyman, son of Noah and —— Lyman; Ann Merwin, daughter of Dan'l and Mary Merwin; and Abigail Parsons, daughter of Moses Parsons.

July 5th, 1747.—Sarah Hawley, daughter of John Hawley; Mary Weld, daughter of Daniel and Elizabeth Weld; and Elizabeth Hull, daughter of Joseph and Cybil Hull.

July 26th, 1747.—John Squire, son of Josiah and Sarah Squire; David Coe, son of David and Hannah Coe; Hannah Averd, daughter of Israel and —— Averd; and Dorcas Hiccock, daughter of Samuel and —— Hiccock.

August 2d, 1747.—Thomas Fairchild made confession a 3d time of the sin of drunkeness, and had remission.

August 9th, 1747.—Edmund Fairchild, son of Thomas and Thankful Fairchild; and Ruth Right, daughter of Sam'l Right.

Jan. 24th, 1747–8 —Ann Lyman, daughter of Thomas and Ann Lyman; and Mary Tibbals, daughter of Abner and Sarah Tibbals; and Bertha, negro child of Jeremy ——; on ye same day, Abner and Sarah Tibbals made confession and owned the covenant.

Jan. 28th, 1747–8.—Israel Godard and his wife made confession of ye sin of fornication and received remission.

Jan. 29th, 1747–8.—Rachel Rockwell, daughter of Ezra and Jeremiah Rockwell, was baptized; and Sarah Spelman, daughter of Tho and Sarah Spelman.

Feb. 6th, 1747–8.—Ann Guernsey, daughter of Lieut. Eben. and Rhoda Guernsey.

Feb. 28th, 1747–8.—Aaron Right, son of John and Lucy Right; Isaac Newton, son of John and Mary Newton; Sarah Norton, daughter of Jonathan and Ruth Norton; Mary Ball, daughter of David and Eliz. Ball

Aug 23d, 1747.—John Wheeler, son of Joseph and Prudence Wheeler.

Aug 30th, 1747.—Moses Camp, son of Abraham and Martha Camp.

Sept 6th, 1747.—John Griswold, son of Samuel and Hannah Griswold of Black Rock

Sept. 20th, 1747.—Esther Fowler, daughter of David and —— Fowler.

Oct. 18th, 1747.—Samuel Fairchild, son of Samuel and Phebe Fairchild, and Abigail Bates, daughter of Samuel and Abigail Bates.

Oct. 25th, 1747.—John Coe, son of John and Anna Coe.

Nov. 22d, 1747.—Sarah Ingham, daughter of Joseph and Abigail; and Rachel Tibbals, daughter of Joseph and Esther Tibbals.

Nov. 29th, 1747.—Stephen Austin, son of Elias and Eunice Austin; and Dorothy Austin, daughter of Moses and Hannah Austin.

Jan. 24th, 1747–8.—Joseph Parsons, son of Samuel and Elizabeth Parsons.

Nov. 6th, 1747.—Robert Stowe, son of Sumner and Sarah Stowe.

Dec. 4th, 1748.—Phinehas Wild, son of Daniel and Elizabeth Wild, and on ye same day, Ephraim Norton, and Mary, his wife, owned ye cov.

Dec. 11th, 1748.—Seth Doney, son of James and Jane Doney; and Charles Norton, son of Ephraim and Mary Norton.

Dec. 18th, 1748.—Henry Crane, son of Serj Henry and Mercey Crane.

Jan. 8th, 1748–9.—Mehitabel Seward, daughter of Ephraim and Abigail Seward.

Jan. 22d, 1748–9.—Ebenezer Curtis, son of David Curtis and his wife; on ye same day, Brotherton Seward and Sarah, his wife, made confession of their sin of fornication, had remission, and owned ye covenant.

Feb. 12th, 1748–9.—Martha Squire, daughter of Josiah and Sarah Squire.

Feb 19th, 1748–9.—Job Merwin, son of Miles and Mary Merwin; and Phebe Griswold, daughter of Dan. Griswold and his wife.

March 9th, 1748–9.—Joseph Coe, son of Josiah Coe and his wife; and Ann Seward, daughter of Brotherton and Sarah Seward.

Apr. 16th, 1749.—John Norton, son of John Norton, 3d.

Apr. ult., 1749.—Reuben Baldwin, son of Ezra and Ruth Baldwin.

June 4th, 1749.—Israel Merwin, son of Daniel and Mary Merwin.

June 11th, 1749.—Stephen Norton and Abigail, his wife, owned ye covenant.

June 25th, 1749.—Mary Meeker, daughter of Nathaniel and Tamar Meeker, was baptized.

July 2d, 1749.—Stephen Hickox, son of Stephen and Lydia Hickox; and Medad Norton, son of Stephen and Abigail Norton.

July 9th, 1749.—Elizabeth Picket, daughter of John and Eliz. Picket.

July 16th, 1749.—Phillis, Negro child of Stephen and Patience Bates.

July 23d, 1749.—Aaron Alvord, son of Aaron and Mehitabel Alvord, were baptized; and Mercy Coe, daughter of John and Anna Coe.

July 30th, 1749.—Phinehas Bates, son of Stephen and Lois Bates; and Abigail Hull, daughter of Cornelious and Abigail Hull.

Aug. 6th, 1749.—Sarah Stowe, the wife of Sumner Stowe.

Aug. 6th.—Daniel Picket, son of Samuel and Hephzibah Picket, was baptized; and Jesse, the Negro child of Ephraim and Hannah Coe.

Aug. 20th, 1749.—Jerushah Parmalee, daughter of Joel and Rhoda Parmalee.

Sept. 10th, 1749.—Rachel Wells, daughter of Serj. Jonathan and Mary Wells.

Nov. 5th, 1749.—Enoch Henman, son of Zechariah and —— Henman; and Aaron Norton, son of Isaac and —— Norton; and Elizabeth Lyman, daughter of Noah and Sarah Lyman; and Hannah Hickox, daughter of Samuel and —— Hickox; and Martha Newton, daughter of Abner and Huldah Newton, all these, on ye same day.

Nov. 12th, 1749.—Mary Francis, daughter of James Francis.

Dec. 3d, 1749.—Elnathan Tibbals, son of Joseph and Esther Tibbals; and Abraham Scranton, son of Abraham and Beulah Scranton.

Dec. 10th, 1749.—Martha Austin, daughter of Elias and Eunice Austin.

Dec. 17th, 1749.—Ruth Crane, daughter of Sergeant Silas Crane and Mercey, his wife.

Dec. 24th, 1749.—Daniel Stephens, son of Allen and Hannah Stevens; and Joseph Hull, son of Joseph and Cybil Hull, and Rosanna Coe, daughter of Simeon and Anna Coe; and Thankful, daughter of Cuff and Kate, Negro.

Dec. ult., 1749.—Deborah, daughter of Cambridge and his wife, Capt Sutlief's Negro servant.

Jan. 7th, 1749–50.—Thomas Tibbals and his wife, owned ye covenant.

Jan 21st, 1749–50.—Rachel Fairchild, daughter of Sam'l and Phebe Fairchild.

Jan. 21st, 1749–50.—Sarah Johnes, daughter of John Johnes and his wife; and Hannah Weld, daughter of Daniel and Elizabeth Weld

Feb. 4th, 1749–50.—Israel Goddard, son of Israel and Ann Goddard.

Feb. 10th, 1749–50.—Abel Lyman, son of Serjeant Thomas and Ann Lyman.

Feb. 11th, 1749–50.—Stephen Tibbals, son of Thomas Tibbals and his wife.

March 4th, 1749–50 —Abijah Curtis, son of John Curtis; and the same day, David Bates, son of John and Elizabeth Bates;

this child was taken with convulsions at noon, on the day it was to be brought forth to baptism, and I went up after meeting and baptized privately, i. e., in Bates' house, a number being present.

March, 11th, 1749-50.—Statira, daughter of Benjamin and Sarah Wells.

March 18th, 1749-50.—Abel Tibbals, son of Abner and Sarah Tibbals; I baptized this child privately, by reason of a swelling on ye head which endangered it.

March 25th, 1750.—John Hawley, son of John Hawley and wife; and Abigail Squire, daughter of Samuel and Sarah Squire; the same day, Joseph Hickox and his wife owned ye covenant.

Apr. 1st, 1750.—Thomas Canfield, son of John Canfield and his wife.

Apr. 8th, 1750.—David Rockwell, son of Ezra and Jemima Rockwell.

May 13th, 1750.—Phebe Norton, daughter of Jonathan and Ruth Norton.

May 20th, 1750.—William Griswold, son of Daniel Griswold and wife; and David Curtis, son of —— Curtis and his wife; and Anne Camp, daughter of Israel and Ann Camp; these three in a day.

May 27th, 1750.—Martha Hickox, daughter of Joseph Hickox and his wife.

June 24th, 1750.—Moses Bates, son of Samuel Bates, born after the death of his father.

June 24th, 1750.—Samuel Ely, son of Samuel Ely and Jerusha, his wife.

July 8th, 1750.—Daniel Bates, son of James and Mary Bates, and Lois Strong daughter of Thomas and Phebe Strong.

July 29th, 1750.—Stephen Bates, with Mindwell, his wife, owned ye covenent; the same day, John Newton, son of John and Mary Newton, was baptized.

Aug. 5th, 1750.—Elizabeth Bates, daughter of Stephen and Mindwell Bates, was baptized.

Sept. 23d, 1750.—Charles Seward, son of Ephraim and Abigail Seward; and Gideon Canfield, son of Gideon and Ann

Canfield; and the same day, Joel Norton, son of Benjamin and Eliz. Norton

Oct. 28th, 1750.—Ithamar Parsons, son of Ithamar and Sarah Parsons; and Rachel Doney, daughter of James and Jane Doney.

Nov. 11th, 1750.—Joseph Tibbals, son of James Tibbals and his wife; Ezra Shelden, son of Moses and Eliz. Shelden; and Abiathar Robinson, son of Daniel and Abigail Robinson; and Katharine Alverd, daughter of Aaron and Mabel Alverd.

Nov. 25th, 1750—Clement Squire, son of Josiah and Sarah Squire.

Dec. 2d, 1750.—Sarah Graves, daughter of Samuel Graves and his wife.

Feb. 3d, 1750-1.—Rhoda Coe, daughter of Josiah Coe and his wife.

March 17th, 1750-1—Samuel Fenn Parsons, son of Samuel and Mary Parsons.

March 17th, 1750-1—Mehetabel Parsons, daughter of Samuel and Eliz Parsons; and Ruth Hull, daughter of Jehiel and Ruth Hull.

Apr. 21st, 1751.—Moses Parmalee, son of Hezekiah Parmalee and his wife.

May 26th, 1751.—Hannah Norton, daughter of Thomas Norton and his wife.

June 23d, 1751—Elizabeth Norton, daughter of Ephraim and Mary Norton.

June ult., 1751—Aaron Norton, son of John Norton, ye 3d, and his wife; and Joseph Snow, son of Abner Snow, and his wife.

July 14th, 1751.—Sybil Hail, wife of Elisha Hail, owned ye covenant.

Aug. 11th, 1751.—Enos Crane, son of Henry and Mercy Crane.

Sept. 8th, 1751.—Linus Bates, son of Stephen Bates, Jun, and his wife.

Sept. 15th, 1751.—Oliver Coe, son of John and Ann Coe.

Sept 22d, 1751.—Thomas Wheeler, son of Joseph and Prudence Wheeler; and Curtis Hail, son of Elisha and Sybil Hail; and Hannah Merwin, daughter of Daniel and Mary Merwin;

on ye same day, Lemuel and Hannah Hand, owned ye covenant.

Sept. 29th, 1751.—Mehitabel Wells, daughter of Jonathan and Mary Wells; and Abraham Austin, son of Moses and Hannah Austin.

Oct. 13th, 1751.—Daniel Sumner Stowe, son of Sumner and Sarah Stowe, on ye same day, Eliakim Strong, son of Eliakim and Hannah Strong.

Oct. 20th, 1751.—Abraham Hand, son of Lemuel and Hannah Hand; and Anne Goddard, daughter of Israel and Ann Goddard; on ye same day, Peter, Negro servant of Mr. Talcott, was baptized, and by baptism, received into full communion.

Oct. 27th, 1751.—Joseph Sothern and his wife, owned ye covenant, and John Canfield, son of John Canfield and his wife, was baptized; and ye same day, Huldah Newton, daughter of Abner and Huldah Newton.

Nov. 3rd, 1751.—David Scranton, son of Abraham and Beulah Scranton; and Samuel Tibbals, son of Thomas Tibbals and his wife.

Nov. 17th, 1751.—David Johnson, Jun, and his wife, owned ye covenant; on ye same day, Helen Curtis, daughter of David Curtis and his wife, was baptized.

Dec. 1st, 1751—James Hickox, son of Joseph Hickox and his wife; and Ruth Sothern, daughter of Joseph and Mary Sothern.

Dec. 8th, 1751.—Phinehas Jones, son of John Jones, and his wife.

Dec. 15th, 1751.—Thomas Johnson, son of David Johnson and Jerushah his wife.

Dec. 29th, 1751.—Eber Tibbals, son of Abner and Sarah Tibbals.

Jan. 14th, 1751–2.—Sam Hull, son of Cornelius and Abigail Hull, whom I baptized privately, being sick.

Feb. 2d, 1751–2.—Elijah Austin, son of Elias and Eunice Austin; and Rhoda Parmalee, daughter of Joel and Rhoda Parmalee.

Feb 9th, 1751–2.—Mary Picket, daughter of John and Elizabeth Picket.

Feb. 16th, 1751-2.—Samuel Benjamin and his wife owned ye covenant, and Asher the son, was baptized; and Rosanna Francis, daughter of James Francis and his wife.

March 1st, 1751-2 —Frederick Crane, son Serjeant Silas and Mercy Crane.

March 22d, 1751-2 —Edmund Fairchild, son of Samuel and Phebe Fairchild; and Ruth Baldwin, daughter of Ezra and Ruth Baldwin; and Sarah Weld, daughter of Samuel and Eliz. Weld, all on ye same day.

Apr. 12th, 1752.—Samuel Hickox, son of Samuel Hickox and his wife; and Moses Shelden, son of Moses and Eliz. Shelden; and Sybill Hull, daughter of Joseph and Sybill Hull; and Mary Griswold, ye daughter of Daniel Griswold and his wife, all these four in a day.

Apr. 19th, 1752.—Samuel, Timothy, Rebeckah, Asher and Rachel, the children of Samuel Seward, deceased.

Apr. 26th, 1752.—Lucy Alverd, daughter of Aaron and Mehetabel Alverd; Elizabeth Bates, daughter of John Bates and his wife, and Phebe Picket, daughter of Samuel and Hephzibah Picket.

Oct. 23d, 1753.—Mary Shelden, daughter of Moses and Elizabeth Shelden; John, son of Timothy Hall and his wife; Martha, daughter of James and Eleanor Picket; and Hannah Camp, daughter of Job and Rachel Camp.

Oct. 30th, 1753.—Charles Parmalee, son of Hezekiah Parmalee and his wife.

Nov. 11th, 1753.—Wilson Cook, and Mary his wife, with John Smith and his wife owned ye covenant, and Lewis, yr son was baptized.

Nov 25th, 1753.—Enos Scranton, son of Abraham and Beulah Scranton.

Dec. 2d, 1753.—Phebe Griswold, daughter of Jeremy and Bathsheba Griswold, and Mary Cook, daughter of Wilson and Mary Cook.

Dec. 9th, 1753.—David Grave and his wife owned ye covenant; and John, the son of James and Jane Dony, was baptized on ye same day.

Jan. 6th, 1754.—Hannah, daughter of Abner Snow and his wife, was baptized.

Jan. 13th, 1754.—Thomas Tibbals, son of Thomas Tibbals and

his wife; Timothy Grave, son of David Grave and his wife, Joseph Brooks, son of Charles Brooks and his wife; and Lois Bates, daughter of Stephen Bates and his wife.

Jan. 27th, 1754.—Jonathan Wells, son of Jonathan and Mary Wells.

Jan. 27th, 1754.—Hannah, daughter of Jehial Hull and his wife.

Feb. 3d, 1754.—Archibald Austin, son of Elias and Eunice Austin; Ann Norton, daughter of John Norton and his wife; and Amy Newton, daughter of Abner and Huldah Newton.

Feb. 24th, 1754.—Esther Hand, daughter of Lemuel Hand and his wife.

March 10th, 1754.—Abiather Newton, son of Burwell and Eunice Newton

March 17th, 1754.—Rosanna Parmalee, daughter of Joel and Rhoda Parmalee; and Edith, daughter of John Bates and his wife; and Abigail, daughter of John —— and his wife.

March 24th, 1754.—Nathaniel Hickox, son of Sam'l Hickox and his wife; Rhoda Bishop, daughter of William and Patience Bishop; and Huldah Camp, daughter of Israel and Annie Camp.

April 14th, 1754.—Joseph Sothern, son of Joseph and Mary Sothern.

May 5th, 1754.—Charles Squire and his wife owned ye covenant.

May 12th, 1754.—George Fairchild, son of John and Rhoda Fairchild was baptized.

May 26th, 1754.—James Tibbals, son of James Tibbals and his wife; and James Francis, son of Thomas Francis and his wife.

June 2d, 1754.—Daniel Bishop, son of Abraham and Mabel Bishop; and Elizabeth Weld, daughter of Daniel and Elizabeth Weld.

June 16th.—Thaddeus Austin, son of Moses and Hannah Austin; and Sarah Tibbals, daughter of Abner and Sarah Tibbals; John Sutlief owned the covenant.

June 30th, 1754.—Dan. Canfield, son of Gideon and Ann Canfield.

June 7th, 1754.—Mehetabel Hull, daughter of Joseph and Sybil Hull.

Phebe, daughter of Elisha and Sybel Hail; and Sarah, daughter of John Sutlief, Jun

June 14th, 1754.—Rachel Gillum, daughter of Benj. and Elizabeth Gillum.

June 25th, 1754.—John Picket, son of John and Eliz. Picket; and Abigail Norton, daughter of Stephen and Abigail Norton.

Aug 20th, 1754.—Jemima Rockwell, daughter of Ezra and Jemima Rockwell.

Sept. 1st, 1754.—Abiather Fowler, son of David Fowler and his wife.

Sept. 8th, 1754.—Mary Squire, daughter of Charles and Mary Squire.

Sept. 22d, 1754.—Nathan Crane, son of Serj. Silas and Mercy Crane.

Sept. 22d, 1754.—Hezekiah Francis, son of James Francis and his wife.

Oct. 27th.—Thankful, negro child, the daughter of Cambridge, Capt. Sutlief's negro servant.

Nov. 3d, 1754—David Spelman, son of John Spelman and his wife of Bedford, and Ebenezer Robinson, son of James and Amy Robinson; and Phebe Strong, daughter of Thomas and Phebe Strong

Nov. 10th, 1754.—Rebecca Rossetter, daughter of Rowland and Mary Rossetter. Mary Rossetter owned the covenant on ye same day David Seaward and his wife owned the cov.

Nov. 17th.—Timothy, son of David Johnson, Jun. and his wife.

Nov. 24th, 1754.—Huldah Right, daughter of Joseph and Helen Right.

Dec 1st, 1754.—Gideon Warner, son of Gideon and Mary Warner.

Dec 8th, 1754.—Daniel Smith, son of Daniel Smith and his wife; and Lucy Rossetter, daughter of Rowland and Mary Rossetter.

Jan. 12th, 1755.—Hannah Curtis, the daughter of John and Dinah Curtis.

Feb. 9th, 1755.—Anne Hull, daughter of Cornelius and Abigail Hull.

Feb 16th, 1755.—Simeon Coe, son of Simeon and Ann Coe; and Elnathan Seward, son of Jared Seward and his wife.

Feb. 16th, 1755.—Phinehas Spelman and his wife made confession.

Feb. 23d, 1755.—Samuel Ely, son of Dr. Samuel Ely and Jerusha his wife; and Aaron Camp, son of Job and Rachel Camp

March 23d, 1755.—James Picket, son of Samuel and Hepzibah Picket.

March 30th, 1755.—Comfort Newton, daughter of John and Mary Newton; and Hannah Spelman, daughter of Phinehas and Eliz Spelman

Apr. 6th, 1755.—John Right, son of John and Lucy Right his wife; and Catherine Coe, daughter of John and Ann Coe.

Apr. 13th, 1755.—Joel Fairchild, son of Samuel and Phebe Fairchild; and Joseph Grave, son of Samuel and his wife; and Rhoda Robinson, daughter of Dan and Abigail Robinson.

Apr 20th, 1755.—Stephen Seward, son of Brotherton and Abigail Seward; and Naomi Parsons, daughter of Serj. Ithamar and Sarah Parsons; the child was baptized privately.

May 11th, 1755.—John Strong, son of Eliakim and H Strong, his wife; and Asher Wright, son of Daniel Wright

May 18th, 1755.—Samuel Crittenden and Sarah his wife, owned ye covenant.

May 18th, 1755.—Elnathan and Elizabeth Norton, twin children of Benjamin and Eliz. Norton were baptized; and Sarah Curtis, daughter of David Curtis and his wife.

May 25th, 1755.—Amy Alverd, daughter of Aaron and Mehetabel Alverd; and Mary Merwin, daughter of Miles and Mary Merwin.

June 15th, 1755.—Phinehas Robinson and his wife owned the covenant.

June 29th, 1755.—Mary Bates, daughter of James and Mary Bates

July 13th, 1755.—Thomas Cooke, Jun and his wife owned the covenant.

July 27th, 1755.—Josiah Parsons, son of Samuel and Mary Parsons; and Phebe, daughter of Charles Brooks and his wife.

Aug. 17th, 1755.—Ruth Robinson, daughter of Phinehas and Susannah Robinson.

Aug. 24th, 1755.—Benjamin Sutlief, son of Sergn't John and

Sarah Sutlief; and Hannah Cook, daughter of Thomas Cook, Jun. and his wife.

Aug 31st.—Lemuel Bates, son of Stephen and Mindwell Bates.

Sept. 14th, 1755.—Ithamar Coe, son of Aaron and Phebe Coe

Sept. 28th, 1755.—Miles Coe, son of Josiah Coe and his wife; and Samuel Crittenden, son of Samuel and Sarah Crittenden.

Sept. ult., 1755.—Rhoda Hickox, daughter of Joseph Hickox and his wife.

Oct. 19th, 1755 —Ebenezer Tibbals, son of Eben. Tibbals and Submit Tibbals.

Oct. 26th, 1755.—Zipporah Norton, daughter of Isaac Norton and his wife; and Abigail Cook, daughter of Wilson and Mary Cook.

1755, Nov 9th.—David Grave.

These following were baptized after Mr Chauncey's death, and before the next settlement:

Feb. 8th, 1756.—Cyrus, son of Abner Newton; Stephen, son of John Newton; grand-son of John Sutlief; John, son of Abraham Bishop; Phebe, daughter of Stephen Bates, Jun.

Feb. 15th.—Walker, son of Tim. Hall

Mar 24th.—A daughter of Daniel Weld.

May 2d.—Benjamin, son of Joseph Ingham; Rachel, daughter of Joel Parmalee; Prudence, daughter of Sumner Stowe; Lucy, daughter of Merwin More.

May 16th —Anne, daughter of Isaac Bartlet; Abner, son of Abner Tibbalds; Hamlet, son of John Fairchild; Concurrence, daughter of Joseph Southworth.

July.—Elizabeth, daughter of Ens. Sam. Parsons.

Aug. 15th.—Asher, son of Samuel Vinton; Rhoda, daughter of Israel Camp; Jeremiah, son of Jeremiah Griswold; Rosannah, daughter of William Bishop.

Nov. 14th —Nathan, son of Lemuel Hand.

Nov. 14th.—Mindwell, daughter of Ephraim Norton; Jerusha, daughter of David Johnson.

REV. ELIZUR GOODRICH'S RECORD

A Record of Persons admitted to full Communion in the Church of Christ, at Durham, beginning with the ministry of Elizur Goodrich, Pastor, Nov. 24th, 1756.

Dec. 19th, 1756 —James Doney; Lemuel Gurnsey and Ruth Gurnsey, his wife; removed—Elihu Norton and Dinah Norton, his wife; Samuel Camp and Phebe Camp, his wife

Jan. 9th, 1757 —Samuel Squire and his wife, Anne Squire.

Jan. 16th, 1757.—Hazael Hinman and his wife, Anne Hinman; Lucretia, wife of Silas Crane, Jun.

Feb. 6th, 1757.—Abiel Baldwin.

Feb. 27th, 1757.—James Robinson.

March 13th, 1757.—Brotherton Seaward; Mehetabel, wife of Abiel Baldwin; Mary, daughter of Isaac Norton.

Feb. 6th, 1757.—Lois, wife of Roswel Graves; Mercy, wife of Hezekiah Parmalee, by a Recommendation from the Church in Kensington, dated Dec. 10th, 1756.

Aug. 10th, 1757.—Anne, daughter of Samuel Griswold.

Sept. 11th, 1757.—Mindwell, wife of Stephen Bates; Ruth, wife of Jehiel Hull.

Sept. 25th, 1757.—David Parsons, admitted.

Oct. 30th, 1757 —Daniel Weld, and his wife, by a Letter of Recommendation from the Church in Long Meadow, dated Oct. 10th, 1757; Catherine, wife of Capt. James Wadsworth; Samuel Sutleif and his wife, Eunice.

Nov. 21st, 1757.—Sarah, wife of Timothy Hall.

Jan. 29th, 1758.—Joseph Ingham, admitted; and Susannah, wife of Isaac Barlet, Jun.; Isaac Barlet, Sen., by a Recommendation from the Church of Haddam, dated July

Feb. 5th.—Elah, son of Nathan Camp; Ozias, son of Nathan Camp; Adah, daughter of Nathan Camp.

March.—Hannah, wife of Ozias Camp.

May 7th —Phebe, daughter of Henry Crane.

June 4th.—Ann, wife of Thomas Canfield, by a Recommendation from the 1st Church in Middletown, Benjamin Picket; Phebe Baldwin; Esther Crittenden; Mary Brown, admitted.

July 23d—Sarah Fowler, admitted.

Sept. 3d, 1758.—David Camp; admitted,—Jemima, wife of Ezra Rockwel; Mary, wife of Miles Merwin; Lydia, wife of Daniel Smith; Esther, wife of John Wadsworth; Rhoda, daughter of Ens. Hezekiah Talcot; Ebenezer Gurnsey, by a Recommendation from the First Church in Springfield.

Oct. 15th.—Katherine Chauncey; Margery Butler.

Oct. 29th.—Mary, wife of Joseph Southworth.

Nov. 26th.—Ezra Baldwin, son of Dea. Baldwin.

Jan. 7th, 1759—Ephraim Coe, Jun., and Ann, his wife, by a Recommendation from the Church in Middlefield.

Feb 4th.—Jesse Austin and Elizabeth, his wife.

Feb 4th.—Lucy Richardson; Sarah Brown, by baptism.

March 25th.—Anne, wife of Caleb Fowler, admitted.

June 10th.—Simeon Parsons and Eunice, his wife, admitted.

July 15th.—Sarah, wife of James Hinman, admitted.

Aug. 26th.—Elizabeth, wife of Phineas Spelman, admitted.

Sept. 23d.—Capt. Joseph Barlet and Mindwell, his wife, were received by a Letter of Recommendation from the First Church in Guilford, dated 11th inst.

March 16th, 1760—Elnathan Camp and Eunice, his wife; Elizabeth, wife of Lieut. Elnathan Chauncey, by a Recommendation from the Church in Saybrook.

Apr 13th—Noah Parsons, son of Ensign Samuel Parsons, Mary, wife of John Norton, of N. Chh., Killingworth.

June.—Abigail, wife of Samuel Seaward, recommended from the Church in N. Killingworth

Apr. 5th, 1761—Hannah, wife of Josiah Coe; Jerusha, wife of David Johnson, Jun.

May 3d—Stephen Norton, and Prudence, wife of Abel Coe.

May 10th.—Sarah Picket, admitted.

May 24th—Noah Baldwin and Mehetabel, his wife.

June 21st.—Elizabeth, wife of Jonah Frisbee.

Oct 25th—Mary, wife of Jared Seaward.

Jan. 17th, 1762.—Samuel Parsons, Jun, and Mary, his wife; Moses Seaward, and Sarah, his wife.

Feb. 7th —Nathan Curtis and Anna, his wife

Aug 8th.—Sarah, wife of Jeremiah Griswold.

Sept. 5th.—Freelove, wife of Gideon Warner, recommended from Mr. Eells.

Jan. 2d, 1763.—Ensign Daniel Hall and Joanna, his wife, recommended from the Church of North Guilford.

Jan. 16th.—Jesse Cook and Ruth, his wife.

Apr. 17th, 1763.—Mary Coe, daughter of Ephraim Coe.

June 26th.—Daniel Dimock, admitted, and some time after, Thankful, his wife.

Oct. 16th.—Rose, negro servant of Lieut. John Camp, was admitted by baptism.

Apr. 21, 1764.—Phebe, negro servant of Ensign Simeon Parsons, by baptism.

May 20th.—Judah Howd and Naomi, his wife, by a Recommendation from Mr. Williams, of Northford; also Hannah, wife of Thomas Cook, by letter from Mr. Huntington, of Middletown.

Sept. 30th.—Samuel Johnson, admitted.

May 12th, 1765 —Israel Wheadon, admitted.

Nov. 3d, 1765.—Hannah Stevens, admitted.

Dec. 8th, 1765.—John Johnson, admitted.

Apr. 11, 1766 —Mary Brown, admitted by baptism.

Aug. 10th, 1766.—Charles Chauncey, Sarah Chauncey, and Elizabeth Camp, admitted.

Sept. 7th, 1766.—James Bates, Jun., and Anne, his wife, were admitted to full communion.

Sept 21st —Joseph Wright, Jun , admitted.

Oct. 5th, 1766 —Lucy Rose, by baptism.

Oct. 26th, 1766.—Daniel Meeker and Mary, his wife, admitted.

Nov. 16th, 1766.—Desire Squier, admitted.

June 21st, 1767.—Mary, wife of Robert Crane, admitted.

Apr. 1768 —Hannah, the wife of Lemuel Hand, by Recommendation from the Chh. in Branford.

March 27th, 1768.—Joseph Camp, admitted

June 26th, 1768.—Elias Camp and Ruth his wife, by Recommendation from 1st Chh. in Middletown; Admitted—Heth Camp and Mary his wife; Elah Crane and Mehetabel his wife.

Dec. 4th, 1768.—Miles Merwin, Jun. and Mary his wife; David Talcot and Anne his wife.

Jan. 1st, 1769.—Samuel Dane Cook and Rebecca his wife, admitted to Communion.

Jan. 29th, 1769.—Widow Mary Hubbard, admitted

March 26th.—Mary, wife of Jesse Atwell, admitted.

Apr. 16th.—William Bishop, and Patience his wife; and Eunice, wife of John Camp, Jun., admitted.

June 11th.—Hannah Hickox, admitted.

Aug. 13.—Susanna, wife of Thomas Francis.

Oct 15th, 1769.—Phebe, wife of Timothy Coe, admitted.

Jan. 14th, 1770.— ———, wife of Samuel Parsons, Jun. by Recommendation from the Church of Christ in Kensington.

Mar. 4th —Sharp and Phillis, negro servants of Mr. Elah Camp. Sharp, by baptism.

Apr. 29th, 1770.—Samuel Bowman Wetmore and Anne, his wife, were admitted

May 27th, 1770.—Elihu Atkins, admitted.

Aug. 5th, 1770.—Daniel Merwin and Rebecca his wife.

Sept. 9th, 1770.—John Jones, admitted.

Nov. 18th, 1770.—Rebecca, wife of Timothy Stowe, admitted.

June 2d, 1771.—Dolphia, negro servant of Lieut. Samuel Parsons; and Zillah, wife of Dolphin, negro servant of Ephraim Coe, admitted on baptism.

July ———. —Hannah, wife of Capt William Warner.

Aug. 18th.—Samuel Hart, and Bridget his wife; Eliphaz Parmalee, and Anne his wife

Sept. 1st.—Daniel Hall, 3d, and Elizabeth, his wife.

Feb. 16th, 1772.—David Curtiss, Jun and Prudence, his wife.

Feb. 23d, 1772.—Moses Bates and Martha, his wife.

Aug. 2d, 1772.—James Hinman and Abigail, his wife.

Aug 3d, 1772.—Samuel Parsons and Martha, his wife

Oct. 18th, 1772.—Anne, wife of William Burrit, and Ruth Wadsworth, admitted.

Nov. 15th, 1772—Josiah Squier and Betty, his wife.

Dec 13th, 1772.—Joseph Chedsey recommended from the Church in North Guilford; Abraham Hand and Ruth, his wife.

Jan. 31st, 1773.—Timothy Stowe, admitted.

March 21st.—Phineas Jones, admitted.

Apr 11th.—Abraham Scranton and Hannah, his wife, admitted.

May 16th.—Thomas Stevens and Mary, his wife.

Dec 12th.—David Squire and Huldah, his wife, Nathan Bristol and Hannah, his wife.

Feb 27th, 1774.—Reuben Baldwin and Abigail, wife of John Johnson, 2d, admitted.

Apr. 24th, 1774.—Ithamar Parsons, Jun. and Mehetabel, his wife; also, Rachel, wife of Nathan Seaward, admitted.

June 19th, 1774—William Bishop, Jun. and his wife

Sept. 25th, 1774.—Noah Merwin and Lemuel Parsons were admitted.

April 2d, 1775—Henry Crane and Jerusha, his wife.

1776.—Dan. Canfield and Comfort, his wife; Huldah, wife of Gurdon Hull; James Hickox, and his wife Rhoda, Widow Mary Rossetter; Morris Coe and Lucy, his wife; Abigail, wife of John Johnson; Remembran, wife of Eliakim Strong, Jun.; Hannah, wife of Medad Strong, Thomas Lyman and Rachel Lyman.

1777.— ———, wife of Levi Parmalee, recommended; Col. James Arnold and Tabiatha, his wife; Rosanna and Rachel Parmalee.

1778—Abijah Curtiss and Ann, his wife, Dan. Parmalee and his wife.

1779.—Joseph Parsons and Mercey, his wife; Katharine, wife of Rev. Lemuel Parsons.

1780.—Timothy Dunn, Jun. and Lucy, his wife

1781.—Charles Parmalee and his wife; Lois, wife of John N. Wadsworth, Jun.; Gloriana Austin, Huldah Camp.

1782.—David Scranton and Phebe, his wife; Hannah Curtiss; wife of Jacob Cornwell, Martha, wife of John Fairchild, by recommendation.

1782.—Dec. Richard Spelman and Rhoda, his wife; Sarah Camp.

Jan. 1783.—Reuben Rose Fowler and Anne Fowler.

March.—Sarah Coe.

A RECORD OF THOSE WHO OWN AND ACKNOWLEDGE THEIR BAPTISMAL COVENANT.

ELIZUR GOODRICH, Pastor.

Dec. 26th, 1756.—Roswel Graves and Lois, his wife.

Jan. 9th, 1757.—Oliver Bates and Lois, his wife; Sarah, wife of William Carr; Mehetabel, wife of Timothy Dunn.

Jan. 16th.—Jane Lowis.

Feb. 27th —William Clarke and his wife, Elizabeth

Sept. 11th.—Nathaniel Bishop and his wife, Huldah.

Feb. 12th, 1758 —Urania, daughter of Lieut. John Camp.

Apr. 30th, 1758.—John Norton, Jun. and Hannah, his wife.

Aug. 6th, 1758 —Sarah Torney

Oct. 1st.—Margaret, wife of Caleb Carr.

Jan. 7th, 1759 —Joseph Franeis, and Martha, his wife.

June 3d, 1759.—Abraham Barlet, and Submit, his wife.

July 22d.—Reuben Bishop and Anne his wife.

Sept 2d.—Noah Norton.

June 21st, 1761.—Phineas Parmalee, and Eunice, his wife, by a Recommendation from Mr Todd, of East Guilford.

Sept. 20th, 1761.—David Squire, and Huldah, his wife.

July 11th, 1762.—John Crane, and Abigail, his wife.

Aug. 8th, 1762 —Samuel Hart owned the Cov.

Nov. 27th, 1763.—Abiather Squire owned the Covenant.

Jan ——1764.—Mary, wife of Abiather Squire, owned the Covenant.

July ——1764 —Richard and Sarah Lucas; Recommended by Mr. Robbins, Branford.

March 10th, 1765.—Samuel and Sarah Bates owned their Covenant.

Apr. 14th, 1765 —Eunice, wife of John Camp, 3d

Feb.——1766.—Beriah Murray, and Mary, his wife.

July 13th, 1766 —Hezekiah Talcott, and Sarah, his wife.

Nov. 23d, 1766.—Daniel Hall, Jun. and Ann, his wife

May 24th, 1767.—Phineas Camp, and Martha, his wife.

Oct. 30th, 1768 —Robert Smithson, and Phebe, his wife.

Dec. 4th, 1768.—Moses Griswold, and Anna, his wife.

Dec. 11th, 1768.—Jonathan Walkley, and Anne, his wife.

Jan. 1st, 1769.—Amtrose Field, and Sarah, his wife.

Jan. 1st, 1769.—Joseph Smith, and Rhoda, his wife.

July 2d, 1769.—Samuel Barlet, and Abigail, his wife.

Aug. 13th, 1769.—Asa Chamberlain, and Martha, his wife.

Sept. 10th, 1769.—Lemuel Moffet, and Ann, wife of Israel Goddard

Nov. 12th, 1769.—Charles Norton, and Elizabeth, his wife.

Dec. 3d, 1769.—James Ferguson and Martha Ferguson.

Jan. 14th, 1770.—Jacob Clark, and Katharine, his wife, owned the Covenant.

Apr. 29th, 1770.—Esther, wife of John Jones, owned the Covenant.

May 13th, 1770.—Jeremiah Butler, and Anna, his wife, owned the Covenant.

Oct. 28th, 1770.—Charles Bishop, and Martha, his wife.

———, 1771.—Timothy Hall, Jun and Deborah his wife.

Dec. 12th, 1773.—Noah Lyman, and his wife.

June —, 1774.—Cornelius Hull, and Mercy, his wife.

July —, 1774.—Phineas Canfield, and Amy, his wife.

Dec. 25th, 1774.—Jonathan Squire, and Sarah, his wife.

Sept. 10th, 1775.—Jerusha, wife of Lemuel Johnson.

Sept. 17th, 1775.—Rhoda, wife of William Trench.

A RECORD OF BAPTISMS.

Nov. 28th, 1756.—James, son of John and —— Jones; John, son of Joseph and Sybil Hull; James, son of James and Amy Robinson.

Dec. 5th, 1756.—Louren, son of James and Jane Doney; Asa, son of Charles and Mehetabel Brooks.

Dec. 19th, 1756.—Content, daughter of Lemuel and Ruth Gurnsey.

Dec. 26th, 1756.—Ezra, son of Roswel Graves, and Lois, his wife.

Jan. 9th, 1757.—Asher, son of Gideon and Ann Canfield; Gad, son of Job and Rachel Camp, Timothy, son of Timo. and Mehetabel Dunn; William, son of William and Sarah Carr; Lucy, daughter of Oliver and Lois Bates.

Jan. 16th.—Burwell, son of Burwell and Eunice Newton;

Nathan, son of Elihu and Dinah Norton; Edmund Adams, son of Charles and Mary Squire; Statyra, daughter of Samuel and Phebe Camp; Elizabeth, (Austin,) daughter of Jane Lewis.

Jan. 30th —Nathan, son of James and Sarah Francis; Anne, daughter of Phinehas and Eliz. Spelman.

Feb. 6th —Rhoda, daughter of Abiel and Mehetabel Baldwin.

Feb. 20th.—Anne, daughter of Sam'l and Anne Squire.

Feb 27th.—Mehetabel, daughter of Wm. and Eliz. Clarke.

Mar. 13th.—Samuel, son of Dan'l and Elizabeth Weld; Levi, son of Ab'm Camp, of Middlefield; Beulah, daughter of Eliakim and Hannah Strong; Catherine, daughter of Rowland and Mary Rossetter.

Mar. 20th, 1757.—Elijah, son of Abel and Prudence Coe; Lorraine, daughter of Thos. and Phebe Strong.

April 10th.—Sarah, daughter of Simeon and Anna Coe; also baptized, privately, Hophni and Phineas, twin children of Elias and Eunice Austin, which died soon after.

Apr 17th.—Hannah, daughter of Silas and Lucretia Crane.

Apr. 24th.—Seth, son of Daniel and Lydia Smith; Sarah, daughter of Hazael and Anne Henman.

May 8th.—Eli, son of John and Mary Norton, B. R.; John, son of John and Dinah Curtiss: Phebe, daughter of Ebenezer and Submit Tibbals.

May 29th.—Elizabeth, daughter of Benjamin Gillum and wife.

July 3d.—Samuel, son of Daniel and Lucy Wright; Dan, son of Cambridge and wife, negro servants of Capt. N. Sutlief.

July 17th.—James, son of Hezekiah and Mercy Parmalee; Joseph, son of Joseph and Martha Hickox—by Mr. Stiles of N. H.

Aug. 14th.—Robert, son of James and Mary Bates; Sarah, daughter of Brotherton and Abigail Seaward.

Aug. 21st. —Rhoda, daughter of Miles and Mary Merwin—by Mr. Clarke of ——.

Aug. 28th.—Timothy, son of Ezra and Jemima Rockwell.

Sept. 4th.—Catharine, daughter of Samuel and Mary Parsons.

Sept. 11th.—Asher, son of Josiah and Sarah Coe; Ann, daughter of Ephraim and Ann Coe, of Middlefield.

Sept. 18th.—Seth, son of David and Rebecca Parsons.

Sept. 25th.—Phineas, son of Samuel and Hephzibah Picket; Wilson, son of Wilson and Mary Cook.

Oct. 23d—Ebenezer, son of Samuel Crittenden and wife; Thalmene, son of Nathaniel and Huldah Bishop.

Nov. 6th.—Aaron, son of Stephen and Mindwel Bates.

Dec. 4th.—John, son of James and Amy Robinson.

Dec. 25th, 1757.—Ebenezer, son of Timothy and Sarah Hall; Abigail, daughter of Capt. James and Kath. Wadsworth; ——, daughter of Marvin Reynold More and wife.

Jan. 1st, 1758.—Hinsdel, son of Oliver and Lois Bates; Benjamin, son of Samuel Graves and wife.

Jan. 22d.—Elizabeth, daughter of Abraham Bishop.

Jan. 26th.—Baptized *Submit*, daughter of John Canfield and wife, privately. The child died 29th.

Feb. 5th.—Lois, daughter of Ozias and Hannah Camp.

Feb. 12th.—Louisa Fairchild, daughter of Urania Camp.

Feb. 26th.—Sarah, daughter of Phineas and Susanna Robinson.

Mar. 12th.—Ichabod, son of Abraham and Elenor Scranton; Huldah, daughter of Cornelius Hull and wife.

Apr. 23d.—Giles, son of Giles Millar, of Middlefield.

May 7th.—Ashbel, (Bradley,) son of Phebe Crane, Sarah, daughter of John Newton and wife.

May 14th—Hannah, daughter of John and Hannah Norton.

June 4th.—Mary Brown, (adult); Santon, son of Samuel Squire and Anne, his wife.

June 11th.—Bridgman, son of Lemuel and Ruth Gurnsey; Jonathan, son of Abiel and Mehetabel Baldwin.

June 18th, 1758.—Roswel, son of Roswel and Lois Graves; Nathan, son of Samuel and Eunice Sutleif—by Mr. Seaward.

June 25th, 1758.—Hannah, daughter of Jared Seaward and wife.

Aug. 13th.—Joel, son of Joel and Rhoda Parmalee.

Aug. 20th.—Stephen, son of Abner and Sarah Tibbals—by Mr. Ely.

Sept. 10th.—Nathaniel, son of David and Margery Camp—by Mr. Williams.

Sept. 17th.—Levi, son of Thomas Norton and wife.

Sept. 24th.—Diana, daughter of David and Jerusha Johnson.

Oct. 1st.—John Noyes, son of John Noyes and Esther Wadsworth; Hannah, daughter of Moses Austin and his wife.

Oct. 29th.—James, son of John Jones and wife; Phebe, daughter of Charles Brooks and wife; Nabby (Henman,) daughter of Sarah Torry.

Nov. 12th.—Aaron, son of Ithamar and Sarah Parsons; William, son of William and Elizabeth Clark; Charity, daughter of Benjamin and Elizabeth Norton. This child was born after its Father's death. Sarah, daughter of Silas and Lucretia Crane.

Nov. 26th.—Justus, son of Charles and Mary Squire.

Dec. 3d.—Richard, son of Phineas and Eliz. Spelman.

Dec. 10th.—Rosanna, daughter of Joseph and Mary Southworth.

Dec. 17th.—Rachel, daughter of Job and Rachel Camp; David, (Meeker,) son of Jane Lewis.

Dec 31st.—Enoch, son of Hazael Hinman and Anne, his wife; Ozias, son of Samuel and Phebe Camp.

Jan. 7th, 1759.—Selah, son of Eliakim Strong and his wife.

Jan. 28th, 1759.—Sarah, daughter of Joseph and Martha Francis.

Jan. 28th, 1759.—Statyra, daughter of Jehiel and Ruth Hull.

Feb. 4th, 1759.—Abigail, daughter of Jesse and Elizabeth Austin.

Feb. 11th, 1759.—Lucy Richardson, age, 19; Sarah Brown, age, 17; Gloriana, daughter of Elias and Eunice Austin.

Feb. 18th.—Ruth, daughter of Caleb and Margaret Carr.

Mar. 4th.—Notwithstanding, daughter of Jeremiah Griswold and his wife, baptized privately. Died March 5.

Mar. 11th.—Darius, son of Joseph Hickox and wife, Martha; Sarah, daughter of Robert and Sarah Akins.

Mar. 18th.—Abigail, daughter of Abraham and Mehetabel Bishop.

Mar. 27th.—Anne, daughter of Daniel Weld and his wife, Elizabeth.

Apr. 8th.—Josiah, son of Joseph and Sybil Hull.

Apr. 15th.—Katharine, daughter of Thomas and Phebe Strong; Mary, daughter of Burwell and Eunice Newton.

Apr. 22.—Abigail, daughter of Daniel and Lucy Wright.

May 6th.—Polycarp, son of Daniel and Lydia Smith; Sarah, daughter of Benjamin and Elizabeth Gillum.

May 13th.—Submit, daughter of Ebenezer and Submit Tibbals.

June 3d.—Abraham, son of Abraham Barlet and his wife.

June 10th.—Asher, son of Abner Newton, Jun., and Huldah, his wife.

July 22d.—James and Jonathan, sons, twins, of James and Sarah Francis.

July 29th.—Joseph, son of Elihu Norton and Dinah, his wife; Stephen, son of Stephen Bates and Lois, his wife.

Aug 5th.—Timothy, son of Gideon Canfield and Anne, his wife; Phebe, daughter of Cambridge and Cloe, his wife, negro servants to Capt. Sutlief.

Sept. 16th —Lucy, daughter of John Picket and Elizabeth, his wife.

Sept. 23, 1759.—Experience, daughter of Noah and Experience Norton.

Oct. 7th —David, son of Samuel Parsons, Jun, and Mary, his wife; Joel, son of Reuben Bishop and Anne, his wife

Oct. 21st.—Chauncey, son of Elizur and Katharine Goodrich.

Oct. 28th.—Rejoice, son of Israel and Anne Camp.

Nov. 11.—Daniel, son of Timothy and Mehetabel Dun.

Nov. 18th.—Josiah, son of William and Sarah Carr.

Nov. 25th.—Ruth, daughter of Benjamin and Adah Picket; Rebekah, daughter of John and Hannah Norton.

Jan. 6th, 1760 —Ozias, son of Stephen Norton and wife.

Jan. 20th, 1760 —Osee, son of Samuel and Sarah Crittenden, Katharine, daughter of Capt James and Ruth Wadsworth

Feb. 10th.—Silas, son of Brotherton and Abigail Seaward.

Feb 17th.—Gad, son of Timothy and Sarah Hall.

Feb. 24th.—Baptized three children at Middlefield.

Mar. 2d.—Gurnsey, son of Abraham and Eleanor Scranton; Ann, daughter of Stephen and Mindwell Bates; Rhoda, daughter of Lemuel and Ruth Gurnsey.

Mar. 16th, 1760.—Rebekah, daughter of Ezra and Jemima Rockwell.

Apr 6th.—Hannah, daughter of James and Mary Bates

Apr. 27th.—Eunice, daughter of Elnathan and Eunice Camp.

May 4th.—Anne, daughter of Samuel and Anne Squire.

May 11th.—Charles, son of Cornelius and Abigail Hull; Amy, daughter of James and Amy Robinson.

June 8th.—Samuel, son of Samuel and Hephzibah Picket,, Sarah, daughter of Miles and Mary Merwin.

July 13th.—Charles, son of Abel and Prudence Coe.

July 13th, 1760.—Rhoda, daughter of John and Mary Newton.

July 20th.—David, son of Samuel and Eunice Sutlicf; Lois, daughter of John and Dinah Curtiss

Aug. 10th.—Eunice, daughter of Abiel and Mehetable Baldwin.

Aug 17th.—Noah, son of Thomas and Rachel Tibbals.

Aug. 24th.—Titus, son of Joseph and Martha Francis, Susanna, daughter of Phinehas and Susanna Robinson; Hannah, daughter of Hazael and Anne Hinman

Sept. 7th.—Bryan, son of Rowland and Mary Rosseter.

Sept. 16th.—Timothy, son of Ephraim Coe, Jun., and Ann, his wife, privately.

Sept. 21.—Seth, son of Roswel and Lois Groves, of Granville; Mahetabel, daughter of Abr'm and Mehetabel Bishop.

Oct. 5th.—Rhoda, daughter of Oliver and Lois Bates.

Oct. 29th.—Eunice, daughter of David and Mary Wood.

Nov. 30th.—Rebekah, daughter of Wilson and Mary Cook.

Dec 28th.—Reuben, son of Joseph Hickox and wife—Martha.

Feb 1st. 1761.—Manoah, son of Job and Rachel Camp; Tryphena, D of William and Patience Bishop; Adah, daughter of Benjamin and Adah Picket

March 8th.—Miles, son of Elihu and Mary Crane; Nabby, daughter of Jess and Elizabeth Austin.

March 22d.—Abigail, daughter of Ebenezer and Submit Tibbals.

March 29th.—Elizur, son of Elizur and Katharine Goodrich.

May 3d.—Ruth, daughter of Abner and Sarah Tibbals.

May 10th.—Seth, son of Eliakim and Hannah Strong.

May 31st.—Abigail, daughter of Benjamin and Elizabeth Gillum.

June 4th.—Phebe, D. of Noah and Mehetabel Baldwin, privately; it died the same day.

June 7th.—Samuel, son of Samuel and Phebe Camp; Hannah, daughter of Joseph and Sibil Hull.

June 14th.—I baptized at Middletown, John, the son of John Cotton; and Ruth, the daughter of David Starr.

June 21st.—Constant, son of Phineas and Eunice Parmalee.

July 5th.—Esther, D of Samuel and Abigail Seaward.

July 12th.—Thadeus Grannis, son of Jonah and Elizabeth Frisbe; William, son of John Noyes and Esther Wadsworth

Aug. 9th.—Ruth, daughter of Elah Camp, and Phebe his wife.

Sept 6th.—Olive, son of William and Elizabeth Clark; Hannah, daughter of Joel and Rhoda Parmalee.

Sept. 20th.—Nathaniel William, son of Lieut Elnathan and Elizabeth Chauncey, Phinehas, son of David and Huldah Squire.

Oct. 4th, 1761.—Lewis, son of Caleb and Margaret Carr.

Oct. 11th, 1761 —Moses, son of Elias and Eunice Austin.

Nov. 1st.—John, son of Samuel and Sarah Crittenden, Anne, daughter of Caleb and Anne Fowler.

Nov. 22d.—I baptized Elijah, son of Simeon Roberts; Elijah, son of Ebenezer Roberts; Ebenezer, son of Harris Prout; Experience, daughter of William Hamlin, at Middletown.

Nov. 29th.—Sarah, daughter of William and Sarah Carr.

Jan. 3d, 1762.—Nathan, son of Thomas and Phebe Strong.

Jan. 10th, 1762.—Lemuel, son of Lemuel and Ruth Gurnsey.

Jan. 24th, 1762.—Titus, son of Gideon and Anne Canfield; Paul, son of Ens. Samuel and Elizabeth Parsons.

Jan. 31st, 1762.—Lydia, D. of Charles and Mary Squier.

Feb. 7th, 1762.—Bethiah, D. of John and Bethiah Canfield.

Feb. 14th.—James, son of Nathan and Anna Curtiss; Enos, son of Silas Crane, Jun. and Lucretia, his wife.

Feb. 21st.—Eunice, daughter of Simeon and Anna Coe.

Feb. 28th, 1762.—Torry, son of Sarah Torry.

Mar. 7th —Talcott S and Damaris D., twins of Elnathan and Eunice Camp; Sarah, D. of Timothy and Sarah Hall; Sarah, D. of Josiah and Hannah Coe.

March 28th.—Sutlief, son of Moses and Sarah Seaward.

Apr. 4th.—Lament (Crane,) daughter of the widow Lois Bates.

Apr. 11th.—Katharine, D. of Samuel and Ann Squier.

Apr. 18th.—Rachel, D. of Asher and Margery Robinson.

June 6th.—Reuben, son of Reuben and Anne Bishop; Submit, D. of Burwel and Eunice Newton.

July 4th —Abel, son of John and Mary Norton, N. Killingworth; Bela, son of Stephen and Mindwell Bates; John, son of Reuben Clarke, and his wife; Abigail, daughter of Joseph and Martha Francis.

July 11th.—Giles, son of Cornelius and Abigail Hull.

July 25th.—Abraham, son of Abraham and Mehetabel Bishop; Seth, son of Robert and Sarah Akins.

Aug. 1st.—Clarissa, D. of John and Abigail Crane.

Aug. 8th.—Sarah, wife of Jeremiah Griswold, baptized; Mary, daughter of Samuel Hart, and his wife, Bridget.

Aug. 15th, 1762.—Robert, son of Reuben Coe; Eder, son of Ens. Edward Camp; Elihu, son of David Wetmore, at Middlefield.

Aug. 29th, 1762 —Abiel, son of Abiel and Mehetabel Baldwin.

Sept. 5th, 1762.—Ichabod, son of Abr'm and Eleanor Scranton.

Oct. 17th, 1762.—Sarah, D. of John and Dinah Curtiss.

Nov. 28th, 1762 —David, son of David and Huldah Squire.

Dec. 5th, 1762.—Jerusha, D of Abel and Prudence Coe.

Dec. 12th, 1772.—Ozias, son of Benjamin and Adah Picket.

Dec. 19th, 1762.—Hannah, daughter of Samuel and Eunice Sutlief; Abigail, D. of Simeon and Sarah Walkley, Hannah, D. of Noah and Mehetabel Baldwin.

Jan. 16th, 1763.—Samuel, son of Elizur and Katharine Goodrich.

Jan. 23d, 1763.—Millesant, D. of Jesse and Ruth Cook.

Feb. 6th, 1763.—Adah, D. of Sam'll and Abigail Seaward.

Feb. 27th, 1763 —Nathan Ozias, S. of Elah and Phebe Camp; Elihu, son of Elihu and Mary Fowler; James, son of Phineas and Eunice Parmalee.

March 13th.—David, son of Miles and Mary Merwin; James, son of Jesse and Elizabeth Austin.

March 20th.—Robert, son of Jesse and Ruth Cook, Jerusha, daughter of Job and Rachel Camp.

May 1st—I baptized at Killingworth, Isaac, son of Jared Elliott.

May 8th.—Stephen, son of Eliakim and Hannah Strong; James, son of James and Amy Robinson; Sarah, D. of Israel and Anne Camp.

May 8th, 1763.—Mary, daughter of John and Mary Newton; Mary, daughter of Ebenezer and Submit Tibbals.

May 22d, 1763.—James, son of Nathan and Anna Curtiss; Samuel, son of Samuel and Anne Squire.

June 12th—Olive, daughter of Gideon and Freelove Warner, by Mr. Huntington.

June 19th.—Reuben Rose, son of Caleb and Anne Fowler; John, son of John Norton, 3d, and Hannah, his wife, Eunice, daughter of Ezra and Jemima Rockwell; Mary, daughter of Joseph and Mary Southworth; Katharine, daughter of Joseph and Martha Hickox.

June 26th.—Thankful, daughter of Daniel and Thankful Dimock.

Aug. 21st.—Huldah, daughter of Thomas Cook, Sen. and wife.

Sept. 4th.—Rachel, daughter of Josiah and Elizabeth Frisbie.

Oct. 9th.—Robert, son of William and Sarah Carr

Oct. 16th.—Rose, negro servant of Lieut. John Camp; Jenny, the daughter of Rose.

Oct. 30th.—Ebenezer, son of Samuel Camp, and his wife.

Nov. 6th—Charles, son of Charles and Mary Squier

Nov. 13th.—Oroondates, son of John and Abigail Crane.

Nov. 27th.—Asher, son of Abiather and Mary Squier.

Dec. 4th.—Phebe, D. of Noah and Mehetabel Baldwin.

Dec. 11th.—Asher, son of Benjamin and Elizabeth Gillum.

Dec. 25th.—Silas, son of Silas and Lucretia Crane.

Jan 15th, 1764.—Moses, son of Moses and Sarah Seaward; Stephen, son of Asher and Margery Robinson.

Feb. 5th, 1764.—Ebenezer, son of Lemuel and Ruth Gurnsey.

Feb. 19th, 1764.—Samuel, son of Samuel and Bridget Hart.

Feb 19th, 1764.—Lucy, daughter of Thomas and Phebe Strong.

Apr. 8th, 1764.—Hannah, D. of Benjamin and Adah Picket.

Apr. 15th, 1764.—Submit, daughter of Abraham and Submit Barlet.

Apr. 29th, 1764.—Notwithstanding, D. of Jeremiah and Sarah Griswold; Phebe, negro servant of Ensign Simeon Parsons was baptized after her own profession; Lydia, daughter of Richard and Phebe, servant of Ens Simeon Parsons, was baptized.

May 6th, 1764.—Reuben, son of Reuben Clark and wife.

May 27th, 1764.—Silas, son of Joseph and Sybil Hull; Medad, son of Samuel and Sarah Crittenden; Mehetabel, D of Abiel and Mehetabel Baldwin.

June 3d, 1764.—Zebulon, son of Simeon and Sarah Wackly; Lois, daughter of Eliakim and Hannah Strong.

June 24th.—Job, son of Gideon and Anne Canfield; Eunice, daughter of Elnathan and Eunice Camp.

July 8th —Ahaziah, son of Richard and Sarah Lucas; Peter, son of Richard and Phebe, N. servants of Ens. Simeon Parsons.

Aug. 12th.—Katharine, daughter of Capt. Elnathan and Elizabeth Chauncey.

Aug. 19th.—Thaddeus, son of David and Huldah Squire.

Sept. 9th.—Phebe Ann, D. of Nathan and Anna Curtiss; Eunice, D. of Rowland and Mary Rosseter

Sept. 23d.—Bristol, son of Timothy and Sarah Hall; Elihu, son of Elizur and Katharine Goodrich; Elizabeth, D. of Lemuel and Huldah Newton

Sept. 30th, 1764.—Statyra, D. of Phineas and Susanna Robinson.

Nov., 1764 —Amos, son of John and Mary Norton; Irene, daughter of Caleb and Anne Fowler.

Jan. 20th, 1765.—Abner and Roger, twins of Burwell and Eunice Newton.

Jan. 27th, 1765.—Sarah, daughter of Jesse and Ruth Cook.

Feb. 1765.—Abiathar, son of Elihu and Mary Crane.

March 10th, 1765.—Samuel, son of Abner and Sarah Tibbals; Samuel, son of Samuel and Sarah Bates.

March 17th, 1765.—Camp, son of Joel and Rhoda Parmalee.

March 31st, 1765.—Caroline, D. of Samuel and Abigail Seaward.

Apr. 14th, 1765.—Stephen, son of Stephen and Mindwell

Bates; Samuel, son of Samuel and Eunice Sutlief; John, son of Patrick and Lucy.

Apr 28th.—Giles, son of Joseph and Martha Hickox; Asher, son of Benjamin and Elizabeth Gillum.

May 12th—Melinda, daughter of Eunice and John Camp; Elizabeth, daughter of Jared and Sarah Wheadon.

June 16th.—Miles, son of Thomas Cook, Jun, and his wife.

July 7th.—Sarah, daughter of Jess and Elizabeth Austin.

July 21st.—Benjamin, son of Benjamin and Adah Picket, Katharine, daughter of Samuel and Anne Squier.

Sept 1st.—Elias, son of Elah and Phebe Camp; Jonah, son of Jonah and Elizabeth Frisbie; Samuel, Timothy, William, and Tryphena, children of William and Tryphena Lucas, were baptized, &c.

Sept. 8th, 1765.—Luke, son of Job Camp and Rachel his wife.

Sept. 29th, 1765.—Lucy, D. of John Norton, Jun and his wife.

Oct. —, 1765.—Lucy, D. of Stow Hawley and wife.

Nov. 17th, 1765.—Sarah, daughter of Noah and Mehetabel Baldwin; Asher, son of Asher and Margery Robinson.

Dec. 8th, 1765.—Rhoda, daughter of Lemuel and Ruth Gurnsey; Rachel, daughter of John and Concurrence Johnson.

Jan. 26th, 1766.—Dinah, daughter of John and Dinah Curtiss.

Feb. 9th, 1766—Sabra, D. of Beriah and Mary Murray

March.—Zelek, son of John and Abigail Crane; Immer, son of Samuel and Sarah Crittenden.

Apr. —, 1766.—Hannah, daughter of John and Mary Newton; Seth, son of Moses and Sarah Seaward; Ishmael, son of Richard and Phebe, negro servants of Ens. Simeon Parsons.

May 4th.—Lewis, son of Stephen and Elizabeth Norton; Mehetabel Brown, of adult age.

May 11th.—Hannah, D. of Josiah and Hannah Coe; Olive, daughter of William and Tryphena Lucas, by Mr. Denison.

Apr. 28th.—Dudley, son of Abiathar and Mary Squier.

May ——,—Stephen, son of Ens. Eliakim and Hannah Strong; Sarah, daughter of Daniel and Thankful Dimock.

June 8th.—Olive, daughter of Abraham and Submit Barlet.

June 15th.—Ruth, daughter of Samuel and Bridget Hart; ——— ———, son of Abiel and Mehetabel Baldwin.

July 13th.—Phebe, daughter of Hezekiah and Sarah Talcot.

Aug 3d.—Ozias, son of Caleb Fowler and Anne, his wife.

Aug. 10th, 1766.—Joel, son of Ephraim and Anne Coe; Ambrose, son of Abiather and Mary Squire.

Sept. 14th, 1766.—Aaron, son of Aaron and Phebe Coe.

Sept 21st, 1766.—David, son of Elnathan and Eunice Camp

Oct. 5th, 1766.—Sarah, daughter of Samuel and Phebe Camp; Lucy Rose, an adult.

Oct. 12th, 1766.—Augustus, son of Nathan and Anne Curtiss.

Oct 26th, 1766.—Nathan, son of Thomas and Phebe Strong; Rosamond and Rossetta, twin daughters of Jeremiah and Sarah Griswold; Katharine, daughter James Bates, Jun. and Anne, his wife.

Nov. 16th, 1766.—Tryphena, D. of David and Huldah Squire.

Dec. 20th, 1766.—Deborah, D. of Timothy Hall and Sarah, his wife.

Dec 27th, 1766.—Samuel, son of Jared and Sarah Whedon; Melinda, son of Aaron Hinman dec'd and Elizabeth, his wife.

Jan. 25th, 1767.—Israel, the son of Rhoda Wells, was baptized.

Feb. 8th, 1767 —Robert, son of Phineas Spelman and Elizabeth, his wife.

Feb. 8th.—Luther, son of Daniel Hall, Jun and Ann, his wife.

March 1st —Elihu, son of Samuel and Sarah Bates; Sally, daughter of Richard and Sarah Lucas.

March 22d.—Elnathan Elihu, son of Capt. Elnathan Chauncey and Elizabeth, his wife; Eunice, daughter of Samuel and Eunice Sutlief

Apr. 12th.—Daniel, son of Dan'll Maddocks and Hannah his wife.

May 17th.—Elisha, son of Thomas Cook, Jun. and Hannah, his wife

May 17th, 1767.—Clement, son of William and Sarah Carr; Molly, D. of Timothy and Mehetabel Dunn.

June 7th, 1767.—Seth, son of Phineas and Martha Camp.

June 28th, 1767.—Stephen, son of Ebenezer Tibbals and Submit, his wife; Roger, son of Stephen and Rhoda Spencer; Abigail, D. of Lemuel and Huldah Moffet.

July 19th, 1767.—Rebekah, D. of Job and Rachel Camp; Dorcas, D. of Jonas and Elizabeth Frisbie.

Aug. 9th, 1767.—Mary, daughter of Robert and Mary Crane.

Aug. 31st, 1767 —Aaron (Henman,) son of Sarah Torry, since wife of Samuel Wilkinson ; John Edward, son of Sam'll and Sarah Wilkinson.

Sept. 27th —Phebe, daughter of Samuel Squier, and wife.

Oct. ——. —Elisha, son of Jesse and Elizabeth Austin.

Nov. 8th.—Nathan, son of Benj'n and Elizabeth Gullum.

Nov 29th.—Edmund, son of Jesse and Rhoda Cook.

Dec. 6th —Clarinda, D of Elihu and Mary Crane.

Jan. 3d, 1768.—Curtiss, son of Beriah and Mary Murray.

Jan. 10th, 1768.—Daniel, son of Joseph and Martha Hickox.

Jan. 31st, 1768 —Israel, son of Ens Israel and Mary Camp

Feb. 14th, 1768.—Elah, son of Elah and Phebe Camp.

Feb 28th, 1768.—Noah, son of Noah and Mehetabel Baldwin.

March 6th.—Charles Augustus, son of Rev. Elizur and Katharine Goodrich , Beulah, D of Samuel and Abigail Seaward.

Apr 3d, 1768.—Anne, D. of Daniel Weld and Elizabeth his wife.

Apr. 28th, 1768.—James, son of Capt. John Noyes Wadsworth and Esther, his wife.

May 1st.—Julius, son of Caleb and Anne Fowler.

May ——. —Clarissa, D. of Nathan and Anna Curtiss , Patty, D. of Daniel and Thankful Dimock.

May 29th.—Roger, son of Burwell and Eunice Newton ; Abiathar, son of Abiathar and Mary Squier.

June 19th —David, son of Joseph and Mehetabel Ingham.

July 13th, 1768.—Daniel, son of Samuel and Bridget Hart ; Rachel, D. of Joseph and Martha Hickox ; Mary, D. of Lemuel and Hannah Hand.

June 28th.—Seth, son of Asher and Margery Robinson.

July 24th —Abel, son of Abel and Prudence Coe ; Sam., son of Daniel and Mary Meeker.

July 31st.—Elam, son of John and Abigail Crane.

Aug. 7th.—Stephen, son of Lieut Eliakim and Hannah Strong.

Aug 14th.—Joel, son of William and Tryphena Lucas ; Noah, son of Samuel and Sarah Crittenden.

Aug. 21st.—Rebeckah, D. of Heth and Mary Camp.

Sept. 18th —Elizabeth, D. of Stephen and Rhoda Spencer.

Sept. 25th.—Eleanor, D. of Silas and Lucretia Crane.

Oct. 30th.—Rhoda, daughter of Robert and Phebe Smithson.

Nov. 6th.—Clarinda, daughter of Phineas and Eunice Parmalee.

Dec. 4th.—David, son of Abiel and Mehetabel Baldwin; Jerusha, D. of Miles Merwin, Jun. and Mary his wife; Noah, son of David and Anne Talcot.

Dec. 25th.—Robert, son of Robert and Mary Crane.

Dec. 25th, 1768.—Mehetabel, D. of Elah and Mehetabel Crane.

Dec. 12th, 1768.—Mary, daughter of Ephraim and Ann Coe.

Jan. 1st, 1769.—Elizabeth, D. of Daniel Hall and Anne, his wife.

Jan. 15th, 1769.—Noah, son of Samuel Done Cook and Rebekah, his wife.

Jan. 29th, 1769.—Daniel, son of Phineas and Martha Camp; Phebe, daughter of Joseph and Sybil Hull; Damaris, D. of Elnathan and Eunice Camp; Hannah, daughter of Jonathan and Anne Wackley.

Feb. 5th, 1769.—Benjamin, son of John and Concurrence Johnson; Content, D. of Rowland and Mary Rosseter.

March 12th.—Millesant, D. of David and Huldah Squier.

March 19th.—Jared, son of Moses and Ann Griswold.

March 26th.—John, son of Joseph Southward and wife; Molly, D. of Jesse Atwell and Mary his wife.

Apr. 16th.—Stephen, son of Richard and Sarah Lucas.

Apr. 23d.—Timothy, son of Jonas and Elizabeth Frisbie; James, son of Joseph and Rhoda Smith; Concurrence, D. of Jared and Sarah Wheadon.

May 7th.—Phebe, D. of Sam'll Done and Rebekah Cook.

May 28th.—Levi, son of Samuel and Eunice Sutlief.

June 4th.—Samuel, son of Jeremiah and Sarah Griswold; Sarah, D. of Moses and Sarah Seaward.

June 11th.—Reuben Hickox, son of Hannah Hickox; William, son of Samuel and Abigail Seaward.

June 18th.—Samuel, son of Ebenezer and Submit Tibbals.

July 2d.—Nathan, son of Thomas and Phebe Strong.

July 2d, 1769.—Samuel, son of Samuel and Abigail Barlet; Ruth, D. of Timothy and Mehetabel Dunn.

July 30th, 1769.—Asher, son of Job and Rachel Camp; Dinah, D. of Thomas Cook and Hannah, his wife.

Aug. 13th, 1769.—Joanna, D. of William and Sarah Carr; Elizabeth, D. of Asa and Martha Chamberlain.

Sept. 10th —Hannah, D. of Lemuel and Huldah Moffett; Phebe, D of Israel and Ann Goddard; Ruth, D. of Jess and Rhoda Cook; Daniel, son of James Bates, Jun. and Anne his wife; Eunice, D. of Samuel Bates and Sarah, his wife.

Oct. 22d.—Joseph, son of Benjamin and Adah Picket; Olive, D. of Samuel and Anne Squier.

Oct. 8th.—Elizabeth, D. of Jesse and Elizabeth Austin.

Oct. 29th —Nathan, son of Ens James and Amy Robinson, Peg, daughter of Richard and Phebe, negro servants of Ensign Simeon Parsons.

Nov. 12th.—Miles, son of Charles and Elizabeth Norton.

Nov. 19.—Rejoice, son of Timothy and Phebe Coe; Anne, daughter of Reuben and Sarah Bishop

Dec. 3d.—Samuel and James, sons of James and Martha Ferguson.

Dec. 10.—James, son of Noah and Mehetabel Baldwin; Sally, daughter of Joseph Wright, Jun. and Sarah, his wife.

Jan. —, 1770.—Joseph, son of Joseph and Mehetabel Ingraham.

Feb. 4th, 1770.—Olive, D. of Jacob and Katharine Clark.

Mar. 4th, 1770.—Edmund, son of Caleb and Anne Fowler; Sharp, negro servant of Elah Camp; Cambridge, son of Sharp and Phillis, his wife.

Mar. 11th, 1770 —Statyra, D. of Abiathar and Mary Squier.

Apr. 29th.—Eunice, D. of Miles Merwin, Jun., and Mary, his wife.

May 6th.—Olive, daughter of Daniel Weld and Eliz., his wife.

May 13th —Anna, daughter of Nathan and Anna Curtiss; Polly, daughter of Jeremiah Butler and Anna, his wife.

May 27th.—Nathaniel, son of John and —— Seaward; Rachel, daughter of Stephen and Rhoda Spencer.

June 17th.—Robert, son of Ambrose and Sarah Field.

July 1st.—Phebe, D of Benjamin and Elizabeth Gillum.

July 8th.—Stephen, son of Joseph and Martha Francis; Mindwell, D. of Abraham and Submit Bartlett.

July 22.—Samuel, son of Samuel and Bridget Hart; Nathan, son of Samuel Bowman Whetmore and Anne, his wife.

July 29th.—Samuel, son of Asher and Margery Robinson.

Aug 5th —Anne, daughter of David and Anne Talcot.

Aug 26th.—Eli, son of Eli and Mehetabel Crane.

Sept. 9th.—Nathan, son of Elizur and Katharine Goodrich; Rufus, son of Asa and Martha Chamberlain; Hannah, D. of Lieut. Eliakim and Hannah Strong; Mabel, daughter of Daniel and Thankful Dimock; Daniel, son of Daniel and Rebecca Merwin.

Oct. 28th.—Charles, son of Charles and Martha Bishop; Mary, daughter of Samuel Parsons and wife.

Nov. 4th.—Ezra, son of Elah and Phebe Camp.

Nov 11th, 1770.—Aaron, son of Abiel and Mehetabel Baldwin.

Nov. 18th, 1770.—Ebenezer, son of Capt. Israel and Mary Camp.

Dec., 1770.—Isaac, son of Burwell Newton and wife.

Jan. 6th, 1771.—Amos, son of Phineas Camp and his wife.

Jan. 13th, 1771.—Sarah, D of John and Esther Jones.

Feb 3d, 1771.—Miranda, daughter of John Crane and wife.

Feb. 17th, 1771 —Phebe, daughter of Lemuel and Hannah Hand; Joel, son of Samuel and Abigail Barlet; Polly, daughter of Daniel Wetmore, at his house.

Mar. 10th.—Phebe, daughter of Timothy Hall, Jun., and Deborah, his wife

Mar. 17th, 1771.—Jenny, negro girl of Capt. James Wadsworth; Chipman, son of Jared and Sarah Wheadon; Joel, son of John Norton and Hannah Norton; Jeremiah, son of Jeremiah Butler and wife.

April.—Susa, an infant negro, belonging to Eph. Coe, privately.

May —Elizabeth, D of Joseph and Rhoda Smith.

May 26th —Schuyler and Nathan, sons of Rebecca Meeker; since, the wife of Timothy Stow; Timothy, son of Timothy and Rebecca Stow; Bishop, son of David and Huldah Squire; Anne, daughter of Timothy and Anne Coe.

June 2d.—Dolphin and Zillah, his wife, adult negroes; Anne,

daughter of Elnathan and Eunice Camp; Lemuel, son of Lemuel and Huldah Moffet.

July.—Joel, son of William and Tryphena Lucas.

July 28th.—Samuel, son of Samuel Done Cook and Rebecca, his wife.

July 29th, 1771.—Daniel and Jon, sons of Tim. and Mabel Dunn.

Aug. 11th, 1771 —Content, D. of William and Sarah Carr.

Aug. 18th, 1771.—Ruth, D. of Eliphaz and Anne Parmalee.

Sept. 1st, 1771.—Eleanor, D. of Job and Rachel Camp; Hezekiah, son of Noah and Mehetabel Baldwin.

Oct. 6th, 1771.—Seth, son of Ephraim and Ann Coe.

Oct. 13th, 1771.—Dan, son of Sharp and Phyllis, negroes of Elah Camp.

Oct. 20th, 1771.—Anne, D. of Robert and Phebe Smithson

Oct. 27th, 1771.—Tryon, son of Thomas Cook, Jun., and Hannah, his wife.

Dec. 1st, 1771.—Esther, D. of Ebenezer and Submit Tibbals; Adah, D. of Ens. Samuel and Phebe Camp.

Dec. 8th.—Henry, S. of Daniel Hall, Jun., and Anne, his wife.

Dec. 15th.—Richard, son of Ens. James and Anne Robinson; Ozias, son of Eliphaz and Amy Parmalee.

Dec. 22d.—Sally, D. of Charles and Martha Bishop.

Jan. 19th, 1772.—Sarah, D. of Jonathan and Ann Walkley.

Jan. 20th, 1772.—Nathan, son of Elah and Mehetabel Crane.

Feb. 16th, 1772.—Charles, son of David Curtiss, Jun., and Prudence, his wife; Rhoda, D. of Samuel Sutlief and Eunice, his wife.

Feb. 23d.—Clarissa, D. of Moses and Martha Bates.

March 1st.—Hannah, D. of Nathan and Anna Curtiss.

March 8th.—Miles, son of Miles and Mary Merwin.

March 15th.—Clary, daughter of Samuel and Anne Squire; Abigail, D of Ambrose and Sarah Field

March 22d.—Gurnsey, son of James Bates, Jun., and Anne, his wife; Sally, daughter of Jesse and Mary Atwell.

Apr. 12th, 1772.—Worthington Gallup, son of Capt. Elnathan and Eliz. Chauncey.

May 10th, 1772.— ———, ——— of Reuben Bishop and his

wife; ———, daughter of Jess Austin and Elizabeth, his wife; Lucretia, daughter of Caleb and Anne Fowler; also, Peter, negro servant of Elah Camp; Lucretia, D of Silas Crane and Lucretia, his wife.

June 28th, 1772.—Augustus, son of Stephen and Rhoda Spencer; Anna, daughter of Elnathan and Eunice Camp; Sarah, daughter of Samuel and Sarah Bates.

July.—Daniel, son of Daniel and Mary Meeker; Mabel, daughter of Timothy and Mehetabel Dunn.

Aug. 9th —Sylvia, Burroughs, James, William and Freelove, children of James and Abigail Hinman; also, Jerusha, D. of Daniel Hall and Eliz., his wife.

Aug. 16th.—Rhoda, D. of Jesse and Anne Cook; Eleanor, D. of Samuel Fenn Parsons and Martha, his wife.

Aug 23d.—Rhoda, D. of David and Anne Talcot.

Sept. 6th.—Daniel, son of Daniel Whitmore and wife.

Oct. 4th, 1772.—Joseph, son of James and Martha Ferguson.

Oct. 18th, 1772.— —— ——, of Moses Seaward and Sarah Seaward; Sarah, daughter of William and Anne Burrit.

Oct. 25th, 1772.—John and Rebecca, twin children of Samuel Hart and Bridget, his wife.

Nov. 15th.—George, Nathan, and Rebecca, children of Josiah Squier and Betty, his wife

Nov. 2d.—Ruth, D. of Abiel and Mehetabel Baldwin.

Dec. 6th.—Samuel, son of Daniel and Rebekah J. Merwin.

Dec. 20th.—Huldah, daughter of Asa and Huldah Chamberlain.

Jan. 3d, 1773.—John, son of Abraham and Ruth Hand.

Feb. 14th.—Elizur, son of Benjamin and Elizabeth Gillum; Phebe, son of Elah and Phebe Camp.

Feb. 20th.—Eunice and Lois, twin daughters of Phinehas and Eunice Parmalee.

Feb. 28th.—Jemmy, son of William and Sarah Carr.

March 14th —John Immanuel, son of John and Esther Jones.

April 4th.—Edward Welles, son of James and Abigail Hinman

April 11th.—Ichabod, son of Joseph Wright, Jun., and Sarah, his wife; Clarissa, D. of Samuel and Abigail Barlett.

April 18th.—Adah, daughter of Noah and Mehetabel Baldwin.

Apr. 28th, 1773.—Rhoda, D. of Elihu and Rhoda Hinman, baptized privately.

May 2d, 1773.—Hamlet, son of Abraham Scranton, Jun., and Hannah, his wife.

May 16th.—Mary, the wife of Thomas Stephens; also, Elnathan, Diana, Huldah, Daniel, Abigail, and Phebe, children of Thomas and Mary Stephens.

May 23d.—John, son of Capt. Israel and Mary Camp.

May 30th.—Wait Cornel, son of Thomas and Susanna Francis; Abraham, son of Phinehas and Martha Camp.

June 27th.—Miles, son of Timothy and Deborah Hall.

July 11th.—Aaron, son of Thomas and Mary Stephens; Anne, D. of Lemuel and Anne Moffat.

July 18th.—Katharine, D. of Samuel Done Cook and Rebecca, his wife.

July 25th.—Timothy, son of Timothy and Phebe Coe

Aug. 1st, 1773.—Asa, son of Lieut Joseph and Martha Hickox, Hamlet, son of Joseph and Rhoda Smith.

Aug. 8th, 1773.—Timothy Botsford, son of John Crane and his wife; Sarah, D. of Charles Norton and his wife.

Aug. 29th, 1773.—Elias, son of Moses and Martha Bates; Chloe, D of Sharp and Phyllis, servants of Elah.

Sept. 19th.—Benoni, son of Cornet Job Camp and Rachel, his wife; Hannah, D. of Lieut. Eliakim Strong and Hannah Strong

Oct. 17th.—Phebe, daughter of Jacob and Katharine Clarke

Nov. 21st.—Linus, son of David and Prudence Curtiss.

Nov. 28th.—Noah, son of Eliphaz Parmalee and Anne, his wife

Dec. 12th.—Stephen, son of Stephen and Rhoda Spencer.

Dec. 26th.—Noah, son of Noah and Eleanor Lyman; Ruth, daughter of Abraham and Submit Barlett.

Jan. 2d, 1774.— ——— daughter of Abel Coe and his wife.

Feb. 10th, 1774.—Peggy, negro servant of Theoph. Merriman.

Feb 20th, 1774.—Asher, son of Samuel B. Wetmore and Anne, his wife; Olive, D. of Miles Merwin and Mary, his wife.

Feb. 27th.—Nathan, son of Charles and Martha Bishop; ——, daughter of Thomas Cook and his wife.

March 12th.—Thomas, son of Jesse and Elizabeth Austin.

March 13th.—Maurice, son of John Johnson, Jun., and Abigail, his wife; Delight, daughter of Jesse and Anne Cook.

March 27th.—Ezra, son of Reuben Baldwin and Eunice, his wife.

Apr. 24th.—Nathaniel, son of Nathan and Rachel Seward.

May 1st.—Josiah, son of Josiah Squire and wife.

May 1st, 1774.—Sybil, daughter of Eli Crane and wife; Jared, son of William Burrit and his wife.

son of Cornelius Hull and wife, Mary.

son of Phinehas Canfield and wife, Amy.

Ozias, son of Caleb Fowler and his wife.

Rachel, D. of David Talcott and his wife.

D. of Phinehas Spelman and his wife.

Benoni, son of Wm. Bishop, Jun , and his wife.

son of Daniel Dimock and his wife.

son of Samuel Seward and his wife.

son of John Johnson and his wife, Concurrence.

Fanny, D. of Jesse Atwel and his wife, Mary.

Rachel, D of Daniel Merwin and his wife Rebekah.

D. of Jeremiah Butler and his wife.

D. of Daniel Hall, 3d, and his wife.

D. of Abraham Bishop and his wife.

Oct 9th, 1774.—Elizur, son of Benjamin Gillum, and his wife; Ebenezer, son of James Bates, Jun., and his wife; Phebe, D of Ensign Samuel Camp, and his wife.

Oct. 21st, 1774.—Elizabeth, daughter of William Coe, and his wife.

Oct. 23d, 1774.—Augustus, son of Nathan and Anna Curtiss; Medad, son of David and Huldah Squire

Nov. 6th.—Benjamin, son of Reuben Bishop, and his wife.

Nov. 13th.—John, son of Timothy and Mehetabel Dunn.

Nov. 20th.—Rachel, daughter of Lemuel and Anna Moffet; Phebe, daughter of Thomas Parsons, Jun. and Mehetabel, his wife.

Nov. 27th, 1774.—Hannah, D. of Noah and Mehetabel Baldwin.

Dec. 18th, 1774.—Rebekah, D. of Timothy and Rebekah Stowe.

Dec. 25th, 1774.—Sarah, D. of Jonathan and Sarah Squire.

Jan. 1st, 1775.—————— of Samuel Bates and wife; —————— of Timothy Hall, and wife.

Feb. 19th. —Rachel, daughter of Henry and Jerusha Crane

Feb. 19th.—Dennis, son of Elnathan and Eunice Camp.

March 5th.—Jerusha, D. of Abiathar Squire and wife.

March 12th.—Lois, daughter of Samuel and Bridget Hart.

March 26th.—William, son of John and Esther Jones.

Apr. 16th —Calvin, son of Nathan and Hannah Bristol.

Apr. 30th.—Seth, son of Abiel and Mehetabel Baldwin; Sarah, daughter of John Norton and wife; Phebe, daughter of Robert Smithson and wife.

May 7th.—Amy Maltby, daughter of William Maltby and Rosanna, his wife; born after its father's death.

May 29th.—Hannah, D. of Samuel Bartlet and wife.

June 11th.—Adah, D. of William Bishop, Jun. and wife.

June 18th.—Henry, son of Abraham Scranton, Jun and wife.

June 25th.— ———, of Timothy Coe and wife.

July 23d.—Parsons, son of Moses Bates and wife.

July 31st.—Sarah, the daughter of Sarah Wilkinson

Aug. 13th.— ————, of Ambrose Field and wife; Polly, daughter of Asa Chamberlain and wife; Anne, daughter of Jonathan Walkly and wife.

Sept. 3d.—Ephraim, son of Charles Norton and wife.

Sept. 10th.— ——, son of Phineas Camp and wife.

Sept. 10th, 1775.—Lewis, son of Lemuel Johnson and wife.

Sept. 17th, 1775.—James, son of Wm. and Rhoda Trench.

Oct. 15th, 1775.—Joyie, daughter of Jesse Cook and wife; Abigail, daughter of —— Johnson and wife; Rachel, daughter of James Hinman and wife.

Dec. 10th.—Jess, son of Joseph Smith and wife; Martha, daughter of Benjamin Picket and wife; Content, daughter of Thomas Cook and wife.

Dec. 17th.—James, son of Henry Crane and wife; Statyra, daughter of Phinehas Canfield and wife.

Jan. 14th, 1776.—Rejoice, son of John Crane and wife; Katharine, daughter of Rev. Elizur Goodrich and Katharine his wife.

June 8th, 1777.—Huldah, daughter of Joseph Francis.

June 22d, 1777.—Sylvester, son of Elnathan and Eunice Camp; Sarah, daughter of James Hinman and wife.

June 29th, 1777.—Lemuel, son of Lemuel Moffet and wife.

July 6th.—Rachel, daughter of Timothy Stowe and wife.

Aug. — ——— of Jesse Cook and wife.

Aug 31st.—Jesse, son of Phineas Canfield and wife.

Sept. 7th, ——— son of David Squier and wife; Mary, daughter of Abiathar Squire and wife, Phebe, daughter of Daniel Dimock.

Sept 14th.— ——— of Daniel Merwin and wife.

Sept. 28th.—Joel, son of Widow Sarah Griswold.

Oct 5th.—Elizabeth, daughter of John Newton and wife; Elizabeth, daughter of Thomas Addres and wife.

Oct. 12th, 1777.—Abigail, daughter of Samuel Barlet and wife.

Oct. 19th, 1777.—Samuel and James, sons of Giles Rosseter and wife; John, son of Richard Terry and wife.

Oct 26th, 1777.—Nathan, son of Phinehas Spelman and wife.

Nov. 9th, 1777.—Stephen, son of Samuel Bates and wife, Hannah, D. of Capt. Samuel Camp and wife; Eunice, D of Johnson and wife.

Dec. —, 1777.—Jonathan, son of Jonathan Loveland and wife.

Dec. —, 1777.—Elizur, son of Ithamar Parsons, Jun. and wife.

Jan 25th, 1778.—Rhoda, daughter of Eliphaz Parmalee and wife.

Jan. 3d, 1779.— ——— of Gudon Hull and his wife.

March 21st.—Katharine, D. of Jeremiah Butler and wife; Rhoda, daughter of Timothy Hull and wife; Jerusha, daughter of Lemuel Johnson and wife.

March 28th.—Jerusha, daughter of Henry Crane and wife; Phebe, daughter of Robert Smithson and wife.

March —, 1783.—Nancy and Sally, twin daughters of Capt. ——— Johnson and Abigail, his wife; Lewis, son of Ens. Jacob Clarke and his wife; Jesse, son of Miles Merwin, Jun. and wife.

March 23d, 1783.—Dan, son of Dan Parmalee and wife; Lemuel, son of Lemuel Johnson and wife.

MARRIAGES RECORDED.

Jan. 12th, 1735.—James Gridley, of Farmington, and Hannah Clarke, of Durham.

Jan. 13th.—Capt. James Wadsworth and Katharine Gurnsey.

Feb. 11th.—Caleb Carr and Margaret Adams.

March 21st.—Samuel Sutlief, of Haddam, and Eunice Curtiss, of Durham.

May 10th, 1757.—Abraham Scranton and Eleanor, widow of James Picket.

June 29th.—Nathaniel Bishop, of Durham, and Huldah Francis, of N. Killingworth.

Oct 6th —Ozias Camp and Hannah Camp.

Oct. 27th.—John Noyes Wadsworth and Esther Parsons.

Dec. 21st —John Norton and Hannah Bishop.

Dec. 29th.—Noah Norton and Experience Strong.

Mar. 23d, 1758 —Robert Akins and widow Sarah Lyman.

June 20th, 1758.—Ensign Edward Camp, of Middletown, and Esther Crittenden, of Durham.

Nov. 8th.—Noah Robinson, of Granville, and Hannah Parmalee, of Durham.

Dec. 5th.—Benjamin Picket and Adah Camp.

Dec 14th.—Miles Norton, of Goshen, and Esther Norton, of Durham.

March 5th, 1759.—Ebenezer Baldwin, of Granville, and Lois Wetmore, of Middletown.

Apr. 26th.—Elihu Crane and Mary Fowler.

May 7th.—Asa Page, of Wallingford, and Eunice Page, of Brandford.

May 23d.—Elnathan Camp and Eunice Talcott.

Nov. 1st.—David Wood, of Greenwich, and Mary Brown, of Haddam.

May 14th, 1760.—Elah Camp and Phebe Baldwin.

July 30th.—Noah Baldwin and Mehetabel Parmalee.

July 31.—Elisha Johnson, of Middletown, and Mary Seward, of Durham.

Oct. 21st.—Jesse Cook, of Durham, and Ruth Fairchild, of Haddam.

Nov. 5th, 1760—Nathaniel Page, of Goshen, and Eleanor Wright, of Durham.

Jan. 29th, 1761.—Benjamin Smith and Mehetabel Barnes, of Middlefield.

Jan. 29th.—David Stone, of Haddam, and Sarah Lucas, of Durham.

March 26th.—Moses Austin, of Wallingford, and Lucy Seaward, of Durham.

Apr. 9th, 1761.—Moses Seaward and Sarah Thomas, both of Durham.

June 11th.—Asher Robinson and Margery Butcher, both of Durham.

March 25th, 1762.—Solomon Rose, of Granville, and Rhoda Moultrup, of Durham.

May 20th.—Amos Harrison, of Northford, and Elizabeth Fowler, of Durham.

May 27th—Daniel Dimoch and Thankful Merriman, of Durham.

June 6th.—James Cornel, of Middletown, and Urania Camp, of Durham.

June 15th.—Richard and Phebe, negro servants of Ensign Simeon Parsons, of Durham.

Dec. 7th.—John Hamilton, of Granville, and Rebecca Canfield, of Durham.

Jan. 19th, 1763.—Jonas Bishop and Phebe Crane, of Durham.

March 3d.—Jesse Crane and the widow Rebekah Seward.

May 11th, 1763—Aaron Curtis, of Granville, and Hannah Griswold, of Durham.

May 12th.—Benjamin Barns, of Granville, and Mary Coe, of Durham

Oct. 12th.—Reuben Parmalee, of Guilford, and Lydia Griswold, of Durham.

Oct. 21st.—Lemuel Moffet and the widow Huldah Newton.

Feb. 26th, 1764—Giles Porter, of Haddam, and Susannah Hill, of Durham.

Feb. 29th.—John Camp, 3d, and Eunice Coe, of Durham.

May 11th.—Dolphin, negro servant of Capt. Abraham Camp,

of Norfolk, and Zill, negro servant of Lieut. David Coe, of Middletown, with consent of their masters.

May 16th.—Ezra Baldwin, Jun., and Elizabeth Lyman, both of Durham.

May 17th.—Samuel Bates and Sarah Spelman, both of Haddam.

May 24th.—Jared Wheadon and Sarah Chipman, both of Durham.

Oct. 18th, 1764.—Elisha Millar, of Farmington, and Sarah Fowler, of Durham.

Jan. 15th, 1765.—John Johnson and Concurrence Crane, both of Durham.

Feb. 21st, 1765.—Lieut. James Arnold and Tabatha Parsons, both of Durham.

March 28th, 1765.—Hezekiah Talcott, of Durham, and Sarah Johnson, of Middletown.

Apr. 9th, 1765.—Titus Fowler, of Granville, and Hannah Burrit, of Durham.

Oct. 21st, 1765.—Aaron Hinman and Elizabeth Welles, both of Durham.

Oct. 31st, 1765.—Robert Crane and Mary Camp, both of Durham.

Dec. 24th, 1765.—Thomas Lewis, of Farmington, and Sarah Gurnsey, of Durham; also, James Bates, Jun., of Haddam, and Anne Gurnsey, of Durham.

Jan. 23d, 1766.—Asahel Cooley, of Wallingford, and Sarah Merwin, of Durham.

Feb. 7th, 1766.—James Brown and Peninnah Meeker, were married.

Apr 7th, 1766.—Amos Millar, Jun., and Elizabeth Tibbals, of Middlefield, were married

Apr. 23d, 1766.—Humfrey Ball, of Lebanon, and Ruth Griswold, of Durham.

July 29th, 1766.—Timothy Coe and Phebe Thomas, both of Durham.

Sept. 21st, 1766.—Daniel Hall, Jun, and Ann Crane

Oct. 27th, 1766.—Jesse Cook and Rhoda Talcot

Nov. 20th, 1766.—Heth Camp and Mary Tibbals.

Dec. 4th, 1766.—Samuel Done Cook, of Durham, and Rebekah Picket, of Haddam.

Dec. 5th, 1766.—Josiah Squire, of Durham, and Betty Dudley, of Guilford; and Stephen Spenar, of Killingworth, and Rhoda Squire, of Durham.

Jan. 8th, 1767.—Phineas Camp and Martha Hall, both of Durham

Apr. 30th, 1767.—Dando, negro servant of Col. Elihu Chauncey, and Rose, negro servant of Mr. John Canfield, were married.

June, 1767.—Giles Rose and Zipporah Camp, both of Durham

Aug 13th.—Sharp and Phyllis, negro servants of Mr. Elah Camp, were married.

Aug. 19th.—Joseph Ingraham and Mehetabel Brown, both of Durham, were married.

Aug. 20th.—Daniel Bacon, of Williamstown, and Hannah Robinson, of Durham, were married.

Sept. 10th.—Joseph Smith and Rhoda Picket, both of Durham

Sept. 15th.—Levi Chapman, of Saybrook, and Elizabeth Hull, of Durham, were married.

Sept 16th.—David Talcot and Anne Lyman, both of Durham, were married.

Sept. 17th.—Timothy Wackley, of Durham, and Anne Bates, of Haddam; also, Ambrose Field, of Durham, and Sarah Bates, of Haddam, were married.

Nov. 4th, 1767.—Miles Merwin, Jun., and Mary Parmalee, both of Durham, were married.

Dec 17th.—Joseph Wright, Jun., of Durham, and Sarah Bishop, of Guilford.

Feb. 3, 1768.—Moses Griswold and Ann Smithson, both of Durham.

Feb. 18.—Capt Ebenezer Gurnsey and the widow Anne Lyman, both of Durham, were married.

June 16th.—Samuel Barlet and Abigail Ingraham, both of Durham, were married.

Aug. 3d.—Eliphaz Parmalee, of Middletown, and Anne Handy, of Guilford, were married.

Nov. 6th, 1768.—Enoch Coe, of Granville, and Katharine Camp, of Durham.

Nov. 7th, 1768.—Samuel Bowman Wetmore and Anna Canfield.

Dec 12th.—Charles Bishop and Martha Hickox.

Dec. 12th.—Reuben Bishop, of Durham, and the widow Sarah Walkley, of Haddam.

Feb. 3d, 1769.—Israel Goddard and Ann Camp, of Durham.

Oct. 26th.—Jacob Clark, of Haddam, and Katharine Canfield, of Durham

Dec. 14th, 1769.—Daniel Merwin and Rebekah Seward, both of Durham.

Feb. 15th, 1770.—Timothy Bishop, of Guilford, and widow Abigail Ingraham, of Durham, married.

Apr. 19th, 1770—Lieut. John Camp and the widow Hannah Maddocks, were married.

May 2d, 1770.—Timothy Hall and Deborah Hull, were married

May 2d, 1770.—Benjamin Holt, of Wallingford, and Anne Merwin, of Durham, were married.

Dec. 27th, 1770.—David Curtiss, Jun., and Prudence Bishop, were married.

Jan 7th, 1771.—Samuel Fenn Parsons and Martha Picket, were married.

Jan. 30th, 1771.—Thomas Lyman and Rachel Seaward, were married.

July 4th, 1771.—Capt. William Ward, of Middletown, and the widow Hannah Spencer, of Durham.

Oct. 20th.—Jesse Cook and the widow Anne Griswold

Nov 7th.—Reuben Hopson, of Wallingford, and Sarah Tibbles, of Durham.

Dec. 5th—Phinehas Bates and Esther Curtiss.

Dec. 25th.—Cæsar and Candace, negro servants of Joseph Camp, with his consent.

Jan. 1st, 1772—Abraham Scranton, Jun, and Hannah Camp.

Jan 2d, 1772—Timothy Parsons, Jun, and Phebe Camp

Jan. 8th, 1772.—Thomas and Thankful, negro servants of Caleb Fowler, with his consent.

——————Abraham Hand and Ruth Southworth.

May 6th.—Nathan Seward and Rachel Gillum.

May 21st.—Ithamar Parsons, Jun., and Mehetabel Hull.

Oct. 29th, 1772.—Elihu Atkins and Ruth Baldwin.

Nov. 9th.—Elias Austin and widow Sarah Akins.

Nov. 11th.—Lemuel Johnson, of Middletown, and Jerusha Norton, of Durham

Nov. 12th.—Gershom Birdsey and Hannah Barlett, both of Middletown.

Nov. 30th.—Ensign Simeon Parsons, of Durham, and widow Abigail Bates, of Haddam.

Dec 28th—Ensign David Camp, of Woodbury, and the widow Mary Hubbard, of Durham.

Nov. 19th—Stephen Tuttle, of New Haven, and Rhoda Coe, of Durham.

Feb. 18th, 1773.—The Rev. Samuel Johnson, of New Lebanon, in the County of Albany, and Elizabeth Camp, of Durham.

Jan., 1773.—Nathan Bristol and Hannah Merwin, were married.

Apr. 1st, 1773—Phineas Canfield and Amy Newton

May 27th, 1773.—Reuben Baldwin and Eunice Camp.

June 24th, 1773.—Henry Crane and Jerusha Parmalee were married.

Aug. 4th, 1773.—Peruda Stevens, of Kensington, and Sarah Seward, of Durham.

Oct. 7th, 1773—Abraham Bishop and Mary Thomas, both of Durham; also, Nathaniel Hickox and Rebeckah Rosseter, of Durham.

Nov. 10th, 1773.—Gurdon Hull, of Killingworth, and Huldah Crane, of Durham; also, William Trench and Rhoda Hickox of Durham.

March 15th, 1774.—Beriah Chittenden and Huldah Newton were married.

April 8d, 1774—Joel Robinson and Hannah Wilcocks were married.

May 9th, 1774.—Jonathan Squire and Sarah Ingraham were married.

Dec. —, 1774.—James Hickox and Rhoda Parmalee were married.

Jan 18th, 1775.—Gideon Canfield, Jun., and Statyra Camp were married.

Feb 14th, 1775.—Samuel Weeks, of Woodbury, and Abigail Hull, of Durham, were married.

Feb 9th, 1775.—Medad Strong and Hannah Kelsey, both of Durham, were married.

March 16th, 1775.—Eliakim Strong, Jun., and Remembrance Wright were married.

May 22.—Ashur Wright and Beulah Strong.

June 15th, 1775.—Morris Coe and Lucy Rosseter were married.

Nov. 22d.—Dan. Canfield and Comfort Newton were married.

Dec. 7th.—Joseph Parsons and Mercy Coe were married.

May 15th, 1777.—Phinehas Parmalee and Lucy Rose were married.

Aug. 27th, 1777.—Reuben Bailey, of Haddam and Rhoda Fairchild, of Durham.

Oct. 15th, 1777.—Roswel Francis, of Killingworth, and Anne Hull, of Durham, were married.

March 23d, 1778.—Stephen Norton, Jun. and Mary Merwin were married.

March 25th, 1778.—Robert Smithson and Mehetabel Hull were married.

Oct. 4th, 1778.—Phinehas Picket and Anne Squire were married.

Oct. 5th, 1778.—Timothy Butler and Sarah Hull were married.

Jan. 17th, 1779.—Benjamin Tainter and Hannah Norton were married.

Jan. 28th, 1779.—Lemuel Parsons and Katharine Coe were married.

Feb. 8th, 1779.—Saxton Squire and Dorcas Bulkley were married.

Feb. 25th, 1779.—Abraham Stow and Rachel Seward were married.

March 1st, 1779.—Joel Palmer, of Greenwich, and Abigail Squire, of Durham, were married.

March 14th, 1779.—Rejoice Camp and Ruth Picket.

June 2d, 1779.—Judah Benjamin, of Milford, and the Widow Rhoda Trench, of Durham.

Aug. 19th, 1779.—Charles Sears, of Haddam, and Diana, daughter of Thomas Stevens, of Durham.

REV. DAVID SMITH'S RECORD.

May 1st, 1804.

Names belonging to the Church of Christ in Durham, Ct. The following persons were admitted before my ordination, which took place Aug 15th, 1799.

James Arnold and wife, Thomas Curtiss and wife; Mrs. Mary Chauncey; Old Jack, Negro; Widow Catharine Goodrich, Widow Sarah Bishop; Abiel Baldwin and wife, Noah Baldwin; Widow ——— Bishop, Curtis Bates and wife, Reuben Baldwin and wife, Widow Rachel Camp; Joseph Camp; Samuel Camp and wife, Elnathan Camp and wife; Widow Anna Canfield, Elias Camp and wife, Wife of Timothy Coe; Abijah Curtis and wife; Rejoice Camp and wife; Daniel Dimock and wife; Ashur Canfield and wife; Oliver Coe and wife; David Camp and Charles Goodrich; Ebenezer Camp and wife; Nathan O Camp and wife; Ezra Camp and wife, Elah Camp and wife, Wife of Jabez Chalker; Gad Camp, John Curtiss; James Curtiss; Abel Coe; Lois Curtiss, Sarah Curtiss, since married to D. Johnson and Elnathan Camp, Widow Anna Curtiss; Caleb Fowler; Reuben Fowler, Bridgman Guernsey, Widow Sarah Guernsey; Samuel Hart and wife, Widow Rachael Hickox; Wife of James Hinman; Wife of John Hall; Deacon John Johnson; Wife of Capt. John Johnson; Miles Merwin and wife; Daniel Meeker, Capt. Stephen Norton; Burwel Newton; Burwell Newton, Jun.; Samuel Parsons and wife; Wife of Benjamin Picket; James Picket, Dea. Dan. Parmalee and wife; Eliphaz Parmalee and wife, Levi Parmalee and wife, Joel Parmalee and wife; Joseph Parsons and wife; Samuel F. Parsons and wife; Ozias Norton and wife; Ashur Robinson; Timothy Stowe and wife; Wife of Gurdon Hull, Abraham Scranton and wife; Seth Seward and wife; Eliakim Strong and wife; Wife of John Spencer; Wife of Russel Strong; Daniel Southmayd; Joseph Southmayd and wife; Hamlet Scranton and wife; Ebenezer Tibbals and wife;

Wife of Hon. James Wadsworth; Ashur Wright and wife; Wife of John N Wadsworth; Richard, (colored man), Widow Hope Davis; Nathan Kelsey, Samuel Wright and wife; Nancy Merwin, Widow Sarah Fowler; Boardman Wetmore and wife; Joseph Southworth; Samuel Meeker and wife.

The following are the names of those who have been admitted into the Church, during my ministry, which commenced Aug 15th, 1799. D. SMITH.

1800.—Aaron Baldwin and wife, date is lost.

August.—Dennis Camp and wife.

Nov —Sylvester Camp and wife; Nathan Wetmore and wife

March 28th, 1802.—Josiah Jewett and wife; Wife of Charles Coe, Esq; Wife of Guernsey Bates

Sept. 5th.—Wife of Jacob Harrison. Recommended from Chh. in Branford.

March 5th, 1803.—Wife of Job Canfield

April 24th.—Wife of Rev. David Smith, Wife of Reuben Fowler; Wife of John Butler.

Sept. 4th —Hezekiah Baldwin and wife; Seth Baldwin and wife; Jesse Smith, Josiah Parsons.

Sept. 4th.—Wife of Asher Coe; Wife of Roger Newton; Nabby Johnson; Phebe Scranton, Catharine Rose, Polly Norton; Phebe Curtiss; Polly Smith

Nov. 6th.—Wife of Stephen Norton, Jun.; Wife of John Norton, Rhoda Hawley, Sally Johnson, daughter of Capt J Johnson, Hannah Bowin; Clarissa Hosmer; Ada Camp.

Nov. 6th, 1803 —Bolinda Hinman.

Nov. 6th 1803.—Roxana Squire; Timothy Tuttle, afterwards a minister; Noah Coe, afterwards a minister; James Hickox; John Tibbals and wife; Wife of Charles White; Wife of Israel Camp; Widow Phebe Johnson; Abigail Seward, afterwards wife of M Merwin; Lois Hart; Anna Wetmore; Wife of Dr. William Foote; Nancy Robinson.

1804.—Augustus Curtis, Ozias Camp, date lost; Ashur Coe; Seth Tibbals; Wife of James Picket; Wife of John Curtiss; Wife of Capt. Noah Cone; Wife of Capt. John Hart.

1805.—Capt. Noah Cone, Roger Newton; Adah Baldwin.

Aug. 25th.—Samuel Lucas and wife; Ashur Wetmore and

wife; Wife of Giles Rose; Wife of James Rose; Wife of Elisha Harvey; Wife of James Clarke; Lucretia Fowler; Eunice Parmalee, afterwards wife of Dr. Stone.

July 6th, 1806.—Wife of George Sheldon; Mary Barnes.

Aug. 23d, 1807.—Rachel Hubbard.

Sept. 16th, 1808.—Wife of Abraham Coe.

Nov 6th.—Wife of Daniel Bates; Dan. Parmalee, Jun. and wife, Wife of Anson Squire; Wife of Seth Tibbals; Mahetabel Parmalee, Nabby Parmalee; Sally Parmalee; Alpha Bates; Phebe Bates; Polly Coe, afterwards wife of J. Chedsey; Sally Coe; Eurana Lyman; Eunice Baldwin; Betsey Hall, afterwards wife of R Parmalee; Hannah Hall, afterwards wife of Dr. Catlin; Almira Johnson; Sally Johnson, 2d, daughter of widow Johnson; Sophronia Reynold; Betsey Robinson; Sally Robinson, Hannah Robinson; Dency White; Sophronia White; Orpha Seward; Electa Strong; Phebe Strong; Eunice Norton; Amanda Camp; William White; Aaron Hosmer; Collins Hosmer, Stephen Turner; James Parmalee, Jun.; Phinehas Parmalee, Henry Canfield; Chauncey Stephens; Miles Merwin, Jun.; Wife of Timothy Coe, Jun. by letter from the Churh in Rocky Hill.

Nov. 15th, 1808.—Wife of William Thomas; Charles Baldwin; Leverett Norton.

Jan. 1st.—David Hull; William Smith.

April 2d.—Wife of Asahel Strong, died Oct. 27th, '62; Samuel Curtiss; Joseph Hull, Jun., Ozias Camp, 2d; Lyman C. Camp; Elah Camp, 2d; Dr. William Foote, by letter from ye Church in Goshen, Isaac Newton by letter.

Oct. 29th.—Ichabod Camp; Samuel Hall; Wife of John King; Wife of John Loveland; Sally, daughter of Ebenezer Camp; Abigail Dalaby; Hannah Strong.

July 1st, 1810.—Wife of Samnel F. Parsons, by letter from Wallingford.

Oct., 1811.—Wife of Thomas Richmond.

1812.—Second wife of Nathan Wetmore; Catharine Parsons; Wife of Burwell Newton.

Oct. 17th, 1813—Wife of John Strong.

Aug. 14th, 1814.—Timothy Stone and wife, admitted by letter from the Church in Guilford.

Sept. 4th —Samuel C. Camp and wife, by letter from Hartford; Amherst Hayes and wife admitted by letter; Polly, wife of Jehiel Hull, admitted by letter; Wife of Joseph Smith.

June 25th, 1815 —Heth F. Camp; Roxana Cone.

Jan. 7th, 1816.—Wife of John Camp; Wife of Lyman C. Camp; Sally, daughter of widow Israel Camp; Sally Hall; Adah Johnson; Achsa Camp; Phebe Merwin; Samuel Johnson and wife, Enos Camp; Alfred Camp.

Sept. 1st.—Widow Betsey Everest; Wife of Ozias Camp; Widow Hannah Strong; Mary Tuttle; Anna Baldwin.

Sept. 7th, 1816.—Wife of Ozias Camp, 2d; Sally, daughter of Nathan O. Camp; Pamela Bagg.

Nov. 3d —Widow Potter.

Nov. 2d, 1817.—Thadeus Camp; Ira T Bates, afterwards a minister.

July 4th, 1819.—Rachel Stone, by letter from the Church in Geneva, New York.

Nov. 7th.—Elijah Coe, Esq, by letter from the Church in Hartland.

March 2d, 1820.—Wife of Elah Camp, 2d, by letter from the Church in Guilford.

May 7th.—Widow Alice C. Wadsworth, by letter from a Church in New York.

Sept. 3d.—George Camp, by letter from New Haven.

Jan. 1st, 1821.—Widow Lucy Parsons; Widow Anna Picket; second wife of Elah Camp; Wife of Wedworth Wadsworth.

Jan. 21st —Wife of Samuel Curtiss; Anna Squire; Delia Norton; Lucy Camp; Ruth Merwin; Anna Stevens; Daniel Howd; Joel Parmalee; Joseph Thomas; Horace Fitch, (coloured.)

March 4th, 1821.—Charlotte Hyde; Lydia Curtiss; Betsey H. Parmalee.

July 15th.—Lola Hall; Wife of James Wheadon; Phebe Parmalee; Mary Ann Bowers

July 15th.—Maria, Eliza, and Nancy Seward; Mary Parmalee; Cynthia Ann Shelley; Samuel Newton.

Nov. 4th.—Betsey, daughter of Elah Camp; Catherine C. Smith.

March 3d, 1822.—George W. Jewett; Wealthy, wife of Miles Merwin, Jun., by letter from 2d Church in Middletown.

June 16th.—Olive, wife of Amos Smith, by letter from the Church in Haddam.

July 7th.—Betsey, wife of Joseph Thomas, by a letter from North Bristol.

Dec. 24th.—Charles Coe, Esq., admitted at his own house and received the ordinance of Lord's Supper.

Oct 26th, 1823.—Dr Jared Kirtland.

Dec.—Wife of Joseph Andrews.

Jan. 22d, 1824.—Fanny, wife of Dr. C. Andrews, admitted by letter from the Church in Haddam.

March 4th.—Dr. John J. Catlin, by letter from ye Church in Canaan.

Dec.—Lois, wife of Reuben Brainard, by letter from ye Church in Haddam.

June 30th, 1825.—Perez Sturtevant, by letter from the Church in Middletown

Dec. 11th.—Althea, wife of David Pardee.

March 5th, 1826.—Martha Stevens, by letter from Haddam

Aug. 13th.—Mary P. Spencer, by letter from the Church in East Haddam.

Oct. 29th.—Widow Sarah Pierson, re-admitted by letter from the Church in North Killingworth.

Nov. 5th.—David Johnson.

Dec. 31st.—Henry B. Camp, afterwards a minister

Aug. 26th, 1827.—Elias Meigs, by letter from ye Church in East Guilford; Wife of Noah Parmalee; Guernsey Camp, Orrin Camp, admitted by letters.

Sept. 2d.—Betsey, daughter of Thadeus Camp, admitted at her father's house, and received the ordinance of ye Lord's Supper. A solemn season.

Oct.—Wife of George Camp, admitted by letter from ye Church in Wilbraham, Mass.

Nov 4th.—Samuel Hart; Capt. John Hart; Roswell Thorpe and wife; Abraham Camp; Nathan Camp, Jun.; Chauncey Swathel; Merick Coe.

Nov. 4th.—Edmund Hart; Wife of Dr. Abner Newton; Wife of Elijah Coe, Esq.; Eunice Manser; Betsey Ann Parker, Mary

Parker; Marietta Loveland; Eurania E. Stone; Phebe Stone; Wife of Edwin Coe; Esther Lyman.

Jan. 6th, 1828.—Abraham Coe.

July 3d, 1828.—Mrs Achsah Goodwin, by letter from a Church in Detroit.

Aug 31st.—Charles Miller and wife; John A. Graves and wife; Wife of John S. Camp; Lunora Camp; Rhoda Merwin; Nancy Merwin; Catharine Foote; Silas Merriman, by letter from ye Church in Wallingford.

Apr. 4th, 1830.—Wife of Isaac Loveland, by letter from ye Church in Haddam.

Sept. 4th, 1831.—Joseph P. Camp and wife; Augustus Howd and wife; Elias H. Pratt and wife.

Sept.—Wife of George W. Jewett; Eli Camp; Betsey B. Camp; Betsey Thomas; Adaline Stone; Eliza B. Camp; Eliza Ann Miller; Abner Newton, Jun. was admitted by a letter from Hartford; date forgotten.

PROPRIETORS' RECORD.

Mary, daughter of Joel Parmalee, was born 12th of ——, 1706.

Eunice, the daughter of Nathaniel Sutlief, was born the seventh day of August, 1706.

Deborah, ye daughter of Joseph Norton, was born the first day of November, 1707.

Concurrence, ye daughter of Henry and Abigail Crane, was born ye 25th day of March, 1708, entered Nov. ye 3d day, 1708, pr Jas. Wadsworth.

Mary, ye daughter of Nathaniel and Sarah Sutlief, was born July ye 16th day, 1708.

John, ye son of Joel and Abigail Parmalee, was born Oct ye 17th day, 1708.

Caleb Seward and Lydia, his wife, the first inhabitants that —— came to settle —— with four children, ye 4th day of May, 1699, the s'd Caleb Seward being then almost six months above 37 years old, who was born the 14th of March, 1662, his wife, Lydia, being then about 35 years old at the time of their coming to Durham Daniel, the son of Caleb and Lydia Seaward, was born the 16th Oct., 1687, and died the 28th of Apr., 1688, being their first child. Lydia, the daughter, and 2d child of Caleb and Lydia Seward, was born ye 22d of May, 1689. Caleb, the son, and 3d child of Caleb and Lydia Seward, was born the 2d of Jan., 1691. Thomas, the son, and 4th child of Caleb and Lydia Seward, was born the 19th December.

Joseph Gailord, born the 22d of ———, 1674, entered June 20th, 1706, now in her 33d year.

Mary, the wife of Joseph Gailord, born the 25th of May, 1678, entered January, 1706, being now in they 29th year of her age.

Mary, the daughter of Joseph and Mary Gailord, was born the 22d of November, 1700.

Thankful, daughter of Joseph and Mary Gailord, was born the 25th of Jan, 1703-4.

Timothy, ye son of Joseph and Mary Gailord, was born ye 29th of November, 1706.

Rachel, the daughter of —— and Sarah Buck, was born ye 22d of March, 1708.

. Samuel, the son of Joseph and Mary Gailord, was born ye 5th day of July, 1709. Entered August 15th, 1710

Sarah, the daughter of Jonathan and Mahetabel Wells, was born the 26th day of February, 1709-10

Moses, the son of Moses and Abigail Parsons, was born Oct. ye 19th day, 1710. Entered Dec. 28th, 1710.

Elihu, the son of Mr. Nathaniel and Mrs. Sarah Chauncey, was born March the 24th, 1710. Entered Jan. 6th, 1710-11.

Joseph, the son of Nathaniel and Sarah Sutliff, was born June 29th, 1710. Entered Jan. 18th, 1710-11.

Joseph, the son of Benjamin and Dinah Beach, was born Oct. 24th day, 1710. Entered Jan 19th, 1710-11.

Deborah, the daughter of John and Hannah Sutliff, was born Apr. 10th, 1710. Entered Jan. 10th, 1710.

Henry, the son of Henry and Abigail Crane, was born the 20th of March, 1710. Entered Feb. 27th, 1710-11.

Elihu, the son of Mr. Nathaniel and Mrs. Sarah Chauncey, was born March, 24th day, 1710.

Sarah, daughter of Mr. Nathaniel and Mrs. Sarah Chauncey, was born Feb. the 24th, 1711-12.

Katherine, the daughter of the sd. Nathaniel and Sarah Chauncey, was born Sept., 22d day, 1714.

Abigail, the daughter of the sd. Nathaniel and Sarah Chauncey, was born Oct., 2d day, 1717.

Nathaniel, the son of the sd. Nath'll Chauncey and the sd Sarah, his wife, was born Jan. 21st, 1720–21.

Elnathan, the son of Mr. Nath'll Chauncey and Sarah, his wife, was born Sept. 10th, 1724.

Abel, the son of Benjamin and Dinah Beach, was born February, the 9th day, 1711–12.

Samuel, the son of Stephen and Ruth Hickox, was born Sept., the 23d day, 1712.

John, the son of Mr Hezekiah and Jemima Tallcot, was born November, the 26th day, 1712

John, the son of Samuel and Mary Parsons, was born the 12th day of June, 1713.

Jonathan, the son of John and Elizabeth Norton, was born the 18th day of February, 1711–12.

Abigail, the daughter of Moses and Abigail Parsons, was born February, the 10th day, 1712–14.

John, the son of John and Hannah Sutliff, was born the 8th of March, 1713–14.

Eleanor, the daughter of Joseph and Eleanor Seward, was born Oct. 9th, 1714.

Phebe, the daughter of Thomas and Mary Wheeler, was born ——, the first day, 1711.

Ephraim, the son, and sixth child of Caleb and Lydia Seward, born the 6th day of Aug., 1700, being the first English child born in Cogingchaug alias Durham.

Ebenezer, the son, and seventh child of Caleb and Lydia Seward, was born ye 7th day of Jan., 1703, being the second English child born in Durham.

Joseph, the son of Nathaniel and Sarah Sutliff, deceased, June 22d, 1711.

Joseph Gaylord, Senior, deceased, Feb., second day, 1711–12, and Sarah, his wife, deceased, upon the 12th day of Feb

Samuel, the son of Samuel and Mary Fairchild, was born the 10th of August, 1708. Entered Dec. 1st, 1709, per James Wadsworth, Town Clerke.

Joseph, the son of Joseph and Deborah Norton, was born Sep. ye 2d day, 1709 Entered Dec. ye 27th, 1709, pr James Wadsworth, Town Clerke.

Jonathan, the son of Robert and Barbarah Coe, was born —— the 13th, 1710. Entered —— 2d, 1710, pr James Wads worth, Town Clerke.

Mr. Nathaniel Chauncey of Durham, and Mrs. Sarah Judson, the daughter of Capt James Judson, of Stratford, were married Oct, 12th day, 1708, by ye Rev. Mr. Charles Chauncey, Pastor of the Church of Christ in Stratfield.

Edmund, the son of Mr. Samuel and Mary Fairchild, was born the 12th day of August, 1714.

Samuel, the son of Samuel and Dinah Norton, was born March, the 20th day, 1714.

Daniel, the son of Jonathan and Abigail Rose, was born Jan., 12th day, 1716-17.

Amos, the son of Amos and Anne Camp, was born Sept., 22d day, 1717.

Eleanour, the wife of Joseph Seward, Jun., departed this life Dec. 20th, 1714.

Joseph Seward, Jun., and Hannah Crane, were married Apr. 26th, 1720, by Mr. Jared Elliott, Pastor of the Church at Killingworth.

Marcey, the daughter of David Johnson and Ruth his wife, was born March, 6th day, 1727-8.

Samuel Parsons and Mary Wheeler were married Dec. 15th, 1711, by the Rev. Mr. Nath'll Chauncey, Pastor of the Church of Christ in Durham.

Caleb Seward, Jun. and Sarah Carr, were married Jan. 21st day, 1713-14, by Nath'll Chauncey, pastor of the Church of Christ in Durham.

Hezekiah, the son of Joel and Abigail Parmalee, was born the tenth day of Jan. 1710-11.

Abigail, the daughter of Richard and Hannah Beach, was born Feb. 5th, 1710-11.

Lois, the daughter of Joseph and Mary Gaylord, was born April, the — day, 1711.

Aaron, the son of Lieut. Samuel and Rhoda Parsons, was born Sep., the 3d day, 1711.

Martha, the daughter of John and Hannah Sutliff, was born Apr, ye 19th day, 1712.

Isaac, the son of Joseph and Deborah Norton, was born Aug. the 17th day, 1712.

Jonathan, the son of Jonathan and Mehethabel Wells, was born Nov, the 16th day, 1712.

Abigail, the daughter of Henry and Abigail Crane, was born June, 6th day, 1712

Mary, the daughter of Jun. Sam'll and Mary Fairchild, was born the first day of July, 1712.

Matthew, the son of Ephraim and Phebe Hawley, was born Feb., ye first day, 1713–14.

Dinah, the daughter of John and Deborah Monger, was born Apr., the 5th day, 1712.

Lucie, the daughter of John and Deborah Monger, was born Sep., 10th day, 1713.

Joel, the son of Joel and Abigail Parmalee, was born January, the — day, 1713–14

November 27th, 1729, Silas Crane and Marcey Griswold were joined in marriage.

September 10th, 1730, Abigail, the daughter of Silas Crane and Marcey, his wife, was born

———, the wife of James Wright, departed this life March 11th, 1715–16

Joseph Seward and Elenour Wheeler were married January the 14th, 1713–14; by the Rev. Mr. Nath'll Chauncey.

William Seward and Damaris Punderson were married Sept, 19th day, 1710, by Abraham Bradley, one of her majesties Justices of the Peace for the County of New Haven

Stephen Bate and Patience Seward were married Dec 29th, 1715, by James Wadsworth, Justice of the Peace.

Jeremiah Leming and Abigail Turner were married July 4th, 1716, by Thomas Ward, Justice of the Peace.

Amos Camp and Anne Andrus were married Dec. 18th, 1716, by James Wadsworth, Justice of the Peace.

Stephen, the son of Stephen and Ruth Hickox, was born July 17th, 1714.

Sarah, the daughter of Stephen and Ruth Hickox, was born Apr. 14th, 1716.

Abraham, the son of Abraham and Sarah Crittenden, was born August third, 1714.

Sarah, the daughter of James and Hannah Curtis, was born March, the 15th day, 1712–13

Esther, the daughter of James and Hannah Curtiss, was born August 22d, 1715.

Certified by Thomas Hastings, Clerke at Hatfield, that Jonathan, son of John and Sarah Wells, was born December 14th, 1682.

Joseph Wright, the son of James and Hannah Wright, was born Nov. 1st, 1713.

John, the son of John and Elizabeth Norton, was born Feb., the 16th day, 1714–15.

Sarah, the daughter of Abraham and Sarah Cruttenden, was born Sept 12th, 1718.

Mary, the daughter of Caleb Seward, Jun., and Sarah, his wife, was born Apr. 8th, 1719.

William, the son of William and Damaris Seward, was born July the 27th, 1712.

David, the son of William and Damaris Seward, was born June the 23d, 1714

Sarah, the daughter of Caleb and Sarah Seward, was born Jan 8th, 1714–15.

Anna, the daughter of Nath'll and Sarah Sutlief, was born the 30th day of May, 1715.

Sarah, the daughter of Abraham and Sarah Cruttenden, was born May, 10th day, 1715.

Thomas, the son of Thomas and Deborah Norton, was born May, the 13th day, 1715.

Ebenezer, the son of Robert and Barbarah Coe, was born Aug. 21st, 1715.

Abigail, the daughter of Richard and Hannah Beach, was born the 15th day of Feb., 1710–11.

Hannah, the daughter of Richard and Hannah Beach, was born the 15th day of May, 1714.

Margarret, the daughter of Abrahm and Rebecca Jelit, was born the 8th of Feb. 1715–16.

Ebenezer, the son of James and Hannah Wright, was born Feb., 26th day, 1715–16

Martha, the daughter of Moses and Abigail Parsons, was born Oct. 5th, 1716.

Abigail, the daughter of Jonathan and Mehethabel Wells, was born the 21st day of June, 1715.

Dinah, the daughter of John and Hannah Sutlief, was born Sep., the 7th day, 1716.

Henry, the son of Henry and Concurrence Crane, was born Oct. 25th, 1671. Entered from an attested copy from Killingworth Records.

Martha, the daughter of Robert and Barbarah Coe, was born March 21st, 1713.

Ebenezer, the son of Robert and Barbarah Coe, was born August 21st, 1715.

Mary, the daughter of Robert and Barbarah Coe, was born Apr. 11th, 1717.

Robert, the son of Ensign Robert and Barbarah Coe, was born June 11th, 1719.

Cornelius Hull and Mahethabel Grave were married Feb, the first day, 1714–15, by Abraham Fowler, Esq., assistant.

Joseph, the son of the sd. Cornelius and Mahethabel Hull, was born Apr. 29th, 1716.

John, the son of the sd. Cornelius and Mahethable Hull, was born 14th of Jan. 1717–18.

Cornelius, the son of the sd. Cornelius and Mahethabel Hull, was born the 5th of Oct., 1719.

Sarah, the daughter of James and Hannah Curtis, was born March 15th, 1712–13.

Esther, the daughter of the sd. James and Hannah, was born Aug. 22d, 1715.

Mary, the daughter of the sd. James and Hannah, was born July 4th, 1717.

Phebe, the daughter of the sd. James and Hannah, was born Oct. 4th, 1719.

Ruth, the daughter of Stephen and Ruth Hickox, was born August 31st, 1719.

Benjamin, the son of John and Elizabeth Norton, was born July 12th, 1719.

Susannah, the daughter of Abraham and Sarah Cruttenden, was born September the 5th, 1720.

Jemimah, the daughter of Mr. Hezekiah Tallcot and Jemimah, his wife, was born the 20th of November, 1719.

Samuel Roberts and Rachel Webb were married March the 22d, 1716–17, by James Wadsworth, Justice of Peace.

Elizabeth, the daughter of Samuel and Rachel Roberts, was born Jan. 24th, 1717–18.

Samuel, the son of Samuel and Rachel Roberts, was born March the 9th, 1719–20.

Thomas Seward and Sarah Camp were married March 31st, 1720, by James Wadsworth, Assistant.

Solomon, the son of the sd. Thomas and Sarah Seward, was born Jan. 19th, 1720–21.

Eunice, the daughter of Richard and Hannah Beach, was born March 28th, 1716.

Benjamin, the son of Richard and Hannah Beach, was born May, 5th day, 1720–1.

John, the son of James and Hannah Curtiss, was born November 21st, 1721.

Elizabeth, the daughter of Cornelious and Mahethabel Hull, was born the 25th of Apr., 1721.

Cornelious, the son of Cornelious and Mahethabel Hull, departed this life the last day of June, 1722.

Mary, the daughter of Abraham and Sarah Cruttenden, was born Sep. the 27th, 1722.

November 30th, 1719, Timothy Parsons and Mary Robinson were joined in marriage, by Rev, Mr. N. Chauncey.

Mary, the daughter of the sd. Timothy and Mary Robinson. was born Nov., the 3d day, 1722.

Noahdiah Seward and Hannah Smith were married Oct. the 19th, 1721, by Phinehas Fisk, minister of the Gospel at Haddam,

Lydia, the daughter of the sd. Noahdiah and Hannah, was born January 17th, 1722–23.

Hannah, the daughter of Abraham Thomas and Hannah, his wife, was born Apr. 23d day, 1723.

Mary, the daughter of Mr. Hezekiah Talcott and Jemima, his wife, was born Feb. 16th, 1722–23.

Ann, the daughter of Mr. Hezekiah Talcott and Jemima, his wife, was born Sep. 6th, 1725.

Rachel, the daughter of Mr. Hez. Talcott and Jemima, his wife, was born Sep. 30th, 1728.

David Fowler and Mary Miles were married June 15th, 1724–25.

Miles, the son of David Fowler and Mary, his wife, was born March 9th, 1726–7.

David, the son of David Fowler and Mary, his wife, was born Jan. 21st, 1728–9.

Jehiel, the son of Cornelious Hull and Mahethabel, his wife, was born Feb. 28th, 1728–9.

Jearid, the son of Joseph Seward and Hannah, his wife, was born Feb. 22d, 1727–8.

Patience, the daughter of Stephen and Patience Bate, was born Jan. 11th, 1716–17.

Anna, the daughter of Stephen and Patience Bate, was born Feb. 5th, 1719–20.

Stephen, the son of Stephen and Patience Bate, was born March 20th, 1722–23.

Hephzibah, the daughter of Joseph and Hannah Seward, was born Nov. 27th, 1722.

Elizabeth, the daughter of Daniel and Sarah Merwin, was born Feb. 14th, 1722–23.

Elizabeth, the daughter of Stephen and Ruth Hickox, was born March 21st, 1722–3, and dyed Jan. 30th, 1723–4.

Joseph, the son of Joseph and Abigail Coe, was born Sep. 5th, 1718

David, the son of Joseph and Abigail Coe, was born Feb. 18th day, 1717.

Cornelious, the son of Cornelious and Mahethabel Hull, was born Oct. 31st, 1723.

Mehethabel, the daughter of Cornelious and Mahethabel Hull, was born Sep. 30th, 1725.

Samuel, the son of Timothy and Mary Parsons, was born July first, 1726.

Brotherton, the son of Joseph and Hannah Seward, was born the 28th day of July, A. D. 1724.

Beula, the daughter of Joseph Seward, was born the 8th day of May, A. D. 1727.

Alvin, the son of John Leete and Abigail, his wife, was born Oct. 20th, 1728.

Mary, the daughter of David and Abigail Baldwin, was born March 22d, 1723.

Abner, the son of David Baldwin and Abigail, his wife, was born May 27th, 1726.

Martha, the daughter of David Baldwin and Abigail, his wife, was born Dec. 23d, 1728.

Noah, the son of Samuel Norton and Dinah, his wife, was born January 24th, 1728–9.

Timothy Rossetter, the son of Mr. Josiah Rossetter, and ——, his wife, was born June the 5th, 1683.

Timothy Rossetter and Abigaile Penfield were joined in marriage, by Mr Thomas Ruggles, Pastor, &c., February 4th, 1711.

Bryan, the son of the sd. Timothy Rossetter and Abegaile, his wife, was born Oct. 22d, 1713.

Asher, the son of the sd. Timothy Rossetter and Abegaile, his wife, was born Oct. 16th, 1715.

Rebeccah, the daughter of the sd. Timothy and Abegaile, was born January 5th, 1718–19.

Rowland, the son of the sd. Timothy and Abegaile, was born May 8th, 1721.

Timothy, the son of the sd. Timothy and Abegaile, was born June 10th, 1725.

Ephraim, the son of John and Elizabeth Norton, was born August 21st, 1721.

Stephen, the son of John and Elizabeth Norton, was born June 7th, 1724.

Thankful, the daughter of John and Mary Hickox, was born March 30th, 1723.

Gideon Leete and Abegail Rossetter were joined in marriage, by Mr. Nath'll Chauncey, Pastor, &c., Sept. 6th, 1727.

Abraham Blatchley, of Durham, and Elizabeth Stone, of Guilford, were joined in marriage, November 16th, 1727.

John, the son of John and Mahethabel Sutlief, was born Jan. 28th, 1727–8.

Ruth, the daughter of John and Ruth Seward, was born June first, 1719

Abegail, the daughter of John and Ruth Seward, was born Dec. the 2d, 1720.

Deborah, the daughter of John and Ruth Seward, was born June the 2d, 1722, and died upon 15th sd. June.

Mary, the daughter of John and Ruth Seward, was born Feb. 17th, 1725.

John, the son of John and Ruth Seward, was born May 15th, 1726.

Moses, the son of John and Ruth Seward, was born Nov. 7th, 1727.

Samuel Norton and Dinah Beach were married May the 13th, 1713, by the Rev. Mr. Nath'll Chauncey.

Samuel, the son of the above named Samuel and Dinah, was born March 20th, 1714, and died March 21st, 1718.

Ebenezer, the son of sd. Samuel Norton and Dinah, his wife, was born Dec. 30th, 1715.

Samuel, the son of sd. Samuel and Dinah, was born March 6th, 1718.

Dinah, the daughter of sd. Samuel and Dinah, was born November —, 1723

David, the son of sd. Samuel Norton and Dinah, his wife, was born Feb. —, 1726.

Annie, the daughter of Richard Spelman and Margerie, his wife, was born December 7th, 1729.

Elinour, the daughter of Ebenezer Gurnsey and Rhoda, his wife, was born June 22d, 1727.

Rhoda, the daughter of Ebenezer Gurnsey and Rhoda, his wife, was born Oct. 23d, 1728.

David Robinson and Rebecca Miller were joined in marriage, Jan. 26th, A. D. 1719–20.

Anna, the daughter of David Robinson and Rebecca, his wife, was born Dec. the 5th, 1720.

David, the son of David Robinson and Rebecca, his wife, was born the 4th of March, A. D 1720–21.

John, the son of David Robinson and Rebecca, his wife, was born June 25th, A. D. 1722.

Dan. the son of David Robinson and Rebeccah, his wife, was born May 2d, 1725.

Rebecca, the daughter of David Robinson and Rebeccah, his wife, was born Dec. 5th, A D. 1727.

Timothy, the son of David Robinson and Rebeckah, his wife, was born Apr. 29th, A. D. 1728.

Phinehas, the son of David Robinson and Rebeckah, his wife, was born July 24th, A. D. 1730.

TOWN RECORDS.

Mary, the daughter of John Norton and Mary, his wife, was born the 13th day of Apr., A. D. 1743.

Rosa, the daughter of John Norton and Mary, his wife, was born the 16th day of Aug, A. D. 1745

Moses, the son of John Norton and Mary, his wife, was born the 28th day of Dec., A. D. 1746.

John, the son of John Norton and Mary his wife, was born the 23d day of Feb. A. D. 1748.

At the desire of the sd. John Norton, who dwells at Killingworth, I make the above entryes of his children.

John, the son of John Canfield and Bethiah, his wife, was born Oct., the 23d day, A. D. 1751.

Brotherton Seaward and Abigail Crane were joined in marriage, Nov. 9th, A. D 1752.

Abigail, the daughter of Brotherton Seaward and Abigail, his wife, was born July 28th, A. D. 1753.

Remembrance, the daughter of Daniel Wright and Lucie, his wife, was born Aug. 22d, 1753.

John Sutlief and Lucy Stocking were joined in marriage, Apr. 23d, A. D. 1754.

Lidia, the widow and Relict of Caleb Seaward, the first settler in Durham, departed this life, Aug. 24th, A. D 1753.

Eliakim Strong departed this life, Jan. 24th, A. D. 1745.

Margaret, the wife of Thomas Canfield, departed this life, March 15th, A D 1757.

Jemimah, the wife of Hezekiah Talcott, departed this life Feb. 2d, A. D. 1757.

Moses Parsons departed this life, Sept. 26th, A. D. 1754, and Abigail. his wife, died Dec. 4th, A. D. 1760.

Paul Chipman departed this life, Sept. 2d, A. D. 1760.

Jonathan Wells departed this life, Nov. 7th, A. D. 1760.

Jonathan Wells departed this life, May 12th, A. D. 1755, and Mehethabel, his wife, died Apr. 16th, A. D 1759

Samuel Seaward departed this life, Dec. 19th, A. D 1751.

Mary Canfield departed this life, Jan. 16th, A. D. 1761.

Lucy, the wife of Daniel Wright, departed this life, Nov. 8th, 1760.

Thomas Canfield departed this life, Dec. 1st, A. D. 1760.

Margaret, the wife of Thomas Canfield, departed this, life March 15th, 1757.

Thomas Lyman departed this life, Apr. 20th, A. D. 1761.

John Jones departed this life, November 25th, A. D. 1759; Hannah, his wife, departed this life Dec. 4th, 1759.

Sarah, daughter of John Jones and Hannah, his wife, died Nov. 28th, A. D. 1759.

Hazard Hinman departed this life, Dec. 14th, 1760.

Josiah Fowler departed this life. Sep. 7th, A D. 1757.

Silas Crane departed this life, Jan. 15th, A. D. 1763.

Samuel Squier departed this life, March 13th, A D. 1752.

John Sutlief departed this life, May 18th, A. D. 1757.

Mary, the wife of David Fowler, departed this life, Dec. 2d, 1734.

Mary, the wife of Thomas Canfield, departed this life, July 30th, 1740.

Capt. Henry Crane departed this life, Apr. 11th, A. D. 1741.

Sarah, the wife of Caleb Seaward, departed this life, May 7th, 1746.

Mrs. Mary Robinson, the wife of David Robinson, departed this life, Oct. the 17th day, A. D. 1746.

Abigail, the wife of James Wadsworth, Jun., departed this life Feb. 14th, A. D. 1748.

Samuel Squier departed this life, March 13th, 1751.

Abigail, the widow and relict of Capt Henry Crane, departed this life, Aug. the 31st, A. D. 1754, in the 78th year of her age.

Ephraim Coe and Ann Canfield were joined in marriage, Oct. 17th, 1754.

William Park, of Haddam, and Elizabeth Sutlif of Durham, were joined in marriage, May 29th, 1755.

Col. James Wadsworth departed this life Jan. 10th, A. D. 1756.

Capt. James Wadsworth and Katharine Guernsey were joined in marriage by the Rev. Mr. Elizur Goodrich, Jan 13th, A. D. 1757.

Abigail, the daughter of Capt. James Wadsworth and Catharine, his wife, was born Dec. 8th, A. D. 1757, and departed this life Feb. 2d, 1759.

Catharine, the daughter of Capt. James Wadsworth and Katharine, his wife, was born Jan. 19th, 1760, A. D, and departed this life, May 28th, 1763.

Ruth, the widow and Relict of Col. James Wadsworth, departed this life, June 5th, A. D. 1774

James Wadsworth, Esq., departed this life July 21st, A. D. 1777.

Catharine, the wife of Gen. James Wadsworth, departed this life Dec. 13th, A. D. 1813.

Gen. James Wadsworth departed this life, Sept. 22d, 1817.

Moses Parsons was born in Northampton, Mass., Jan. 15th, 1687, and married Abigail Ball, of Springfield, Jan 20th, 1710 He removed to Durham about 1710. He was the seventh son of Joseph Parsons, of Northampton. His uncle, Samuel Parsons, removed from Northampton to Durham the same time, and married Mary Wheeler, of Durham, in 1711.

Martha, the daughter of Abner Newton and Huldah, his wife, was born Oct. 16th, A. D. 1749.

Samuel, the son of Samuel Ely and Jerushah, his wife, was born June 21st, A. D. 1750.

Moses Sheldon and Elizabeth Grave were joined in marriage, Apr. 20th, Anno Domini, 1749.

Ezra, the son of Moses Sheldon and Elizabeth, his wife, was born Nov. 7th, A D. 1750.

Enos, the son of Henry Crane and Mercy, his wife, was born Aug 10th, A. D. 1751, and departed this life Aug. 28th, A. D. 1751.

Medad, the son of Stephen Norton and Abigail, his wife, was born June 30th, 1749.

Israel Camp and Ann Talcott were joined in marriage, Dec. 24th, 1747.

Phebe, the daughter of Israel Camp and Ann, his wife, was born Oct. 26th, A. D. 1748

Ann, the daughter of Israel Camp and Ann his wife, was born May 20th, 1756

Hezekiel, the son of Israel Camp and Ann, his wife, was born May 21st, 1752.

David Curtiss and Thankful Thomson were joined in marriage, Jan. 22d, 1747.

Ebenezer, the son of David Curtiss and Thankful, his wife, was born Jan. 17th, A. D. 1749

David, the son of David Curtiss and Thankful, his wife, was born May 19th, A. D 1750.

Esther, the daughter of David Curtiss and Thankful, his wife, was born Nov 15th, A. D. 1751.

Daniel, the son of David Curtiss and Thankful, his wife, was born Oct. 7th, A. D. 1753.

John Curtiss and Dinah Norton were joined in marriage, Nov. 18th, A. D 1747.

Abijah, the son of John Curtiss and Dinah, his wife, was born March 2d, A. D. 1750.

Phebe, the daughter of John Curtiss and Dinah, his wife, was born June 16th, A. D 1752.

Job Camp and Rachel Talcott were joined in marriage, Dec. 28th, 1752.

Hannah, the daughter of Job Camp and Rachel, his wife, was born Oct. 15th, A. D. 1753.

Josiah Fowler and Hannah Baldwin were joined in marriage, June 6th day, A. D. 1723.

Josiah, the son of Josiah Fowler and Hannah, his wife, was born March 31st, 1724.

Hannah, the daughter of Josiah Fowler and Hannah, his wife, was born Apr. 12th, A. D. 1725.

Caleb, the son of Josiah Fowler and Hannah, his wife, was born Jan. 7th, A. D 1727.

Elizabeth, the daughter of Josiah Fowler and Hannah, his wife, was born Oct. 11th, A. D. 1728.

Jonathan, the son of Josiah Fowler and Hannah, his wife, was born Aug. 20th, A. D. 1730

Joseph Norton and Prudence Osborn were joined in marriage, Sept. 16th, A D. 1729.

Mehetabel, the daughter of Joseph Norton and Prudence, his wife, was born July 12th, A. D. 1730.

Jerusha, the daughter of Abraham Thomas and Hannah, his wife, was born March 10th, A. D. 1730.

Mary, the daughter of David Fowler and Mary, his wife, was born Feb. 2d, 1731.

Nathaniel, the son of Abraham Cruttenden and Sarah, his wife, was born July 21st, A. D 1731.

James, the son of David Robinson and Rebeckah, his wife, was born June 10th, 1731.

Elihu, the son of Jesse Norton, Jun., and Prudence, his wife, was born Jan. 11th, 1732.

Henry Crane, Jun., and Marcey Francis were joined in marriage, June, the seventh day, A. D. 1732.

Abraham, the son of Abraham Thomas and Hannah, his wife, was born Jan. 9th, 1732.

Huldah, the daughter of Richard Spellman and Margery, his wife, was born July 9th, 1732.

Jesse, the son of Silas Crane and Mercy, his wife, was born June 5th, 1732.

Mary, the daughter of Stephen Bate and Patience, his wife, was born June 11th, 1732.

Phineas, the son of John Camp and Damaris, his wife, was born June 15th, 1731.

Abiathar, the son of John Camp and Damaris, his wife, was born Nov. 16th, 1732.

Simeon, the son of Simeon Parsons and Mehethabel, his wife, was born Nov. 25th, 1732.

Joel Parmalee and Abigail Andrus were joined in marriage, June 30th, 1706.

Mary, the daughter of Joel Parmalee and Abigail, his wife, was born Nov. 11th, 1707.

John, the son of Joel Parmalee and Abigail, his wife, was born Sep. 22d, 1709

Hezekiah, the son of Joel Parmalee and Abigail, his wife, was born Jan. 10th, 1712.

Joel, the son of Joel Parmalee and Abigail, his wife, was born March 8th, 1714.

Abigail, the daughter of Joel Parmalee and Abigail, his wife, was born July 12th, 1715.

Hannah, the daughter of Joel Parmalee and Abigail, his wife, was born Aug 27th, 1717.

Sarah, the daughter of Joel Parmalee and Abigail, his wife, was born Aug. 28th, 1719.

Jerusha, the daughter of Joel Parmalee and Abigail, his wife, was born April 10th, 1721.

Job Wheeler and Jane Squire were joined in marriage, Apr. 29th, 1731.

Jane, the daughter of Job Wheeler and Jane, his wife, was born Feb. 15th, 1732.

Israel, the son of Daniel Squire and Patience, his wife, was born the 27th of June, 1732.

Adonijah, the son of Adonijah Morris and Sarah, his wife, was born Oct. 26th, 1723.

John, the son of Adonijah Morris and Sarah, his wife, was born Nov. 15th, 1725.

Anna, the daughter of Adonijah Morris and Sarah, his wife, was born Feb. 24th, 1728.

Timothy, the son of Adonijah Morris and Sarah, his wife, was born Jan. 27th, 1730.

Hannah, the daughter of Joseph Seward and Hannah, his wife, was born Feb. 21st, 1730–1.

Lucretia, the daughter of Joseph Seward and Hannah, his, wife, was born Jan. 15th, 1732–3.

Joseph Wheeler and Prudence Graves were joined in marriage, Apr. 13th, 1732.

Sarah, the daughter of Joseph Wheeler and Prudence, his wife, was born Feb. 18th, 1732–3.

Phebe, the daughter of Ithamar Parsons and Sarah, his wife, was born Sept. 13th, 1732.

John, the son of Henry Crane, Jun., and Mercey, his wife, was, born March 27th, 1733.

Ann, the daughter of Aaron Parsons and Abigail, his wife, was born Nov. 13th, 1733.

Phinehas, the son of Simeon Parsons and Mehetabel, his wife, was born March 7th, 1733.

Nathaniel Seward and Concurrence Crane were joined in marriage, Feb. 2d, A. D. 1730.

Lucy, the daughter of Nathaniel Seaward and Concurrence, his wife, was born Nov. 7th, 1732

Enos, the son of Nathaniel Seward and Concurrence, his wife, was born July 14th, 1734

John Camp and Hannah Hickox were joined in marriage, June 27th, 1728.

Ruth, the daughter of John Camp and Hannah, his wife, was born Oct. 9th, 1733.

Oliver, the son of Stephen Bates and Patience, his wife, was born Aug. 26th, 1734.

Anne, the daughter of Jabez Wetmore and Abigail, his wife, was born Sept. 29th, 1734.

Sarah, the daughter of Noahdiah Grave and Sarah, his wife, was born March 20th, 1720-1.

Noahoriah, the son of Noahdiah Grave and Sarah, his wife, was born June the 20th, 1721.

Elizabeth, the daughter of Noahdiah Grave and Sarah, his wife, was born June 21st, 1723

Abigail, the daughter of Noahdiah Grave and Sarah, was born Sep. 25th, 1725.

David, the son of Noahdiah Grave and Sarah his wife, was born Oct. 5th, 1728.

Rozwell, the son of Noahdiah Grave and Sarah, his wife, was born Dec. 5th, 1731.

Elihu, the son of Henry Crane, Jun., and Mercy, his wife, was born June 24th, 1735.

Samuel, the son of Abraham Crittenden and Sarah, his wife, was born Feb. 7th, 1733.

Mary, the daughter of John Guthrie and Abigail, his wife, was born Dec. 20th, 1735.

Joseph Fowler and Ruth Baker were joined in marriage, by the Rev. Mr. Nathaniel Chauncey, Apr. 2d, 1736.

Simeon Parsons, of Durham, and Mehetabel Clapp, of Northampton, were joined in marriage, Oct. 12th, A. D. 1731, by Mr. Jonathan Edwards, Pastor.

Daniel Squire and Patience Barnes were joined in marriage, Sep. 1st, A. D. 1730, by John Russell, Justice of the Peace.

Flood, the son of Silas Crane and Mercy, his wife, was born Feb. 12th, 1734.

Phebe, the daughter of Joseph Fowler and Ruth, his wife, was born Sep 19th, 1735.

Samuel, the son of John Camp and Hannah, his wife, was born Nov. 11th, 1735.

Catharine, the daughter of Jabez Wetmore and Abigail, his wife, was born July 20th, 1736.

Jonathan, the son of Jonathan Wells, Jun., and Mary, his wife, was born July 28th, 1736.

Eunice, the daughter of Mr. Hezekiah Talcott and Jemimah, his wife, was born Feb. 1st, 1735.

Samuel Stent, the son of Ephraim Squire and Mehetabel, his wife, was born June 15th, 1733.

John, the son of Henry Crane, Jun., and Mercy, his wife, departed this life, Dec. 12th, 1736.

Anne, the daughter of Richard Spelman and Margery, his wife, was born July 3d, 1734.

Phinehas, the son of Richard Spelman and Margery, his wife, was born Feb. 9th, 1736.

Eunice, the daughter of Mr. Hezekiah Talcott and Jemimah, his wife, was born Feb. 1st, A. D. 1735.

Elizabeth, the daughter of John Norton and Elizabeth, his wife, was born Jan. 15th, 1725–6.

Hannah, the daughter of Joseph Sanford and Mary, his wife, was born July 23d, 1729.

Sarah, the daughter of Joseph Sanford and Mary, his wife, was born July 28th, 1731.

Oliver, the son of Joseph Sanford and Mary, his wife, was born Aug. 22d, 1732.

Jonah, the son of Joseph Sanford and Mary, his wife, was born Aug. 1st, A. D. 1737.

Abiel, the son of Edward Camp and Mary, his wife, was born Aug. 29th, 1734.

Caleb, the son of Edmund Fairchild and Mary, his wife, was born Jan. 27th, 1737.

Aaron, the son of Thomas Spelman and Sarah, his wife, was born Jan. 22d, 1735.

Mary, the daughter of Thomas Spelman and Sarah, his wife, was born Aug. 18th, 1736.

Gideon, the son of Gideon Leete and Abigail, his wife, was born May 5th, 1731.

Phebe, the daughter of Henry Crane, Jun., and Mercey, his wife, was born Feb. 6th, 1737–8.

Sarah, the daughter of Jonathan Wells, Jun., and Mary, his wife, was born Feb. 2d, 1737.

April 21st, 1736, David Fowler and Elizabeth Hall were joined in marriage, by Theophilus Yale, Justice of Peace.

Oliver, the son of David Fowler and Elizabeth, his wife, was born June 2d, 1737.

Titus, the son of David Fowler and Elizabeth, his wife, was born Nov. 29th, 1738.

Hezekiah, the son of John Talcott and Sarah, his wife, was born June 19th, 1739.

March 28th, 1739, Capt. Elihu Chauncey and Mary Griswold (the daughter of Mr. Samuel Griswold, late of Killingworth, deceased,) were joined in marriage, by Capt. David Buil, Justice of the Peace in New London County.

Eunice, the daughter of Benjamin Johnson and Eunice, his wife, was born Sept. 16th, 1733.

Mehetabel, the daughter of Benjamin Johnson and Eunice, his wife, was born Nov. 23d, 1734.

Submit, the daughter of Benjamin Johnson and Eunice, his wife, was born Sept. 28th, 1736

John, the son of Benjamin Johnson and Eunice, his wife, was born July 28th, 1739

Mary, the daughter of Henry Crane, Jun, and Marcey, his wife, was born Nov. 24th, 1739.

Ira, the son of Jabez Wetmore, and Abigail, his wife, was born on the third day of April, 1740.

Silas, the son of Silas Crane and Mercey, his wife, was born Nov. 9th, 1737.

Samuel Roberts and Rachel Webb were joined in marriage, March 22d, 1716.

The children of the sd. Samuel Roberts and Rachel, his wife, were here entered Jan. 28th, 1739, sd. Roberts being present, gave the account.

Elizabeth, the daughter of Samuel Roberts and Rachel, his wife, was born March 24th, 1717–18.

Samuel, was born March 9th, 1719–20.

Anna, was born March 16th, 1722–23.

Sarah, was born Sept 26th, 1725.

Rachel, was born Dec. 7th, 1728

Mary, was born Aug 7th, 1731.

John, was born July 16th, 1734.

Joel, was born Oct. 27th, 1736.

Noah, was born Oct. 21st, 1739.

Daniel Merwin, Junior, of Durham, and Elizabeth Wells, of Haddam, were joined in marriage, Dec. 20th, 1738, by Mr. Henry Brainard, Justice of the Peace.

James, the son of Daniel Merwin, Jun., and Elizabeth, his wife, was born Oct. 19th, 1739, and the above named Elizabeth, the wife of Daniel Merwin, Jun., departed this life, Oct. 29th, 1739.

Charles, the son of Capt. Elihu Chauncey and Mary, his wife, was born Dec. 28th, A. D. 1729, died Jan'y 13th, 1740–41.

Ephraim, the son of John Guthrie and Abigail, his wife, was born March 1st, 1737.

Ebenezer, the son of John Guthrie and Abigail, his wife, was born July 29th, 1740.

Robert, the son of Silas Crane and Marcey, his wife, was born Feb. 18th, 1739.

Gideon Canfield and Anne Robinson were joined in marriage, Oct. 28th, 1740.

Thomas, the son of Thomas and Tabatha Philips, was born Oct. 1st, 1740.

Oliver, the son of Simeon Burton and Mary, his wife, was born June 9th, 1740.

Mr. Thomas Canfield and Miss Margaret Brainard were joined in marriage, Nov. 26th, 1740.

Sumner Stow and Sarah Seward were joined in marriage, Dec. 1st, A. D. 1736.

Sarah, the daughter of Sumner Stow and Sarah his wife, was born Feb. 10th, A. D. 1737.

Abraham, the son of Sumner Stow and Sarah, his wife, was born March 5th, A. D. 1740.

Israel Auered and Abigail Beach were joined in marriage, Aug. 25th, 1731, by Mr. Bliss, minister at Hebron.

Mical, the son of Israel Auered and Abigail, his wife, was born July 29th, 1732.

Abigail, the daughter of Israel Auered and Abigail, his wife, was born March 1st, 1733–4.

Ann, the daughter of Israel Auered and Abigail, his wife, was born Jan. 15th, 1740–1.

Samuel, the son of Lieut. Joseph Seward and Hannah, his wife, was born Jan. 30th, A. D. 1734–5.

John, the son of Lieut. Joseph Seward and Hannah, his wife, was born May 11th, 1737.

Caroline, the daughter of Lieut. Joseph Seward and Hannah, his wife, was born Aug. 6th, 1739.

Thomas Norton and Mary Stedman were oined in marriage, Nov. 5th, 1740.

Elisha, the son of Thomas Norton and Mary, his wife, was born Nov. 21st. 1741.

Daniel, the son of Joseph Norton, Jun., and Prudence, his wife, was born the second day of March, A D. 1735–6.

Esther, the daughter of Joseph Norton, Jun., and Prudence, his wife, was born Dec. 18th, A. D. 1738.

Sarah, the daughter of John Talcott and Sarah, his wife, was born Sept. 1st, A. D. 1741.

Israel, the son of Gideon Canfield and Anne, his wife, was born Sept 15th, 1741.

May 11th, 1741, Daniel Merwin, Jun., and Mary Burrett were joined in marriage, by Mr. Nathaniel Chauncey, pastor of the Church in Durham.

John, the son of Henry Crane and Mercey, his wife, was born July 1st, 1741.

Benjamin, the son of Ephraim Coe and Hannah, his wife, was born March 7th, A. D. 1741.

Hannah, the daughter of Samuel Hickox and Hannah, his wife, was born Oct. 17th, 1740.

Mary, the daughter of Jonathan Wells and Mary, his wife, was born March 17th, 1739.

Jonathan, the son of Jonathan Wells, Jun., and Mary, his wife, was born Apr. 1st, 1742. Died, Sept. 9th, 1746.

Timothy, the son of Sumner Stowe and Sarah, his wife, was born Apr. 27th, 1742.

Abigail, the son of John Guthrie and Abigail, his wife, was born July 21st, 1742.

Paul, the son of Silvanus Chipman and Elizabeth, his wife, was born Jan. 16th, A. D. 1740

Hannah, the daughter of John Bates and Edith, his wife, was born July 28th, 1742.

Catharine, the daughter of Capt. Elihu Chauncey and Mary, his wife, was born Apr 11th, 1741.

Sarah, the daughter of Major Elihu Chauncey and Mary, his wife, was born Sept. 22d, 1742. Died, Aug 15th, 1744.

Ambros, the son of Samuel Hickox and Hannah, his wife, was born Oct. 23d, A. D. 1742.

Joseph, the son of Joseph Sutlief and Sarah, his wife, was born Jan. 1st, A. D. 1733.

John, the son of Thomas Phillips and Tabitha, his wife, was born Oct. 6th, 1742.

John Parmalee, of Durham, and Sarah Boardman, of Weathersfield, were joined in marriage, Nov. 24th, 1730.

Rosemon, the daughter of John Parmalee and Sarah, his wife, was born Oct. 24th, 1731.

Ann, the daughter of John Parmalee and Sarah, his wife, was born Jan. 6th, 1732

Phinehas, the son of John Parmalee and Sarah, his wife, was born Oct. 16th, 1734.

Aaron, the son of John Parmalee and Sarah, his wife, was born Sept. 17th, 1736.

John, the son of John Parmalee and Sarah, his wife, was born Feb. 18th, 1738.

Samuel, the son of John Parmalee and Sarah, his wife, was born Oct. 20th, 1740.

Sarah, the daughter of John Parmalee and Sarah, his wife, was born June 24th, 1742.

Thomas Strong and Phebe Seward were joined in marriage, Jan 16th, 1746.

Isaac Norton and Mary Rockwell, of Windsor, were joined in marriage, Nov. 12th, A. D. 1735.

Abigail, the daughter of Isaac Norton and Mary, his wife, was born Oct. 14th, 1736.

Mary, the daughter of Isaac Norton and Mary, his wife, was born July 1st, 1737.

Lydia, the daughter of Isaac Norton and Mary, his wife, was born March 5th, 1739–40.

Silvanus, the son of Isaac Norton and Mary, his wife, was born July 16th, 1742

Henry, the son of Ensign Nathaniel Seward and Concurrence, his wife, was born July 7th, 1736.

Nathaniel, the son of Ensign Nathaniel Seward and Concurrence, his wife, was born Oct. 16th, 1738.

Enos, the son of Ensign Nathaniel Seward and Concurrence, his wife, departed this life, Oct. 5th, 1742.

John, the son of Curtis Fairchild and Mercy, his wife, was born Feb 15th, 1728.

the son of Curtis Fairchild and Mercey, his wife, was 6th, 1730.

Zipporah, the daughter of Curtis Fairchild and Mercey, his wife, was born Jan. 1st, 1732. Since is deceased.

Reuben, the son of Curtis Fairchild and Marcey, his wife, was born Dec. 18th, 1734

Alexander, the son of Curtis Fairchild and Marcey, his wife, was born Dec 14th, 1736.

Robert, the son of Curtis Fairchild and Marcey, his wife, was born Jan. 16th, 1738.

Anne, the daughter of Curtis Fairchild and Marcey, his wife, was born Oct. 1st, 1740.

Zipporah, the daughter of Curtis Fairchild and Marcey, his wife, was born Nov. 7th, 1732 *Memorandum.*—There was no double dating in C. Fairchild's certificate.

Katharine, the daughter of Ebenezer Guernsey and Rhoda, his wife, was born Jan. 15th, 1732–3.

Mary, the daughter of Ebenezer Guernsey and Rhoda, his wife, was born Oct. 12th, 1734

Ebenezer, the son of Ebenezer Guernsey and Rhoda, his wife, was born Feb. 26th, 1737–8.

Sarah, the daughter of Ebenezer Guernsey and Rhoda, his wife, was born May 22d, 1742.

Aaron Alvord and Mehetabel Strong were joined in marriage, Nov. 6th, A D. 1739.

Elenor, the daughter of Joseph Wright and Elenor, his wife, was born May 2d, 1740.

Margery, the daughter of Joseph Wright and Elenor, his wife, was born Jan. 5th, A. D 1741–2.

Stephen, the son of Jonathan Norton and Ruth, his wife, was born June 21st, A. D. 1741.

Belah, the son of Aaron Alvord and Mehethabel, his wife, was born Aug. 31st, 1741.

Selah, the son of Aaron Alvord and Mehethabel, his wife, was born March 26th, A D. 1743.

Eli, the son of Silas Crane and Mercey his wife, was born Nov. 27th, 1742.

Flood, the son of Silas Crane and Mercey, his wife, departed this life, June 2d, 1743.

Sarah, the daughter of Stephen Hickox and Lydia, his wife, was born Oct. 3d, A. D. 1743.

John, the son of David Fowler and Elizabeth, his wife, was born May 7th, 1740.

Elizabeth, the daughter of David Fowler and Elizabeth, his wife, was born Feb. 27th, 1742.

Robert, the son of Samuel Fairchild and Mary, his wife, was born Nov. 19th, 1703.

Ann, the daughter of Ephraim Curtis and Elizabeth, his wife, was born Sep. 1st, 1740.

May 18th, 1730, the above named Robert Fairchild and Ann Curtis were joined in marriage.

June 14th, 1743, Elizabeth, the daughter of Capt. Robert Fairchild and Anne, his wife, was born.

Concurrence, the daughter of Henry Crane and Marcey, his wife, was born Nov. 14th, 1744.

John, the son of John Camp (the second) and Hannah, his wife, was born March 2d, A. D. 1738.

Hannah, the daughter of John Camp (the second) and Hannah, his wife, was born Feb. 11th, A. D 1739–40.

Phebe, the daughter of John Camp (the second) and Hannah, his wife, was born Feb. 3d, A. D. 1741–2.

Katherine, the daughter of John Camp (the second) and Hannah, his wife, was born Jan 16th, A. D. 1744–5.

Rebeckah, the daughter of Gideon Canfield and Ann, his wife, was born Oct 16th, A. D. 1743.

Samuel Parsons and Elizabeth Chipman were joined in marriage, Jan. 21st, A. D. 1746–7.

Flood, the son of Silas Crane and Marcey, his wife, was born Feb. 27th, 1744–5. Departed this life, Jan. 6th, A. D. 1763.

Ephraim Seward and Abigail Wetmore were joined in marriage, Oct. 19th, 1743.

James, the son of Ephraim Seward and Abigail, his wife, was born Oct. 20th, A. D 1744.

Rachel, the daughter of Samuel Hickox and Hannah, his wife, was born Nov. 13th, 1745.

Mahethabel, the daughter of Aaron Aluord and Mehethabel, his wife, was born Oct. 1st, A. D. 1745.

Ruth, the daughter of Jonathan Norton and Ruth, his wife, was born Aug. 20th, 1743.

Jonathan, the son of Jonathan Norton and Ruth, his wife, was born Aug 27th, 1745.

John, the son of Lieut William Smithson and Anne, his wife, was born Feb. 19th, A. D. 1742–3.

Robert, the son of Lieut. William Smithson and Anne, his wife, was born June 25th, 1744.

Anne, the daughter of Lieut. William Smithson and Anne, his wife, was born July 19th, A. D. 1746.

Anne, the daughter of Gideon Canfield and Anne, his wife, was born March 30th, 1746

Timothy, the son of Simeon Coe and Anne, his wife, was born Oct. 21st, 1746.

Job, the son of Ephraim Seward and Abigail, his wife, was born Nov. 8th, A D. 1746

Ann, the daughter of Henry Crane and Marcey, his wife, was born Oct 8th, A. D. 1746.

Sarah, the daughter of Silvanius Chipman and Mary, his wife, was born Feb 17th, 1742–3.

Darcos, the daughter of Samuel Hickox and Hannah, his wife, was born July 19th, 1747.

Joseph Hull and Sibel Coe were joined in marriage, Jan. 1st, A D. 1746.

Elizabeth, the daughter of Joseph Hull and Sibel, his wife, was born July 1st, A. D. 1747.

Samuel, the son of Ezra Rockwell and Jemimah, his wife, was born March 30th, 1745–6

Joel, the son of David Robinson and Rebeccah, his wife, was born March 31st, 1733.

Mary, the daughter of David Robinson and Rebecca, his wife, was born Dec. 7th, 1734.

Noah, the son of David Robinson and Rebecca, his wife, was born May 29th, 1736.

Abigail, the daughter of David Robinson and Rebecca, his wife, was born the 9th of March, 1737–8.

Asher, the son of David Robinson and Rebeccah, his wife, was born May 4th, 1740.

Huldah, the daughter of Silas Crane and Mercey, his wife, was born Apr. 30th, 1747.

Joel, the son of John Norton (the second) and Deborah, his wife, was born Sept. 20th, 1745, and died July 2d, 1746.

Katherine, the daughter of Gideon Canfield and Ann, his wife, was born June 16th, 1748.

Joseph, the son of Samuel Parsons (the first) and Elizabeth, his wife, was born Dec. 25th, A. D. 1747.

Hannah, the daughter of Benony Hills and Hannah, his wife, was born in Suffield, Oct. 5th, 1724, and the other children of the sd Benoni Hills and Hannah, his wife, were born in times as followeth:

Zimry, was born Dec. 16th, 1725.

Beriah, was born Aug. 31st, 1727

Medad, was born Apr. 27th, 1729

John, was born Dec. 13th, 1732.

Mary, was born Sep. 25th, 1734.

Seth, was born Sept. 13th, 1736

Ratchel, was born July 8th, 1739

Belah, was born in Goshen, Aug. 24th, 1741.

Ann, was born in Goshen, June 11th, 1743.

Henry, the son of Henry Crane and Mercey, his wife, was born Dec. 11th, 1748.

Phebe, the daughter of Samuel Ely and Jerusha, his wife, was born Jan 24th, A. D. 1742, and died Jan. 28th, 1748–9.

John Canfield and Bethiah Moss were joined in marriage, Jan. 19th, 1748–9.

Joseph Seward, Jun , and Elizabeth Norton were joined in marriage, Jan. 14th, 1748–9.

Noah, the son of Nanthaniel Howe and Mary, his wife, was born in Wallingford, where his parents were inhabitants, Oct. 13th, 1745.

Anne, the daughter of Ebenezer Gurnsey and Rhoda, his wife, was born Feb. 3d, 1747.

Ruth, the daughter of Silas Crane and Marcey, his wife, was born Dec. 12th, A. D. 1749.

Thomas Spelman and Sarah, his wife, children's births:

Aaron, was born Jan 22d, 1733–4.

Mary, was born Aug. 18th, 1736.

Daniel, was born July 12th, 1738.

Elizabeth, was born July 14th, 1740.

Martha, was born March 21st, 1742–3.

Charles, was born Dec 24th, 1743.

Stephen, was born Dec. 5th, 1745.

Sarah, was born Jan. 30th, 1747–8

Hannah, the daughter of Samuel Hickox and Hannah, his wife, was born Oct. 17th, A. D. 1749.

Rosannah, the daughter of Simeon Coe and Anna, his wife, was born Dec. 22d, A. D. 1749.

Thomas, the son of John Canfield and Bethiah, his wife, was born Feb. 14th, A D. 1749–50.

Anna, the daughter of Samuel Roberts and Rachel, his wife, was born March 16th, 1723.

Sarah, the daughter of Samuel Roberts and Rachel, his wife, was born Sept. 26th, 1725.

Rachel, the daughter of Samuel Roberts and Rachel, his wife, was born Dec 7th, 1728

Mary, the daughter of Samuel Roberts and Rachel, his wife, was born Aug. 7th, 1731.

John, the son of Samuel Roberts and Rachel, his wife, was born July 16th, 1734.

Joel, the son of Samuel Roberts and Rachel, his wife, was born Oct. 27th, 1736.

Noah, the son of Samuel Roberts and Rachel, his wife, was born Oct. 21st, 1739.

Joseph, the son of Joseph Hull and Sibel, his wife, was born Dec. 24th, A. D 1749.

Sarah, the daughter of Jonathan Norton and Ruth, his wife, was born Feb. 23d, A D. 1747–8.

Phebe, the daughter of Jonathan Norton and Ruth, his wife, was born May 10th, A D. 1750

Rachel, the daughter of Ezra Rockwell and Jemima, his wife, was born Jan 26th, 1747–8.

Daniel, the son of Ezra Rockwell and Jemima, his wife, was born April 5th, 1750

Brotherton Seward and Sarah Camp were joined in marriage, the 23d day of Nov., 1748

Ann, the daughter of Brotherton Seward and Sarah, his wife, was born March 7th, 1748.

Gideon, the son of Gideon Canfield and Anne, his wife, was born Sept. 10th, A. D. 1750.

Sarah, the daughter of Thomas Strong and Phebe, his wife, was born Feb. 20th, 1747.

Thomas, the son of Thomas Strong and Phebe, his wife, was born July 23d, 1748.

Lois, the daughter of Thomas Strong and Phebe, his wife, was born July 1st, 1750.

Joseph, the son of Josiah Coe and Sarah, his wife, was born March 18th, A. D. 1748–9.

Rhoda, the daughter of Josiah Coe and Sarah, his wife, was born Feb. 1st, A. D. 1750–1.

Joseph, the son of Joseph Tibbals and Abigail, his wife, was born May 27th, 1718.

James, the son of Joseph Tibbals and Abigail, his wife, was born July 21st, 1720.

Thomas, the son of Joseph Tibbals and Abigail, his wife, was born Sept. 25th, 1722.

Abigail, the daughter of Joseph Tibbals and Abigail, his wife, was born July 1st, 1725.

John, the son of Joseph Tibbals and Abigail, his wife, was born Oct. 29th, 1727.

Ebenezer, the son of Joseph Tibbals and Abigail, his wife, was born Jan. 19th, 1730.

Mary, the daughter of Joseph Tibbals and Abigail, his wife, was born Nov. 20th, 1733.

Samuel, the son of Joseph Tibbals and Abigail, his wife, was born May 29th, 1735.

Bryan Rossetter and Catharine Strong were joined in marriage, Sept. 2d, A. D. 1736

Katherine, the daughter of Bryan Rossetter and Katherine, his wife, was born Nov. 10th, 1737. Dyed, March 28th, A. D. 1756.

Susanna, the daughter of Bryan Rossetter and Catharine, his wife, was born Dec. 6th, 1739. Died, Apr. 2d, 1753.

Bryan, the son of Bryan Rossetter and Catharine, his wife, was born Aug. 6th, A. D. 1742. Dyed, July 28th, 1755

Abigail, the daughter of Bryan Rossetter and Katharine, his wife, was born Dec. 11th, 1744.

Phinehas, the son of John Canfield and Bethiah, his wife, was born Apr. 10th, 1753.

Charles Brooks and Mehethabel Norton were joined in marriage, Oct. 13th, 1753.

Joseph, the son of Charles Brooks and Mehethabel, his wife, was born Jan. 8th, A. D. 1754.

Charles, the son of Ephraim Seward and Abigail, his wife, was born Sept 14th, A. D. 1750.

Aaron, the son of John Norton (of Kilingworth) and Mary, his wife, was born in Durham, June 24th, 1751

Ebenezer, the son of Samuel Squire and Abigail, his wife, was born Apr 7th, 1745.

Daniel, the son of Samuel Squire and Abigail, his wife, was born Oct. 11th, 1746.

Jonathan, the son of Samuel Squire and Abigail, his wife, was born July 21st, 1748.

Abigail, the daughter of Samuel Squire and Abigail, his wife, was born March 19th, 1750.

Frederick, the son of Silas Crane and Abigail, his wife, was born Feb. 24th, 1751-2.

Abraham, the son of Abraham Scranton and Beulah, his wife, was born Dec 3d, 1749.

David, the son of Abraham Scranton and Beulah, his wife, was born Oct. 27th, 1751.

Sibil, the daughter of Joseph Hull and Sibil, his wife, was born Apr. 6th, A. D. 1752

Charles, the son of Ephraim Norton and Mary, his wife, was born Dec. 8th, 1738.

Elizabeth, the daughter of Ephraim Norton and Mary, his wife, was born June 19th, 1751.

Samuel, the son of Samuel Hickox and Hannah, his wife, was born Apr. 5th, 1752.

Josiah Squires' and Sarah his wife, children's births, are as follows:

Sarah, their daughter, was born Nov. 22d, 1737.

Josiah, their son, was born Sept. 15th, 1742.

Ruth, their daughter, was born May 25th, 1744.

Rhoda, their daughter, was born Nov. 25th, 1745

John, their son, was born July 19th, 1747.

Martha, their daughter was born Feb 7th, 1749-50

Clement, their son, was born Nov. 22d, 1750.

Abner Tibbals and Sarah Crittenden were joined in marriage, Aug. 26th, 1747.

Mary, the daughter of Abner Tibbals and Sarah, his wife, was born Oct. 2d, 1747.

Abel, the son of Abner Tibbals and Sarah his wife, was born March 4th, 1750.

Eber, the son of Abner Tibbals and Sarah, his wife, was born Dec. 27th, 1751.

Jerusha, the daughter of Samuel Ely and Jerusha, his wife, was born Jan. 3d, 1753.

Phinehas, the son of Josiah Coe and Sarah, his wife, was born the 5th day of June, A. D. 1753.

Charles, the son of Samuel Squire and Abigail, his wife, was born August 28th, A. D. 1732.

Jared Seaward and Mary Bishop were joined in marriage, Sep. 12th, A. D. 1753.

Daniel Wright and Lucy Stevens, were joined in marriage, Nov. 9th, A. D. 1752.

Miles, the son of Miles Merwin and Mary, his wife, was born May 1st, 1744.

Daniel, the son of Miles Merwin and Mary, his wife, was born May 30th, 1746.

Job, the son of Miles Merwin and Mary, his wife, was born Feb. 16th, 1749.

Noah, the son of Miles Merwin and Mary, his wife, was born Nov. 9th, A. D 1752.

Mary, the daughter of Daniel Weld and Elizabeth, his wife, was born July 9th, 1747.

Phinehas, the son of Daniel Weld and Elizabeth, his wife, was born Nov 25th, 1748, and died Jan. 1st, 1749.

Hannah, the daughter of Daniel Weld and Elizabeth, his wife, was born Jan. 27th, 1750–1

Sarah, the daughter of Daniel Weld and Elizabeth, his wife, was born March 20th, 1752–3.

Elizabeth, the daughter of John Camp (second) and Hannah, his wife, was born Oct. 20th, 1748.

Thomas Tibbals, and Rachel Doud were joined in marriage, Dec. 22d, 1748.

Stephen, the son of Thomas Tibbals and Rachel, his wife, was born Feb. 8th, 1749–50, and died March 28th, 1751.

Samuel, the son of Thomas Tibbals and Rachel, his wife, was born Nov 2d, 1751.

Thomas, the son of Thomas Tibbals and Rachel, his wife, was born Jan. 10th, 1754.

Sarah, the daughter of Thomas Norton and Mary, his wife, was born March 26th, 1756.

Phinehas, the son of Thomas Norton and Mary, his wife, was born Apr. 23d, 1748

Hannah, the daughter of Thomas Norton and Mary, his wife, was born May 22d, 1751.

James Tibbals and Martha Spencer were joined in marriage, Apr. 4th, A. D. 1744.

Sarah, the daughter of James Tibbals and Martha, his wife, was born Sep. 5th, 1745

Asher, the son of James Tibbals and Martha, his wife, was born Apr. 4th, 1748.

Joseph, the son of James Tibbals and Martha, his wife, was born Nov. 10th, 1750.

Abigail, the daughter of James Tibbals and Martha, his wife, was born Nov. 27th, 1752

Timothy, the son of David Grave and Hannah, his wife, was born Feb. 1st, 1754.

Anne, the daughter of Isaac Norton and Mary, his wife, was born December 19th, 1743.

Aaron, the son of Isaac Norton and Mary, his wife, was born March 26th, 1749.

Isaac, the son of Isaac Norton and Mary, his wife, was born March 23d, 1747.

Joel, the son of Isaac Norton and Mary, his wife, was born May 13th, 1753.

Nathaniel, the son of Samuel Hickox and Hannah, his wife, was born March 21st, A. D. 1754.

Aaron, the son of Ezra Rockwell and Jemimah, his wife, was born May 20th, O. S., A. D. 1752

Nathan, the son of Silas Crane and Mercy, his wife, was born Sep. 18th, A. D. 1754.

Mahithabel, the daughter of Joseph Hull and Sibil, his wife, was born July 3d, 1754.

Asher, the son of Daniel Wright and Lucy, his wife, was born May 9th, A. D. 1755.

Simeon, the son of Simeon Coe and Annah his wife, was born Feb. 12th, A. D. 1755.

Eliakim Strong and Hannah Seward were joined in marriage, June 4th, A. D. 1751.

John Sutlif and Sarah Squire were joined in marriage, Jan 19th, 1754.

Jehiel Hull and Ruth Phelps were joined in marriage, Nov. 8th, A. D. 1750.

Stephen Bates, 3d, and Mindwell Seward were joined in marriage, March, A. D. 1749.

Abijah, the son of Sumner Howe and Sarah, his wife, was born May 14th, 1746.

Robert, the son of Sumner Howe and Sarah, his wife, was born Nov. 2d, 1748.

Daniel, the son of Sumner Howe and Sarah, his wife, was born Oct 9th, 1751

Jemimah, the daughter of Ezra Rockwell and Jemimah, his wife, was born Aug. 20th, A. D. 1754.

Benjamin, the son of John Sutlif and Sarah, his wife, was born Aug. 23d, 1755.

Eliakim, the son of Eliakim Strong and Hannah, his wife, was born Oct. 6th, A. D. 1751

Medad, the son of Eliakim Strong and Hannah, his wife, was born July 4th, A. D. 1753.

John, the son of Eliakim Strong and Hannah, his wife, was born May 7th, A. D. 1755.

Ruth, the daughter of Jehiel Hull and Ruth, his wife, was born Feb. 1st, A. D. 1751

Hannah, the daughter of Jehiel Hull and Ruth, his wife, was born Jan. 21st, A. D 1754.

Stephen, the son of Brotherton Seward and Abigail, his wife, was born Apr. 19th, A. D. 1755.

Rowland Rossetter and Mary Strong were joined in marriage, Apr. 11th, A. D. 1753.

Rebeckah, the daughter of Rowland Rossetter and Mary, his wife, was born Oct. 23d, A. D 1753.

Lucy, the daughter of Rowland Rossetter and Mary, his wife, was born Dec. 8th, A. D. 1754.

Abigail, the daughter of Stephen Norton and Abigail, his wife was born July 14th, A. D. 1754.

Stephen, the son of Stephen Norton and Abigail, his wife, was born Jan. 26th, A. D 1756.

Sylvanus, the son of William Bishop and Patience, his wife, was born July 16th, A. D. 1738.

Ann, the daughter of William Bishop and Patience, his wife, was born May 29th, A. D. 1740.

Huldah, the daughter of William Bishop and Patience, his wife, was born June 24th, 1742.

Charles, the son of William Bishop and Patience, his wife, was born July 26th, A. D. 1744.

William, the son of William Bishop and Patience, his wife, was born Aug. 11th, A. D. 1746.

Prudence, the daughter of William Bishop and Patience his wife, was born March 8th, 1749.

Rhoda, the daughter of William Bishop and Patience, his wife, was born March 21st, A. D. 1754

Ruth, the daughter of Joseph Southworth and Mary, his wife, was born Nov 27th, A. D. 1751

Joseph, the son of Joseph Southworth and Mary, his wife, was born Apr. 7th, A. D. 1754.

Elizabeth, the daughter of Stephen Bates, 3d, and Mindwell, his wife, was born Aug. 3d, A. D. 1750.

Keziah, the daughter of Stephen Bates, 3d, and Mindwell, his wife, was born Sep 6th, A. D. 1753.

Lemuel, the son of Stephen Bates, 3d, and Mindwell, his wife, was born Aug 29th, A. D. 1755

Lewis, the son of David Grave and Hannah, his wife, was born Nov. 7th, A. D. 1755

Dan, the son of Gideon Canfield and Ann, his wife, was born June 27th, A. D. 1754.

Abiel Baldwin and Mehethabel Johnson were joined in marriage, Apr. 1st, A. D. 1756

Phebe, the daughter of Charles Brooks and Mehethabel, his wife, was born July 19th, A D. 1755

Lemuel Gurnsey and Ruth Camp were joined in marriage, Dec. 18th, A. D. 1755.

Joseph Frances and Sarah Buek were joined in marriage, Oct. 2d, A. D 1750

Sarah, the wife of Joseph Frances, departed this life, Oct. 11th, A. D. 1753.

Sarah, the daughter of David Curtiss and Thankful, his wife, was born May 7th, A. D 1755.

Hazael Hinman and Ann Torrey were joined in marriage, May 11th, A. D 1756.

Rosanna, the daughter of William Bishop and Patience, his wife, was born July 2d, A. D. 1756.

Ashur, the son of Samuel Hickox and Hannah, his wife, was born June 27th, A. D. 1756

Asa, the son of Charles Brooks and Mehethabel, his wife, was born Nov. 19th, A D 1756.

Content, the daughter of Lemuel Gurnsey and Ruth, his wife, was born Sept. 9th, A. D. 1756.

Mary, the daughter of Charles Squire and Mary, his wife, was born Sept. 4th, A D 1754

Edward Adams, the son of Charles Squire and Mary, his wife, was born Jan. 15th, A. D. 1757.

Miles, the son of Josiah Coe and Sarah, his wife, was born Sept. 24th, A. D 1755

John, the son of Joseph Hull and Sybil, his wife, was born Nov 20th, A. D. 1756.

Mindwell, the daughter of Ephraim Norton and Mary, his wife, was born Oct. 21st, A. D. 1756

Ruth, the daughter of Phineas Robinson and Susanna, his wife, was born Aug. 10th, A. D. 1755

Balah, the daughter of Eliakim Strong and Hannah, his wife, was born March 13th, A. D. 1757.

Hannah, the daughter of Silas Crane, Jun., and Lucretia, his wife, was born Apr 15th, A D 1757.

Rhoda, the daughter of Abiel Baldwin and Mehethable, his wife, was born Jan. 25th, A. D. 1757.

Gad, the son of John Sutlief, Jun., and Lucy, his wife, was born Jan 2d, 1756.

Sarah, the daughter of Hazael Hinman and Ann, his wife, was born Apr. 21st, A. D. 1757.

Abner, the son of Abner Tibbals and Sarah, his wife, was born May 29th, A. D. 1756.

Ashur, the son of Josiah Coe and Sarah, his wife, was born Sept. 9th, A. D 1757.

Sarah, the daughter of Daniel Weld and Elizabeth, his wife, was born Mar. 20th, A D 1752

Elizabeth, the daughter of Daniel Weld and Elizabeth, his wife, was born May 26th, A. D. 1754.

Samuel, the son of Daniel Weld and Elizabeth, his wife, was born March 10th, A. D. 1757.

Sarah, the daughter of Brotherton Seaward and Abigail his wife, was born Aug. 8th, A. D. 1757.

Samuel, the son of Daniel Wright and Lucy, his wife, was born June 22d, A. D. 1757.

Submit, the daughter of John Canfield and Bethiah, his wife, was born Jan. 26th, 1758, and departed this life Jan. 29th, 1758.

Abraham, the son of Lemuel Hand and Hannah, his wife, was born Oct. 17th, A. D. 1751.

Esther, the daughter of Lemuel Hand and Hannah, his wife, was born Feb. 21st, A. D. 1754.

Nathan, the son of Lemuel Hand and Hannah, his wife, was born Sept. 10th, A D. 1756.

Mehethabel, the daughter of Samuel Parsons and Elizabeth, his wife, was born March 5th, A D 1750–1.

Lemuel, the son of Samuel Parsons and Elizabeth, his wife, was born May 2d, A. D. 1753.

Elizabeth, the daughter of Samuel Parsons and Elizabeth, his wife, was born July 14th, A. D. 1756.

Joseph Francis and Martha Porter were joined in marriage, Jan. 26th, A. D. 1758.

Sarah, the daughter of Silas Crane, Jun., and Lucretia, his wife, was born Nov. 7th, A D. 1758.

William, the son of William Clarke and Elizabeth, his wife, was born Nov. 8th, A. D 1758.

Jonathan, the son of Abiel Baldwin and Mehethabel, his wife, was born June 6th, A. D 1758

Justice, the son of Charles Squire and Mary, his wife, was born Nov. 20th, A D 1758.

Enoch, the son of Hazael Hinman and Ann, his wife, was born Dec. 30th, A. D. 1758.

Ashbel, the son of Phebe Crane, was born Dec. 10th, 1757.

Amos Hubbard and Mary Bristol were joined in marriage, June 15th, A. D. 1758.

Hannah, the daughter of John Curtiss and Dinah, his wife, was born Jan. 8th, 1755.

John, the son of John Curtiss and Dinah, his wife, was born May 5th, A. D. 1757.

Samuel Parsons, Jun., and Mary Fenn were joined in marriage, Dec. 1st, 1758.

Samuel Fenn, the son of Samuel Parsons, Jun., and Mary, his wife, was born Jan. 24th, A. D. 1751.

Josiah, the son of Samuel Parsons, Jun., and Mary, his wife, was born July 20th, A D. 1755.

Catharine, the daughter of Samuel Parsons, Jun., and Mary, his wife, was born Aug 30th, A. D. 1757.

Sarah, the daughter of Joseph Parsons and Martha, his wife, was born Jan. 28th, A. D. 1759.

Josiah, the son of Joseph Hull and Sybil, his wife, was born Apr. 4th, A. D. 1759.

Stephen, the son of Abner Tibbals and Sarah, his wife, was born Aug 2d, A. D. 1758.

Bridgman, the son of Lemuel Guernsey and Ruth, his wife, was born June 11th, A. D. 1758.

The children of Benjamin Norton and Elizabeth, of Killingworth, was born as followeth, viz:

Benjamin, July 10th, A. D. 1746; Noahdiah, Aug. 17th, A. D. 1748; Joel, Sep. 17th, 1750; Hannah, Sep. 17th, 1752; Elnathan and Elizabeth, May 10th, 1755; Charity, Sep. 24th, A. D. 1758.

Abigail, the daughter of Joseph Ingham and Abigail, his wife, was born May 13th, A. D. 1745.

Sarah, the daughter of Joseph Ingham and Abigail, his wife, was born Nov. 21st, A. D. 1747.

David, the son of Joseph Ingham and Abigail, his wife, was born Sep. 5th, A. D. 1750.

Samuel, the son of Joseph Ingham and Abigail, his wife, was born June 7th, A. D. 1753.

Benjamin, the son of Joseph Ingham and Abigail, his wife, was born March 29th, A. D 1756.

Mr. Elnathan Chauncey and Elizabeth Gale were joined in marriage, Feb. 6th, 1760.

Abraham, the son of Abraham Bartlet and Submit, his wife was born Apr. 14th, A. D. 1759.

Titus, the son of Joseph Frances and Martha, his wife, was born Aug. 22d, A. D. 1760.

Anne, the daughter of Samuel Squier and Anne, his wife, was born Feb. 20th, A. D. 1759.

Saxton, the son of Samuel Squier and Anne, his wife, was born June 4th, A. D. 1758.

Anne, the daughter of Samuel Squier and Anne, his wife, was born Apr. 30th, A. D. 1760.

Eunice, the daughter of Abiel Baldwin and Mehithabel, his wife, was born Aug. 2d, A. D. 1760.

Joseph Hickox and Martha Willcoks were joined in marriage, Dec. 8th, 1748.

The children of Joseph Hickox and Martha, his wife, was born as follows, (viz.)

Martha, May 24th, A. D. 1750; James, Nov. 23d, A. D. 1751; William, Aug. 31st, A. D. 1753; Rhoda, Oct. 6th, A. D. 1755; Joseph, July 12th, A. D. 1757; Darius, March 8th, A. D. 1759

Mary, the daughter of Miles Merwin and Mary, his wife, was born May 24th, A. D. 1755.

Rhoda, the daughter of Miles Merwin and Mary, his wife, was born Aug. 19th, A. D 1757.

Sarah, the daughter of Miles Merwin and Mary, his wife, was born June 7th, A. D. 1760.

Samuel, the son of Samuel Crittenden and Sarah, his wife, was born Sep. 27th, A. D 1755

Ebenezer, the son of Samuel Crittenden and Sarah, his wife, was born Oct. 18th, A. D. 1757.

Osee, the son of Samuel Crittenden and Sarah, his wife was born Jan. 18th, A D. 1760.

Charles, the son of Abel Coe and Prudence, his wife, was born July 12th, A D. 1760.

Selah, the son of Eliakim Strong and Hannah, his wife, was born Jan. 6th, A. D. 1759.

Eunice, the daughter of Thomas Strong and Phebe, his wife, was born Aug 16th, A. D. 1752

Phebe, the daughter of Thomas Strong and Phebe, his wife, was born Nov 1st, A. D. 1754.

Lorain, the daughter of Thomas Strong and Phebe, his wife, was born March 18th, A. D. 1757.

Katharine, the daughter of Thomas Strong and Phebe, his wife, was born Apr. 14th, 1759.

David Johnson, Jun., and Jerusha Thomas were joined in marriage, March 14th, A. D. 1751, and their children born as follows:

Thomas, Dec. 13th, A. D. 1751; Rebecka, June 7th, A. D. 1753; Timothy, Nov. 12th, A. D. 1754; Jerusha, Sept. 21st, A. D. 1756; Diana, Sept. 24th, A. D. 1758.

The Rev. Mr. Elizur Goodrich and Mrs. Katharine Chauncey were joined in marriage, Feb. 1st, A. D. 1759.

Chauncey, the son of the Rev. Mr. Elizur Goodrich and Katharine, his wife, was born Oct. 20th, A. D. 1759.

Elizabeth, the daughter of Jonathan Wells and Mary, his wife, was born June 25th, A. D. 1744.

Rhoda, the daughter of Jonathan Wells and Mary, his wife, was born July 15th, A. D. 1746.

Rachel, the daughter of Jonathan Wells and Mary, his wife, was born Sept. 24th, A. D. 1749.

Mehithabel, the daughter of Jonathan Wells and Mary his wife, was born Sept. 9th, A. D. 1751

Jonathan the son of Jonathan Wells and Mary his wife, was born Jan. 24th, A. D. 1754.

Samuel Squier and Anne Bishop were joined in marriage, Sep. 30th, A. D 1756.

Benjamin Gillum and Elizabeth Seward were joined in marriage, June 26th, A. D. 1754.

Rachel, the daughter of Benjamin Gillum and Elizabeth, his wife, was born July 12th, A. D. 1754.

Elizabeth, the daughter of Benjamin Gillum and Elizabeth, his wife, was born May 24th, A. D. 1757.

Sarah, the daughter of Benjamin Gillum and Elizabeth, his wife, was born Apr. 24th, 1759.

Sarah, the daughter of Simeon Coe and Anna, his wife, was born March 4th, A. D. 1757.

Lois, the daughter of John Curtiss and Dinah, his wife, was born July 15th, A. D 1760.

Elizabeth, the daughter of Jane Lewis, was born May 28th, 1755.

David, the son of Jane Lewis, was born July 10th, A. D. 1758.

Rachel, the daughter of Jane Lewis, was born Dec. 18th, A. D. 1760.

Elah Camp and Phebe Baldwin were joined in marriage, May 14th, A. D. 1760.

Samuel Seward and Rebecca Rossetter were joined in marriage, May 17th, A. D. 1739.

The children of Samuel Seward and Rebeckah, his wife, were born as follows, (viz:)

Samuel, was born Apr. 1st, A. D. 1740.

Timothy, was born Aug. 30th, A. D. 1741, and dyed Aug. 2d, A. D. 1759.

Rebecca, was born Oct. 2d, A. D. 1743

Ashur, was born Oct. 14th, A. D. 1745.

Rachel, was born July 11th, A. D. 1750.

Daniel, the son of Ephraim Coe, Jun., and Ann, his wife, was born Aug. 4th, A. D. 1755.

Ann, the daughter of Ephraim Coe and Ann, his wife, was born Sept. 5th, A D. 1757.

Timothy, the son of Ephraim Coe and Ann, his wife, was born Sept. 16th, A. D. 1760.

Samuel Seaward and Abigail Hull were joined in marriage, May 7th, A. D. 1760.

Elihu Crane and Mary Fowler were joined in marriage, Apr. 26th, A. D 1759.

Miles, the son of Elihu Crane and Mary, his wife, was born Feb 18th, A. D. 1761.

Sarah, the daughter of Col. Elihu Chauncey and Mary, his wife, was born May 8th, A. D. 1745.

Charles, the son of Col. Elihu Chauncey and Mary, his wife, was born May 30th, A. D. 1747.

Seth, the son of David Fowler and Elizabeth, his wife, was born Jan. 1st, A. D. 1744.

Amos, the son of David Fowler and Elizabeth, his wife, was born Aug 1st, A. D. 1752.

Abiathar, the son of David Fowlor and Elizabeth, his wife, was born Aug. 31st, A. D. 1754.

Silas, the son of Brotherton Seaward and Abigail, his wife, was born Feb. 4th, A. D 1760

Samuel Camp and Phebe Coe were joined in marriage, Sept. 3d, A. D. 1756

Statira, the daughter of Samuel Camp and Phebe, his wife, was born Jan. 9th, A. D. 1757

Ozias, the son of Samuel Camp and Phebe, his wife, was born Dec 26th, A. D. 1758.

Elnathan Camp and Eunice Talcott were joined in marriage, May 23d, A. D. 1759.

Eunice, the daughter of Elnathan Camp and Eunice, his wife, was born Apr 25th, A. D. 1760.

John Camp, Jun., and Damaris Strong were joined in marriage, A. D 1730.

Elnathan, the son of John Camp, Jun., and Damaris, his wife, was born Jan. 24th, A. D. 1734–5.

Urania, the daughter of John Camp, Jun., and Damaris, his wife, was born Aug 14th, A. D. 1737.

Damaris, the wife of John Camp, Jun., departed this life, Aug. 25th, A. D. 1737.

John Camp, Jun., and Sarah Merwin were joined in marriage, July 11th, A. D. 1739.

Sarah, the wife of John Camp, Jun, departed this life, Jan. 14th, A. D. 1740–1.

John Camp, Jun., and Jerusha Parmalee were joined in marriage, March 17th, A. D. 1742.

Phinehas, the son of John Camp, Jun., and Damaris, his wife, dyed Oct. 7th, A. D. 1743.

Phinehas, the son of John Camp, Jun., and Jerusha, his wife, was born Jan. 13th, A. D. 1744–5.

Jerusha, the wife of John Camp, Jun., departed this life, Jan. 22d, A D. 1744–5.

John Camp, Jun., and Abigail Field were joined in marriage, Apr 13th, A. D. 1749.

Ruth, the daughter of Abner Tibbals and Sarah, his wife, was born May 3d, A. D. 1761.

Jess Austin and Elizabeth Ward were joined in marriage, Jan. 26th, A. D 1758.

Abigail, the daughter of Jess Austin and Elizabeth, his wife, was born Dec. 4th, A D. 1758, and dyed Sept. 12th, A. D 1760.

Nabe, the daughter of Jess Austin and Elizabeth, his wife, was born March 7th, A. D. 1761.

Elizur, the son of the Rev. Mr. Elizur Goodrich and Katharine, his wife, was born March 24th, A D 1761.

Abigail, the daughter of Benj'n Gillum and Elizabeth, his wife, was born May 29th, A. D. 1761.

Samuel, the son of Samuel Camp and Phebe, his wife, was born June 2d, A. D. 1761.

Nathaniel William, the son of Mr. Elnathan Chauncey and Elizabeth, his wife, was born Sept. 12th, 1761.

James Curtiss, Jun , and Hannah Bull were joined in marriage, Sept. 12th, A. D. 1734.

Nathan, the son of James Curtiss, Jun., and Hannah, his wife, was born June 23d, A. D. 1735.

Aaron, the son of James Curtiss, Jun., and Hannah, his wife, was born Sept. 9th, A. D. 1737.

Nathan Curtiss and Anna Booth were joined in marriage, May 13th, A. D. 1761.

James, the son of John Jones and Hannah, his wife, was born Oct. 16th, A. D. 1758.

Moses Seward and Sarah Thomas were joined in marriage, Apr. 9th, A. D. 1761.

Olive, the son of William Clarke and Elizabeth, his wife, was born Sept. 5th, A. D. 1761.

Noah Baldwin and Mehitabel Parmalee were joined in marriage, July 30th, A. D. 1760.

Phebe, the daughter of Noah Baldwin and Mehitabel, his wife, was born June 3d, A. D. 1761, and died June 4th, A. D. 1761.

Eunice, the daughter of Simon Coe and Anna, his wife, was born Jan. 14th, 1762.

Enos, the son of Silas Crane, Jun., and Lucretia, his wife, was born Feb. 13th, A. D. 1762.

Seth, the son of Eliakim Strong and Hannah, his wife, was born May 8th, A. D 1761

Hannah, the daughter of Hazael Hinman and Ann, his wife, was born June 27th, A. D. 1760.

Ruth, the daughter of Elah Camp and Phebe, his wife, was born Aug 8th, A. D. 1761.

Caleb Fowler and Anne Rose were joined in marriage, Jan. 10th, A. D. 1759.

Anne, the daughter of Caleb Fowler and Anne, his wife, was born Oct. 28th, A. D. 1761.

Bethiah, the daughter of John Canfield and Bethiah, his wife, was born Feb. 4th, A. D. 1762.

John Crane and Abigail Camp were joined in marriage, Apr. 7th, A. D. 1762.

The children of Stephen Bate, Jun., and Lois, his wife, were born as follows, (viz :)

Phinehas, was born July 26th, A. D. 1749; Linus, was born Sept. 6th, A. D. 1751; Lois, was born Jan. 7th, 1754; Phebe, was born Feb. 4th, A D. 1756; Stephen, was born July 10th, 1762.

Lament, the daughter of Lois Bate was born Jan. 7th, 1762.

David Squier and Huldah Bishop were joined in marriage, Feb. 9th, 1761.

Phinehas, the son of David Squier and Huldah, his wife, was born Apr. 13th, A. D. 1761.

Abigail, the daughter of Joseph Francis and Martha, his wife, was born July 3d, A. D. 1762.

Daniel Dimock and Thankful Merriman were joined in marriage, May 27th, A. D 1762.

Ichabod, the son of Abraham Scranton and Elenor, his wife, was born Aug. 31st, A. D. 1762.

Sarah, the daughter of John Curtiss and Dinah, his wife, was born Oct. 11th, A. D. 1762.

Abiel, the son of Abiel Baldwin and Mehitabel, his wife, was born Aug. 28th, A. D. 1762.

Jonas Bishop and Phebe Crane were joined in marriage, Jan. 20th, A. D. 1763.

Clarissa, the daughter of John Crane and Abigail, his wife, was born July 31st, A. D. 1762.

Elihu, the son of Elihu Crane and Mary, his wife, was born Jan 18th, A. D 1763.

Statira, the daughter of Jehiel Hull and Ruth, his wife, was born Jan. 25th, A. D. 1759.

David, the son of Miles Merwin and Mary, his wife, was born Feb. 10th, A. D. 1763.

James, the son of Jess Austin and Elizabeth, his wife, was born March 5th, A. D. 1763.

Samuel, the son of Rev. Mr. Elizur Goodrich and Mrs. Katharine, his wife, was born Jan. 12th, A. D. 1763.

Hannah, the daughter of Joseph Hull and Sybil, his wife, was born June 5th, A. D. 1761.

Ashur Robinson and Margery Butcher were joined in marriage, June 11th, A. D. 1761.

Rachel, the daughter of Ashur Robinson and Margery, his wife, was born Apr. 16th, A D. 1762.

Stephen, the son of Eliakim Strong and Hannah, his wife, was born May 8th, 1763, and departed this life, June 4th, A. D. 1763.

Hezekiah Parmalee and Mehitabel Hall were joined in marriage, Apr. 18th, 1737, and their children were born as follows, (viz:)

Hannah, Apr 14th, A. D. 1738; Simeon, Aug. 3d, A. D. 1740; Mehithabel, Aug. 31st, A. D 1742; Hezekiah, June 20th, 1745; Dan, May 15th, A. D. 1748; Moses, Apr. 15th, A. D. 1751, and Charles, Sept. 17th, A. D. 1753.

Mehithabel, the wife of Hezekiah Parmalee, departed this life, Feb. 14th, A. D. 1755.

Hezekiah Parmalee and Mercy Smith were joined in marriage, June 10th, A. D. 1756.

James, the son of Hezekiah Parmalee and Mercy, his wife, was born July 15th, A. D. 1757, and dyed Nov. 30th, A. D. 1759.

Erastus, the son of Israel Godard and Ann, his wife, was born March 27th, A. D. 1748

Israel, the son of Israel Goddard and Ann, his wife, was born Jan. 30th, A. D. 1750.

Anne, the daughter of Israel Goddard and Ann, his wife, was born Oct. 16th, A. D. 1752.

Eunice, the daughter of Ezra Rockwell and Jemima, his wife, was born May 21st, A. D. 1763.

Eunice, the daughter of Elnathan Camp and Eunice, his wife, died March 31st, A. D. 1762.

Talcott, the son of Elnathan Camp and Eunice, his wife, was born March 4th, A D. 1762.

Damaris, the daughter of Elnathan Camp and Eunice, his wife, was born March 4th, A. D 1762, and died March 30th, 1762.

Ozias, the son of Stephen Norton and Abigail, his wife, was born Dec 31st, A. D. 1759.

Lyman, the son of Stephen Norton and Abigail, his wife, was born June 1st, A. D. 1763.

Silas, the son of Silas Crane and Lucretia, his wife, was born Dec 13th, A. D. 1763.

Oorondates, the son of John Crane and Abigail, his wife, was born Nov. 10th, A. D. 1763.

Canfield, the son of Ephraim Coe, Jun, and Ann, his wife, was born Sept. 26th, A. D. 1763.

Paul, the son of Samuel Parsons and Elizabeth, his wife, was born Jan. 17th, A. D 1762.

Aaron Coe and Phebe Parsons were joined in marriage, Nov. 28th, A. D. 1754.

Ithamar, the son of Aaron Coe and Phebe, his wife, was born Sept. 10th, A. D. 1755.

Simeon Parsons, Jun, and Eunice Rossetter were joined in marriage, March 16th, A. D. 1758.

Hezekiah Talcott departed this life, Feb. 18th, 1764.

Ashur, the son of Benjamin Gillum and Elizabeth, his wife, was born Dec. 4th, A. D. 1763, and dyed Jan. 4th, A. D. 1764.

Lucretia, the daughter of Joseph Frances and Martha, his wife, was born Apr. 24th, A. D. 1764.

Submit, the daughter of Abraham Bartlet and Submit, his wife, was born Apr. 10th, A. D. 1764.

Silas, the son of Joseph Hull and Sibil, his wife, was born May 26th, A D. 1764.

Thankful, the daughter of Daniel Dimock and Thankful, his wife, was born June 22d, A. D. 1763.

Katharine, the daughter of Samuel Squier and Ann, his wife, was born Apr. 5th, A. D. 1762, and died June 8th, A. D. 1762

Samuel, the son of Samuel Squier and Ann, his wife, was born May 16th, A. D. 1763.

Lucy, the daughter of Oliver Bate and Lois, his wife, was born Jan. 25th, A. D. 1756.

Hinsdel, the son of Oliver Bate and Lois, his wife, was born Dec. 25th, 1757.

Rhoda, the daughter of Oliver Bate and Lois, his wife, was born Sept. 1st, A. D. 1760.

Ebenezer, the son of Samuel Camp and Phebe, his wife, was born Nov. 28th, A. D. 1763.

Henry Seaward departed this life May 10th, 1764.

Elihu, the son of Rev. Mr. Elizur Goodrich and Katharine, his wife, was born Sept. 16th, A. D. 1764.

Mehithabel, the daughter of Abiel Baldwin and Mehithabel, his wife, was born May 21st, 1764.

Lois, the daughter of Eliakin Strong and Hannah, his wife, was born May 29th, A. D. 1764.

Sarah, the wife of Daniel Merwin, departed this life, Sept. 23d, 1764.

Eunice, the daughter of Elnathan Camp and Eunice, his wife, was born June 23d, A. D. 1764.

John, the son of Samuel Crittenden and Sarah, his wife, was born Oct. 27th, A. D. 1761.

Medad, the son of Samuel Crittenden and Sarah, his wife, was born May 23d, A. D. 1764.

Torry, the son of Sarah Torry, was born Oct. 6th, 1761.

Patrick Nief and Lucy Richardson were joined in marriage, Aug. 4th, A. D. 1764.

John, the son of Patrick Nief and Lucy, his wife, was born Dec 30th, A. D. 1764.

Reuben Bishop and Anne Wright were joined in marriage, March 9th, A. D. 1758.

Joel, the son of Reuben Bishop and Anne, his wife, was born Oct. 2d, A D. 1759.

Reuben, the son of Reuben Bishop and Anne, his wife, was born June 4th, A. D. 1762.

Anne, the wife of Reuben Bishop, departed this life, Jan. 17th, A. D. 1765.

Samuel, the son of Abner Tibbals and Sarah, his wife, was born March 9th, A. D. 1765.

Abiathar, the son of Elihu Crane and Mary, his wife, was born Jan 29th, A. D. 1765.

Aaron, the son of Zachariah Hinman and Hannah, his wife, was born Jan. 6th, O. S., A. D. 1740.

Jared Whedon and Sarah Chipman were joined in marriage, May 24th, A. D. 1764.

Elizabeth, the daughter of Jared Whedon and Sarah, his wife, was born Apr. 28th, A. D. 1765.

Ashur, the son of Benjamin Gillum and Elizabeth, his wife, was born Apr. 13th, A. D. 1765.

Rejoice, the son of Israel Camp and Ann, his wife, was born Oct. 23d, A. D. 1759.

Sarah, the daughter of Israel Camp and Ann, his wife, was born Apr. 30th, A. D. 1763.

Ann, the wife of Israel Camp, departed this life, March 18th, A. D. 1765.

Catharine, the daughter of Samuel Squier, and Ann, his wife, was born July 21st, A. D. 1765.

Stephen, the son of Ashur Robinson and Margery, his wife, was born Jan. 14th, A. D. 1764.

David, the son of Samuel Parsons, Jun., and Mary, his wife, was born Oct. 1st, A. D. 1758.

Daniel Merwin, Jun., departed this life, May 15th, 1758.

Hannah, the daughter of Noah Baldwin and Mehcthabel, his wife, was born Dec. 15th, A. D. 1762, and died Feb. 4th, A. D. 1763.

Phebe, the daughter of Noah Baldwin and Mahethabel, his wife, was born Dec. 4th, A. D. 1763, and died Dec. 31st, A. D. 1763.

Nathan Ozias, the son of Elah Camp and Phebe, his wife, was born Feb. 10th, A. D. 1763.

Elias, the son of Elah Camp and Phebe, his wife, was born Aug. 28th, A. D. 1765.

Joel Parmalee and Rhoda Camp were joined in marriage, Jan 6th, A. D. 1742–3, and their children were born as follows, (viz:)

Eliphaz, Dec 27th, A. D. 1743; Levi, June 22d, A. D. 1745; Mary, May 27th, A. D. 1747; Jerusha, Aug. 15th, A D 1749; Rhoda, Feb. 1st, A. D. 1752; Rosanna, March 5th, 1754; Rachel, Apr. 24th, A. D. 1756; Joel, Aug 6th, A. D. 1758; Hannah, Sept. 2d, A. D. 1761; Camp, March 17th, A D. 1765.

Hannah, the daughter of John Norton, Jun., and Hannah, his wife, was born May 7th, A. D. 1758.

Rebeckah, the daughter of John Norton Jun., and Hannah, his wife, was born Nov. 20th, A. D. 1759.

John, the son of John Norton, Jun., and Hannah, his wife, was born June 10th, A. D 1763.

Lucy, the daughter of John Norton, Jun , and Hannah, his wife, was born Sept. 27th, A. D. 1765

Concurrence, the daughter of Joseph Frances and Martha, his wife, was born Feb. 17th, A. D. 1766.

Lieut Joseph Seward departed this life, Nov. 19th, 1764.

Zeleck, the son of John Crane and Abigail, his wife, was born Feb 23d, A. D. 1766.

Beriah Murry and Mary Meeker were joined in marriage, July 21st, A. D. 1765.

Sabra, the daughter of Beriah Murry and Mary, his wife, was born Aug. 24th, A D. 1765.

David, the son of David Squier and Huldah, his wife, was born Oct 8th, A. D 1762.

Thaddeus, the son of David Squier and Hulda, his wife, was born Aug. 19th, A. D. 1764.

Daniel Merwin departed this life Apr. 11th, A. D. 1766.

Oorondates, the son of John Crane and Abigail, his wife, died May 12th, A. D. 1766.

Sarah, the daughter of Daniel Dimock and Thankful, his wife, was born May 9th, 1766.

Dinah, the daughter of John Curtiss and Dinah, his wife, was born Jan. 21st, A D. 1766.

Olive, the daughter of Abraham Bartlett and Submit, his wife, was born June 6th, A. D. 1766.

Ashur, the son of Ashur Robinson and Margaret, his wife, was born Nov. 21st, A. D. 1765.

Rhoda, the daughter of Abiel Baldwin and Mehethabel, his wife, died May 30th, A. D. 1766.

Curtiss, the son of Abiel Baldwin and Mehethabel, his wife, was born June 20th, A. D. 1766.

Samuel Hart and Abredgget Fowler were joined in marriage, Oct 9th, 1759.

Mary, the daughter of Samuel Hart and Abredgget, his wife, was born June 24th, A. D. 1762.

Samuel, the son of Samuel Hart and Abredgget, his wife, was born Feb. 23d, A. D 1764.

Ruth, the daughter of Samuel Hart and Abredgget, his wife, was born June 8th, A. D. 1766.

Mehitabel, the wife of Simeon Parsons, departed this life, Aug. 9th, A. D 1766.

Mary, the daughter of Silas Crane and Lucretia, his wife, was born Nov. 27th, 1766.

Sutlief, the son of Moses Seaward and Sarah, his wife, was born March 25th, A D. 1762.

Moses, the son of Moses Seaward and Sarah, his wife, was born Jan. 11th, A. D. 1764.

Seth, the son of Moses Seaward and Sarah, his wife, was born Apr. 15th, A. D. 1766.

Sarah, the daughter of Noah Baldwin and Mehethabel, his wife, was born Nov. 13th, 1765.

Sarah, the daughter of Samuel Camp and Phebe, his wife, was born Sept. 26th, 1766.

Daniel, the son of Ezra Rockwell and Jemima, his wife, was born Dec. 11th, A. D 1765.

Samuel, the son of Jared Whedon and Sarah, his wife, was born Dec. 27th, A. D. 1766.

Phebe, the daughter of Hezekiah Talcott and Sarah, his wife, was born May 29th, A. D. 1766.

Hezekiah Talcott and Sarah Johnson were joined in marriage, March 28th, A. D. 1765.

James Arnold and Tabitha Parsons were joined in marriage, Feb. 27th, A. D. 1765.

Rhoda, the daughter of Lemuel Gurnsey and Ruth, his wife, was born Feb. 24th, A D 1760, and died Dec. 4th, A. D. 1760.

Lemuel, the son of Lemuel Gurnsey and Ruth, his wife, was born Jan. 8th, A. D. 1762.

Ebenezer, the son of Lemuel Gurnsey and Ruth, his wife, was born Feb. 3d, A. D. 1764.

Rhoda, the daughter of Lemuel Gurnsey and Ruth, his wife, was born Dec. 6th, 1765.

Jesse Cook and Ruth Fairchild were joined in marriage, Oct. 22d, A. D. 1760.

Millecent, the daughter of Jesse and Ruth Fairchild, was born Nov. 19th, A. D. 1761.

Robert, their son was born March 11th, A. D. 1763.

Sarah, their daughter was born Jan. 17th, A. D. 1765.

Ruth, the wife of Jesse Cook departed this life, Apr. 5th, A. D. 1766.

Jesse Cook and Rhoda Talcott were joined in marriage, Oct. 27th, A. D. 1766.

John Camp departed this life, Jan. 6th, A. D. 1767.

Israel Camp and Mary Gurnsey were joined in marriage, Dec. 24th, A. D. 1766.

The children of Job Camp and Rachel his wife, were born as follows, (viz:)

Aaron, born Feb. 18th, A. D. 1755

Gad, born Jan. 3d, A. D. 1757.

Rachel, born Dec. 13th, A. D. 1758.

Manoah, born Dec. 31st, A. D. 1760.

Jerusha, born March 19th, A. D. 1763.

Luke, born July 28th, A. D. 1765.

Immer, the son of Samuel Crittenden and Sarah, his wife, was born March 17th, A. D. 1766.

Joseph Ingham and Mehithabel Brown were joined in marriage, Aug 19th, 1767.

Lucy, ye daughter of John Norton, Jun., and Hannah, his wife, died Nov. 20th, A D 1766.

Nathan, the son of Thomas Strong and Phebe, his wife, was born Jan. 3d, A. D. 1762, and died Apr. 28th, 1763.

Lucy, ye daughter of Thomas Strong and Phebe, his wife, was born March 4th, A. D. 1764.

Nathan, the son of Thomas Strong and Phebe, his wife, was born Oct. 13th, A. D. 1766, and died Nov. 23d, A. D. 1767.

Samuel Norton departed this life July 13th, A. D. 1767.

Daniel Hall, Jun., and Ann Crane were joined in marriage, Sept. 21st, A. D. 1766.

Luther, the son of Daniel Hall, Jun., and Ann, his wife, was born Feb. 3d, A. D. 1767.

Reuben Rose, the son of Caleb Fowler and Anne, his wife, was born June 17th, A. D. 1763

Irene, the daughter of Caleb Fowler and Anne, his wife, was born Nov 5th, A. D. 1764.

Ozias, the son of Caleb Fowler and Anne, his wife, was born July 25th, A. D. 1766; died Apr. 14th, 1767.

Clarinda, the daughter of Elihu Crane and Mary, his wife, was born Nov. 23d, A. D. 1767.

Stephen, the son of Eliakim Strong and Hannah, his wife, was born May 12th, 1766, and died Sept 26th, 1767.

The children of Rowland Rossetter and Mary, his wife, were born as follows, (viz:)

Catharine, born March 6th, A. D. 1767.

Bryan, born Sept. 6th, A. D. 1760.

Eunice, born Sept. 9th, A. D. 1764.

Rhoda, the wife of Capt. Ebenezer Gurnsey, departed this life, Oct. 14th, A. D. 1767.

Mr. Henry Crane departed this life Feb. 1st, 1768.

Dr. Amos Hubbard departed this life Nov. 15th, 1767.

Joseph Wright, Jun., and Sarah Bishop were joined in marriage, Dec. 17th, 1767.

David Talcott and Anne Lyman were joined in marriage, Sept. 17th, 1767.

Tryphene, ye daughter of David Squier and Huldah, his wife, was born Nov. 9th, A. D. 1766.

Samuel Doan Cook and Rebeckah Picket were joined in marriage, Dec. 4th, A. D 1766.

Noah, ye son of Samuel Doan Cook and Rebeckah, his wife, was born Dec. 11th, 1767.

Salle, ye daughter of John Norton, Jun., and Hannah, was born Dec. 10th, A. D. 1767.

Israel, the son of Israel Camp and Mary, his wife, was born Jan. 29th, A. D. 1768.

Elah, the son of Elah Camp and Phebe, his wife, was born Feb. 11th, A. D. 1768.

Nathan, the son of Benj. Gillum and Elizabeth, his wife, was born Nov. 4th, A. D. 1767.

Rachel, the daughter of Joseph Frances and Martha, his wife, was born July 2d, 1768.

Patte, the daughter of Daniel Dimock and Thankful, his wife, was born May 7th, 1768.

Elenor, the daughter of Silas Crane and Lucretia, his wife, was born Sept. 19th, 1768.

David, the son of Elnathan Camp and Eunice, his wife, was born Sept. 23d, A. D. 1766.

David, the son of Abial Baldwin and Mehithabel, his wife, was born Nov. 23d, A. D. 1768.

Edmund, the son of Jesse Cook and Rhoda, his wife, was born Nov. 17th, A. D. 1767, and died Feb. 17th, A. D. 1768.

Charles Augustus, the son of Rev. Mr. Elizur Goodrich and Katharine, his wife, was born March 2d A. D. 1768.

Elizabeth, the daughter of Daniel Hall, Jun., and Ann, his wife, was born Dec. 25th, A. D. 1768.

The children of Thomas Lyman and Anne, his wife, were born as follows, (viz:)

Sarah, was born May 29th, A. D. 1741.

Elizabeth, was born March 4th, A. D. 1744.

Thomas, was born Feb 14th, A. D. 1746.

Anne, was born Jan. 10th, A. D. 1748.

Abel, was born Feb. 12th, A. D. 1750.

James, was born June 10th, A. D. 1753.

Daniel, was born Jan. 27th, A. D. 1756.

Thomas Lyman departed this life Apr. 20th, A. D. 1761

Noah, the son of David Talcott and Anne, his wife, was born Aug. 7th, A. D. 1768.

Melinda, the daughter of Aaron Hinman and Elizabeth, his wife, was born Apr. 15th, A. D. 1766.

Rebeckah, the daughter of Heth Camp and Mary, his wife, was born July 26th, A. D. 1768.

Mary, the daughter of Robert Crane and Mary, his wife, was born Aug. 7th, A. D. 1767.

Robert, the son of Robert Crane and Mary, his wife, was born Nov. 12th, A. D. 1768.

Abel, the son of Abel Coe and Prudence, his wife, was born July 20th, A. D. 1768.

Israel, the son of Rhoda Wells, was born Apr. 29th, A. D. 1766.

Hannah Seaward departed this life Apr. 23d, A D. 1769.

Sarah, the daughter of Josiah Coe and Hannah, his wife, was born March 5th, A D 1762.

Hannah, the daughter of Josiah Coe and Hannah, his wife, was born May 1st, A. D. 1766

Cornelius Hull and Abigail Chipman were married, Jan. 1st, A. D. 1746.

The children of Cornelius Hull and Abigail, his wife, were born as follows, (viz:)

Sylvanus, was born Oct. 13th, A. D. 1746.

Cornelius, was born Mar. 5th, A. D. 1748.

Abigail, was born July 26th, A. D. 1749.

Samuel, was born Dec. 10th, A. D. 1752.

Ann, was born Feb. 3d, A. D. 1755.

Huldah, was born March 6th, A. D. 1758.

Charles, was born May 5th, A. D. 1760.

Giles, was born July 4th, A. D. 1762

Concurrence, ye daughter of Jared Whedon and Sarah, his wife, was born Apr. 19th, 1769.

John Seaward, of Durham, and Sarah Burr, of Haddam, were joined in marriage, May 10th, A. D. 1769.

Elam, the son of John Crane and Abigail, his wife, was born July 23d, A. D. 1768.

Ambrose Field and Sarah Bate were joined in marriage, Sept. 17th, A. D. 1767.

John Edwards, the son of Samuel Wilkinson and Sarah, his wife, was born Apr. 2d, A. D. 1766.

Ruth, the daughter of Jesse Cook and Rhoda, his wife, was born July 27th, A. D. 1769.

Amaziah, the son of Richard Lucas and Sarah his wife, was born July ——, A. D. 1764.

Salle, the daughter of Richard Lucas and Sarah, his wife, was born March 2d, A. D. 1767.

Sarah, the daughter of Moses Seaward and Sarah, his wife, was born June 3d, A. D. 1769.

Phebe, the daughter of Joseph Hull and Sybil, his wife, was born Jan. 21st, A. D. 1769.

Mr. Joseph Tibbals and Mrs. Elizabeth Lane were joined in marriage, Oct., A. D. 1752.

Sally, the daughter of Joseph Wright, Jun., and Sarah, his wife, was born Dec. 3d, A. D. 1769.

Ebenezer Tibbals and Submit Seaward were joined in marriage, May 23d, A. D. 1754

The children of Ebenezer Tibbals and Submit, his wife, were born as follows, (viz:)

Ebenezer, was born Oct. 16th, A. D. 1755.

Phebe, was born May 7th, A. D. 1757.

Submit, was born May 8th, A. D. 1759.

Abigail, was born March 22d, A. D. 1761.

Mary, was born Apr. 30th, A. D. 1763.

Hannah, was born July 22d, A. D. 1765.

Stephen, was born June 23d, A. D. 1767.

Samuel, was born June 18th, A. D. 1769.

Timothy Stow and Rebeckah Meeker were joined in marriage, June 13th, A. D. 1769.

David, the son of Elnathan Camp and Eunice, his wife, was born Sept. 23d, A. D. 1766.

Damaris, the daughter of Elnathan Camp and Eunice, his wife, was born Dec. 21st, A. D. 1768.

Elah, the son of Elah Camp and Phebe, his wife, was born Feb. 11th, A. D 1768.

Daniel Merwin and Rebeckah Seaward were joined in marriage, Dec. 14th, A. D. 1769.

Jonathan Wackley and Anne Bates were joined in marriage, Sep. 17th, A. D. 1767.

Hannah, the daughter of Jonathan Wackley and Anne, his wife, was born Jan. 18th, A. D. 1769

James, the son of Jonah Frisbee and Elizabeth, his wife, was born July 31st, A. D. 1771.

Phinehas Camp and Martha Hall were joined in marriage, Jan. 8th, A. D. 1767.

Seth, the son of Phinehas Camp and Martha, his wife, was born May 31st, A. D. 1767.

Daniel, the son of Phinehas Camp and Martha, his wife, was born Dec. 4th, A. D. 1768.

Lieut. Nathaniel Seward departed this life, Apr. 2d, 1770.

Samuel Bartlett and Abigail Ingham were joined in marriage, June 16th, A. D. 1768.

Samuel, the son of Samuel Bartlet and Abigail, his wife, was born Apr. 23d, A. D. 1769.

Nathaniel, the son of John Seaward and Sarah, his wife, was born May 21st, A. D. 1770.

Nathan, the son of Thomas Strong and Phebe, his wife, was born June 29th, A. D. 1769.

Moses Griswold and Ann Smithson were joined in marriage, Feb. 3d, A. D. 1768.

Jared, the son of Moses Griswold and Ann, his wife, was born March 13th, A. D. 1769.

Moses Griswold departed this life, Sept. 30th, A. D. 1770.

Ezra, the son of Elah Camp and Phebe, his wife, was born Oct. 31st, A. D. 1770.

Lemuel, the son of Israel Camp and Mary, his wife, was born Nov. 15th, A. D. 1770.

Aaron, the son of Abial Baldwin and Mehitabel, his wife, was born Nov. 8th, A. D. 1770.

Thomas Canfield departed this life Nov. 25th, 1770.

Lieut. John Norton departed this life, Nov. 4th, 1770.

Miles Merwin, Jun., and Mary Parmele were joined in marriage, Nov 4th, A. D. 1767.

Jerusha, the daughter of Miles Merwin, Jun., and Mary, his wife, was born Aug. 27th, A. D. 1768.

Eunice, the daughter of Miles Merwin, Jun, and Mary, his wife, was born Apr. 27th, A. D. 1770.

Daniel, the son of Daniel Merwin and Rebeckah, his wife, was born Sept. 29th, A. D. 1770.

Robert, the son of Ambrose Field and Sarah, his wife, was born June 10th, A. D 1770.

Eli Crane and Mehitabel Chapman were joined in marriage, Jan. 18th, A. D. 1768.

Mehitabel, the daughter of Eli Crane and Mehitabel, his wife, was born Nov. 15th, A D. 1768.

Eli, the son of Eli Crane and Mehitabel, his wife, was born July 9th, A. D. 1770.

Phebe, ye daughter of Samuel Doan Cook and Rebeckah, his wife, was born May 6th, A D. 1769.

Nathan, the son of the Rev. Mr. Elizur Goodrich and Katharine, his wife, was born Aug 1st, A. D 1770.

Lewis, the son of Stephen Norton and Abigail, his wife, was born Apr. 28th, A D 1766, and departed this life, Jan. 8th, A. D. 1770.

Mary, the daughter of Samuel Parsons, Jun., and Abigail, his wife, was born Oct. 23d, A. D. 1770.

Miranda, the daughter of John Crane and Abigail, his wife, was born Jan. 20th, A. D. 1771.

Chipman, the son of Jared Whedon and Sarah, his wife, was born Feb. 9th, A. D 1771

Charles, the son of Ephraim Seaward and Abigail, his wife, was born Sept. 14th, A. D. 1750.

Lydia, the daughter of Ephraim Seaward and Abigail, his wife, was born Jan. 18th, A. D. 1753.

Abigail, the daughter of Ephraim Seward and Abigail, his wife, was born March 8th, A. D. 1758.

Jonah Frisbie and Elizabeth Hickox were joined in marriage, Sept. 27th, A. D. 1758.

The children of Jonah Frisbie and Elizabeth, his wife, were born as follows, (viz:)

Thaddeus Grannice, was born Jan. 5th, A. D. 1760.

Elizabeth, was born Feb. 23d, A. D. 1761.

Rachel, was born Aug. 27th, A. D. 1763.

Jonah, was born Aug. 25th, A. D. 1765.

Dorcas, was born June 10th, A. D. 1767.

Timothy, was born Apr. 20th, A. D. 1769.

Timothy Hall departed this life, July 29th, 1771.

Jeremiah Butler and Anna Coe were joined in marriage, Sept. 20th, A. D. 1769.

Polly, the daughter of Jeremiah Butler and Anna, his wife, was born March 18th, A. D 1770.

Jeremiah, the son of Jeremiah Butler and Anna, his wife, was born May 4th, A. D. 1771.

Benjamin Picket and Adah Camp were joined in marriage, Dec. 5th, A. D. 1758.

The children of Benjamin Pickett and Adah, his wife, were born as follows, (viz:)

Ruth, was born Nov. 19th, A. D. 1759.

Adah, was born Dec. 22d, A. D. 1760, and died June 29th, 1765

Ozias, was born Dec. 7th, A. D. 1762.

Hannah, was born Mar. 4th, A. D. 1764.

Benjamin, was born July 19th, A. D. 1765.

Adah, was born Sept. 11th, A. D 1766.

Rhoda, was born Sept. 7th, A. D. 1768.

Joseph, was born Sept. 13th, A. D. 1769.

Dolle, the daughter of Ann Allen, was born Feb. 13th, A. D. 1771.

Lucretia, the daughter of Silas Crane and Lucretia, his wife, was born July 19th, 1772.

Nathan Seaward and Rachel Gillum were joined in marriage, May 6th, A. D. 1772.

Jerusha, the daughter of Daniel Hall, 3d, and Elizabeth, his wife, was born Aug. 4th, A. D. 1772.

The children of Jeremiah Griswold and Sarah, his wife, were born as follows, (viz:)

Notwithstanding, was born Apr. 16th, A D. 1764.

Rosamond and Rosetta, were born Oct. 20th, A. D 1766.

Samuel, was born May 29th, A. D. 1769.

Henry, the son of Daniel Hall, Jun., and Ann, his wife, was born Dec. 3d, A. D. 1771.

Ruth, the daughter of Abial Baldwin and Mehitabel, his wife, was born Oct. 30th, A. D. 1772.

Polly, the daughter of Daniel Whitmore and Sarah his wife, was born Nov. 7th, A. D 1770

Daniel, the son of Daniel Whitmore and Sarah, his wife, was born Sept. 4th, A. D. 1772.

Polly, the daughter of Jesse Atwell and Marah, his wife, was born Feb. 16th, A. D. 1768.

Jesse, the son of Jesse Atwell and Marah, his wife, was born Feb. 28th, A. D. 1770.

Salle, the daughter of Jesse Atwell and Marah, his wife, was born March 17th, A. D. 1772.

Rhoda, the wife of Jesse Cook, departed this life, July 29th, 1771.

Jesse Cook and Ann Griswold were joined in marriage, Oct. 20th, A. D. 1771.

Rhoda, the daughter of Jesse Cook and Ann, his wife, was born July 15th, A. D. 1772.

Joseph Smith and Rhoda Pickett were joined in marriage, Sept. 10th, A D. 1767.

James, the son of Joseph Smith and Rhoda, his wife, was born Apr 17th, 1769.

Elizabeth, the daughter of Joseph Smith and Rhoda, his wife, was born Apr. 23d, A. D. 1771, and died May 9th, 1773.

Joel, the son of John Norton and Hannah, his wife, was born Apr. 24th, A. D. 1771

Hannah, the wife of John Norton, departed this life, Dec. 18th, A D. 1772.

Miles, the son of Charles Norton and Elizabeth, his wife, was born May 30th, A. D. 1769.

Eunice, the daughter of Charles Norton and Elizabeth, his wife, was born March 6th, A. D. 1771.

John, the son of Israel Camp and Mary, his wife, was born May 18th, A. D. 1773.

Katharine, the daughter of Heth Camp and Mary, his wife, was born Aug. 20th, A. D. 1770.

Libbeus, the son of Heth Camp and Mary, his wife, was born Nov. 20th, A. D. 1772.

Zerujah Chidsey departed this life, Nov. 24th, A. D. 1771.

Ichabod Lewis, the son of Ichabod Higgins and Jane, his wife, was born Apr. 1st, A. D. 1771.

Anne, the daughter of Daniel Weld and Elizabeth, his wife, was born Feb. 21st, A. D. 1758

Olive, the daughter of Daniel Weld and Elizabeth, his wife, was born May 2d, A. D. 1770.

Abiathar, the son of Samuel Squier and Abigail, his wife, was born Nov. 15th, A D. 1740.

Abiathar Squier and Mary Dudley were joined in marriage, March 9th, A. D. 1763, and their children were born as follows, viz:

Asher, was born Nov. 16th, A. D. 1763.

Dudley, was born March 31st, A. D. 1765.

Ambrose, was born Aug. 2d, A. D. 1766.

Abiathar, was born May 19th, 1768.

Statira, was born March 6th, A. D. 1769.

Noah, was born May 25th, A. D. 1772.

Sarah, the daughter of Moses Seaward and Sarah, his wife, was born June 3d, A. D 1769.

Abram, the son of Moses Seward and Sarah, his wife, was born Oct. 11th, A. D. 1772.

Jared, the son of Jared Whedon and Sarah, his wife, was born Oct. 24th, A. D. 1773.

Hamlet, the son of Joseph Smith and Rhoda, his wife, was born June 29th, A. D. 1773.

The children of Job Camp and Rachel, his wife, were born as follows, (viz.)

Rebeckah, was born July 12th, A D. 1767.

Ashur, was born July 29th, A. D 1769.

Elenor, was born Aug. 28th, A. D. 1771.

Benoni, was born Sept 7th, A. D. 1773.

Julius, the son of Caleb Fowler and Anne, his wife, was born Apr., A. D, 1768.

Edmund, the son of Caleb Fowler and Anne, his wife, was born Feb. 25th, A. D. 1770.

Lucretia, the daughter of Caleb Fowler and Anne, his wife, was born March 10th, A. D. 1772.

Mindwell, the daughter of Abraham Bartlett and Submit, his wife, was born July 6th, 1770.

Phebe, the daughter of Benjamin Gillum and Elizabeth, his wife, was born June 19th, A. D. 1770.

Elizur, the son of Benjamin Gillum and Elizabeth, his wife, was born Feb. 11th, A. D. 1773, and died Feb. 16th, A. D. 1773.

Mary, the daughter of Abel Coe and Prudence, his wife, was born Jan. 1st, A. D. 1774.

Phinehas Canfield and Anne Newton were joined in marriage, Apr. 1st, 1773.

Thomas, the son of Phinehas Canfield and Anne, his wife, was born March 28th, 1774.

John, the son of Jeremiah Butler and Anna, his wife, was born Sept. 13th, A. D. 1772

Rayner, the son of Jeremiah Butler and Anna, his wife, was born Aug. 15th, 1774.

Mary, the daughter of Daniel Hall, 3d, and Elizabeth, his wife, was born Sept. 7th, A. D. 1774.

Timothy Botchford, the son of John Crane and Abigail, his wife, was born June 10th, A. D. 1773.

Mr. Noah Parsons departed this life at Hispaniola, in May A. D. 1774.

Stephen, the son of Eliakim Strong and Hannah, his wife, was born July 31st, A. D. 1768

John Norton and Sarah Tainter were joined in marriage, March 24th, A. D. 1774.

Rebeckah, the daughter of Timothy Stow and Rebeckah, his wife, was born Dec. 4th, A. D. 1774.

Hannah, the daughter of Eliakim Strong and Hannah, his wife, was born July 4th, A. D. 1773.

Elizur, the son of Benjamin Gillum and Elizabeth, his wife, was born Oct. 4th, A. D. 1774.

James, the son of James Tibbals and Martha, his wife, was born May 23d, A. D. 1754.

Anne, the daughter of Heth Camp and Mary, his wife, was born July 16th, A. D. 1776.

Samuel, the son of John Laws and Abigail, his wife was born Jan. 16th, A. D. 1770.

Hannah, the daughter of John Laws and Abigail, his wife, was born May 28th, A. D. 1772.

Daniel, the son of Jown Laws and Abigail, his wife, was born June 2d, A. D. 1775.

Seth, the son of Abial Baldwin and Mehitabel, his wife, was born Apr. 27th, A. D. 1775.

Rejoice, the son of John Crane and Abigail, his wife, was born Oct. 10th, A. D. 1775.

Mary Coe departed this life, Oct. 26th, A. D. 1776.

Daniel, the son of Daniel Hall, 2d, and Ann, his wife, was born March 16th, 1776.

Daniel Hall, 2d, departed this life, Aug. 17th, 1776.

John, the son of Jared Whedon and Sarah, his wife, was born Apr. 26th, 1777.

Dan Parmalee and Abigail Norton were joined in marriage, Jan. 11th, A. D. 1776.

Hannah, the daughter of Dan Parmalee and Abigail, his wife, was born Nov. 1st, A. D. 1776.

Stephen, the son of Jeremiah Butler and Anne, his wife, was born March 26th, A. D. 1776.

Concurrence Seaward departed this life, Sept. 1st, A. D. 1776.

Moses, the son of John Las and Abigail, his wife, was born Sep. 23d, A. D. 1777.

Rejoice, the son of John Crane and Abigail, his wife, died Feb. 17th, A. D. 1777.

Eli, the son of Eli Crane and Mehitabel, his wife, was born July 9th, A. D. 1770, and died the 3d day of Dec. A. D. 1776.

Nathan, the son of Eli Crane and Mehitabel, his wife, was born Jan. 14th, A. D. 1772.

Sybil, the daughter of Eli Crane and Mehitabel, his wife, was born Apr. 17th, A. D. 1774.

Eli, the son of Eli Crane and Mehitabel, his wife, was born Feb. 24th, A. D. 1777.

Amos Fowler and Sarah Hinman were joined in marriage, Jan. 2d, A. D. 1777.

Betsey, the daughter of Dan Parmalee and Abigail, his wife, was born Oct. 24th, A. D. 1781.

Tabitha, the daughter of Col. James Arnold and Tabitha, his wife, was born Dec. 27th, 1776.

Rejoice, the son of John Crane and Abigail, his wife, was born May 31st, A. D. 1778.

Abijah Curtiss and Ann Bishop were joined in marriage, Aug. 13th, A. D. 1777.

Olive, the daughter of Abijah Curtiss and Ann, his wife, was born Apr. 24th, A. D. 1778.

Mary, the daughter of Heth Camp and Mary, his wife, was born Sept. 26th, A. D. 1778.

Anne, the daughter of Abijah Curtiss and Ann, his wife, was born Dec. 6th, A. D. 1779.

Abel Tibbals and Jane Kelsey were joined in marriage, Oct. 7th, A. D. 1776.

Anna, the daughter of Abel Tibbals and Jane, his wife, was born May 7th, A. D. 1778.

Hannah, the daughter of Abel Tibbals and Jane, his wife, was born Oct. 7th, A. D. 1779.

Ens'n Simeon Parsons departed this life Jan. 6th, 1781.

The children of John Johnson, Jun., and Abigail, his wife, were born as follows, viz:

Morris, was born Dec. 12th, A. D. 1773.

Rhoda, was born Oct. 6th, A. D. 1775.

Mercy, was born May 2d, 1778.

Nabbe, was born Oct. 22d, A. D. 1780.

The children of Eliphaz Parmalee and Anne, his wife, were born as follows, viz:

Ruth, was born Sept. 27th, A. D. 1769.

Ozias, was born Dec. 7th, A. D. 1771.

Noah, was born Nov. 25th, A. D. 1773.

Rhoda, was born Jan. 20th, A. D. 1778.

Eli, was born Feb. 9th, A. D. 1781.

Lidia, the daughter of Eli Crane and Mehitabel, his wife, was born Dec. 14th, A. D. 1779.

Jesse, the son of Eli Crane and Mehitabel, his wife, was born Apr. 28th, A. D. 1782.

Eli Crane departed this life, Oct. 5th, A. D. 1781.

Thaddeus, the son of Heth Camp and Mary, his wife, was born Nov. 19th, A D. 1780

Dan, the son of Dan Parmalee and Abigail, his wife, was born Feb. 3d, A D. 1783.

Joseph, the son of John Loas and Abigail, his wife, was born Sept. 18th, A. D. 1780

The children of Phinehas Spelman and Elisabeth, his wife, were born as follows, viz:

Hannah, was born Mar. 26th, A. D. 1755; Ann, was born Jan. 27th, A. D. 1757; Richard, was born Dec. 3d, A. D. 1758; Robert, was born Feb 7th, A. D 1767; Elisabeth, was born May 13th, A. D. 1774; Nathan, was born Sep. 23d, A. D. 1777; Elizur, was born Aug. 7th, A. D. 1780.

Phinehas Spelman departed this life, Dec. 31st, 1783.

Benjamin, the son of John Loas and Abigail, his wife, was born May 4th, A. D. 1784.

Thaddeus, the son of Thaddeus Manning and Elisabeth, his wife, was born Feb. 23d, A. D. 1780.

Hannah, the daughter of Heth Camp and Mary, his wife, was born May 17th, A. D. 1784.

Frederick Crane and Anne Babcock were joined in marriage, Jan. 1st, A. D. 1778.

The children of Frederick Crane and Anne, his wife, were born as follows:

Rebeckah, was born Aug. 25th, A. D 1778; Asa, was born March 12th, A. D. 1780; Charles, was born Feb. 1st, 1782; Eunice, was born Jan. 13th, A. D. 1784.

Mercy Crane, widow of Silas Crane, departed this life, Aug. 29th, A. D. 1782

Eunice, the daughter of Levi Parmalee and Phebe, his wife, was born Apr. 3d, 1778.

Phebe, the daughter of Levi Parmalee and Phebe, his wife, was born Apr. 18th, 1782.

Ozias, the son of Abel Tibbals and Jane, his wife, was born Aug. 20th, 1783.

Joseph Parsons and Mercy Coe were joined in marriage, Dec. 7th, A D 1775.

Charles, the son of Joseph Parsons and Mercy, his wife, was born Dec. 7th, A. D. 1778.

Katharine, the daughter of Joseph Parsons and Mercy, his wife, was born Sept. 2d, A. D. 1781.

Eunice, the daughter of Joseph Parsons and Mercy, his wife, was born Apr. 26th, A. D. 1784.

John Camp, the son of Abraham Bartlet, Jun., and Melinda, his wife, was born Dec. 24th, 1785.

Mehitable, the daughter of Dan Parmelee and Abigail, his wife, was born March 4th, 1785.

Nabby, the daughter of Dan Parmelee and Abigail, his wife, was born Jan. 2d, 1792.

Mr. Ithamar Parsons departed this life, Jan. 21st, A. D. 1786.

Elisabeth Parsons, wife to Lieut. Samuel Parsons, departed this life July 6th, 1785

Aaron Parsons, son to Ithamar Parsons and Sarah, his wife, was born Nov. 10th, 1758.

Aaron Parsons and Lucy, his wife, were joined in marriage, Oct. 3d, A. D. 1782.

Curtiss, the son of Aaron Parsons and Lucy, his wife, was born Apr. 23d, 1783.

Hannah, the daughter of Aaron Parsons and Lucy, his wife, was born Jan. 22d, A. D. 1785.

Jesse Atwell and Mary, his wife, were joined in marriage, June 16th, 1767.

The children of Jesse Atwell and Mary, his wife, were born as follows, (viz:)

Polly, Feb. 16th, 1768; Jesse, Feb. 28th, 1770; Sally, March ye 17th, 1772; Fanny, Aug. 8th, 1774; Electa, March 5th, 1776; William, July 2d, 1778, Harriet, June 25th, 1781.

Jesse Atwell departed this life, July 11th, A. D. 1781.

Charles Coe and Hannah Bates joined in marriage, Oct. 30th, 1784

Noah, the son of Charles Coe and Hannah, his wife, was born May 24th, 1786.

Chauncey Graham and Sarah Merwin were joined in marriage, Nov. 11th, A. D. 1782.

Chauncey, the son of Chauncey Graham and Sarah, his wife, was born July 26th, 1783.

Sarah, the daughter of Chauncey Graham and Sarah, his wife, was born Sept. 18th, 1784.

Stephen, the son of Chauncey Graham and Sarah, his wife, was born Dec. 13th, 1736.

Isaac, the son of Moses Seaward and Sarah, his wife, was born June 19th, 1776.

Joseph, the son of John Loas and Abigail, his wife, was born Sept. 28th, 1780.

Henry, the son of John Loas and Abigail, his wife, was born June 9th, 1786.

Nathan, the son of Aaron Parsons and Lucy, his wife, was born May 9th, 1787.

Bridgman Gurnsey and Phebe Ann Curtiss were joined in marriage, Feb. 5th, 1786.

Daniel, son to John Loas and Abigail, his wife, departed this life Jan. 12th, 1788.

Jacob, the son of Jacob Cornwell and Hannah, his wife, was born Apr. 25th, 1778.

Phebe Strong, wife to Mr. Thomas Strong, departed this life, Feb. 3d, 1787.

Polly, the daughter of Charles Coe and Hannah, his wife was born Sep. 13th, 1788.

Miles, the son of Miles Merwin and Mary, his wife, was born Feb 2d, 1772.

Olive, was born Dec. 12th, 1773, Ruth, was born June 25th, 1776; Nancy, Oct. 25th, 1778; Rhoda, Nov. 11th, 1780; Jesse, was born Dec 23d, 1782; Mary, May 14th, 1785, and Hannah, was born Aug. 31st, 1787.

James Gurdon, the son of Hope Whitmore, was born Oct. 30th, 1779.

Luca, the daughter of Amos Davis and Hope, his wife, was born Jan. 24th, 1787.

Amos, the son of Amos Davis and Hope, his wife, was born Sept. 1st, 1788.

Marcus, the son of Aaron Parsons and Lucy, his wife, was born Feb. 23d, 1789.

Nilit, the daughter of Jin, servants to the widow Esther Wadsworth, was born May 7th, 1784; and Mille, servant to the sd Esther Wadsworth, was born May 5th, 1787.

James, the son of James Arnold and Tabatha, his wife, was born Oct. 26th, 1782.

Whiting, the son of James Arnold and Tabatha, his wife, was born Sept. 25th, 1785.

Eunice, the wife of Simeon Parsons, Esq., departed this life, Apr. 12th, 1791.

Samuel, the son of Richard Barret and Sarah, his wife was born June 10th, 1781.

Parsons, the son of Richard Barret and Sarah, his wife, was born June 7th, 1784.

Sally, the daughter of Richard Barret and Sarah, his wife, was born Dec. 20th, 1790.

Calvin Hawley, the son of Aaron Parsons and Lucy, his wife, was born Sept. 20th, 1791.

Parsons, the son of Charles Coe and Hannah, his wife, was born Feb. 4th, 1792.

Mary, the daughter of Dr. Chauncey Graham and Sarah, his wife, was born Apr. 7th, A. D. 1789.

Mr. Elah Camp departed this life, Oct. 17th, 1787.

Nathan O. Camp and Phebe Spencer joined in marriage, May 16th, 1787.

Sally, the daughter of Nathan O. Camp and Phebe, his wife, was born Jan. 27th, 1788.

Enos Spencer, son to Nathan O. Camp and Phebe, his wife, was born Dec. 30th, 1789.

Elah, son to Nathan O. Camp and Phebe, his wife, was born July 22d, 1792.

James Curtiss and Sally Morrow were joined in marriage, the 2d of Nov., 1791.

James Robinson, Jun., and Thankful Dimmock joined in marriage. Mar 16th, 1785.

Samuel, the son of James Robinson, Jun., and Thankful, his wife, was born Dec. 5th, 1785.

Henry, the son of James Robinson, Jun., and Thankful, his wife, was born Oct. 23d, 1787.

Israel, the son of James Robinson, Jun., and Thankful, his wife, was born Apr. 12th, 1789.

James, the son of James Robinson, Jun., and Thankful, his wife, was born Nov. 14th, 1791.

Eliakim Hull was born Aug 1st, 1752.

Rachel Hull was born Sept. 20th, 1750.

Eliakim Hull and Rachel Welles were joined in marriage, March 14th, 1787.

Rachel, the daughter of Eliakim Hull, was born Feb. 11th, 1783.

Jehiel, the son of Eliakim Hull and Rachel, his wife, was born July 31st, 1789.

Dency, the daughter of Joseph Parsons and Marcy, his wife, was born May 25th, 1786.

Samuel, the son of Joseph Parsons and Marcy, his wife, was born Aug 29th, 1788.

Curtiss Bates and Clarissa, his wife, were joined in marriage, Dec. 14th, 1776.

John, the son of Curtiss Bates and Clarissa, his wife, was born Oct. 20th, 1787, and died Apr. 22d, 1792.

Alvey, the daughter of Curtiss Bates and Clarissa, his wife, was born Nov. 24th, 1789.

Clarissa, the daughter of Curtiss Bates and Clarissa, his wife, was born Feb. 4th, 1792.

Samuel Bates, Jun., and Hannah Southmayd were joined in marriage Nov. 13th, 1786.

Abiah Southmayd, daughter to Samuel Bates, Jun., and Hannah, his wife, was born Dec. 15th, 1787.

William, the son to sd. Bates was born July 9th, 1790.

Hannah, the daughter to Samuel Bates and Hannah, his wife, was born Feb. 24th, 1793.

James Bates, Jun., and Anne Gurnsey were joined in marriage, Dec. 24th, 1766.

Katharine, the daughter of James Bates and Anne, his wife, was born Oct. 26th, 1767.

Daniel, the son of James Bates and Anne, his wife, was born Sept. 25th, 1770.

Gurnsey was born Feb. 1st, 1772; Ebenezer, was born Oct. 3d, 1775, and died June 6th, 1779.

Anne, the daughter of the sd. James and Anne, was born May 9th, 1780.

Lieut. Miles Merwin departed this life, Dec. 12th, 1786.

Mary Merwin, wife to Lieut. Miles Merwin, departed this life, Jan. 18th, 1793.

Daniel Bates and Anne Smithson were joined in marriage, Oct. 24th, 1790.

Phebe, the daughter of Daniel Bates and Anne, his wife, was born Feb. 13th, 1792.

William Butler was born Apr. 16th, 1752.

Sarah Butler, wife to William Butler, was born Feb. 23d, 1758.

William Butler and Sarah Hull were joined in marriage, Sept. 29th, 1778.

Charles, the son of William Butler and Sarah, his wife, was born March 21st, 1779.

Elizur, the son of William Butler and Sarah, his wife, was born March 3d, 1781.

Sarah, the daughter of William Butler and Sarah, his wife, was born March 7th, 1784.

William, the son of William Butler and Sarah, his wife, was born June 16th, 1786.

Harriet, the daughter of William Butler and Sarah, his wife, was born Aug. 11th, 1788.

Chauncey, the son of William Butler and Sarah, his wife, was born May 7th, 1791.

Betcy, the daughter of William Butler and Sarah, his wife, was born May 20th, 1793.

Hannah, the daughter of Samuel Bates and Hannah, his wife, departed this life, Feb. 13th, 1794.

Rhoda, the daughter of Aaron Parsons and Lucy, his wife, was born March 13th, 1794.

Sarah, the wife of Ithamar Parsons, departed this life, Apr. 13th, 1794.

Mr. Lemuel Gurnsey departed this life, July 17th, 1794.

Clarissa, the daughter of Curtiss Bates and Clarissa Bates, his wife, departed this life, May 10th, 1794.

Elias Camp, Jun., and Elizabeth Spencer were joined in marriage, Oct. 17th, 1788.

Betsey, the daughter of Elias Camp, Jun., and Elisabeth, his wife, was born Apr. 4th, 1789.

Thomas Spencer, son of Elias Camp, Jun., and Elisabeth, his wife, was born Jan. 3d, 1791.

Lucinda, daughter to Elias Camp, Jun., and Elisabeth, his wife, was born Jan. 28th, 1793.

Elize, daughter of Elias Camp, Jun., and Elizabeth, his wife, was born Apr. 20th, 1795.

Samuel, the son of Morris Coe and Lucy, his wife, was born May the 4th, 1776.

Sally, the daughter of Morris Coe and Lucy, his wife, was born March the 30th, 1778.

Jesse, the son of Morris Coe and Lucy, his wife, was born Apr. the 2d, 1780.

Morris, the son of Morris Coe and Lucy, his wife, was born March the 20th, 1783.

Hamlet, the son of Morris Coe and Lucy, his wife, was born Aug. 22d, 1785.

Alandon, the daughter of Morris Coe and Lucy, his wife, was born Aug. 16th, 1789.

Tenta, the daughter of Morris Coe and Lucy, his wife, was born July 26th, 1791.

Simeon, the son of Morris Coe and Lucy, his wife, was born June 22d, 1794.

Simeon Parsons, Esq., and Sarah Gurnsey were joined in marriage, Feb. 19th, 1795.

Henry, the son of John Loas and Abigail, his wife, departed this life, the 26th day of Sept., 1794.

Ebenezer Squire and Lucy Wilcox were joined in marriage, Nov. 26th, 1778.

Daniel, the son of Ebenezer Squire and Lucy, his wife, was born Sept. 12th, 1780.

Ebenezer, the son of Ebenezer Squire and Lucy, his wife, was born Dec. 14th, 1782.

Katharine, the daughter of Ebenezer Squire and Lucy, his wife, was born Dec. 6th, 1787.

Anne, the daughter of Ebenezer Squire and Lucy, his wife, was born Aug. 26th, 1791.

Polly, the daughter of Richard Barret and Sarah, his wife, was born Apr. 9th, 1794

Sally, the daughter of Richard Barret and Sarah, his wife, departed this life, Apr. 19th, 1794.

Prudence, the wife of Abel Coe, departed this life, Nov 23d, A. D. 1795.

Nathan Ozias Camp, the son of Nathan O. Camp and Phebe, his wife, was born Jan. 4th, 1796.

Col. Elihu Chauncey departed this life, Apr. 11th, 1791.

Capt. Elnathan Chauncey departed this life, May 4th, 1796.

Joseph, the son of Eliphaz Nettleton and Lydia, his wife, was born Jan. 10th, 1793.

Mimemery, daughter to Eliphaz Nettleton and Lydia, his wife, was born May 27th, 1795.

Nathaniel Thayer and Anne Fowler were joined in marriage, Nov. 6th, 1791.

William Austin, son to Nathaniel Thayer and Anne, his wife, was born Aug. 5th, 1792.

Phebe, the daughter of Aaron Parsons and Lucy, his wife, was born March 8th, 1796.

Phebe, the daughter of Abijah Curtiss and Ann, his wife, was born Feb 27th, 1783.

Dinah, the daughter of Abijah Curtiss and Ann, his wife, was born July 23d, 1785.

Samuel, the son of Abijah Curtiss and Ann, his wife, was born July 13th, 1787.

Ichabod, the son of Abijah Curtiss and Ann, his wife, was born May 17th, 1790.

Ichabod, the son of Abijah Curtiss and Ann, his wife, departed this life May 10th, 1791.

Ichabod, the son of Abijah Curtiss and Ann, his wife, was born Apr. 3d, 1792.

David, the son of Abijah Curtiss and Ann, his wife, was born Jan. 31st, 1795.

Lucius Fowler Thayer, son of Nathaniel Thayer and Anne, his wife, was born June 21st, A. D. 1797.

Israel Camp and Rhoda Smithson were joined in marriage, May 3d, 1789.

William Smithson, son to Israel Camp and Rhoda, his wife, was born Jan. 2d, 1790.

Two sons, twins of Israel Camp and Rhoda, his wife, was born Jan. 18th, 1792.

Sally, daughter to Israel Camp and Rhoda, his wife, was born Sept. 5th, 1794.

William Smithson, son to Israel Camp and Rhoda, his wife, was born Apr. 23d, 1796.

William Smithson, eldest son to Israel Camp and Rhoda, his wife, died Sept. 20th, 1795.

Joel Coe, son to Ephraim Coe, was born Aug. 10th, 1766.

Sally Talcott, daughter to Hezekiah Talcott, was born July 30th, 1768.

Joel Coe and Sally Talcott were joined in marriage, Jan. 31st, 1791.

Talcott Coe, son to Joel Coe and Sally, his wife, was born Dec. 21st, 1791.

Eunice Coe, daughter to Joel Coe and Sally, his wife, was born Apr. 21st, 1794.

Lester and Chester, twins, sons to Joel Coe and Sally, his wife, were born Sept. 13th, 1796.

John Curtiss, Jun., and Lydia Hall were joined in marriage, Dec. 29th, 1794.

Rev. Elizur Goodrich departed this life at Norfolk, Nov. 21st, 1797.

John Coe and Susannah Swaddle were joined in marriage, Dec 10th, 1797. Abel Coe departed this life Jan. 10th, 1798. Josiah Coe departed this life, Feb. 14th, 1798.

Samuel Tibbals and Esther Swaddle joined in marriage, Apr. 27th, 1794.

John Spencer, son to Elias Camp and Elizabeth his wife, was born July 17th, 1797.

John Turner and Elizabeth Chatfield joined in marriage, Oct. 18th, 1792.

Hannah Eli, daughter to John Turner and Elisabeth, his wife, was born Aug. 26th, 1793.

Danforth, daughter to John Turner and Elisabeth, his wife, was born Jan. 3d, 1795.

Oreb, son to John Turner and Elisabeth, his wife, was born Dec. 21st, 1796.

Elisabeth, wife to John Turner, departed this life, Dec. 13th, 1798.

Mr. David Smith was ordained over the Church and Congregation of this town, Aug. 15th, 1799.

Harry Chamberlin, son to Asa Chamberlin and Martha, his wife, was born Apr 9th, 1782. Entered Sept. 10th, 1700.

Elisabeth, was born Dec. 4th, 1768; Rufus, was born Aug. 31st, 1770; Huldah, was born Dec. 15th, 1772; Polly, was born Aug. 8th, 1775; Parmelee, was born Nov. 14th, 1777; Asa, was born Jan. 26th, 1779. Entered Sept. 10th, 1799.

Amanda, the daughter of Aaron Parsons and Lucy, his wife, was born July 11th, 1799.

Lydia, the wife of John Curtiss, Jun., departed this life, July 6th, 1799.

Lieut. Abraham Scranton and Hannah Camp were joined in marriage, Jan 1st, 1772.

Hamlet Scranton, son to Abraham Scranton and Hannah, his wife, was born Dec. 1st, 1772; Henry, was born May 10th, 1775; Israel, was born Apr. 4th, 1778; Joy, was born March 7th, 1781; Content, was born March 11th, 1783; Manda, was born Apr. 13th, 1785, Abraham, was born May 3d, 1787.

Moses Seaward and Sarah Fowler were joined in marriage, May 5th, 1791.

Harvey, the son of Moses Seaward and Sarah, his wife, was born Aug. 18th, 1792.

Polly, the daughter of Moses Seaward and Sarah, his wife, was born March 8th, 1795.

Moses Seward departed this life, Oct. 17th, 1799.

John, the son of Curtiss Bates and Clarissa, his wife, was born the 19th of Aug. 1798

Mr. John Curtiss departed this life July 1st, 1800.

Mrs. Mary Chauncey, widow to Col. Elihu Chauncey, departed this life, March the first, 1801.

William, the son of Richard Barret and Sarah, his wife, was born June 10th, 1799.

Dinah, the widow of Mr. John Curtiss, departed this life, Sept. 6th, 1800.

John Curtiss and Ruth Parmele joined in marriage, June 2d, 1801.

Rachel, the wife of Abraham Stowe, departed this life, Sept. 20th, 1800.

Enos Seaward departed this life July 14th, 1801.

Nathaniel Seward departed this life Dec. 28th, 1801.

Lydia, the daughter of Eliphaz Nettleton was born Dec. 9th, 1798.

Polly, the daughter of Eliphaz Nettleton, was born Oct. 16th, 1801.

Timothy Parsons departed this life, March 12th, 1802

Abiel Baldwin departed this life, Aug. 11th, 1802.

Sarah Allen departed this life, Feb. 25th, 1803.

Concurrence, the wife of Dea. John Johnson, departed this life, Feb. 24th, 1803.

Pernel, daughter to Israel Camp and Rhoda, his wife, was born Oct. 6th, 1799.

Meriah, the daughter of Daniel Bates and Ann, his wife, was born Apr. 12th, 1796.

Anne, the daughter of Daniel Bates and Anne, his wife, was born Aug. 14th, 1799

Otis, the son of Aaron Parsons and Lucy, his wife, was born May 4th, 1803.

Charles Augustus Goodrich, son to the Rev. Elizur Goodrich, departed this life, Jan. 25th, 1804.

Elihu Chauncey Goodrich, Esq., departed this life at Neighigary, Aug. 20th, 1802.

Dr. Lyman Norton and Olive Weld were joined in marriage, June 18th, 1795.

The children of Joseph Hull and Diana, his wife:

Joseph, was born Oct. 28th, 1786; Diana, was born Aug. 19th, 1788; David, was born Nov. 26th, 1790; Stephen, was born July 19th, 1794; Elisabeth, was born Aug. 19th, 1796.

Delia W., daughter to Lyman Norton and Olive, his wife, was born May 28th, 1798.

Stephen Lyman, son to Dr. Lyman Norton and Olive, his wife, was born Sept. 5th, 1799.

Eunice, the wife of Mr. Elnathan Camp, departed this life, Aug. 2d, 1804.

John, son to Joseph Southmayd and Cynthia, his wife, was born June 11th, 1794.

Jonathan, son to Joseph Southmayd and Cynthia, his wife, was born March 2d, 1797.

Freeman Bailey, son to Joseph Southmayd and Cynthia, his wife, was born May 26th, 1801.

Nathan, the son of Abner Tibbals and Elisabeth, his former wife, was born May 16th, 1786.

Oliver Coe and Lydia Swathel were joined in marriage, Jan. 1st, 1794, and the said Oliver and Lydia had a son still born, Sept. 28th, 1794.

Anna, the daughter of Oliver Coe and Lydia, his wife, was born Apr. 11th, 1796, and died May 13th, 1796.

Katharine, the daughter of Oliver Coe and Lydia, his wife, was born Apr. 5th, 1797.

Oliver Bates, son to Oliver Coe and Lydia, his wife, was born Aug. 5th, 1798.

William, son to Oliver Coe and Lydia, his wife, was born Apr. 24th, 1801.

Sally, the daughter of Oliver Coe and Lydia, his wife, was born Apr. 8th, 1805.

Ebenezer Guernsey, son to Daniel Bates and Anne, his wife, was born May 14th, 1805.

Israel Burrit departed this life, May 25th, 1806.

Col. James Arnold departed this life Aug. 25th, 1806.

Lydia, daughter of John Curtiss and Ruth, his wife, was born Oct. 7th, 1802.

Maranda, daughter to Wait C. Frances and Mary, his wife, was born Feb. 11th, 1796.

Phebe, the daughter of Wait C. Frances and Mary, his wife, was born Feb. 2d, 1799.

Mary, the daughter of Wait C. Frances and Mary, his wife, was born May 6th, 1801.

James, the son of Wait C. Frances and Mary, his wife, was born Apr. 30th, 1806.

Eliza F. Strong, daughter to Russel H. Strong and Sarah, his wife, was born Aug. 24th, 1802.

Mr. Elnathan Camp departed this life, May 12th, 1807.

Mr. Caleb Fowler departed this life, June 21st, 1807.

Israel Camp departed this life, Nov 5th, 1807

Ebenezer Guernsey, son to Daniel Bates and Anne, his wife, was born May 14th, 1805.

Timothy Stowe departed this life, March 16th, 1808.

Mr. Asher Robinson departed this life, May 4th, 1808.

David Camp departed this life, Oct. 13th, 1808

Allen Clarke and Sally Swathel joined in marriage, Sept 22d, 1803.

Susan, daughter to Allen Clarke and Sally, his wife, was born March 12th, 1805.

Fanny, daughter to Allen Clarke and Sally, his wife, was born June 14th, 1807.

Capt. Stephen Norton departed this life, Nov. 13th, 1808.

Edward Henry, son to George Lyman and Sally, his wife, was born Jan. 8th, 1802.

Ozias, son to Stephen Norton and Abigail, his wife, was born Dec. 31st, 1759.

Hannah, daughter to Joel Parmalee and Rhoda, his wife, was born Sept. 2d, 1761.

Ozias Norton and Hannah Parmalee joined in marriage, March 14th, 1790.

Leverett, son to Ozias Norton and Hannah, his wife, was born Nov. 28th, 1791.

Clarissa, daughter to Ozias Norton and Hannah, his wife, was born Aug. 15th, 1794.

William, son to Ozias Norton and Hannah, his wife, was born Apr. 19th, 1797, and died the 24th day of the same month.

Alfred, son to Ozias Norton and Hannah, his wife, was born July 16th, 1798.

Ozias P., son to Ozias Norton and Hannah, his wife, was born Dec. 4th, 1800.

Joseph Chedsey, of Guilford, and Polly Coe, of Durham, were joined in marriage, March 16th, 1809.

Elias, son to Luke Camp and Grace, his wife, was born Feb. 4th, 1794.

Noyes Camp, son to Luke Camp and Grace, his wife, was born Nov. 21st, 1797.

Henry, the son of Thaddeus Camp and Betsey, his wife, was born Apr. 26th, 1802.

Edwin Stiles, son of Thaddeus Camp and Betsey, his wife, was born Dec. 1st, 1803.

Leunora, daughter of Thaddeus Camp and Betsey, his wife, was born Aug. 19th, 1805.

Betsey, daughter of Thaddeus Camp and Betsey, his wife, was born June 25th, 1808.

Col. Samuel Camp departed this life, Nov. 3d, 1810.

Day Hall departed this life, Dec. 19th, 1810.

Elenor Parsons departed this life, Dec. 23d, 1810.

Anne, the wife of Israel Scranton, departed this life, Dec. 24th, 1810.

Penina, the wife of James Brown, deceased, departed this life, Jan 4th, 1811.

Ruth, daughter of Daniel Hart and Hannah, his wife, was born Aug. 6th, 1800.

Harriet, the daughter of Henry Hall and Electa, his wife, was born Aug. 31st, 1806.

Malvina, the daughter of Henry Hall and Electa, his wife, was born Jan. 20th, 1809.

The children of Samuel Hart and Patience, his wife, were born as follows:

William, Apr. 26th, 1806; Edward, Jan. 12th, 1808; George, Apr. 14th, 1810.

Thomas William, the son of George Lyman and Sally, his wife, was born Apr. 23d, 1810.

Capt. John Hart and Sally Coe were joined in marriage, July 15th, 1800.

Emeline Rebeckah, the daughter of John Hart and Sally, his wife, was born Sept. 28th, 1802.

Leander, the son of John Hart and Sally, his wife, was born Jan. 30th, 1809.

Harriet, the daughter of John Hart and Sally, his wife, was born June 20th, 1811.

Thomas S. Camp and Almira Coles were joined in marriage, Dec. 23d, 1813.

John B. Southmayd, the son of Joseph Southmayd and Cynthia, his wife, was born June 11th, 1794.

Ozias Camp, the son of Samuel Camp and Phebe, his wife, was born Jan. 28th, 1780.

Christian Byington, daughter of Joel Byington and Christian, his wife, was born Dec. 22d, 1779.

Ozias Camp and Christian Byington were joined in marriage, Apr. —, 1807.

Mary, the daughter of Ozias Camp and Christian, his wife, was born Aug. 23d, 1808.

Edward, the son of Ozias Camp and Christian, his wife, was born Jan. 19th, 1809.

Betsey Byington, the daughter of Ozias Camp and Christian, his wife, was born Feb. 5th, 1812.

Phebe, the daughter of Ozias Camp and Christian, his wife, was born June 24th, 1813, and died Jan. 5th, 1814.

Lavinia, the daughter of Mr. Timothy Stone and Eunice, his wife, was born 25th day of May, 1814.

James, the son of Jonathan Clarke and Ruth, his wife, was born at Romney, in N. H., Oct. 23d, 1773.

Tamza, the daughter of Eliakim Stephens and Prudence, his wife, was born at Killingworth, Sept., 1774.

James Clarke and Tamza Stephens were joined in marriage, Nov. 5th, A. D. 1799.

Lavinia, the daughter of James Clarke and Tamza, his wife, was born Oct. 10th, 1800, and died Feb. 25th, 1802.

Lewis, the son of Stephen Norton and Mary, his wife, was born Oct. 15th, 1785.

Lewis Norton and Hannah Swathel were joined in marriage, Dec 16th, 1805.

Andrew Talcott, the son of Lewis Norton and Hannah, his wife, was born Jan. 23d, 1809.

Lyman Lewis, the son of Lewis Norton and Hannah, his wife, was born July 4th, 1810.

Abigail Clarissa, the daughter of Lewis Norton and Hannah, his wife, was born Jan. 1st, 1813.

John Coe, the son of Allen Clarke and Sally, his wife, was born Jan. 23d, 1810.

Betsey, the daughter of Allen Clarke and Sally, his wife, was born May 14th, 1812.

Frederick, the son of George Lyman and Sally, his wife, was born Oct. 11th, 1812.

Adeline, the daughter of Timothy Stone and Eunice, his wife, was born May 15th, 1817

Katherine, the daughter of John Hart and Sally, his wife was born Jan. 25th, 1814.

Simeon Parsons, Esq., departed this life, July 12th, 1819.

Samuel Curtiss and Lucretia Brooks were joined in marriage, Oct. 3d, 1810.

John, the son of Samuel Curtiss and Lucretia, his wife, was born Nov. 2d, 1811.

Samuel Brooks, the son of Samuel Curtiss and Lucretia, his wife, was born July 13th, 1813.

Anna Elizabeth, the daughter of Samuel Curtiss and Lucretia, his wife, was born May 11th, 1815.

Phebe, the daughter of Samuel Curtiss and Lucretia, his wife, was born Apr. 12th, 1817

Sarah, the daughter of Samuel Curtiss and Lucretia, his wife, was born May 31st, 1819.

Timothy Coe, Jun., and Polly Callender were joined in marriage, Jan. 10th, 1803.

Edwin Thomas, the son of Timothy Coe, Jun., and Polly, his wife, was born Dec. 4th, 1803.

William Callender, the son of Timothy Coe, Jun, and Polly, his wife, was born Jan. 1st, 1808.

Maryann, the daughter of Timothy Coe, Jun., and Polly, his wife, was born Nov. 1st, 1809.

Henry Moulthrop, the son of Timothy Coe, Jun., and Polly, his wife, was born Oct. 12th, 1811.

Timothy Jewett, the son of Timothy Coe, Jun., and Polly, his wife, was born June 19th, 1819.

Heury, the son of Jesse Atwell and Phebe, his wife, was born Dec. 7th, 1791.

William, the son of Jesse Atwell and Phebe, his wife, was born Dec. 9th, 1809.

George, the son of Jesse Atwell and Phebe, his wife, was born Oct. 17th, 1805.

Bishop, the son of Jesse Atwell and Phebe, his wife, was born Dec. 4th, 1812.

David, the son of James Tibbals and Hannah, his wife, was born March 5th, 1801.

Asher, the son of James Tibbals and Hannah, his wife, was born Nov. 14th, 1802.

Olive, the daughter of James Tibbals and Hannah, his wife, was born Nov. 30th, 1804.

Anna, the daughter of James Tibbals and Hannah, his wife, was born May 2d, 1806.

James, the son of James Tibbals and Hannah, his wife, was born June 6th, 1808.

James Tibbals, the son of James Tibbals and Martha, his wife, was born May 7th, 1754.

Hannah Richmond was born in Killingworth, March 6th, 1770.

James Tibbals and Hannah Richmond were joined in marriage, Apr. 21st, 1799.

Burwell Newton, the son of Burwell Newton and Eunice, his wife, was born Jan. 6th, 1757.

Sally Harvey, the daughter of Elisha Harvey and wife, was born Aug. 7th, 1766.

Burwell Newton and Sibyl Harvey were joined in marriage, Nov. 19th, 1795.

Samuel, the son of Burwell Newton and Sibyl, his wife, was born Dec. 30th, 1796.

John, the son of Burwell Newton and Sibyl, his wife, was born Aug. 5th, 1798.

Sophia, the daughter of Burwell Newton and Sibyl, his wife, was born Feb. 7th, 1810.

Sibyl, the wife of Burwell Newton, departed this life, Apr. 19th, 1813.

Burwell Newton and Betsey Hall were joined in marriage, Dec. 20th, 1814.

Manoah Camp and Clarissa Bartlet were joined in marriage, Apr. 24th, 1794.

The children of Manoah Camp and Clarissa, his wife, were born as follows, viz:

Benoni, was born Feb. 10th, 1795; Herschal, born Jan. 15th, 1798; Frederick, born Nov. 21st, 1800; Elizur, born Aug. 22d, 1804.

Charles, the son of Ebenezer Camp and Sarah, his wife, was born Jan. 16th, 1791.

Anne, the daughter of Caleb Miller and wife, was born at Middletown, ———, 1791.

Charles Camp and Anne Miller were joined in marriage, Jan. 1st, 1817.

Josiah, the son of Charles Camp and Anne, his wife, was born Jan. 24th, 1818.

Anne, the wife of Charles Camp, departed this life, Feb. 14th, 1818.

John Swathel, Jun., and Sophronia Robinson were joined in marriage, Nov. 3d, 1820.

Jane Maria, the daughter of John Swathel, Jun., and Sophronia, his wife, was born May 2d, 1821.

John William, the son of John Swathel, Jun., and Sophronia, his wife, was born Jan. 25th, 1822.

Dan. Parmalee, Jun., and Mary Linley were joined in marriage, March 27th, 1803.

Theodore Nelson, the son of Dan Parmalee, Jun., and Mary, his wife, was born Jan. 7th, 1804.

Betsey A., the daughter of Dan Parmalee, Jun., and Mary, his wife, was born Dec. 23d, 1805.

Mary R., the daughter of Dan. Parmalee, Jun., and Mary, his wife, was born July 8th, 1809.

Hezekiah, the son of Dan. Parmalee, Jun., and Mary, his wife, was born July 25th, 1811

Charles, the son of Dan. Parmalee, Jun., and Mary, his wife, was born Oct. 5th, 1815.

Timothy Sherman, the son of Timothy Stone and Eunice, his wife, was born Oct. 21st, 1820.

Catharine Chauncey, the daughter of Rev. David Smith and Catharine, his wife, was born Aug. 27th, 1800

Elizur Goodrich, the son of Rev. David Smith and Catharine, his wife, was born May 30th, 1802.

Betsey Marsh, the daughter of Rev. Mr. David Smith and Catharine, his wife, was born May 20th, 1806.

Chauncey Goodrich, the son of Rev. David Smith and Catharine, his wife, was born Oct. 19th, 1807.

Simeon Parsons, the son of Rev. David Smith and Catharine, his wife, was born July 31st, 1809.

Gustavus Walter, the son of Rev. David Smith and Catharine, his wife, was born June 16th, 1815.

Henry, the son of John Reed and Catharine, his wife, was born March 23d, 1807.

Chauncey, the son of John Reed and Catharine, his wife, was born March 25th, 1809.

Vila, the daughter of Nehemiah Desbury and his wife, departed this life, Nov. 28th, 1822.

Richard Barret departed this life, May 5th, 1822.

Elizabeth, the wife of Elnathan Chauncey, departed this life, Feb. 9th, 1791.

William, the son of Reuben Fowler and Catharine, his wife, departed this life, June 26th, 1792.

Charles Augustus, the son of Ozias Camp, 2d, and Polly, his wife, was born May 10th, 1822.

Elijah Coe, the son of Joseph Tuttle and Margaret, his wife, was born Dec. 22d, 1821.

Richard, the servant of Abel Coe, deceased, a man of color, departed this life, Oct. 31st, 1822.

Eliza, the daughter of Richard Robinson and Tabathy, his wife, was born Nov. 16th, 1794.

Orpha, the daughter of Richard Robinson and Tabathy, his wife, was born July 23d, 1796.

Tabathy, the daughter of Richard Robinson and Tabathy, his wife, was born Jan. 31st, 1800.

Sophronia, the daughter of Richard Robinson and Tabathy, his wife, was born Oct. 17th, 1802.

Caroline, the daughter of Richard Robinson and Tabathy, his wife, were born Sept. 16th, 1805.

Angelina, the daughter of Richard Robinson and Tabathy, his wife, was born Oct. 29th, 1809.

Emma, the daughter of Richard Robinson and Cynthia, his wife, was born Apr. 26th, 1815.

Richard P., the son of Richard Robinson and Cynthia, his wife, was born Apr. 9th, 1817.

Henry, the son of Richard Robinson and Cynthia, his wife, was born Aug 17th, 1819.

Cynthia, the daughter of Richard Robinson and Cynthia, his wife, was born Dec. 19th, 1821.

Phinehas, the son of Charles Robinson and Concurrence, his wife, was born May 22d, 1798.

Content, the daughter of Charles Robinson and Concurrence, his wife, was born Jan 3d, 1799.

Harriet, the daughter of Charles Robinson and Concurrence, his wife, was born Oct. 13th, 1801.

John, the son of Charles Robinson and Concurrence, his wife, was born July 13th, 1803.

Charles, the son of Charles Robinson and Concurrence, his wife, was born Sept. 30th, 1805.

George, the son of Charles Robinson and Concurrence, his wife, was born Jan. 28th, 1808.

Lyman, the son of Charles Robinson and Concurrence, his wife, was born Apr. 20th, 1810.

Betsey, the daughter of Charles Robinson and Concurrence, his wife, was born March 24th, 1813.

William, the son of Charles Robinson and Concurrence, his wife, was born Aug. 2d, 1818.

James, the son of Charles Robinson and Concurrence, his wife, was born July 13th, 1822.

Israel C., the son of Elisha Newton and Sally, his wife, was born March 23d, 1822.

William Augustus, the son of William S. Camp and Margaret, his wife, was born Sept. 22d, 1822.

James, the son of James Hickox and Rhoda, his wife, was born June 9th, 1788.

James Hickox and Hope Smith were married, Sept. 30th, 1815.

Walter Smith, the son of James Hickox and Hope, his wife, was born Nov. 17th, 1816.

Tamzin Mariah, the daughter of James Hickox and Hope, his wife, was born Dec. 27th, 1818.

James Lawrence, the son of James Hickox and Hope, his wife, was born Oct. 4th, 1820.

Mary M., the daughter of Marcus Parsons and Orpha, his wife, was born June 23d, 1814.

Harriet M., the daughter of Marcus Parsons and Orpha, his wife, was born Oct. 10th, 1816.

Aaron A.. the son of Marcus Parsons and Orpha, his wife, was born Oct. 31st, 1819.

Leander R., the son of Marcus Parsons and Orpha, his wife, was born Jan. 23d, 1822.

Amelia, the daughter of Jabez Bailey and Lucretia, his wife, was born Dec. 10th, 1810.

Henry W., the son of Jabez Bailey and Lucretia, his wife, was born Dec. 20th, 1812.

Julia E., the daughter of Jabez Bailey and Lucretia, his wife, was born Nov. 27th, 1814

Julia E., the daughter of Jabez Bailey and Lucretia, his wife, died Aug. 23d, 1815.

Daniel J., the son of Jabez Bailey and Lucretia, his wife, was born June 10th, 1817.

Julia A., the daughter of Jabez Bailey and Lucretia, his wife, was born Nov. 18th, 1820.

Adah Ann, the daughter of Lyman C. Camp and Emma, his wife, was born March 22d, 1816.

Harriet Parmalee, the daughter of Lyman C. Camp and Emma, his wife, was born Oct. 3d, 1817.

Lyman Coe, the son of Lyman C. Camp and Emma, his wife, was born July 2d, 1820.

Margaret Ann, the daughter of Oren Bartholomew and Emeline, his wife, were born Apr. 2d, 1820.

Eliza Emeline, the daughter of Oren Bartholomew and Emeline, his wife, was born Oct. 8th, 1822.

Sarah Adaline, the daughter of Augustus Howd and Catharine, his wife, was born Feb. 24th, 1820.

Horace, the son of Augustus Howd and Catharine, his wife, was born Aug. 25th, 1822.

Lucy Rose, the daughter of Timothy Elliott and his wife, was born Aug. 7th, 1803.

Lucius, the son of Timothy Elliott and Lydia, his wife, was born July 9th, 1807.

Jenet, the daughter of Timothy Elliott and Lydia, his wife, was born March 2d, 1811

Luzerne, the son of Timothy Elliott and Lydia, his wife, was born March 4th, 1814.

Lydia Mariah, the daughter of Timothy Elliott and Lydia, his wife, was born Jan 16th, 1818.

Elizabeth Mariah, the daughter of Heth F. Camp and Phebe, his wife, was born Sept. 23d, 1821.

Israel Scranton and Anna Curtiss were joined in marriage, Oct 12th, 1800.

Harriet Amanda, the daughter of Israel Scranton and Anna, his wife, was born July 5th, 1803.

Talemachus Norman, the son of Israel Scranton, was born at Camden, in South Carolina, May 12th, 1806.

Mary Aurelia, the daughter of Israel Scranton and Anna, his wife, was born at Camden, South Carolina, Feb. 5th, 1808, and died June 3d, 1809.

Mary Aurelia, the daughter of Israel Scranton and Anna, his wife, was born at Camden, in South Carolina, Oct. 15th, 1809.

Beriah, the son of Israel Scranton and Anna, his wife, was born Dec. 4th, 1810.

Israel Scranton and Clarissa Pardee were joined in marriage, Feb 9th, 1813.

Israel, the son of Israel Scranton and Clarissa, his wife, was born at the village of Rochester, town of Gates, and State of New York, Apr. 4th, 1813.

Alonzo Camp, the son of Israel Scranton and Clarissa, his

wife, was born in the village of Rochester, town of Gates, and State of New York, Nov. 20th, 1814.

Anna Curtiss, the daughter of Israel Scranton and Clarissa, his wife, was born at the village of Rochester, town of Gates, and State of New York, March 21st, 1816.

Abraham, the son of Israel Scranton and Clarissa, his wife, was born Dec. 14th, 1817.

Hiram, the son of Israel Scranton and Clarissa, his wife, was born Sept. 24th, 1819.

Serina, the daughter of Israel Scranton and Clarissa, his wife, was born Feb. 7th, 1821.

Emero, the son of Israel Scranton and Clarissa, his wife, was born Dec. 25th, 1822.

Asahel, the son of Joseph Andrews and Betsey, his wife, was born Dec. 4th, 1816.

Benjamin, the son of Joseph Andrews and Betsey, his wife, was born May 24th, 1819.

Concurrence, the daughter of John Tibbals and Eunice, his wife, was born Aug. 15th, 1798.

Concurrence Tibbals departed this life, March 22d, 1822

Seth, the son of John Tibbals and Eunice, his wife, was born May 21st, 1801.

Angus, the son of John Tibbals and Eunice, his wife, was born Nov. 19th, 1805.

Eunice, the daughter of John Tibbals and Eunice, his wife, was born Jan. 22d, 1808.

John, the son of John Tibbals and Eunice, his wife, was born Jan. 4th, 1812.

Loise, the daughter of John Tibbals and Eunice, his wife, was born July 26th, 1816.

Ozias, the son of Noah Parmelee and Ann, his wife, was born July 12th, 1806.

Zeruiah, the daughter of Noah Parmalee and Ann, his wife, was born Dec. 24th, 1811.

Lucretia, the daughter of Noah Parmalee and Ann, his wife, born Feb. 15th, 1815.

William, the son of Noah Parmalee and Ann, his wife, born Jan. 24th, 1820.

Reuben, the son of Ezra Baldwin and Ruth, his wife, was born Apr. 29th, 1749.

Reuben Baldwin and Mabel Jones joined in marriage, June 4th, 1782.

Eunice, the daughter of Reuben Baldwin and Mabel, his wife, was born June 25th, 1785.

Anna, the daughter of Reuben Baldwin and Mabel, his wife, was born Nov. 18th, 1787.

John, the son of Horace Parmelee and Mary, his wife, was born Feb. 5th, 1818.

Elizabeth, the daughter of Horace Parmelee and Mary, his wife, was born Jan. 14th, 1821.

Ebenezer Tibbals departed this life, May 25th, 1819.

Charles Thompson, of Guilford, and Lydia Nettleton, of Killingworth, were joined in marriage, Apr. 5th, 1810.

Daniel, the son of Charles Thompson and Lydia, his wife, was born in Killingworth, Jan. 24th, 1811.

William, the son of Charles Thompson and Lydia, his wife, was born in Killingworth, Oct. 14th, 1812

Lydia Diana, the daughter of Charles Thompson, was born in Guilford, Dec. 13th, 1814.

Edward, the son of Charles Thompson and Lydia, his wife, was born in Killingworth, March 24th, 1817.

Andrew Jackson, the son of Charles Thompson and Lydia, his wife, was born in Killingworth, Feb. 17th, 1821.

Samuel C., the son of Samuel C. Johnson and Phebe, his wife, was born Feb. 2d, 1820.

Theodore, the son of Samuel C. Johnson and Phebe, his wife, was born Apr. 13th, 1821, and departed this life, Aug. 15th, 1822.

Theodore Nelson, the son of Samuel Johnson and Phebe, his wife, was born Oct. 22d, 1822.

John, the son of John Swathel and Phebe, his wife, was born Sept 8th, 1799.

Mary Ann, the daughter of John Swathel and Phebe, his wife, was born Oct. 1st, 1806.

Elizabeth, the daughter of John Swathel and Phebe, his wife, was born March 24th, 1800.

Margaret, the daughter of John Swathel and Phebe, his wife, was born June 30th, 1811.

Phinehas, the son of John Swathel and Phebe, his wife, was born Aug. 17th, 1814.

Phebe, the daughter of John Swathel and Phebe his wife, was born Nov. 6th, 1815.

Hezekiah Clarke and Olive Lee were joined in marriage, Nov. 3d, 1807.

Hezekiah Post, the son of Hezekiah Clarke and Olive, his wife, was born July 3d, 1808.

Samuel Wilson, the son of Hezekiah Clarke and Olive, his wife, was born Nov. 9th, 1810.

Cornelia, the daughter of Hezekiah Clarke and Olive, his wife, was born June 21st, 1813.

Samuel Wilson, the son of Hezekiah Clarke and Olive, his wife, died Sept. 27th, 1813.

Aaron, the son of Hezekiah Clarke and Olive, his wife, was born June 4th, 1815.

Samuel Wilson Lee, the son of Hezekiah Clarke and Olive, his wife, was born July 22d, 1819.

Hannah Post, the daughter of Hezekiah Clarke and Olive, his wife, was born Feb. 8th, 1822.

Lucy Alvira, the daughter of David Pardee and Althea, his wife, was born at Southington, Jan. 2d, 1815.

Stephen Decatur, the son of David Pardee and Althea, his wife, was born Feb. 10th, 1822.

Lemuel Gurnsey departed this life, Sept. 23d, 1820.

Medad Norton departed this life, Dec. 27th, 1821.

Abel Lyman and Adah Pickett were joined in marriage, March 15th, 1790.

Sophia, the daughter of Abel Lyman and Adah, his wife, was born Dec. 3d, 1790.

Frances Amelia, the daughter of Abel Lyman and Adah, his wife, was born March 4th, 1793.

Dwight Alpheus, the son of Abel Lyman and Adah, his wife, was born Jan. 14th, 1797.

James, the son of Abel Lyman and Adah, his wife, was born June 28th, 1815.

Mary Lyman, the daughter of Daniel Dimock, Jun., and Sophia, his wife, was born Sept. 1st, 1812.

Widow Anne Bray departed this life, June 10th, A. D. 1823.

Albert, the son of Abiael Camp and Lucinda, his wife, was born Oct. 1st, 1804.

Mariah, the daughter of Abiael Camp and Lucinda, his wife, was born Apr. 13th, 1806.

Lemuel, the son of Abiael Camp and Lucinda, his wife, was born Oct. 14th, 1808.

Horace, the son of Abiael Camp and Lucinda, his wife, was born July 14th, 1811.

Frances, the son of Abiael Camp and Lucinda, his wife, was born Sept. 29th, 1814.

Gilbert, the son of Abiael Camp and Lucinda, his wife, was born July 31st, 1817.

Abiael Camp departed this life, Jan. 21st, 1821.

Elah Camp and Orib Lee were joined in marriage, Dec 2d, 1819

David Nelson, the son of Elah Camp and Orib, his wife, was born Oct. 3d, 1820.

Phebe Elizabeth, the daughter of Elah Camp and Orib, his wife, was born Sept 3d, 1822.

Moses, the son of Harvey Seward and his wife, was born Feb. 3d, 1815

Hannah Hall, the daughter of Samuel Curtiss and Lucretia, his wife, was born Aug. 29th, 1823.

David, the son of Samuel Curtiss and Lucretia, his wife, was born July 25th, 1823.

Ann Maria, the daughter of Asher Robinson and Eunice, his wife, was born July 26th, 1820.

Henry Parmalee, the son of Asher Robinson and Eunice, his wife, was born Sept. 29th, 1822.

Seth, the son of Eber. Tibbals and wife, was born at Haddam, May 28th, 1782.

Diana, the daughter of Joseph Hull and Diana, his wife, was born Aug. 29th, 1788.

Seth Tibbals and Diana Hull were joined in marriage, June 11th, 1807.

Alpheus Chalker, the son of Seth Tibbals and Diana, his wife, was born Feb. 15th, 1809, and died Apr. 19th, 1809.

Amelia, the daughter of Seth Tibbals and Diana, his wife, was born June 3d, 1810.

Alpheus, the son of Seth Tibbals and Diana, his wife, was born Apr. 14th, 1812.

Diana, the wife of Seth Tibbals, departed this life, Sept. 5th, 1813.

Sally, the daughter of Asher Gillum and Sally, his wife, was born Dec. 24th, 1788.

Seth Tibbals and Sally Gillum were joined in marriage, March 6th, 1814.

Diana, the daughter of Seth Tibbals and Sally, his wife, was born Dec. 12th, 1814.

Mary, the daughter of Seth Tibbals and Sally, his wife, was born Feb. 21st, 1817.

Sarah, the daughter of Seth Tibbals and Sally, his wife, was born March 19th, 1819.

Samuel Hall, the son of Seth Tibbals and Sally, his wife, was born May 11th, 1821.

Henry, the son of Seth Tibbals and Sally, his wife, was born Dec. 29th, 1822.

Ashael, the son of Eliakim Strong and Remembrance, his wife, was born July 27th, 1781.

Sally, the daughter of Tobe L. Munson and Lucy, his wife, was born March 1st, 1785

Asahel Strong and Sally Munson were joined in marriage, May 12th, 1803.

Munson, the son of Asahel Strong and Sally, his wife, was born Feb. 26th, 1804.

Lucy, the daughter of Asahel Strong and Sally, his wife, was born Feb. 6th, 1807.

Asahel, the son of Asahel Strong and Sally, his wife, was born Aug 6th, 1812.

Asahel, the son of Asahel Strong and Sally, his wife, departed this life, Sept. 6th, 1812.

Nancy, the daughter of Asahel Strong and Sally, his wife, was born Apr. 16th, 1815.

Mary, the daughter of Asahel Strong and Sally, his wife, was born May 8th, 1817.

Sarah, the daughter of Asahel Strong and Sally, his wife, was born Apr. 19th, 1823.

Moses Robinson departed this life, Nov. 14th, 1820.

Moses Austin, the son of Moses Robinson and Electa, his wife, was born Feb. 17th, 1821.

Eliza Ann, the daughter of James Hickox and Hope, his wife, was born June 24th, 1823.

Prudence Melora, the daughter of Charles Thompson and Lydia, his wife, was born Jan. 1st, 1824.

Charles Augustus, the son of Reuben R. Fowler and Catharine, his wife, was born Apr. 13th, 1798.

Harriet Eliza, the daughter of Guernsey Camp and Cynthia Ann, his wife, was born Sept. 18th, 1823.

Eliza Merrel, the daughter of Joseph Tuttle and Margaret, his wife, was born March 3d, 1824.

Henry Nelson, the son of Jefferson Ives and Mary, his wife, was born May 6th, 1824.

Merick Rejoice, son of Abraham Coe and Rebecca, his wife, was born June 27th, 1804.

Hannah Angeline, daughter of Abraham Coe and Rebecca, his wife, was born May 3d, 1809.

Phebe Ann Tabatha, daughter of Abraham Coe and Rebecca, his wife, was born Aug. 13th, 1817.

Ebenezer Gurnsey, the son of Timothy W. Baldwin and Ann, his wife, was born Feb. 22d, 1825.

George Lyman and Sally Smithson were joined in marriage, March 7th, 1801.

Frederick, the son of George Lyman and Sally, his wife, was born Oct. 11th, 1812.

Sally, the wife of George Lyman, departed this life, Sept. 28th, 1825.

Rossetta Fayette, the daughter of Richard Robinson and Cynthia, his wife, was born June —, 1824.

Frederic Nelson, the son of Thaddeus Camp and Betsey, his wife, was born Oct. 7th, 1811.

Katharine Louisa, the daughter of Thaddeus Camp and Betsey, his wife, was born Nov. 15th, 1814.

Theodore Dwight, the son of Thaddeus Camp and Betsey, his wife, was born Jan. 24th, 1815.

Thaddeus, the son of Thaddeus Camp and Betsey, his wife, was born May 13th, 1820.

Frederick Nelson Camp departed this life, July 12th, 1825.

Henry Camp, departed this life, July 15th, 1825.

Samuel Guernsey, the son of Guernsey Camp and Cynthia Ann, was born Dec. 24th, 1825.

Henry L. Simmons, the son of Elisha Simmons and Jerusha, his wife, was born Jan. 10th, 1810.

Elizabeth Gillum departed this life, Feb. 18th, 1827.

Edward Thompson, the son of Charles Thompson and Lydia, his wife, departed this life, Nov. 6th, 1825.

Lucy Ann Thompson, the daughter of Charles and Lydia Thompson, was born July 23d, 1826.

David Thompson, departed this life, July 24th, 1828.

Henry, the son of William Lyman and Weltha Maria, was born July 20th, 1825.

Mary, the daughter of William Lyman and Weltha Maria, was born at Rochester, Vt., June 15th, 1828.

William Augustus, the son of Asher Robinson and Eunice, his wife, Oct. 20th, 1826.

Sarah Chittenden, the daughter of Asher Robinson and Eunice, his wife, was born Oct. 30th, 1828

Olive Smith, the daughter of James Mucket and Ann, his wife, was born July 9th, 1820.

Amos Manwarren, the son of James Mucket and Ann, his wife, was born March 21st, 1822.

Charles Denison, the son of James Mucket and Ann, his wife, was born Mar 6th, 1824.

Martha Ann, the daughter of James Mucket and Ann, his wife, was born Oct. 24th, 1828.

Frances Amelia, the daughter of John A. Graves and Amelia, his wife, was born June 9th, 1821.

Henry, the son of John A. Graves and Amelia, his wife, was born Feb. 4th, 1829.

Sophronia Camp, the daughter of Lemuel Camp and Patty, his wife, born June 30th, 1796.

Mary G. Camp, the daughter of Lemuel Camp and Patty, his wife, was born Aug. 26th, 1800.

Henry T. Camp, the son of Lemuel Camp and Patty, his wife, was born Aug. 30th, 1804.

Edward P. Camp, the son of Lemuel Camp and Patty, his wife, was born Apr. 12th, 1808.

Oren J. Camp, the son of Oren Camp and Delight, his wife, was born June 13th, 1829.

Sarah A. Camp, the daughter of Oren Camp and Delight, his wife, was born Jan. 19th, 1831.

Benjamin Benonia Camp, son of Manoah Camp and Clarissa, his wife, was born Feb. 10th, 1795.

Herschel Camp, son of Manoah Camp and Clarissa, his wife, was born Jan. 15th, 1798.

Frederick Camp, son of Manoah Camp and Charissa, his wife, was born Nov. 21st, 1801.

Elizur Camp, son of Manoah Camp and Charissa, his wife, was born Aug. 22d, 1804.

Betsey Lyman Camp, daughter of Manoah Camp and Charissa, his wife, was born March 11th, 1810.

Betsey Lyman Camp, daughter of Manoah Camp and Charissa, his wife, was born May 5th, 1814.

Mary Temperance Mucket, daughter of James Mucket and Ann, his wife, was born Apr. 3d, 1831.

Ann Elizabeth Norton, daughter of Stephen L. Norton and Jerusha, his wife, was born at Cheshire, Feb. 28th, 1821.

Lyman Warren, son of Stephen L. Norton and Jerusha, his his wife, was born Nov. 13th, 1822.

Charles, son of Stephen L. Norton and Jerusha, his wife, was born July 17th, 1824.

Laura, daughter of Stephen L. Norton and Jerusha, his wife, was born June 20th, 1826.

Jerusha, daughter of Stephen L. Norton and Jerusha, his wife, was born June 3d, 1828.

Jerusha Norton departed this life, Sept. 13th, 1828

Jerusha Norton, daughter of Stephen L. Norton, departed this life, Oct. 27th, 1828.

Isaac Loveland departed this life, July 12th, 1830.

Clarissa Bishop, widow of Zebulon Bishop, died Sept. 29th, 1830.

Ann Bates Baldwin, daughter of Timothy W and Ann Baldwin, was born May 15th, A. D. 1831.

Irena Mattoon, daughter of Sarah Mattoon, was born May 31st, 1824.

William Allen, the son of Allen Clarke and Sally, his wife, was born May 8th, 1818.

Neamiah Murias, the son of James Mucket and Ann, his wife, was born July 21st, 1834.

Frances Edgar, son of James Mucket and Ann, his wife, was born Feb. 2d, 1839.

Manoah Camp, departed this life, March 5th, 1842.

Rosetta F. Robinson, daughter of Richard Robinson and Cynthia, his wife, was born May 26th, 1824.

James Robinson, son of Richard Robinson and Cynthia, his wife, was born June 15th, 1829.

Charles Benjamin, son of Andrew J. and Betsey Ann Thompson, was born on the 28th of Oct. 1843.

The following are the children of Thomas and Lydia D Frances of Durham, born as follows:

Charles C. and Lydia J., (twins) born July 20th, 1837.

William H , born Dec. 28th, 1839.

Henrietta G., born Nov. 22d, 1841.

Thomas A., born June 29th, 1844.

The above is a true copy of the acct given me by Thomas Francis, July 11th, 1844. S. PARSONS, T. Clerk.

Henry Allen Lyman, born July 20th, 1825.

Mary Charlotte Lyman, born June 15th, 1828

Hannah Mariah Lyman, born Jan. 18th, 1830

Julia Ann Lyman, born May 14th, 1831.

William Oliver Lyman, born Nov. 16th, 1832.

Loisa Jane Lyman, born May 16th, 1834.

Gilbert Augustus Lyman, born July 1st, 1836

Richard Melvin Lyman, born Feb. 3d, 1840.

Urbane Lyman, born March 1st, 1842.

Elsa Lavinia Lyman, born Oct. 7th, 1843.

Eugene Lewellyn Lyman, born Oct. 21st, 1845.

The above are the names of the children of William Lyman and Weltha Maria Lyman, his wife. Copy of the original received for record, January 1st, 1846.

WILLIAM WADSWORTH, Town Clerk.

Laura Artelissea Marsh, baptised July 31st, 1853, by Rev. Mr. Pease, in Durham Centre. A true record received Aug. 1st, 1853. WILLIAM WADSWORTH, Town Clerk.

Elisha Newton and Sally Camp were joined in marriage, on the 13th of Dec., and Joseph Tuttle and Margaret Coe on the 25th of the same month, 1820.

Edmond Orton and Amanda Camp were joined in marriage, Jan. 1st, 1821.

Guy Blakeman and Anne Camp were joined in marriage, March 11th, 1821.

Timothy W. Baldwin, of North Guildford, and Ann Bates, of Durham, were joined in marriage, May 16th, 1821.

Marvin Riley, of Middletown, and Catharine Richmond, of Durham, were joined in marriage, May 12th, 1821.

Henry Crowell and Persis Southworth were joined in marriage, July 30th, 1821.

William Hart and Sophia Newton were joined in marriage, Sept. 23d, 1821.

Joseph Ward and Charlotte M. Hyde were joined in marriage, Sept 24th, 1821.

Anson Meigs and Eunice Loveland were joined in marriage, Sept. 26th, 1821.

Samuel Hicks and Sarah Parmalee were joined in marriage, Oct. 8th, 1821.

James Clyme, of New Haven, and Lusina Reed of Durham, were joined in marriage, Oct. 7th, 1821.

Harvey Robinson and Lydia Dickinson were joined in marriage, Oct. 29th, 1821, and Elizur Hall and Deborah Ann Chadeayne on the 30th of sd. month

Sidney Norton and Palina Ives, both of Durham, were joined in marriage, Oct. 31st, 1821.

Henry Maltby and Ruth Hart were joined in marriage, Dec. 12th, 1821.

Phinehas Beers and Mary Curtiss were joined in marriage, June 25th, 1822.

Timothy Russell and Eliza Butler were joined in marriage, Oct. 27th, 1822, and John S Catlin and Hannah Hall were joined in marriage on 28th sd. month.

John S. Camp and Parnel Camp were joined in marriage, Oct. 15th, 1822.

Stephen Tibbals and Adah Camp were joined in marriage, Dec. 8th, 1822.

Jefferson Ives and Mary Frances were joined in marriage, Jan. 16th, 1823.

Wyllys Elliott and Lucy Camp were joined in marriage, Feb. 19th, 1823.

Chauncey C Stevens and Lucinda Hoadley were joined in marriage, March 9th, 1823.

Ebenezer G. Bates and Mary Ann Swathel were joined in marriage, Mar. 26th, 1823.

Ichabod Camp and Sally Johnson were joined in marriage, Mar. 31st, 1823.

Alfred Camp and Phebe Parmalee were joined in marriage, Apr. 2d, 1823.

Abner Newton and Sarah Hall were joined in marriage, Apr 29th, 1823.

Lyman Butler and Eunice B. Southmayd were joined in marriage, May 23d, 1823.

Guernsey Strong and Amanda Parsons were joined in marriage, Sept 7th, 1823.

George W. Jewett and Harriet Camp were joined in marriage, Sept. 11th, 1823.

Isaac Baldwin and Alva Merwin were joined in marriage, Sept. 17th, 1823.

Charles Cornwell and Eunice Jennett Sheldon were joined in marriage, Oct. 5th, 1823.

Benjamin Coe and Lydia Curtiss were joined in marriage, Oct. 13th, 1823.

Jonathan Munson and Sally Johnson were joined in marriage, Nov. 27th, 1823.

Thomas Noble and Mary Merwin were joined in marriage, Apr. 27th, 1824.

Peris Sturtevant and Caroline D. Camp were joined in marriage, Apr 28th, 1824.

George Cruttenden and Eliza A. Strong were joined in marriage, May 19th, 1824.

Peter Hardin and Esther Jack, colored, were joined in marriage, June 2d, 1824; also, William Shelley and Sarah Isbil on the same day of said month.

Lyman Basset and Orpha Parsons were joined in marriage, June 21st, 1824; also, Sylvanus Shelley and Harriet Loveland on the same day of sd. month.

Thorrit Davis and Patty Kelsey were joined in marriage, Sept. 23d, 1824.

Joseph Collins and Tabatha Strong were joined in marriage, Oct. 19th, 1824.

Austin Bailey and Mary R. Brainard were joined in marriage, Oct. 25th, 1824.

Henry Lothrop and Catharine Coe were joined in marriage, Nov. 25th, 1824.

Henry Simons and Clarrissa Phillips, (two persons of color,) were joined in marriage, May 5th, 1825.

Denis Gillum, of Durham, and Mary Isbill, of Killingworth, were joined in marriage, Aug. 7th, 1825.

James Lee, of Guilford, and Ruth Merwin, of Durham, were joined in marriage, Sept. 28th, 1825.

Edwin Hubbard and Lucy Strong were joined in marriage, Sept 17th, 1825.

Albin Shipman and Benilla Isbil were joined in marriage, Sept. 15th, 1826.

Joel Blatchley, of Guilford, and Margery Robinson, of Durham, were joined in marriage, Oct. 10th, 1825.

Giles H. Robinson and Emily Wheeler were joined in marriage, Oct. 13th, 1825.

John Graves and Alelia Bailey were joined in marriage, Dec. 5th, 1825.

Asa Chamberlain and Electa Robinson were joined in marriage, Jan. 17th, 1826.

Lewis Norton and Emily Dunn were joined in marriage, Jan. 22d, 1826.

Erastus Jones and Lucy R. Elliott were joined in marriage, Feb. 21st, 1826.

Selden Stevens and Polly Nettleton were joined in marriage, Mar 12th, 1826

Edwin Coe and Cornelia C. Parmalee were joined in marriage, Mar 16th, 1826

John Robinson and Phebe Scranton were joined in marriage, May 15th, 1826.

Horace Newton and Delight Camp were joined in marriage, May 24th, 1826.

Charles Gay and Lucinda Camp were joined in marriage, June 1st, 1826.

John W. Miller and Polly Miller, both of Middlefield, were joined in marriage, July 10th, 1826

David Johnson and Nancy J. Seward were joined in marriage, July 31st, 1826.

Chauncey Bartholomew and Sophronia Parmalee were joined in marriage, Aug. 1st, 1826.

Hosmer Fowler and Harriett E. Nettleton were joined in marriage, Nov. 6th, 1826

John Z. Howell and Charlotte Ann Lanison were joined in marriage, Nov. 14th, 1826.

——— Rutty and Abiah Southmayd were joined in marriage, Nov. 12th, 1826.

George W. Gorham and Hannah Bemus were joined in marriage, Dec. 1st, 1826.

Samuel Camp and Betsey A. Cone were joined in marriage, Jan. 28th, 1827.

Nelson Holcomb and Fanny Bemus were joined in marriage, Feb. 7th, 1827.

Joel Blatchley and Margery Robinson were joined in marriage, Oct. 10th, 1825.

Israel S. Camp and Clarissa Dickinson were joined in marriage, May 1st, 1827.

Richard Hubbard and Rhoda Graham were joined in marriage, May 20th, 1827.

Elijah Beaumont and Sophronia Nettleton were joined in marriage, May 27th, 1827.

Andrew Merriman and Eliza Peck were joined in marriage, Aug. 6th, 1827.

Samuel Robinson, of Madison, and Ann Baldwin, of Durham, Horatio N Fowler, of Middletown, and Mary Ann Bates, of Durham, were joined in marriage, Sept. 12th, 1827.

Alvin Roberts and Mary A. Parmalee, Elizur Camp and Fanny Clarke were joined in marriage, Oct. 1st, 1827.

Samuel Newton and Betsey H. Parmalee were joined in marriage, Nov. 23d, 1827.

Mr. Orren Camp and Miss Delight Ives, both of Durham, were joined in marriage, Nov. 29th, 1827.

Benjamin Chalker and Polly Pratt were joined in marriage, Apr 6th, 1828.

Lewis Chatfield and Rachel Griswold were joined in marriage, Apr. 17th, 1828.

George W. Jewett and Jennet Camp, Clement Parsons and Phebe Smith, were joined in marriage, Apr. 30th,1828.

Abraham Camp and Mary Ann Coe were joined in marriage, May 28th, 1828

Abraham W. Rice and Rhoda Ann Worthington were joined in marriage, July 30th, 1828.

Ebenezer Goolthraight and Esther Tibbals; also, Samuel G. Tibbals and Harriet Hall were joined in marriage, Sept. 8th, 1828.

Charles Robinson, Jun., and Almira Chalker; also, Jonathan I. Fuller and Martha Stevens were joined in marriage, Nov. 27th, 1828.

Richard H. Hotchkiss and Anne Nettleton were joined in marriage, Aug. 17th, 1828.

Jehiel U. Hand and Eliza Swathel were joined in marriage, May 12th, 1829.

Roswel Stevens and Anna Lynn were joined in marriage, June 24th, 1829.

Edmund Sage and Rhoda Merwin were joined in marriage, June 28th, 1829.

Lewis I. Davis and Harriet Bishop were joined in marriage, Aug. 3d, 1829.

William Thomas and Clarissa Ann Chamberlain were joined in marriage, Aug. 26th, 1829.

Henry C. Camp and Caroline E. Wright were joined in marriage, Sept. 6th, 1829.

Samuel W. Lynn and Sarah Coe were joined in marriage, Jan. 24th, 1829.

John A. Collins and Betsey Clarke were joined in marriage, March 1st, 1830.

Elnathan Conner, of Wallingford, and Barbara Buel, of Killingworth, were joined in marriage, Apr. 21st, 1830.

Blinn I Brainard and Catharine H. Foote were joined in marriage, May 1st, 1830.

Benjamin Thomas and Eliza Crowell were joined in marriage, June 2d, 1830

Lucius Holcomb, of Granby, and Lavina A. Galpin, of Durham, were married, June 21st, 1830.

Julius Rich, of Chatham, and Cecilia A. Camp, of Durham, were joined in marriage, Sept. 12th, 1830.

William A. Baldwin and Betsey Camp were joined in marriage, Sept. 22d, 1830.

Eliakim W. Hull and Betsey Fowler were joined in marriage, Nov. 19th, 1819.

William Y. Bailey and Sarah Stevens were joined in marriage, Nov. 25th, 1830

James C. Arnold and Abigail Flagg were joined in marriage, March 9th, 1831.

Stephen L. Norton and Mary Ann Gorham were joined in marriage, May 16th, 1831.

Hiram Bishop and Mariah Lucass were joined in marriage, July 11th,

Albert Ward, of Durham, and Harriet Beardsley, of Meriden, were joined in marriage, Oct. 7th, 1831.

Allen Way and Sally Simons were joined in marriage, Oct. 7th, 1831.

Amos Harrison and Harriet Hart were joined in marriage, Oct 12th, 1831

Seth R. Parsons and Mary Francis were joined in marriage, May 5th, 1832.

Leander P. Hickox and Lucy Parsons were joined in marriage, May 20th, 1832.

Charles Brown, of Meriden, and Juliet Griffing, of Guilford, were joined in marriage, May 22d, 1832.

Horace Parmalee, of Durham and Zeruiah Leete, of Guilford, were joined in marriage, Oct 18th, 1832.

Bennet B. Beecher, of Woodbridge, and Sarah Bishop, of Durham, were joined in marriage, Nov. 18th, 1832.

Edward P. Church of Middletown, and Amelia M. Clarke, of Durham, have been joined in marriage, Nov. 29th, 1832.

Charles G. Lyman, of Colebrook, and Louisa Hull, of Durham, were joined in marriage, Nov. 29th, 1832.

Joseph Winship, of Hartford, and Mary Ives, of Durham, were joined in marriage, Feb. 10th, 1833.

Brainard Montague of Sandersfield, Mass., and Abigail S. Bolles, of Middletown, were joined in marriage, Feb. 11th, 1833.

Carlos and Betsey B. Camp were joined in marriage, May 9th,

1833; and on the 23d day of the same month, William Southmayd and Mary Tucker were joined in marriage.

Thomas F. Morgan and Lucinda Stevens were joined in marriage, Aug. 6th, 1833.

David P Camp and Nancy E. Strong were joined in marriage, Aug. 11th, 1833.

Phinehas Meigs and Mary Camp were joined in marriage, Aug. 20th, 1833.

Frederic Dowd, of Madison and Charlotte Hickox were joined in marriage, Feb. 24th, 1834.

Leonard Hull and Emily Chalker were joined in marriage, March 16th, 1834.

Huntington Southmayd and Mary Brainard were joined in marriage, Apr. 24th, 1834.

Silas Williams and Elizabeth Bates, of Durham, were joined in marriage, May 1st, 1834.

Jehial Johnson and Betsey Bowles, both of Middletown, were joined in marriage, Jan. 2d, 1834.

Thomas C. Camp and Betsey A. Parker were joined in marriage, June 11th, 1834.

Thomas and Zeruiah Parmelee were joined in marriage, Sept 1st, 1834.

John Wadsworth, of the city of New York, and Maria Chedsey, of Durham, were joined in marriage, Aug. 21st, 1834.

Henry Parsons and Jane White were joined in marriage, Sept 7th, 1834.

Linus Coc and Maria Seward were joined in marriage, Sept. 15th, 1834.

Mr Wedworth Wadsworth, of Monroe, Michigan, and Miss Margaret Swathel, of Durham, were joined in marriage, Dec. 25th, 1833.

Mr. Henry M. Coe and Miss Betsey Robinson, both of Durham, were joined in marriage, Oct. 12th, 1834.

Hinchman Roberts, of Middletown, and Polly Nettleton, of Durham, were joined in marriage, Mar. 23d, 1835.

Cyrus Kelsey and Jane A. Fowler were joined in marriage, May 12th, 1835

Henry Robinson and Phebe A. Southmayd were joined in marriage, Sept. 2d, 1835.

Morgan Davis, of North Madison, and Cynthia E. Davis, of South Killingworth, were joined in marriage, Sept 27th, 1835.

Seneca Barnes, of Northford, and Mary Hart, of Durham, were joined in marriage, Nov 1st, 1835.

Rev. Rollin S Stone, of Brooklyn, N. Y., and Miss Urania E. Stone, of Durham, were joined in marriage, Nov. 27th, 1835.

Evelyn Scranton, of Madison, and Eunice Davis, of Killingworth, were joined in marriage, Jan. 24th, 1836.

Calvin Alby, of Saybrook and Maria Scranton of Durham, were joined in marriage, Jan. 14th, 1836.

Noyes Cone and Polly A. Lynn were joined in marriage, Apr. 30th, 1837.

Samuel Stevens and Harriet Bradley were joined in marriage, May 4th, 1836.

Samuel Wilcox and Eliza A. Parsons were joined in marriage, July 20th, 1836.

Silas Higgins and Susan Ives were joined in marriage, July 31st, 1836.

William Robinson and Jennett Elliott were joined in marriage, August 15th, 1836.

Elias Hale and Eliza Ann Miller were joined in marriage, Sept 26th, 1836.

Lucius P. Bryan, of Waterbury and Jennett White of Durham, were joined in marriage, Aug. 25th, 1836.

Seymour White and Phebe C. Merwin were joined in marriage, Oct. 5th, 1836.

Aralon W. Russell and Emeline Curtiss were joined in marriage, Oct. 12th, 1836.

Talcott Parsons and Betsey M. Savage were joined in marriage, Oct. 31st, 1836.

Thomas Francis and Lydia D. Thompson were joined in marriage, Nov. 15th, 1836.

Obier Blakeslee and Sarah Ann Morse were joined in marriage, Dec. 14th, 1836.

Charles Ives and Phebe Ann Hull were joined in marriage.

Ezekiel W. Lynn and ——— ——— were joined in marriage, Mar. 14th, 1837.

Hartwell and Eliza J. Nettleton were joined in marriage, Apr. 7th, 1838.

Albert M. Sizer and Hannah S. Cone were joined in marriage, Dec. 24th, 1838.

Gaylord Newton and Nancy Merwin were joined in marriage, Dec. 5th, 1838.

Daniel Southmayd and Tamson Hickox were joined in marriage, Dec. 25th, 1838.

Henry Tucker and Rosella Ridel were joined in marriage.

Henry Bailey and Mary Parsons were joined in marriage, Aug. 12th, 1837.

Seth B. Cooper and Elizabeth Strong were joined in marriage, Aug. 6th, 1837.

Samuel W. Clarke and Eliza P. Ranney were joined in marriage, Dec. 6th, 1837.

William Peck and Hannah A. Coe were joined in marriage, Oct. 22d, 1837.

John W. Houseman and Eunice Spiner were joined in marriage, in 1837.

Linas Harrison and Miss E. Jones were joined in marriage, in 1838.

Henry E. Nettleton and Cornelia Camp were joined in marriage, Sept. 6th, 1839.

Heman Stone, Jun., of Madison, and Rachel D. Hale, of Durham, were joined in marriage, June 5th, 1839.

John Bailey and Ursula Scranton were joined in marriage, Jan. 1st, 1839.

Nathaniel P Mason and Orpha M. Squires were joined in marriage, July 1st, 1839.

Luzerne Elliott and Hannah Robinson were joined in marriage, Sept. 24th, 1839.

Samuel C. B. Prat and Phebe A. Coe were joined in marriage, Sept. 28th, 1839.

Israel Camp and Rachel H. Maynard were joined in marriage, Oct. 1st, 1839.

Joel Blatchley and Harriet Hull were joined in marriage, Aug. 8th, 1839.

Edward C Hull and Clarissa Nettleton were joined in marriage, Oct. 9th, 1839.

Alonzo C. Clarke, of Haddam, and Freelove M. Scranton were joined in marriage, Nov. 28th, 1839.

Augustus Seward and Alpha M Bailey were joined in marriage, Feb. 27th, 1840.

Ezra G. Johnson and Frances E. Andrews were joined in marriage, Apr. 19th, 1840.

William A. Parmalee and Mary J. Camp were joined in marriage, Aug. 13th, 1840.

Charles P. Chedsy and Sarah Squires were joined in marriage, June 2d, 1840

John M. Auliffe and Matilda Robinson were joined in marriage, Aug. 16th, 1840.

Smith Samuel Baldwin, of Martinsburg, Lewis County, New York, and Mary Fairchild, of Durham, were joined in marriage, Oct. 17th, 1839.

William E. Graham and Eunice Scranton were joined in marriage, Oct. 11th, 1840.

James N. Phelps, of Wallingford, and Lavinia Meeker, of Durham, were joined in marriage, Dec. 27th, 1840.

Abel Sanford, of Middletown, and Phebe Hull, of Durham, were joined in marriage, Dec 29th, 1840.

Joseph S. Morse, of Durham, and Mary O. Nettleton, of Killingworth, were joined in marriage, May 4th, 1841.

Samuel G. Stevens and Elizabeth Parmalee were joined in marriage. June 23d, 1841.

Joel Austin and Esther Parmalee were joined in marriage, May 12th, 1840.

Phinehas Nettleton, of Killingworth, and Lorinda Burr, of Haddam, were joined in marriage, Nov. 15th, 1840.

Henry D. Fowler, of Middletown, and Cynthia Curtiss, of Durham, were joined in marriage, Nov. 19th, 1840

James Minor and Elizabeth Leete were joined in marriage, Sept. 1st, 1841.

Charles G. Arnold and Betsey M. Smith were joined in marriage, Sept. 19th, 1841.

Daniel B. Coe and Cynthia Robinson were joined in marriage, Sept. 1st, 1841.

Ichabod Avery and Martha Pomeroy were joined in marriage, Aug. 13th, 1841.

John R. Baldwin of Mènden, Illinois, and Mary Ann Coe, of Durham, were joined in marriage, Jan. 23d, 1842.

Alexander Camp and Abigail W. Maynard, of Durham, were joined in marriage, Feb. 22d, 1842.

Moses B. Barns and Martha J. Galpin were joined in marriage, Feb. 1st, 1842.

Timothy J. Coe and Ann M. Hull were joined in marriage, Jan. 3d, 1842

Henry E. Bailey and Martha J. Brooks were joined in marriage, March 27th, 1842.

Henry W. Smith, of Durham, and Harriet M. Wamsley were joined in marriage, April 25th, 1842.

Benj H. Carrier and Mary A. Strong were joined in marriage, May 2d, 1842.

Arelno Thompson and Betsey Lynn were joined in marriage, Sept 11th, 1842.

Elijah Loveland, of Middletown, and Sarah Strong, of Durham, were joined in marriage, June 19th, 1843.

Edward Canfield and Eliza Robinson were joined in marriage, Nov. 22d, 1842.

David B. Rosseter and Caroline M. Rosseter, of North Guilford, were joined in marriage, Nov. 22d, 1842

Hezekiah Bartholomew and Sally Neal, of Wallingford, were joined in marriage, Nov. 22d, 1842.

Isaac W. Hickox and Elizabeth White were joined in marriage, June 6th, 1843.

William Stevens, of Berlin and Adeline Atkins, of Middletown, were joined in marriage, Sept. 25th, 1843.

Thomas H Clarke, of Haddam, and Betsey M. Parsons were joined in marriage, Oct. 3d, 1843.

Alpheus Beach, of Northford, and Mary Skinner, of Durham, were joined in marriage, Oct. 21st, 1843.

Charles Pritchard, of Waterbury, and Harriet E. Jones of New Haven, were joined in marriage, Nov. 13th, 1843.

George H. Welton and Mary Nichols, both of Waterbury, were joined in marriage, Jan. 28th, 1844.

Leveret Marsden Leach and Lydia Maria Thayer, both of Durham, were joined in marriage, Feb. 7th, 1844.

Clement M. Parsons, of Durham, and Sarah Hill, of Haddam, were joined in marriage, Mar. 10th, 1844.

Jacob Johnson, 2d, of Middletown, and Harriet E. Smith, of Durham, were joined in marriage, June 19th, 1844.

Joseph H. Paddock, of Middletown, and Fanny M. Brainard, of Haddam, were joined in marriage, July 10th, 1844.

Noble Lewenronth, of Waterbury, and Louisa E. Davis, of Watertown, were joined in marriage, Oct. 15th, 1844.

Jerome Shelley and Jennette S. Ward were joined in marriage, Aug. 22d, 1844..

Jackson Mann, of Carlisle, Kentucky, and Lydia M. Elliott, of Durham, were joined in marriage, Oct. 6th, 1844.

Alonzo Brainard, of Haddam, and Diana Platt, of Durham, were joined in marriage, Dec. 15th, 1844.

Elisha Lines, of Waterbury, and Ann Carr, of Simsbury, were joined in marriage, Jan. 8th, 1845.

Lyman C. Robinson and Jane E. Canfield, both of Durham, were joined in marriage, Jan. 19th, 1845.

A. M Griswold, of Killingworth, and Sophronia Fowler, of Durham, were joined in marriage, Jan. 23d, 1845.

Worthington Scranton and Lydia Bailey, both of Durham, were joined in marriage, March 10th, 1845.

Henry Riggs, of New Haven, and H. Amelia Hull, of Durham, were joined in marriage, March 9th, 1845.

John Leavitt, of New Haven and Sarah Skinner, of Northford, were joined in marriage, Apr. 6th, 1840.

Hiram Miller, of Middlefield, and Catharine Shelley, of Durham, were joined in marriage, Apr. 8th, 1845.

Justus I Bailey and Eunice E Lynn, both of Durham, were joined in marriage, May 4th, 1845.

John Jackson and Charlotte Angeline Field were joined in marriage, Aug. 31st, 1845.

James Wadsworth and Rosetta [illegible] Robinson were joined in marriage, Sept. 8th, 1845.

Leonidas Maynard and Abigail Scranton were joined in marriage, Sept. 28th, 1845.

Nathan G. R. Southwick and Sarah Ann Nettleton were joined in marriage, Sept. 28th, 1845.

David N. Camp and Sarah A Howd were joined in marriage, Nov. 25th, 1845.

Francis M. Fortes and Jane A. Camp were joined in marriage, Nov. 25th, 1845.

Henry L. Miller and Mariah Miller were joined in marriage, Nov. 30th, 1845.

Nathan H. Parsons and Maria W Sturtevant, both of Durham, were joined in marriage, May 14th, 1846.

Eli Hubbard and Georgiana Leach were joined in marriage, May 20th, 1846.

Timothy Smith and Harriet Ransom, both of Durham, were joined in marriage, Aug 17th, 1846.

Mr. James S. Ely, of Meriden, and Miss Amelia S. Harrison were joined in marriage, Aug 30th, 1846.

Mr. Franklin S. Smith, of Middletown, to Miss Lucy A. Thompson, of Durham, were joined in marriage, Sept. 27th, 1846.

Mr. George S. Morse, of North Haven, and Miss Clarissa Lynn, of Durham, were joined in marriage, Sept. 27th, 1846.

Mr. Stephen Bailey, of Durham, to Miss Nancy Merriman, of Wallingford, were joined in marriage, Oct. 25th, 1846.

Mr. Leander R. Parsons and Frances A. Camp, both of Durham, were joined in marriage, Nov. 26th, 1846.

William R. Reynolds and Miss Martha N. Chamberlain, were joined in marriage, Nov. 26th, 1846.

Mr. Alanson Brainard, of Durham, and Miss Ellen Cook, of Northford, were joined in marriage, Aug. 8th, 1847.

Mr. Timothy Dwight Camp to Miss Mary Page, both of Durham, were joined in marriage, Nov 4th, 1847

Mr. Enoch F. Camp and Miss Mary A. Coe, both of Durham, were married, Nov. 4th, 1847.

Mr. Jerome Shelley and Miss Betsey Ann Thomas, both of Durham, were joined in marriage, Jan. 9th, 1848.

Joseph Adams, Esq., of Cleaveland, Ohio, and Louisa Clarke, of Middletown, were joined in marriage, Oct. 17th, 1847.

Andrew Hull and Ann Parsons, both of Durham, were married, June 5th, 1848.

Lester Cornwall, of Meriden, and Sarah M. Brainard, of Durham, were joined in marriage, Oct. 6th, 1846.

Wm. S. Post and Catharine Elizabeth Howd, of Durham, were joined in marriage, Aug. 1st, 1848.

Samuel S. Spencer, of Middletown, and Mary A. Jackson, of Durham, were joined in marriage, Oct. 1st, 1848.

Horace Wooding, of Hamden, Conn., and Catharine Bailey, of Durham, were joined in marriage, Oct. 1st, 1848.

Stephen D. Lane and Sarah A. Potter were joined in marriage, Dec. 4th, 1848.

Martin M. Chalker and Frances A. Richmond were joined in marriage, July 9th, 1849; also, at the same time, Walter J. Chalker to Hannah Jane Robinson.

Richard H. Hotchkiss and Ann Nettleton were joined in marriage, Aug. 17th, 1823.

F. P. Chaffee, of Middletown, and Ellen A. Hull, of Durham, were joined in marriage, Sept. 15th, 1851.

Henry Ward, of Middletown, and Maria A. Newton, of Durham, were joined in marriage, May 13th, 1852.

Lucius M. Knowles, of Durham, and Elisabeth R. Shelley, of Madison, were joined in marriage, June 13th, 1852.

Levi Fowler and Mary L. Munson, both of Northford, were joined in marriage, Oct. 11th, 1852.

Edwin Gatzmer, of Philadelphia, Penn., and Mary Jane Fowler, of Durham, were joined in marriage, Sept. 1st, 1853.

Joseph P. Camp, Jr., and Caroline E. Robinson, both of Durham, were joined in marriage, June 28th, 1854.

Henry E Bemus and Hannah Sulivan were joined in marriage, Sept. 28th, 1860

TOWN CLERK'S OFFICE,
DURHAM, May 25th, 1866.

I hereby Certify, that the foregoing is a true Copy of the Town Records, as recorded in this Office; and I hereby Certify, that the foregoing Proprietors' Records are a true Copy of the original.

Attest,

WILLIAM WADSWORTH.

Town Clerk.

Town Clerk.—1865.—William Wadsworth.

Select Men.—1865.—L. M. Leach, George Atwell, Gaylord Newton.

Justices of the Peace—1866.—William Wadsworth, Israel C. Newton, Wm. H. Walkley, Henry Tucker, Elias B. Meigs, Henry S. Merwin, Wm. A. Hart.

Electors Admitted.—March 26th, 1866.—Timothy E. Hawley, John W Johnson, Howard A. Camp, Henry H. Church, George D. Seward, Frederick Wimlar, Frederick J. Hart, Wm. T. D. Coe, Charles M. Camp, John D. Hart, Philipp Reinhardt.

Electors Admitted.—March 28th, 1866.—Daniel W. Priest, Robert M. Murdock, Silas W. Fowler, Eckford J. Morse, Frederick H. Parker, Lucius H. Foot.

Representatives.—1866.—William Wadsworth, Oscar Leach.

NOTE AND CORRECTION.

There being an error in the average age at death, in Durham, as published in the Sanitary Article, p. 226, the following table has been prepared to correct that error and to show, at a glance, the healthfulness of Durham, as compared with the State at large, according to the registration returns for ten years,—and with Massachusetts and Rhode Island, those being the only adjoining States that have registration laws; and with the United States, according to the two last census returns.

	Durham.	Conn	Mass.	R Island.	U States.
Death to Population,	1 to 59		1 to 52	1 to 55	1 to 45
Average age at Death,	46	31.40	30	29.40	22.7
Do. do. Males,	43	30.19	29	28.13	22.85
Do. do. Females,	49	32.63	31	30.43	22.55
Consumption, per cent.,	8	15 67	16.7	13	14
Zymotic Disease, do.,	17½	30	29	29½	32

www.ingramcontent.com/pod-product-compliance
Lightning Source LLC
Chambersburg PA
CBHW070146181225
36965CB00015B/898
* 9 7 8 1 0 1 7 0 1 9 7 5 9 *